ADVANCED DIGITAL INFORMATION SYSTEMS

Edited by

Igor Aleksander

Kobler Professor of the Management of Information Technology,
Imperial College of Science, University of London
Formerly of the
Dept. of Electrical Engineering and Electronics, Brunel University

Contributing Authors

Igor Aleksander
Vivienne Begg
Robert Holte

Les Johnson
Chris Reade
John Stonham

of the Advanced Information Initiative at Brunel University

Prentice/Hall International

Englewood Cliffs, NJ London New Delhi Rio de Janeiro
Singapore Sydney Tokyo Toronto Wellington

Library of Congress Cataloging in Publication Data
Main entry under title:

Advanced digital information systems.

  Bibliography: p.
  Includes index.
  1. Electronic digital computers—Addresses, essays,
lectures. 2. Electronic data processing—Addresses,
essays, lectures. I. Aleksander, Igor.
TK7885.A625 1984   004   84–8273
ISBN 0-13-011305-0

British Library Cataloguing in Publication Data

Aleksander, Igor
  Advanced Digital information systems
  1. Digital communications
  I. Title
  621.38'0413   TK5103.7

  ISBN 0-13-011305-0

ISBN 0-13-011305 0

Prentice-Hall International, Inc., *London*
Prentice-Hall of Australia Pty. Ltd., *Sydney*
Prentice-Hall Canada, Inc., *Toronto*
Prentice-Hall of India Private Ltd., *New Delhi*
Prentice-Hall of Japan, Inc., *Tokyo*
Prentice-Hall of Southeast Asia Pte., Ltd., *Singapore*
Prentice-Hall Inc., *Englewood Cliffs, New Jersey*
Prentice-Hall do Brasil Ltda., *Rio de Janeiro*
Prentice-Hall Hispanoamericana, S.A. *Mexico*
Whitehall Books Ltd., *Wellington, New Zealand*

Printed in the United States of America

10 9 8 7 6 5 4 3 2 1

Contents

Preface

Information is beginning to assume a role in engineering which is on a par with that classically held by energy. This has been recognized since Shannon produced a statistical theory of information that closely resembles the theoretical description of the behavior of the molecules of a gas. Systems designers of the pre-digital era used information theory to calculate the losses in information that occur through transmission media and to design equipment in which such losses are avoided. But as technology heads towards the year 2000, the information-energy analogy assumes a more direct and practical meaning. The falling cost of the silicon chip has given rise to digital systems that perform sophisticated functions of storing, transferring and manipulating information in ways that may be described as being 'intelligent'. The resulting equipment is finding ever expanding markets in offices, hospitals, factories and even the home. On a par with energy, information is becoming the life-blood of systems that are growing central to human existence.

It is not only the microprocessor-based personal computer that is responsible for the boom. Office automation demands image and voice communication that requires novel system structures. Industrial systems need to become ever more free of detailed programming so as to bring them under the control of operators not skilled in computer use, while systems in the home too need to be designed to be adaptive to the individual needs of their users.

The ideas and techniques that are required by the designer of information systems who is looking forward to the year 2000, come from a variety of sources. It is the aim of this book to bring these together as seen by a group of experienced designers of advanced digital systems. The authors of this book are all members of an Inter-Faculty Advanced Information Initiative research group at Brunel University in the UK, whose central concern is to anticipate the structure of digital information systems of the future. But this is not a book about computer architectures only. In some sense these change rapidly with advances in Silicon Chip technology, but in another, have changed little since the early proposals by

Von Neumann. The book is about principles that are likely to be the basis of advanced machines that break away from this mould as well as a few examples of novel architectures.

In the earlier sections the mathematical basis for the subject is presented from first principles. In particular, mathematical notations of a discrete kind are shown to give the system designer a language whereby he can be precise. A pleasant characteristic of this type of theory is that it makes virtually no demands on prior mathematical skills. It is based on notations of logical self-consistency that have become the main-stay of mathematics since the turn of the century. Aspects of ´Automata Theory´ are shown to be the applied side of such abstract mathematics. Despite the seeming contradiction in terms, the main use of these theories is to provide a thorough understanding of information handling machinery at a detached level avoiding the need for blind prototyping or even simulation. This philosophy is sustained in a chapter by Les Johnson and Chris Reade, who subject programming notations to abstract modeling. This commends itself to practically minded designers who have a concern for getting the structure of a program design right, without being caught up in the details of a specific programming language.

One of the major changes faced by information systems designers is the role of ´knowledge´ stored in such systems. Knowledge is information, but it is information of a functional kind; information that does things such as helping a robot understand the natural language requests of his user. To this end, ideas in Artificial Intelligence are reviewed together with the way in which digital systems may be designed to make such techniques available. Vision and pattern recognition are given particular attention: the editor, with John Stonham describes digital systems designs for fast, inexpensive intelligent schemes that are close to practical application.

A major chapter of this book presents a comprehensive survey by Rob Holte of ways in which knowledge may be built up in systems. The central problem is to extract concepts from streams of data: chairs, tables, nuts and bolts are concepts, but how does one design algorithms that learn to distinguish between them? Again the accent is on the ideas involved in such programs away from the clutter of programming detail.

In the closing parts of the book, Viv Begg turns advanced
information systems on themselves. She discusses the ideas
needed to implement knowledge-based systems that aid
designers to design other digital systems. The interest here
centers on the fine balance which needs to be achieved
between giving the designer structural access to stored rules
and previous designs and providing for variations in design
style. This is a developing field and Viv Begg's chapter is
one of the first tutorial descriptions of the subject.

In contrast, the final chapter by Mike Lea concentrates on
VLSI computer architecture. This describes the work carried
out in Lea's laboratory over some years relating to
associative processes. Implementation of such processes are
of vital importance in areas of information retrieval and
text processing where the task needs to be done rapidly.

On the whole, this book is written by a group of
practitioners who are concerned not only with the design of
advanced information systems but also with the education that
is necessary for understanding such advances. The authors
and their teams therefore present this book to others whose
educational aims and problems they share.

Acknowledgement

This book could not have been produced without the enormous
dedication shown by Mrs E. Flanagan and Dr Y.H. Ng, whose
perseverance with computer-based text production has made the
book available to the reader in a remarkably short period of
time.

Igor Aleksander
April 1984

Chapter 1

**Research in digital systems
historical hindsight and a look to
the future**

I. Aleksander

It is a curious aberration of technological history and technical language that the phrase ´digital systems´ means more than ´systems that operate using digits´. Its true meaning needs some explanation and it is in this explanation that one discovers the breadth and richness of this field of research. It is intended that this chapter as well as being a trailer for the rest of the book, shall be historical so as best to encompass ´digital systems´ in its full breadth.

At first glance one finds the foundation of digital systems amid the machinery of telephones and electromagnetic relays where from a mixture of ad hoc design methods, emerged the first set of unifying concepts: a technological application of mathematical logic proposed by Shannon in 1938.[*] From that date to the present day, the development of the subject includes not only novel ideas in methods of hardware design – from the giant mainframe to the distributed microprocessor network, or software – from the meticulousness of machine language to communication with machines in near–natural language, but also ideas of the fundamental meaning of concepts such as ´intelligence´, ´memory´, ´information´, and ´computability´ and so on.

In this first chapter we shall take a closer look at some of these ideas, partly because of their historical importance, and partly in order to focus on the significance of certain research areas that will be pursued in greater depth in the rest of the book.

The question of the real meaning of ´digital systems´ posed in the first paragraph still remains to be answered. If there is a common thread it must surely be this. The lifeblood of such systems is not energy, nor is it electricity, it is something much less definable: information.

Curiously enough the French word for ´digital systems´ is ´informatique´. The English translation of this word ´informatics´ is not generally accepted. Nevertheless, informatics is the subject of this book.

---

[*] Details of the references may be found at the end of the chapter.

1.1 INFORMATION AND INFORMATICS

Historically the central theoretical theme in information is
the modelling and definition of <u>information</u> itself.   Painted
with a very broad brush, <u>information</u> is

> ´that which is transacted when one entity
> alters the behavior of, or the state of
> knowledge of, another entity´

This kind of definition has almost a psychological quality
about it, although a psychologist would probably use the
words ´human being´ is place of ´entity´.   In   the
technological world this constraint is relaxed as the
´entity´ could be be a digital computer or a digital system
of some kind.   In the late 1930s, however, manufacturers of
equipment (telephone and radio) saw the need for a
theoretical model for information so that they might in some
way qualify the efficiency of their transmission equipment.
It is evident that if such equipment produces distortions
some of the information which it transmits may well get lost.
We all have experience of bad telephone lines.   In bad
telephone lines one can overcome these distortions either by
repeating words or speaking more slowly. It is possible to do
this too in the design of transmitters and receivers. This
possibility led to the best known theoretical development in
the modelling of information, *and that is Shannon´s
Statistical Theory of Information.*

Probably the most important result of Shannon´s work is the
definition of the ´bit´ and it is worth dwelling on this for
a while.

---

*   Shannon, C.E., and Weaver, W. (1949).
    There are also several undergraduate texts which explain
    information theory at an easily understandable level. One
    of these is Hamming, R.W. (1980)

Even very young microcomputer enthusiasts are now fully aware
of both the mathematical and technical character of the bit.
Its <u>mathematical</u> character is the fact that if the recipient
of the information can identify that he is expecting one of N
equally probable messages, the transmitter will have to send
at least $\log_2 N$ bits, where this number has to be rounded up
to the nearest integer. In other words, if the receiver
wants to know which, out of a pack of 52 cards has been
dealt, the transmitter has to set aside 6 bits of
information. The <u>technical</u> nature of the bit is that in a
system of transmission it is the least detectable signal. In
a slightly deeper look one realizes that distortion or noise
in a transmission system limits the accuracy with which a
signal can be transmitted. For example analog voltages
between 0 and 10 volts could be transmitted, where, if the
uncertainty due to ´noise´ were above one volt, such a signal
could carry up to 10 messages. If pushed to a limit one
finds it when the noise is about 5 volts and one can barely
distinguish whether the signal is there or not. Then one has
a ´two way´ unit of information and hence the name ´bit´
which means ´binary unit´.

Norbert Wiener in 1947 showed that not only was the bit a
fundamental unit of information in the transmission sense,
but also it was a cardinal element when one considers the
storage of information.[*] His argument goes as follows: let
us say that analog electronic devices are available, each of
which has an accuracy of 1 in K. That is, each device can
store precisely K messages. If the total number of messages
to be stored is M, then a number N of such devices is
required so that number N of such devices is required so
that:

$$K^N \text{ exceeds } M$$

At this point Wiener introduces <u>the cost of the storage elements</u>. He argues that it is quite plausible that the
cost of such a device is likely to be monotonically (that is
regularly increasing but not necessarily linearly increasing)
related to the accuracy (K) of the device. Under such
conditions he shows that the total cost of the system

---

[*] This argument can be found in chapter 5 of Wiener´s book
´Cybernetics´, MIT Press (1947). The book deals with
theoretical approaches to a study of living systems and
argues that Shannon´s contribution in the definition of
the ´bit´ was fundamental in a quest to assess the human
being as an information storage and processing machine.

required to store M messages is least when K is at its lowest
value, and consequently N is at its largest value. It has
already been said that the lowest usable value of K is 2 and
this completes the demonstration that the storage of the
information in binary form is likely to be the cheapest.

Although originally criticized for being too theoretical,
Wiener's argument has proved to be true in practice in the
intervening years since 1947.

Attempts at manufacturing analog or multi-message stores can
be found in work on hardware modeling of neural functions.
The two best examples of such work perhaps are the plated
wired memory or 'memistor' of Bernard Widrow (1961), and the
motor driven potentiometers of W.K. Taylor (1968). The lack
of realistic development of this work is now clearly seen as
having been caused by the wildly expensive nature of the
storage devices employed.

The cost of silicon chip binary memories on the other hand
has been plummetting downwards with the advance of Very Large
Scale Integrated technology (VLSI). Much of the research
reported in this book centers around the fact that this
falling cost makes novel informational architectures possible
and economically feasible.

So far, we have only dealt with some beneficial technical
advantages that have been derived from the definition of the
bit. There is, alas, a less beneficial side which is due to
the fact that the technical side of 'the stuff which is
transacted' is only a minor part of the whole.

At a superficial level, one can get a view of this problem by
realizing that 'that which is being transacted' is not only a
series of bits, but also that technically similar series can
have meanings of a widely different human value. A simple
example is the realization that the monetary value of a page
from Macbeth is very different from a page of a manual of a
new secret nuclear submarine, even though the two may contain
exactly the same number of bits. We shall return to this
theme in this chapter when considering advances made in
theoretical representations of language and its meaning.

A second research-provoking inadequacy of the concept of the bit relates to the colloquial or psychological use of the word ´memory´. Consider statements such as ´he has a good memory´; ´suddenly she remembered something she learnt as a child´; ´I can´t remember what he looks like´. The straight measurement of the number of bits going into, say, the human brain, or indeed, a measurement of the number of bits involved in speech, turns out to be a very poor indicator of the technological processes involved in the mechanism of storing information.

Unfortunately even John Von Neumann (1958), a giant of theoretical thought, attempted to say meaningful things about human memory by carrying out computations based on a bit-count.

Even less fortunately, the influence of digital computer memories has been such that psychology students reading fundamental texts* find brain models which structurally resemble digital computers and bear no relation to the structure of the brain itself.

An illustration of this difficulty involving a pseudo-random pulse generator may help at this point.

Consider a typical pseudo-random generator that generates 32 uncorrelated 8-bit characters. A calculation which assumes that such characters are merely stored and then regurgitated requires a mechanism capable of storing 256 bits of information. It is well known that a system consisting of only 8 binary storage elements and a suitable arrangement of feedback connections can achieve this performance. This sort of difficulty is particularly marked in digital learning systems as will be discussed in Chapters 5, 6 and 7. In such systems, incoming information modifies the functions of some crucial elements employed in generating networks (such as the pseudo-random pulse generator), completely re-arranging their behavior. This kind of consideration opens a novel approach to the storage of information which is closer to that found in psychology and brain study. It leads one to enquire into the relationship between stored information and changes in a system´s behavior: a fascinating subject which

----

*   Norman, D.A. (1969).

will be left until later.

1.2 THE ROLE OF LANGUAGE IN INFORMATICS RESEARCH

The development of digital computers and their programming
languages has had a major influence on the definition of what
´information´ might be. ´That which is transacted´ between a
programmer and his computer is usually done through the
medium of a well-developed programming language. It is
interesting that the emphasis in the development of such
languages has changed over the years, and this might be worth
tracing.

Early enthusiasm for computer programming which followed from
Von Neumann´s proposal that program as well as data should be
stored (1946), * was dampened by the sheer tedium of having to
express stored programs in a series of zeros and ones.

Therefore, the early intentions of computer language writers
were to overcome some of this detailed work by use of
mnemonics. Typical of such efforts were ´autocodes´ that
appeared in the late 1950s. Clearly, these efforts were not
wasted as mnemonic languages have survived and are indeed a
vital but intermediate part of the programming chain, having
been given the new name of ´assembly´ languages. The number
of minute steps that have to be taken even in mnemonic
language does not overcome the tedium of programming. For
this reason programming language development effort in the
early and mid 1960s was aimed at developing languages where
instructions of a more global nature could be interpreted or
compiled by the machine itself into its minute constituents.
A deeper intention was an attempt to bring such languages
closer to the natural spoken language. The more widely used
results of these efforts were languages such as Fortran,
Algol and, for business applications, Cobol.

---

* This is the well-known fundamental report on computer
  design: Burks, W.A., Goldstine, H.M., and Von Neumann, J.
  (1946).
  A classical, general text on programming languages is:
  Peterson, W.W. (1974).

Even those who have had minimal experience of computer programming will be aware of occasions when the computer prints out something like ´syntax error´. This simply indicates that the machine and its resident program have not ´understood´ something which the programmer was trying to communicate to them. This illustrates a breakdown of communications which could not be explained by using Shannon´s theory. The line is clear, there is no noise, and yet the information has not struck home. The new concept which has to be accommodated by a theory which deals with this problem is that of breaking or obeying certain rules.

It is generally accepted the most influential creator of such a theory was Noam Chomsky, who, in 1957 and 1965, produced a mathematical theory of language.

Detailed attention will be given to such concepts in Chapter 3, here we merely wish to focus our attention on what linguistic theory adds to our understanding of the word ´information´.

To Shannon, information is simply a string or sequence of symbols. The amount of information transmitted may be calculated simply through a knowledge of the probability of occurrence of these symbols. Linguistic theories on the other hand say that certain strings of symbols carry information whereas others are totally meaningless. Linguistic theory goes on to say that the way in which living beings and computers distinguish between such meaningful and meaningless strings is not because they have memorized all legitimate strings that make up a particular language, but results from remembering the rules which are necessary both to generate and to check the authenticity of such strings.

At this stage it might be worth giving a simple brief example of the way in which Chomsky formulated some of these rules. They are based on a system of replacements.

In the following example we shall show that starting with a symbol such as <sentence> and a string replacement governed by rules, one can generate limited statements about possible relationships between two persons.

The starting symbol in a process of generation is <sentence>. The first rule says that the symbol <sentence> may be replaced by a sequence of precisely three other symbols. The first of these is <subject>, the second is <verb> and the third is <object>. The formal way of writing this is: <sentence> := <subject> <verb> <object>.

The symbol (:=) is read as ˊmay be replaced byˊ.

The next level of ˊproductionˊ consists of replacing the symbols <subject>, <verb> and <object>. For example the rules might say that <subject> may be replaced by the words John or Jack or Mary. Formally this is written as.

<subject> := John/Jack/Mary.

Similarly:

<verb> := loves/hates/ignores.

Also:

<object> := John/Jack/Mary.

We note that in obeying these rules we can generate somewhat simple sentences such as:

John loves Mary

or:

Jack hates John.

It might also strike one as odd that the rules generate sentences such as ˊMary hates Maryˊ. We can let that go for the time being on the understanding that we do not possess the sophistication in our rules that would allow us to say.

Mary hates herself.

It is clear nevertheless, that the rules would not allow sentences such as:

Mary John loves hates ignores.

Shannonˊs concept of information would indeed have failed to distinguish between these two types of sequences.

An important question for the informatician to ask is why
should there be a virtue in grammatical correctness? After
all, the often quoted phrase:

'little green ideas sleep furiously'

although grammatically correct (within the rules of English
grammar) is just as meaningless as one that breaks the rules.

The point about the last sentence above is that its meaning
has gone awry as it does not point to sensible things in the
world as we know it. To the computer expert that is the same
as writing a perfectly legitimate line of program but one
which might cause the computer to cycle endlessly or produce
meaningless results. This is called 'semantic correctness'
which will be tackled in some detail in Chapter 4. Here we
return briefly to the question we have raised earlier on the
necessity for grammatical or 'syntactic' correctness. In the
same way as Shannon draws our attention to the fact that the
transmission medium must contain little noise and must have
sufficient bandwidth for transmission (in other words in
order to transmit information one must have a properly
structured carrier), Chomsky teaches us that grammatical
correctness is a necessary carrier for the conveyance of
meaning.

In other words, phrases and sentences have to be correctly
structured before they can carry meaning at all. From the
point of view of the information engineer this has enormous
importance because it draws attention to mechanisms which
must exist in the machines which receive linguistic
information or, indeed, machines which might generate such
information. The methodology of the design of such machines
will be of central concern to us in Chapter 3.

It is clear that we must, even in this introductory chapter,
go beyond Chomsky's work and return to the question of the
transmission of meaning. As seen in our discussion so far,
meaning is a central element of 'that which is transacted':
if meaning is not transmitted, nothing is transmitted.

In a technical sense there are two inter-related pre-
requisites for the transmission of meaning. The first is
that both the transmitter and the receiver should be endowed
with storage media of both the long term and the short term

nature. Secondly, the transmitter and the receiver must
share some common information stored in their memory. These
points may be illustrated as follows. Consider the following
strings of phrases:

´Champion show-jumper Harvey Smith was ready. He took the
first fence with ease, hesitating a little at the   second.´
Notice how the first phrase acts in a scene setting capacity
for the second.   Clearly the receiver must be endowed with a
short term store which he uses to hold the scenario created
by the first phrase.   Otherwise taken in isolation, the
second phrase might be totally misunderstood as having to do
perhaps with the stealing of fences.   Now note the role of
longer term stores. Very simply, the receiver must possess a
store of knowledge from which he can extract elements for his
short term store triggered by words such as ´champion show-
jumper´.   One notes that nothing that has been said actually
indicates that there are horses in the scene and it is
precisely information such as this that the receiver will
need to extract from his long term store in order to
understand the sentence.   An even more interesting use of
stored information lies in the knowledge that the transmitter
might have the knowledge contained in the receiver.

For example, if the transmitter were to know that the
receiver was an expert in show-jumping, the above group of
phrases need not have contained the phrase ´champion show-
jumper´.

The issue is undoubtedly a complex one and will be treated in
greater detail in Chapter 5 under the heading ´Artifical
Intelligence´.   Here we stress that, in pursuing the
transmission of meaning, the information scientist has found
a need to cope with the concept of stored information as an
integral part of a communications system.   We shall see in
Chapter 5 that the major originators of technical ideas in
this area were Winograd (1972) , Schank and Abelson (1975)
and the larger group of scientists who developed work which
goes under the heading of ´expert systems´.*

At this point we can provide brief trailers of this work so
as not to leave the contribution of meaning in the definition

---

*   See the following for a review of ´Expert Systems´ Michie,
     D. (1980).

of information as too much of a mystery.

One strand among the theoretical approaches to meaning (or
semantics), assumes that words point to sets of objects in a
real world, or relationships between such sets. Indeed, in
order to transmit semantic information is a pseudo-robotic
scenario, Terry Winograd (1972) assumed that a human user was
carrying a natural language conversation with a computer with
both the human being and the computer sharing knowledge above
in a simplified world which contain objects such as blocks,
pyramids, boxes and spheres. A statement such as ´the green
box´ could cause the computer to perform a logical operation
of intersection between the set of green objects and the set
of boxes in its field of view and treat the resulting set of
objects as having the new label ´green boxes´. In this way,
the meaning of complete sentences could be evaluated as sets
of objects in the real world. Should this set turn out to be
empty then the sentence would have no meaning. It is through
this procedure that sentences such as:

               ´little green ideas sleep furiously´

would evaluate to an empty set.

This would happen in an early part of the computation because
even the part of the phrase ´green ideas´ would imply an
intersection of all objects that are green and all objects
that could be labeled as ´ideas´ which is quite clearly an
empty set. But more of this in Chapter 5.

Schank and Abelson (1975), although accepting this approach,
argue that the informational transaction between two
intelligent organisms must be capable of ranging over several
´simple worlds´. They refer to such simple worlds as
´scripts´. According to these principles the major part of
the informational transaction is seen as containing cues
which are used to load the correct scripts into the
recipient´s memory. Indeed in the previous example involving
the show-jumping sentence, the words ´Harvey Smith´ for the
initiated or ´show-jumper´ for the uninitiated were just such
cues.

It will become obvious in Chapter 5 that the field of
Artificial Intelligence often addresses questions related to

the enabling of specific areas of store within the computer
system in response to cues received from the machine's input.
One suspects that some of the definition of information
transactions particularly with regard to scripts, cues and,
as we shall see, 'semantic networks' (Winston, 1977) were
heavily influenced by developments in computer science in the
area of relational databases. These are schemes of storing
information particularly in the backing store (disk or tape)
of a computer, schemes which were originally intended to keep
track of information such as mailing lists or the stock
holdings of commercial organizations. The relations in such
systems are of a simple nature such as, for example, the
relationship between a person's name and his telephone
number. This is just one facet of the importance of role of
memory structure in the history of digital systems research,
one which merits closer attention.

1.3 MEMORY: THE TECHNOLOGICAL CORNERSTONE OF DIGITAL SYSTEMS

In this introductory survey one has already seen hints that
memory is a concept which is inextricably interwoven in
systems that handle information. In the next few paragraphs
concepts of memory will be singled out because, as will be
seen in several other parts of this book, it is research in
memory structures which has led and is likely to lead in the
future to some of the major advances in digital systems.
There are three distinct avenues which can be pursued. The
first relates to advances in memory structures as they apply
to the conventional Von Neumann computer model. The second,
indirectly related to physiological models of brain function,
relates to memory being used as an active logical ingredient
in a digital system. The third strand is theoretical and
centers around the role which memory plays in the structure
of an abstract 'automaton'.

1.3.1 Computer Memories

The word 'memory' crept into engineering jargon in the late
1930s among communication engineers who were involved in
designing switching systems for telephone networks. The
building brick of such networks in the electromagnetic relay
and this was said to have 'memory' in a way which is best

illustrated by means of an example (Fig. 1.1).

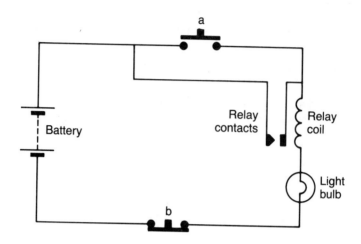

Fig. 1.1 An early 'memory' circuit

In this figure we see a very simple circuit that consists of a battery, a switch ´a´ which is normally open, a switch ´b´ which is normally closed and the electromagnetic relay, all of this being in series with a light bulb.

The coil of the electromagnetic relay is also in series with a pair of its contacts and if at any time a current were to be made to pass through the coil, the magnetic force it creates shuts the contact. We also note that switch ´a´ is in parallel with these contacts. Assume that the contacts are open and that no current flows in the circuit with the consequence that the light is off. If switch ´a´ (which we assume to be a push button) is now pressed a current is caused to flow in the circuit switching the light on and also closing the contacts of the relay. We note that if switch ´a´ is now released allowing it to spring open, the circuit continues to allow the current to flow leaving the light on. Switch ´b´ must be pressed in order to return the circuit to its original state with the light switched off. It will stay in this state even if switch ´b´ is released.

The circuit can rest (that is with no one pushing the buttons) in two states, one with the light switched on and the other with the light switched off. Which of these states is enforced depends on which of the two buttons was last pressed. The word ´memory´ was used in this context because the circuit ´remembers´, and indicates by means of the light, which was the last button to be pressed. This indeed is a feat of electrical memory.

The above is an example of a relay version of the building block of virtually any electronic digital system with memory. the Set-Reset flip-flop. In modern systems such devices are created electronically, of course, and a single silicon chip may have tens of thousands of such flip-flops inside it. Of course in a system with, say, f such flip-flops there can be 2f possible memory states. With systems containing tens of thousands of such flip-flops the number of available memory states in which the system can exist becomes astronomical.

In early electronic computers, flip-flops were organized in banks of, say, ten such devices. These were called <u>registers</u> and the memories of such computers consisted solely of banks of such registers. The registers with ten flip-flops can memorise 2^{10}, that is, approximately 1000 different numbers.

Such registers would be used mainly as temporary stores for numbers which were to be deployed in a calculation. Currently, even the cheapest pocket calculators contain several such registers. As has already been mentioned the contribution made by Von Neumann to the design of digital systems was to show that instructions too could be stored in such registers after being suitably encoded. He also suggested a method of addressing these registers so that the stored instructions would not only be addressed one after the other during the execution of a program, but also could contain information regarding where the data pertaining to the chosen instruction could be found. All this is now familiar knowledge even to teenage enthusiasts who have computing amongst their list of hobbies.

The trouble with this model of ´memory´ is that in a sense it redefines the notion of living memory in rather stultified technological terms. In other words, when a technologically minded person mentions the word ´memory´, a standard structure is implied which at first sight appears to have as much capability as a filing cabinet and a highly restricted filing cabinet at that: one where the file pockets have only numerical indices rather than context indices. Such indices correspond to the addresses that are used in conventional computer memory systems.

There has even been a kind of ricochet effect from this type of structure into the modeling of human memory. Models of memory in texts for psychology students which closely resemble the structures in computer systems are quite common. This is totally at odds with the findings of neurophysiology where the structure of the brain brings to light no evidence of addressing schemes and input/output data flows such as exist in computer structures. We will return to models which more closely resemble the structures of the brain in the next section.

In the meantime it is worth noting that there are enormous opportunities for research into imaginative memory structures that are considerably different from those dominated by the Von Neumann model. For example, in Chapter 10 of this book, a storage structure which can be addressed by content instead of number, will be discussed. Such concepts if implemented in hardware result in enormous speed improvements in the behavior of computing systems applied to specific tasks. The tasks that benefit most are in the areas of text editing and information retrieval as will be seen. This type of work benefits particularly if the implementation is carried out through the medium of special purpose high speed Very Large Scale Integrated circuits (VLSI). Furthermore, there is a great deal that can be done in the design of imaginative storage structures if one treats a conventional commercial memory chip as a logical device. In such a device what is memorized is the function between its input and output terminals. It will be shown in Chapter 6 that such an approach is particularly profitable in the design of large parallel systems such as the WISARD scheme of pattern recognition. The following section deals with this type of approach in a little more detail.

1.3.2 Functional Aspects of Memory

The roots of some of the concepts expressed under this heading go back further in history than the invention of the

Von Neumann computer structure. They may be found among attempts by engineers and physiologists to create artificial models of the fundamental brain cell: the neuron. The best known model is that of McCulloch and Pitts (1943), which was then modified slightly by Brindley (1967). Although details of this will be provided in a later chapter, suffice it to say here that such models see neurons as learning to fire strongly (that is, to emit a rapid succession of electrical impulses) at an output called the axon, for certain selected groups of patterns of such firing at the inputs of the neuron, which are called the synapses.

According to recent hypotheses, in early stages of learning, the neuron is forced to fire by the arrival of pulses at one or more particularly active synapses called the dominant synapses. Whatever learning goes on in this cell seems to be related to its ability to perform an association between patterns of firing at the other synapses which occur in a consistent fashion with the firing at the dominant synapses. Eventually the firing patterns at the non-dominant synapses take over and cause firing in the neuron itself without further action from the dominant synapses.

It can be said that the neuron has ´learnt´ a logical function which relates sets of input firing patterns to the firing at its own output. In earlier parts of this chapter we have already referred to the work of Widrow (1961) and Taylor (1968) in the context of systems which required multi-message memories. This relates to neuron modelling as follows.

It was a team at the Massachusetts Institute of Technology composed of the physiologist Warren McCulloch and the engineer Walter Pitts who, as early as 1943, proposed an electronic model for the neuron in which learning could be represented as changes in synaptic effect. These changes would be recorded in a multi-message or analog memory, one being required for each synaptic input. As mentioned before, implemented in hardware, such analog memories turn out to be unwieldy. It has often been stressed (Aleksander and Burnett, 1984) that in order to achieve an intelligent level of memory such as represented by systems of neurons, one need not do this by means of precise analog models of the neuron itself. The alternative is a ´functional´ model, that is, one which is similar with respect to its outward terminal behavior, but very different in its technological make-up. The prime candidate for such a device is the commercially available Random Access Memory.

This is a conventional computer store shrunk into a single silicon chip which literally only costs a few pence. Functionally this behaves as a neuron in the sense that the output data terminals fire (output logical ones) or don't (output logical noughts) in response to input patterns present at the 'addressing' terminals of the RAM. 'The data input' terminals, which when the chip is 'enabled' to read, and therefore actually determine the desired output for a given addressing input, behave much like the dominant synapses in the neuron. The ability to see the Random Access Memory device as merely a component from which one can create networks opens the possibility of several research areas as will be discussed in Chapter 7. This research is not only technological, but it also enables one to model living systems as networks of memory elements and in this way carry out pseudo-clinical experiments which tell us more about living systems themselves. This too will be discussed in Chapter 7.

1.3.3 Theoretical Approaches to Memory

From a theoretical standpoint the world of information processing machines divides neatly into machines with memory and machines without. Those without generally go under the heading 'combinational' machines, their overriding characteristic being the fact that their outputs are related to their inputs in a most direct, one-for-one manner. A combinational machine which at some stage outputs message n_1 will do so in response to input message i_1 and do so consistently forever. Again in mathematical terminology (see Chapter 2) one could say that every combinational (that is memoryless) machine maps a set of input messages into a set of output messages. On the other hand, a machine with memory produces an output which is a function of not only this current input message but also the entire past history of such messages.

David Huffman (1954) provided an early ingenious mathematical model which showed quite clearly how memory in the shape of flip-flops can be brought into play in a general way in making machines sensitive to such input sequences.

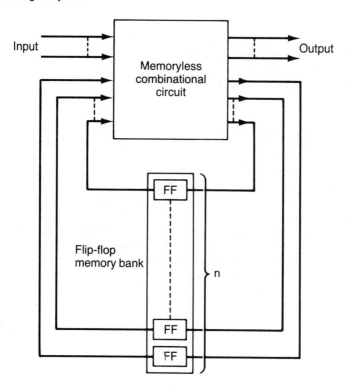

Fig. 1.2 The Huffman sequential circuit model

The model used by Huffman is shown in Fig. 1.2. Here it is seen that the machine is split into two parts. The first is a part without memory and the second is the memory itself which merely consists of a row of n single bit storage elements or flip-flops. It is this group of flip-flops that keeps track of significant historical events at the input while the memoryless or combinational part of the system relates not only the overall output but also the next memory state to the current input and current memory state. Much more will be said of this model (called the ´finite state machine´ or FSM both in Chapter 2 where the mathematics of such systems will be discussed and in Chapter 3 where the scope and limitations of such models will be described.

In the latter we shall discover that one of the main limitations of such models lies in the fact that they become

difficult to handle when it is necessary to keep track of
very long sequences of inputs. In general, if there are n
flip-flops in the system the output can at best be a function
of past history of a large but finite number of input events,
as will be seen in Chapter 2.

A system of computation that does not suffer from this
limitation has been devised by British mathematician Alan
Turing (1936). This achieves its virtually infinite memory
through the conceptual notion of an infinite tape on which
symbols may be written and from which symbols may be read.
Turing devised this idea in order to provide a theory which
defines ´that which may be computed´. He did not wish such
arguments to be hampered by the practical fact that most
computing systems have a limited amount of store. In other
words, he was interested in ´that which may be computed´
given an infinite amount of memory.

1.3.4 Comment

The three aspects of memory outlined above make it quite
clear that storage of information has played an enormous role
in the development of informatic systems. However, it should
be realized that the above three points only encompassed a
particular aspect of storage: the structure and theoretical
aspect.   One ought also to remember that even with
conventional structures of storage and conventional computing
machines, programmers have been able to devise most
significant ´apparent´ memory structures. For example, the
concept of paging has enabled the computer user to address a
great deal more store than would otherwise have been possible
with a limited word size in a machine. The same is true of
´virtual memory´ which makes the power of backing memory
available to the user of the machine as if it were local
storage within the computer. Indeed the entire question of
organizing and interfacing with structured items of
information in the backing store of a computer is a topic on
which much research has been done and on which many advanced
programming techniques rely.

Such work will not be considered in any detail in this book
as it properly belongs to the very center of computer science
and several textbooks are devoted to these subjects.[*]
Although our stated aim in this book is to concentrate on
novel structures and novel techniques that might influence
the digital system of the future, we shall make frequent
reference to such central work in computer science wherever
appropriate.

1.4 THE STRUCTURE OF THIS BOOK: A LOOK TOWARDS THE FUTURE

From the background history of digital systems as described
so far in this chapter, the authors of this book are unified
in thinking that the very nature of Digital Information
Systems is changing from a concern for systems that process
and store information, to systems that in some way or another
may be said to possess 'Intelligence', or process
'Knowledge'. One uses here words, derived from human
attributes, with a great deal of care. They need to be given
a technical meaning and a technical framework, in much the
same way as 'Memory' and 'Information' have been formalized
as seen earlier.

There is no doubt, however, that 'Intelligence' and
'Knowledge' express ideas at a higher level of systems design
than 'Information' and 'Memory'. Our contention therefore is
that the Digital Systems design engineer needs to change his
standpoint, and it is to facilitate this change that this
book is dedicated. It has been divided into three major
sections which we introduce below.

Digital Systems and Formalisms (Chapters 2, 3 and 4)

A formalism is merely a method of expression, one that
sharpens up concepts and removes ambiguity. The next three
chapters of this book look at different aspects of
formalisms, starting in Chapter 2, with 'modern' mathematics
and the way in which it is likely to help those interested in
digital information systems. Some of the ideas presented in

---

[*]   See for example: Teorey, T.J., and Fry, J.P., (1982).

this chapter lie at the very root of formal thought and its relationship to digital systems, which may come as a surprise to classically trained engineers or computer scientists.

The surprise comes from a break with engineering tradition where mathematical equations are <u>used</u> as tools. Digital Systems are much more like expressions of mathematical ideas. So the ´use´ of mathematics is different.

In fact, there are very few ´equations´ that can be used as tools. The chapter concentrates on ´modern´ mathematics (or ´abstract´ mathematics) and the way its formalisms stand away from direct application. The accent is on theories that are consistent in themselves and the way one achieves and structures mathematical systems. This type of thinking is of central importance in digital systems design; it will be seen that consistency is analogous to correct operation, and mathematical structure is related to the functional structure of systems.

The chapter explains how mathematics, of necessity, departed from being closely related to effects in the real world as the main test for correctness, to self-consistency being the main testing criterion. The best known mathematical systems (Boolean Algebra, Semigroups, etc.) and the way they are classified as the basis of their properties is the main theme of the chapter.

Chapter 3 concentrates on those theoretical principles that are of direct relevance to digital information systems and go under the heading of Automata Theory. This is a theory that formalizes the rules governing systems that may be described as having ´internal´ states. The behavior of such systems depends on the interactions between internal states and inputs and applies to almost every non-trivial digital system. The chapter goes on the consider automata that are specifically attuned to information systems that can be described as <u>languages</u>. The chapter not only deals with abstract machinery (or theories), but also with the constraints that are introduced when one thinks of physical implementation.

The third chapter in this group (Chapter 4), by Chris Reade and Les Johnson, continues the theme of concern for formalism. In this case it is not the structure of the automation, or of the general characteristics of language-like systems that comes under scrutiny, but the programming language itself. The links between programming language components and method of abstraction are discussed, showing that in a programming language the process of abstraction is explicit and interesting.

A discussion of data types and control structures as abstraction mechanisms leads to a consideration of the nature of very high level languages whose constructs are based on pure mathematical expressions. These high-level structures go under the headings of 'Functional' and 'Applicative' languages. The structure of such languages is much closer to mathematical notation and its potential for precise expression is likely to be of major importance to the designer of advanced systems.

Digital Systems and the Handling of Knowledge
(Chapters 5, 6 and 7)

The traditional field in which 'Knowledge' was first seen as an important parameter in artificial intelligence. This is briefly reviewed in Chapter 5, stressing those advances that embody interesting engineering principles. In many ways artificial intelligence is maturing, and one aspect of this in an increase of interest in capturing 'Knowledge'. Simply defined, knowledge is stored information about facts in the real world that enable a system to interact with further information with better anticipation and expectation.

In Chapter 6, John Stonham describes a low level system for capturing knowledge of a kind that leads to practical pattern recognition systems. These systems are described as being 'low-level' as they operate on new data as may be, say, generated by a television camera.

In Chapter 7, one examines two principal ways in which the computational level of the systems described in the previous chapter may be raised. The object of the exercise is to make increasingly better use of knowledge.

The first method deals with the application of feedback techniques to low-level systems, essentially to translate acquired knowledge into functional state structures (sequences of internal states).

The second method, suggests that a theory of personality may be used to enhance high-level systems by giving them a technical version of ´curiosity´. But more of that in Chapter 7.

Chapter 8 contains a major contribution by Robert Holte which provides a survey of recent advances in knowledge acquisition, under the heading of ´concept learning´. It is curious that knowledge acquisition received relatively little attention from workers in artificial intelligence in the 1960s and 1970s. This chapter points clearly at the recent revival of interest in this field which is soundly based in algorithmic principles. The chapter forms a clear link back to the first chapter in this group being based in principles largely derived from artificial intelligence.

Aids and Architectures

The last two chapters return to the digital system proper, in two very different ways. Chapter 9 by Vivienne Begg, discusses computer aided design schemes and argues that potentially it is the partnership of man and machine that is going to yield the most powerful design. But where does the future lie in this field which again, has a track record of some 4 years of standing, without striking advances having occurred? Vivienne Begg argues convincingly that the answer may lie in considering known CAD techniques with expert systems. That is, by setting up a conversation between machine and expert designer, it may be possible to acquire better knowledge bases for CAD, than has been done to date by blatant pre-programming.

The final chapter by Michael Lea concentrates on a specific class of computer architecture: the associative processor. This is a practical development that finds application in text processing, image processing and database organization from well-founded hardware principles – a fitting down-to-earth end to the book.

1.5 SUMMARY

We have described the focus of attention in this book on Advances in Digital Systems against a background of the hindsight of history and the realism of a certain degree of rigor. It is intended to provide a springboard for the inventive designer of digital information systems to develop his future contributions.

REFERENCES

Aleksander, I., and Burnett, P. (1984) ´Reinventing Man´ Kogan Page, London.

Brindley, G.S. (1967) ´The Classification of Modifiable Synapses and their Use in Models for Conditioning´, Proc. R. Soc. B 168, 361-376.

Burks, A.N., Goldstine, H.H., and Von Neumann, J. (1946) ´A Preliminary Discussion of the Logical Design of an Electronic Computing Instrument´, Princeton Inst. of Adv. Study.

Chomsky, N. (1957) ´Syntactic Structures´ Mouton, (1957).

Chomsky, N. (1965) ´Aspects of The Theory of Syntax´, Mouton.

Hamming, R.W. (1980) ´Coding and Information Theory´, Prentice-Hall, Englewood Cliffs.

Huffman, D.A. (1954) ´The Synthesis of Sequential Switching Circuits´, J. Franklin Inst., 257, 161-190 and 275-303.

Michie, D. (1980) ´Expert Systems´, Computer Journal 23 (Nov. 1980).

McCulloch, W.S., and Pitts, N.H. (1943) ´A Logical Calculus of the Ideas Immanent in Nervous Activity´, Bull. Math. Biophys. 5, 115-133.

Norman, D.A. (1969) ´Memory and Attention´, John Wiley and Sons, New York.

Peterson, W.W. (1974) ´Introduction to Programming Languages´, Prentice-Hall, Englewood Cliffs.

Schank, R.C., and Abelson R.P. (1975) ´Scripts Plans of Knowledge´, in ´Proc. 4th Int. Joint Conf. on A.I.´, Tbilisi, USSR.

Shannon, E.C., and Weaver, W. (1949) ´The Mathematical Theory of Communication´, University of Illinois Press.

Taylor, W.K. (1968) ´Machines that Learn´, Science Journal 4 (10), 102-107.

Teorey, T.J., and Fry, J.P. (1982) ´Data Base Structures´, Prentice-Hall, Englewood Cliffs.

Turing, A.M. (1936) ´On Computable Numbers with an Application to the Entscheidungs Problem´, Proc. Condon Math Soc. 4R, 230-265.

Von Neumann, J. (1958) ´The Computer and The Brain´, Yale University Press.

Widrow, B., and Hoff, M.E. (1961) ´Adaptive and Switching Circuits´, Inst. of Radio Engineers, Wescon Record.

Wiener, N. (1947) ´Cybernetics´, MIT Press, Boston.

Winograd, T. (1972) ´Understanding Natural Language´, Academic Press.

Winston, P.H. (1977) ´Artificial Intelligence´, Addison Wesley, Menlo Park, California.

Chapter 2

Mathematics and digital systems
A guide to formalisms

I Aleksander

2.1 INTRODUCTION

There are three marks of distinction that make the
relationship between the digital systems scientist and
mathematics different from, say, the classical interaction
between the engineer and mathematics. These are, first, in
some sense the mathematics used in conjunction with digital
systems is ´modern´; second, the mathematics of digital
systems is in some sense ´pure´; finally, the way in which a
digital systems scientist ´uses´ mathematics is what at this
stage can only be described as different. It is the
intention of this chapter to explore all three of these
concepts while at the same time providing some of the basic
ideas which underline such mathematics. Unfortunately the
above issues are inter-twined but will hopefully emerge as
part of our discussion.

2.2 NEW MATHS FOR NEW SYSTEMS

Before the days of digital systems, 90% of what was being
analyzed and designed by engineers and physicists required a
deep knowledge of classical linear algebra and Euclidean
geometry. This is ´old´ mathematics in the sense that some
of it dates back to the ancient Greeks while some ´recent´
discoveries find their roots in the seventeenth and
eighteenth centuries. In a very broad sense ´the ancient´
is the mathematics of continuousness. Digital systems are
clearly discontinuous and are therefore likely to benefit
little from continuous mathematics.

However, continuousness is not the only factor at stake,
there is also a qualitative difference between the ancient
and the modern. The modern mathematician is used to
creating mathematical systems where self-consistency is the
prime requirement rather than a reflection of things in the
world. The digital systems engineer finds this attitude
appealing because he too is interested in creating
structures, whether they be programmed or whether they be
hardware, where self-consistency (that is, correct operation)
is a prime requirement.

It should be stressed, however, that in order to reach a level of abstraction the modern mathematician must be very cautious. Having decided to abandon the safe world of theories which can easily be tested by experiment, the pure mathematician must proceed in small rigorous steps so as to be convincing about his conclusions. This is true too of the digital systems designer. Since he trades in abstractions he must make sure that the steps he takes follow logically from what he has developed already. It is for this reason that designers of computational systems have found an interest in the methodology of rigorous proof procedures. One is arguing therefore that the digital systems designer is inclined to operate more as a ´pure´ mathematician than an ´applied´ mathematician. It is quite common nowadays for papers in digital systems design to be expressed in the language of a logical proof.

Finally one notes that the objects which modern mathematicians use as tools of their trade, that is, various self-consistent mathematical systems with known properties, are also appealing to the digital systems designer. The reason for this is the actual self-consistency of such systems. In other words if a systems designer can identify properties of one of his systems as being in some way parallel to those of a self-consistent abstract mathematical theory he can bring to bear the known characteristics of the mathematical system into an understanding of his own design.

It is for these reasons that in the rest of this chapter we shall first take a look at the way in which modern mathematics has developed from the ancient and relate this to the notion of axiom and proof. We shall then go on to consider some of the best known abstract mathematical systems and try to relate them where possible to systems that are found in the realm of informatics.

It is necessary to end this section by stressing that modern algebraic systems, being abstract, have almost a life of their own. Whether they find sympathetic systems in the real world depends on whether the mathematician/systems designer finds suitable hypotheses whereby he can achieve this connection. The excellence or otherwise of the theory is usually judged by standards of self-consistency and elegance rather than one´s ability to find hypotheses which map theories into the real world. This is the crux of what one means by abstraction, the implication being that there may be some excellent abstract mathematical systems for which no mapping into the real world has yet been found. This is an object lesson for the digital systems designer as it points him towards freedom in understanding systems, and indeed, designing systems, for which the technology might as yet not have produced the right hypotheses for mapping into a real systems. Despite the apparent uselessness of designing such systems it is an appealing notion that through abstraction one reaches higher levels of understanding, both in mathematics and modern digital systems.

2.3 MATHEMATICAL TRUTH AND RIGOR: A BRIEF HISTORY

It is sometimes thought that mathematics provides an intellectual refuge of cold logic where opinion and emotion have no place - an endeavor where statements follow without ambiguity from previous ones. Mathematical history, however, reveals a somewhat different picture. Indeed, statements (or theories) follow logically from one another, but where do the initial statements (or axioms) come from? Clearly, such axioms cannot, by definition, be proved so their validity must be established in some other way.

To stress this point, most who have followed a school curriculum in geometry have slavishly learnt the proofs of one theory after another, most of which were first proved by Euclid in the fourth century BC. However, all of this quite vast structure of theories is underpinned by very few axioms.

The most fundamental of these is:

> ´Given a straight line and a point P not on this
> line, there is one and only one other straight
> line through P which is parallel to the first.´

Very few would choose to question this as it somehow appears to be self-evident. But what are the rules for chosing such ´self-evident´ axioms in a system of mathematics? This question began to be debated in the seventeenth century and developed into a raging controversy by the turn of the twentieth century. At times this debate was so furious that

it made mathematicians wonder whether there was any validity
in mathematical activity at all.

The dominating notion until the seventeenth century was one
due to Plato[*] and saw the objects of mathematics as
generalizations of objects in the real world.

For example, the real world is full of circular objects,
while in mathematics there is only one <u>notion</u> of a ´circle´
with only one determining parameter; its diameter. Thus over
the 2000 or so years since Plato and Euclid, it was thought
that most of the main objects of mathematics had been
discovered and formed a stable set of formal ideas which
could be transferred from generation to generation as the
study of ´mathematics´.

Among those who began to question this attitude was the
French mathematician Blaise Pascal, who, around 1660
suggested that if two salient rules are followed, it
legitimizes the discovery of new axioms. The rules are:

a) No matter how clear an axiom may seem, it must be
widely accepted.

b) Only perfectly self-evident concepts may be chosen
as axioms.

This gave mathematics a status of ´truth by consensus´ and
mathematicians the role of high priests sitting in judgement
over the acceptability of new axioms. Inevitably such
acceptability was gained by looking to one´s experience in
the real world. This meant that mathematics remained
solidly Euclidean as the ancient Greeks had already
encompassed most observable axioms of geometry. It was
about 200 years after the death of Pascal that mathematicians
began to wonder whether observable axioms might not be merely
the tip of an iceberg of grander, but more abstract,
mathematical systems.

---

[*] See ´Plato´s Republic´, Book VI, No. 510.

This was brought into sharp focus by the questioning of Euclid´s axiom (quoted earlier) by the Russian mathematician Lobatchevski (ca. 1840) and the Hungarian Bolyay (see Meschkowski, 1968, for more detail). Independently they suggested that instead of imagining one and only one line passing through a point at some distance from another line and parallel to it, one could define at least two. They suggested that initially one such line be the parallel one and the other not, and that it makes mathematical sense to retain the separate identity of such lines even if the second swings around to become coincident with the first. In Euclidean terms such individual identity is lost. Thus Lobatchevski and Bolyay defined the first non-Euclidean geometry and studied the rather significant effect of the above modification on geometry as a whole. Indeed, this not only provided evidence of the possibility of a perfectly consistent alternative method of mathematics, but also, because of the seeming arbitrariness of the fundamental Euclidean axiom, suggested that there may be of a very large number, indeed an infinite number, of perfectly legitimate, self-consistent, alternative systems of geometry.

The shattering effect of such non-Euclidean geometries was not due to the theories within the newly discovered set, but the fact that the ´axioms´ were in some sense abstract and not easily verifiable in the real world, removing the Platonic basis for deciding ´where axioms come from´. It was at the turn of the twentieth century that the German mathematician David Hilbert (1900)[*] suggested that the real world need only ´hint-at´ the existence of axioms. In other words, there must be another quality that distinguishes the excellence or ´truth´ of an axiom. For Hilbert it is free-dom from contradiction and the independence from other axioms that creates this quality. The importance of this lay in the fact that the objects of a mathematical system could be suggested by ´...love, law, chimneysweeps, tables, chairs and beermugs...´. What is important is the fact that if a theory can be proved it has a value that may be independent of these objects even though it may hold for the objects. The attraction of such an independence of objects in the real world is that once proven, a theory may have an important significance not only in the world of objects which first suggested its axioms, but in a variety of other situations as well.

---

[*]   Hilbert, D. (1900).

Thus the excellence or otherwise of a theory lies in the breadth of self-related properties that form a mathematical system.

The application of such a theory is a double transformation process. First the objects of a particular aspect of the world must be seen as being properly described by an existing set of axioms of a mathematical system. Having established such a correspondence, the theories can be significantly transformed back into this world as a second step. Thus it is possible to conceive theories which are complete and hence ´real´ even if no ´real world´ correspondence has been established.

Before ending this introductory section, it may be worth mentioning that the discovery of ´abstract´ mathematical systems was the beginning and not the end of additional headaches for mathematicians. This arose through an enquiry into which was ´the most fundamental´ of mathematical systems. Was it Euclidean geometry or something else?

The strongest contender for the most ´fundamental´ of mathematical system was ´Set Theory´ suggested by Georg Cantor, again at the turn of the century. We shall look at this more closely later in this chapter, suffice it now to realize that Cantor argued that the concept of a set (i.e. a collection of objects with some common property) is more fundamental than, and, indeed, incorporates, the concept of ´number´ which is the basis for Euclidean mathematics. Hence set theory, its axioms and theories, was thought to be a good candidate for replacing Euclidean mathematics.

Unfortunately, Bertrand Russell, through his well-known paradox of infinite sets showed that set theory was, in fact, not complete as it contained contradictions when one questions whether very large sets contain themselves or not. Although this created a seeming crisis in mathematics, the fundamental value of set theory was not entirely negated by this discovery. One merely learnt that the sets in such mathematical systems must be identified by enumeration of their elements or a clear statement of the properties of such elements. We shall return to this later in this chapter.

A semi-historical survey such as this is not complete without reference to the work of George Boole.   As most students of digital systems know, Boole proposed a system of algebra based on the truth or falsehood of propositions.   The interesting fact about this is that he did this about 40 years before Cantor established set theory and yet, in abstract mathematical terms, Boolean algebra is identical to Cantor's algebra of sets.   Again, we shall return to some details of these concepts later in this chapter, while here we merely note that the above is not a coincidence, but strongly points to the fact that there are useful algebraic abstractions which find a true evaluation in several disparate facets of the real world.

After all, one of Boole's concerns was with finding a mathematical way of evaluating the evidence given in a court of law during a trial, while Cantor thought he was providing an algebra that related to collections of objects.   No one has probably ever used Boolean algebra in legal applications, while Shannon (1938) clearly claimed its applicability for relay switching circuits.   What could be more convincing of the general value of the mathematical system itself?

Finally, we return briefly to Russell's paradox and raise the question, central to this section, of the validity of axioms. The paradox points to the fact that one can have excellent axioms and an excellent theory, where the axioms are, to a certain extent, contradictory.   This difficulty, which sets a certain degree of arbitrariness in the section of abstract mathematical systems has been resolved by Kurt Godel (1930) who has shown that there is no <u>universal</u> mathematical system, but that the mathematical universe consists of a very large (infinite) number of abstract systems, none of which is totally self-consistent, but requires the aid of another system to check the validity of all its axioms.   The importance to the digital system designer here is that a computational process is a little like a mathematical system, and to prove its correctness it may be necessary to step outside that process.

The central question that every digital systems designer should address, is whether a system of his creation can be expressed in terms of its mathematical properties.

The procedure is analogous to the creation of a mathematical system and must follow a laid down procedure which takes the following form.

a) The objects of the system have to be named (integers, bottles, stars, etc.)

b) The operators of the system have to be named (multiplication, raising to the power of, AND, OR, etc.

c) The properties of the operators have to be listed (there is a catalog of these, as will be seen, e.g. commutation absorption)

d) Only then can one try to prove theorems.

The rest of this chapter will be devoted to abstract mathematical systems in which the above procedure has been followed. In particular, those systems that have some relevance to digital systems will be highlighted, and this relevance stressed.

2.4 A STANDARD APPROACH

Even in abstract mathematics, the properties of a mathematical system are not dragged out of thin air. On the contrary, there is a well-founded procedure whose aim is to define all the elements of a group of four sets[*] known as a 4-tuple. This 4-tuple is written

$$\langle S, O, P, E \rangle$$

where

S is a set of objects (e.g. real numbers in everyday arithmetic),
O is a set of operations (e.g. +, -, x, - in arithmetic)
P is a set of elements of S with special characteristics (for example $0 + a = a$ whatever a, a property belonging to O only and no other real number).

---

[*]   Recall that a <u>set</u> is a collection of objects with a known property.

Brackets such as ⟨ ⟩ are generally used to indicate such n-tuples. They will occur again in Chapter 3 in ´finite state machine´ theory. The main task in defining a mathematical system is to define the elements of this 4-tuple.

This can be done abstractly as we shall do in what follows, where we develop an abstract system of algebra as an example, in order to illustrate the meaning of the elements of the 4-tuple. We call the abstract system. ´Algebra A´.

2.4.1 The Set of Objects S

Right from the start, one must distinguish between the objects of an algebra and the labels that such objects carry in an algebraic expression.

In the familiar system of numerical algebra, one can write an expression such as

$$8w - 2x + 3y = z$$

It is conventional, as taught in schools, that one understands that the letters w, y and z stand for ´any number´ (which could be a fraction, an irrational, real number, negative or zero). However the objects of this algebra are not the labels but the elements of the set of real numbers. The complete set of objects in Euclidean algebra is in fact the set of real and imaginary numbers (e.g. such as $j = \sqrt{-1}$).

In algebra A we shall have only two objects

$$S_A = \{r , b\}$$

Clearly in the same way as letters could be used as labels for variable number objects in the conventional algebraic expression, we shall use the labels s_1, s_2, s_3,...to indicate the variables of algebra A.

2.4.2 The Set of Operations O

The word operation needs some explanation. First, it is conventional (and certainly true of any algebraic system

considered in this book) that an operation may be defined in
respect to what its effect is on at most two objects from set
S.   For this reason one often hears of ´binary´ operations
in abstract systems.   In conventional algebra, addition (+)
is an operation, and it is fundamental that one knows what
addition does to any two objects or variables.

For objects, for example, we know that, say

$$14.6 + 1076.482$$

produces a new object

$$1091.082$$

or, for variables, it is quite acceptable to write
expressions such as

$$y = w + z \text{ (which fixes the relationship of w to z)}$$

or $y + 0 = y$ (irrespective of the value of y)

In an abstract mathematical system it is conventional merely
to define how many such operations are evoked and to define
them in terms of the set of properties P, usually in a pair-
wise fashion or with respect to one variable only, where
appropriate.

In algebra A we have three operations

$$0 = \{o, \#, L\}$$

These will be entirely defined by their properties in what
follows.

2.4.3 The Set of Properties

This set is the central item of the 4-tuple as this is where
one begins to find the axioms of the system.   The properties
are usually sought in a standardized format as will become
evident.

First one looks for properties which relate to operations
that are used on single objects.   In conventional algebra,
negation is such an operation and its general property is

that $-(-A) = A$ whatever the value of A.   This particular
property is called complementation.   If a given system for a
given operation has this property it is said that
complementation holds within the system.

Clearly for an operation such as, say   squaring
complementation does not hold as

$$(A^2)^2 \quad A$$

Two properties hold for algebra A and operation L

> Reciprocity holds
> $$Lb = r$$
> $$Lr = b$$ A(1)

(A(1) reads: algebra A property 1, etc.)

Also (and this follows from A(1) and is therefore just
another way of putting it):

> Complementation holds
>
> $$LLs_j = s_j$$ A(2)

Secondly one defines the properties of binary operations
starting with probably the most important: closure.   Closure
is defined as the property which ensures that a binary
operation has a result which is an element of the set of
objects S of the system itself.   Usually, without closure,
one does not have a mathematical system at all.   For example
if one defines S as the integers from 1 to 10 and defines
addition as the operation, closure does not hold (as, for
example $4 + 8$ is 12 and the latter is outside the system and
therefore somewhat meaningless).   In algebra A, one
indicates that closure holds in the following way.

> Closure holds
>
> $$s_j \mathbin{\#} s_k = s_i$$
> $$s_j \circ s_p = s_i \qquad s_i,\ s_j,\ s_k, \in S \ V \ i,\ j,\ k.$$
> A(3)

in the above, the symbol $\in$ reads, 'belongs to', and the symbol V reads 'for all'.

TEXT EXERCISE 1. The reader should attempt to read out A(3) aloud as a verbal statement. (Answers to text exercises are given at the end of the chapter.)

Next, one usually looks for the property of <u>idempotence</u> which, in algebra A is expressed as follows.

$$\boxed{\begin{array}{l} \underline{\text{Idempotence holds}} \\[1em] \qquad\qquad s_j \;\#\; s_j \;=\; s_j \\ \qquad\qquad s_j \;\text{o}\; s_j \;=\; s_j \\ \qquad\qquad\qquad\qquad\quad V_j \qquad\qquad A(4) \end{array}}$$

TEXT EXERCISE 2. Given S = { set of all positive, non-zero integers} and the operation of addition, does idempotence hold?

One generally wishes to know whether the order in which one applies an operation is important. This is the property of <u>commutation</u>. For example in conventional arithmetic 1 + 2 = 2 + 1, etc., hence commutation holds. However, if one defines an operation as exponentiation for S = {integers}

$$a \uparrow b \neq b \uparrow a$$

for example $3 \uparrow 2 \;=\; 9$ and $2 \uparrow 3 \;=\; 8$ hence commutation does <u>not</u> hold.

However, for algebra A we define that.

$$\boxed{\begin{array}{l} \underline{\text{Commutation holds}} \\[1em] \qquad\quad s_j \;\#\; s_k \;=\; s_k \;\#\; s_j \\ \qquad\qquad\qquad\qquad\qquad\qquad Vj,k. \\ \qquad\quad s_j \;\text{o}\; s_k \;=\; s_k \;\text{o}\; s_j \qquad\qquad A(5) \end{array}}$$

One progresses through this definitional process by enquiring about the effect of carrying out two operations in the same procedure. The first property in this context is <u>association</u> which simply asks whether the order in which the <u>same</u> operation is carried out matters. If it does not, association holds.

For example in arithmetic, using brackets to indicate which operation is carried out first, one notes that

$$(6+2) +8 = 6+(2+8)$$
(and indeed may then be written as
6+2+8).

In algebra A we define that

Association holds
$$s_1 \mathbin{\#} (s_2 \mathbin{\#} s_3) = (s_1 \mathbin{\#} s_2) \mathbin{\#} s_3$$
$$s_1 \mathbin{o} (s_2 \mathbin{o} s_3) = (s_1 \mathbin{o} s_2) \mathbin{o} s_3$$
A(6)

Usually, the situation is different if two operations are used.   Clearly,

$$(8x2)+1 \text{ gives a different result from}$$
$$8x(2+1)$$

To resolve this, one looks for a property called distribution.   For example, multiplication is said to distribute over addition as

$$8x(2+1) = 8x2+8x1$$

while addition does not distribute over multiplication as

$$8+(2x1) = (8+2)x(8+1)$$

In algebra A, we shall depart from this characteristic of conventional algebra and insist that distribution should hold both ways.

Distribution holds for both operations

$$s_1 \mathbin{o} (s_2 \mathbin{\#} s_3) = (s_1 \mathbin{o} s_2) \mathbin{\#} (s_1 \mathbin{o} s_3)$$
$$s_1 \mathbin{\#} (s_2 \mathbin{o} s_3) = (s_1 \mathbin{\#} s_2) \mathbin{o} (s_1 \mathbin{\#} s_3)$$
A(7)

At this point we shall do something rather bizarre and take

$$s_1 \text{ o } (s_2 \text{ \# } s_3)$$

and let $s_2 = s_1$ to see if any interesting properties emerge.

$$s_1 \text{ o } (s_1 \text{ \# } s_3) = (s_1 \text{ o } s_1) \text{ \# } (s_1 \text{ o } s_3) \qquad \text{by A(7)}$$

also $\qquad\qquad\quad = s_1 \text{ \# } (s_1 \text{ o } s_3) \qquad\qquad\quad \text{by A(3)}$

So this looks as a kind of theorem: note that in the starting expression the signs can be interchanged.

However this is not the end of the story. We shall insist (note a new axiom is coming up) that in this starting expression s_1 <u>absorbs</u> s_3. There appears to be nothing in the earlier axioms to prevent us from doing this, hence our only rule for generating new axioms, <u>freedom from contradiction</u>, is satisfied.

Hence, we have the final axiom.

<u>Absorption holds</u>

$$s_1 \text{ o } (s_1 \text{ \# } s_3) = s_1 \text{ \# } (s_1 \text{ o } s_3) = s_1 \qquad \text{A(8)}$$

2.4.4 The Set of Special Elements E

So far, all the properties of algebra A have been couched in forms of the variables of the system. What follows is a list of properties that relates to the objects of the algebra. The need for this is seen in conventional algebra where

$$A + B = A \quad \text{if and only if } B = 0$$

Hence one can see

$$A + 0 = A \text{ for all } A$$

In this way one refers to 0 as a special element of S because of the above property with respect to the rest of the variables.

TEXT EXERCISE 3: Describe other similar properties for other special objects and operations in conventional algebra. For algebra A, we

simply list these properties, which since
there are only two objects, involve both of
these objects.

Special properties of elements

$$s_1 \mathbin{\#} b = s_1 \qquad\qquad\qquad A(9)$$
$$s_1 \mathbin{o} b = b \qquad\qquad\qquad A(10)$$
$$s_1 \mathbin{\#} r = r \qquad\qquad\qquad A(11)$$
$$s_1 \mathbin{o} r = s_1 \qquad\qquad\qquad A(12)$$

2.4.5 Theorems

Clearly, one does not know at what point in the definition of
a mathematical system one has defined a <u>complete</u> set of
axioms. A weak clue is the proof that existing axioms are
not sufficient to satisfy the outcome of an equation. This
was the case in the definition of the <u>absorption</u> property in
algebra A. We now move on to situations where interesting
outcomes may be derived merely on the basis of existing
axioms. This may be illustrated by investigating what
happens if one applies the L operator in algebra A to entire
expressions.

For example, one can investigate

$$L\,(s_1 \mathbin{\#} s_2) \qquad\qquad \dotfill (2-1)$$

Scanning down the axioms there is no single property that
applies directly to this expression. However, looking at
the four special properties $A(9) - A(12)$, one realizes that
one can carry out an exhaustive application of these by
letting s_1 and s_2 be r and b in turn.

A good way of getting a ´feel´ for the operations as defined,
is to develop truth tables from properties such as $A(9)$ to
$A(12)$. Such tables evaluate a binary operation for all
possible values of two variables. In conventional
arithmetic this cannot be done exhaustively because there is
an infinity of objects in S. Nevertheless it is done by
taking subsets of S, hence the importance of ´learning one´s
multiplication tables´ at school. For algebra A we have two
basic truth tables, one for o and one for #.

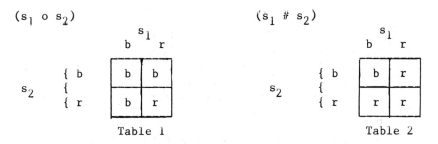

$(s_1 \text{ o } s_2)$

| | | s_1 | |
		b	r
	{ b	b	b
s_2 {			
	{ r	b	r

Table 1

$(s_1 \text{ \# } s_2)$

| | | s_1 | |
		b	r
	{ b	b	r
s_2 {			
	{ r	r	r

Table 2

The way that these are derived from set E may be illustrated as follows.   Take s_1 o s_2 where s_1 = b, then we know that

$$s_1 \text{ o } s_2 = b \text{ from A(10) (and A(5)).}$$

This is true for s_2 = b which fills three boxes in the truth table for o.   Also if s_2 = r, A(12) tells us that s_1 o s_2 = 2 given that s_1 =r in the last box, completing the truth table.

TEXT EXERCISE 4.   Justify the truth table for #.

One can derive a table for L (s_1 o s_2) from Table 1 simply by changing b and r around in the table, which is justified by A(1).

This becomes
           L (s_1 o s_2)

| | | s_1 | |
	?	b	r
	{ b	r	r
s_2 {			
	{ r	r	b

At this point, one notes that if one swaps the b and r columns for s_1 and the b and r rows for s_2 one gets

| | | s_1 | |
		r	b
	{ r	b	r
s_2 {			
	{ r	r	r

One notes that this now is the same (within the table) as
Table 2.

But the ´swapping round´ that has done this is equivalent to
the operation

$$s_1´ = Ls_1$$

$$s_2´ = Ls_2$$

This allows one to replace ? by Ls_1 ≠ Ls_2
The result is that one has a <u>theorem</u>, i.e.

<u>Theorem 2-1</u>

$$L(s_1 \text{ o } s_2) = Ls_1 ≠ Ls_2$$

Notice that the process of truth table manipulation is simply
an aid at arriving at a relationship that constitutes a
theorem, that is a non-obvious relationship which in some way
or another appears to result from the axiomatic system.
There are no rules for generating theorems.   A theorem,
however, requires a <u>rigorous</u> proof; that is, a proof which
relies entirely on the axioms or previously proven theorems.
Here we could have PROOF 2.1:   this proof will be executed by
exhaustive evaluation.

Take the proposition

$$L (s_1 \text{ o } s_2)   =   Ls_1 ≠ Ls_2$$

Substitute $s_2 = b$, then:
$$L (s_1 \text{ o } b) = Ls_1 ≠ r$$

which, by A(10) becomes,
$$Lb = L_1 S_1 ≠ r$$

and by A(11) becomes,
$$Lb = r$$

and this, finally, by A(1)
$$r = r$$

which completes this part of the proof showing that if $s_2 = b$
the theorem holds, irrespectively of the value of s_1.
Similarly, letting $s_2 = r$

then $\quad$ L $(s_1 \cap s_2) = Ls_1 \# Ls_2$

becomes $\quad$ L $(s_1 \text{ o } r) = Ls_1 \# b \qquad$ by A(12)

leading to L $\quad s_1 = Ls_1 \# b \qquad$ by A(9)

$\qquad\qquad$ L $\quad s_1 = Ls_1$

which completes the proof.

TEXT EXERCISE 5: Prove the theorem dual to 2-1:

$$L \ (s_1 \# s_2) = Ls_1 \text{ o } Ls_2$$

2.4.6 Summary of the Standard Approach

The thrust of this section has been to show that one can define an algebra and prove theorems within it merely by making sure that the $\langle S, O, P, E \rangle$ group is properly and self-consistently defined. The discipline in doing this arises from a scan of properties which one can define to exist or not exist at will – the only constraint being that no two definitions should clash. All this has been done without the need to refer to events in the real world for a justification. An essence of such a contact with non-mathematical objects will be seen in the next chapter.

2.5 LOGIC, SWITCHES AND GATES

2.5.1 Boolean Algebra

The objects in the real world of George Boole´s algebra[*] were the truth or falsehood (T, F) of verbal statements, hence S_B in $B = \langle S_B, O_B, P_B, E_B \rangle$ is $S_B = \{T, F\}$.

The suffix B is used to indicate a Boolean algebra. The variables of the system are simple logical statements such as ´dogs are animals´ which can evaluate into T or F usually by definition. Such definition is usually based on either a known fact or a consensus.

---

[*] $\quad$ Boole, G. (1947).

Here we shall use the letters b_1 b_2 ... etc. to indicate a
<u>variable</u> in Boolean algebra. Boole's system was abstract
in the sense that he developed an algebra which did not
require a knowledge of <u>how</u> the truth or falsehood of a
statement is established, it merely assumes that such
statements can have only two values ('maybe' is not
admitted). The operations of the system are the
conjunctions AND, OR and the negation NOT. Let us shorten
these to A, O and N. That is,

$$O_B = \{A, O, N\}$$

One follows a path of examining the system for standard
properties, starting with reciprocity and complementation.
This is done from the real-world meaning and understanding of
the system.

We note that   N (T) = F
        and   N (F) = T

since the negation of a true statement is a false statement
and vice versa.

This leads to the conclusion that <u>complementation</u> and
<u>reciprocity</u> both hold. <u>Closure</u> too is seen to hold since the
evaluation of

           b_1 A b_2
  or b_1 O b_2
  or   N b_1

has always a result of the form T or F. The simple fact is
that all the properties of algebra A do in fact apply in
Boolean algebra. (In passing, however, note that Boolean
algebra is heavily centered on the real-world meaning of its
objects: 'Truth' and 'Falsehood'. It was not necessary to
evoke this meaning when defining algebra A, making the point
about the possible 'abstraction' of mathematical systems.)

It is left for the reader to verify the above assumption by
working through the properties of algebra A. For example
one can verify, in the world of True and False statements,
that property A(8), <u>absorption,</u> makes sense.

Taking

$$b_1 \ A \ (b_1 \ O \ b_2)$$

we note that $(b_1 \ O \ b_2)$ is true whenever either is true and certainly if b_1 is true.   If b_1 is true then

T A T = T hence the expression is T

If b_1 is false, the entire statement must be false

because F A b_2 = F

Hence the expression takes the value of b_1 proving that absorption (in part) holds. The reader may come to verify that

$$b_1 \ O \ (b_1 \ A \ b_2) = b_1$$

by means of a similar process.

Part of the relationship between theory and real-world experience is that having established the validity and application of an abstract set of axioms (say from algebra A) one can rest safely in the knowledge that the theorems tell us something about real world events.   Theorem (2-1), for example, asserts that if it is known that a statement such as:

´It is not true that both John and Harry are dead´

is the same as saying:

´It is true that either John is not dead or Harry is not dead´.

This, indeed, does make sense.

TEXT EXERCISE 6: Provide a similar illustration to be dual of theorem (2 1) (i.e. (2-1)a).

It has been shown that Boolean algebra is an embodiment of abstract algebra A.   This form of correspondence is called an isomorphism.   A similar isomophism exists between algebra A and switching theory as will be seen.

2.5.2 Switching Theory

Most will know that Claude Shannon in 1938 first ´applied´
Boolean algebra to ´switching circuits´.   In fact a better
way of describing that situation may be to say that ´the
algebra of switching circuits´ is isomorphic to Boolean
algebra (and, indeed from what we have seen, to algebra A).

The isomorphism is based on the following

$$\text{Let } \langle S_s, O_s, P_s, E_s \rangle$$

be the 4 -tuple for switching algebra.

Then $S_s = \{ON, OFF\}$ (sometimes abbreviated to 0,1).

A variable s_1 then is a switch that could be either in the <u>on</u>
state or the <u>off</u> state.

The set O_s is seen as having three components.

$$O_s = \{., +, ^-\}$$

$s_1 . s_2$, refers to switches s_1 and s_2 being in series, $s_1 +$
s_2, refers to s_1 and s_2 being in parallel and s_1 refers to a
change in the state of a switch from open to closed or vice
versa.

Moving on to P_s, one refers to switching networks which have
two terminals, and the object of an ´evaluation´ is to
discover whether the <u>network</u> has the property of a switch
being ´on´ or ´off´.   This immediately implies <u>closure</u>
(somewhat of a pun in this system).

Looking for <u>idempotence</u>, for example, one realizes that

$$s_1 . s_1$$

implies two switches in series, the two always having the
same ´value´. Clearly this is equivalent to just one switch

$$\text{hence } s_1 . s_1 = s_1$$
$$\text{similarly } s_1 + s_1 = s_1$$

leading to the realization that <u>idempotence</u> holds.

Again, one can show that all the properties of algebra A hold for switching algebra.   Clearly, the importance of this lies in its engineering repercussions.   For example consider the absorption law

$$s_1 \cdot (s_1 + s_2) = s_1$$

This implies that the circuits shown in Fig. 2.1 are equivalent.   Clearly, one is less costly than the other.

Even more pertinent are the ´minimization´ theorems:

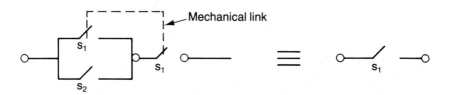

Fig. 2.1 Meaning of the absorption law

THEOREM (2-2)a $(s_1 \cdot s_2) + (\overline{s_1} \cdot s_2) = s_2$

and

THEOREM (2-2)b $(s_1 + s_2) \cdot (\overline{s_1} + s_2) = s_2$

Although it is conventional in switching theory to convince oneself from a knowledge of circuitry that the above relationships are true, it is quite possible to prove them in algebra A.   Taking Theorem (2-2)a, the LHS develops as follows

Lemma* $(\overline{s_1} + s_1) = 1$

Proof: if $s_1 = 0$, $(\overline{s_1} + s_1) = (0+1) = 1$ by A(10)
                          if $s_1 = 1$, $(1 + 0) = 1$ by A(10) again,
                          proving the lemma.

Main Proof
                    $(s_1.s_2) + (\overline{s_1} . s_2) = s_2 (\overline{s_1} + s_1)$ by
                    distribution
                                        $= s_2 . 1$ by lemma 1
                                        $= s_2$ by A(9)
                                                  QED

(The reader may care to prove (2-2)b, the dual version of this theorem.)   The engineering implication of this theorem is demonstrated in Fig. 2.2 with a more complex example.

Figure 2.2(a) shows the arrangement of six switches which are mechanically linked to become just two switches.   Note that the arrangement where a switch opens when another closes makes the two related as s_1 and $\overline{s}_1$ respectively, hence for Fig. 2.2(a), the expresion representing the switching function between A and B is

$$(s_1.s_2) + (s_1 . \overline{s_2}) + (\overline{s_1} . s_2)$$

This may be manipulated as follows.   In the first instance it becomes
$$(s_1.s_2) + (s_1 . \overline{s_2}) + (s_1 . s_2) + (\overline{s_1} . s_2)$$

by idempotence, then applying Theorem (2-2)a twice, this becomes $(s_1 + s_2)$ which is shown in Fig. 2.2(b) as representing a saving of hardware.

---

* A lemma is a mini-theorem required to prove a major one

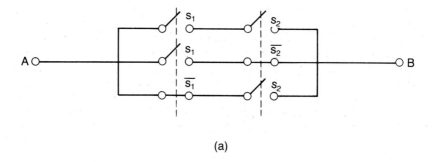

(a)

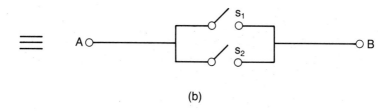

(b)

Fig. 2.2 Minimization example

Indeed most of what goes under the heading of 'logic circuit minimization' is based on repeated applications of the procedure just illustrated.

2.5.3 Gate Theory

Switching theory is more usually applied to circuits such as AND, OR, NOT 'gates', rather than contact switches. Here one notes that, knowing the meaning of the three functions

$$AND, \quad OR, \quad NOT$$

one can develop a system of algebra, again isomorphic to algebra A, by letting

$$\{AND, OR, NOT\} \text{ be equivalent to } \{\#, o, L\}.$$

While the reader may wish to work through this notion, here we shall pursue the theoretical reasoning which underpins the well-known proposition that any switching or gate system that may be achieved by means of AND, OR and NOT gates may also be constructed solely from NAND (or alternatively NOR) functions. The first step in this is to show that there exists a single-operation algebra (say the NAND system) which is isomorphic to algebra A.

Define n_1/n_2 as the NAND operation, and define it in terms of algebra A as follows:

$$n_1/n_2 = L (n_1 \text{ o } n_2)$$
$$(\text{where} = \text{reads: is equivalent to})$$

where n_1 and n_2 are the labels in NAND algebra and / is the NAND operation.

In the NAND system labels such as n_1, n_2, etc.... can take on values of 0 and 1 (as in gate algebra) which correspond to r and b respectively in algebra A.

The next objective is to show that operations L, o and $\#$ in algebra A may be expressed in terms of / only.

First take, n_1 / n_1 – $L (n_1 \text{ o } n_1)$
                                      = $L\ n_1$ by idempotence in A.

Hence one can write, n_1 / n_1 = n_1 (as a definition)

Then, $/n_1$ = Ln_1 .....Result 1

Now, $L (n_1 \text{ o } n_2)$ = n_1 / n_2 by definition

so, by result 1 $n_1 \text{ o } n_2$ = $/(n_1/ n_2)$ .....Result 2

This shows that o can be expressed solely in terms of /.

Now, note that $L\ n_1 \text{ \# } L\ n_2$ = $L (n_1 \text{ o } n_2)$ by Theorem (2-1)
                                      = n_1 / n_2 by definition

By 'inverting' n_1 and n_2 this becomes
                      $n_1 \text{ \# } n_2 = (/n_1) / (/n_2)$ .....Result 3

which shows that the \# operation may be expressed in terms
of / only.

It is now possible to see that there is a NAND algebra that
is isomorphic to algebra A as for every axiom and theorem in
the latter there is a translation into the former.

So far what has been shown is that any system of gates of the
AND OR NOT type may be replaced by a NAND system of gates.
It is left as an exercise for the reader to work through the
same reasoning for the NOR operation which starts with the
proposition:
                 $n_1 \text{ ! } n_2 = L (n_1 \text{ \# } n_2)$
                 ! being the symbol for NOR.

Now we attack the proposition that any switching task may be
achieved either by the NAND or the NOR system of gates. It is
well known that the AND OR NOT system of gates is sufficient
for achieving any switching duty (a direct result of the
closure property of the algebra) and it therefore follows
that NAND on its own or NOR on its own is a complete system
just in this way.

2.6 SETS, MAPPINGS, RELATIONS AND LATTICES

2.6.1 Sets and Algebra A

From the mathematical ideas triggered off by the needs of the
technical world of digital systems, we now step into
mathematics triggered off by the need of mathematics itself.
As seen earlier Georg Cantor sought to re-establish a
foundation for mathematics once it was clear that Euclidean
ideas, although sound and widely applicable, were somewhat
arbitrary being related to real-world measurement only.
Cantor replaced ´number´ by ´set´ as the fundamental object
of a system of mathematics. We define this as ´a collection
of objects with a given property, which may be identified
either by denumeration, or by a well-defined property common
to all the elements of the set.´
Sets are <u>generally</u> defined as:

$$A = \{ a/a \text{ has property } P \}$$

which reads: A is the set of elements a all of which have
property P.

$\langle S,O,P,E \rangle$ in set theory goes as follows. S has already been
defined, while the set of operation O is given by

Intersection $C = A \cap B$ where $C = \{x/x \in A \underline{\text{ and }} x \in B\}$

(the symbol $\in$ reads ´belongs to´)

union $C = A \cup B$ where $C = \{x/x \in A \underline{\text{ or }} x \in B\}$

negation $C = -A$ where $C = \{x/x \notin A\}$

(Naturally, $\notin$ reads ´does not belong to´).

Skipping over to E now, special elements are

I the set of <u>all</u> elements in a frame of discourse
and Q the set of <u>no</u> elements, or <u>empty</u> set

It now becomes possible to run down the list of properties P
for this system.

Reciprocity holds with respect to the special elements

$$-I = Q$$
$$-Q = I$$

and complementarity holds

$$-(-A) = A$$

Again, it comes as no surprise that all the properties of algebra A hold for set algebra.

To check these, consider some of the more intricate properties such as distribution and absorption. It is conventional to develop an understanding of axioms in set algebra by using Venn diagrams and a graphical representation of these two axioms is shown in Fig. 2.3 for one of the distributive laws.

$$A \cup (B \cap C) \quad = \quad (A \cup B) \cap (A \cup C)$$

The reader may wish to verify the dual to this

$$A \cap (B \cup C) \quad = \quad (A \cap B) \cup (A \cap C)$$

A similar approach may be taken with relationships that involve negation. For example Theorem 2-1 may be illustrated as in Fig. 2.4. The set theory formulation for this theorem is

$$-(A \cap B) \quad = \quad (-A) \quad \cup \quad (-B)$$

2.6.2 Mappings

There is more to set theory than just the algebra related to operations of Union, Interaction and Negation. For example the process of operating on one set to produce another is fundamental. It is called the process of mapping and is analogous to a 'function' in numerical algebra.

A formal definition of a mapping is:
a set of pairs (a, b) is a mapping from A to B iff

i) $a \in A$, $b \in B$

ii) to each a A there corresponds only one pair (a,b).

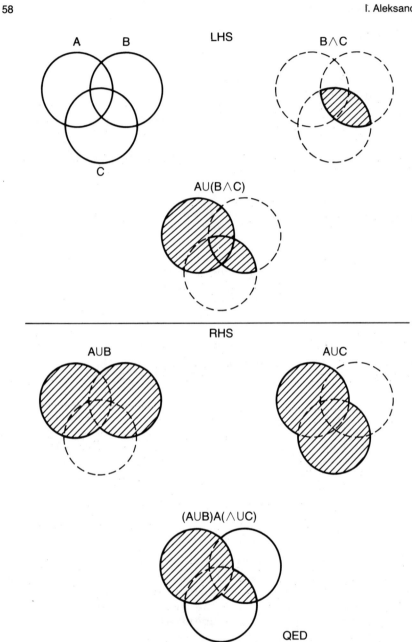

Fig. 2.3
AXIOM: AU(B∧C) = (AUB) ∧ (AUC)
VENN VERIFICATION

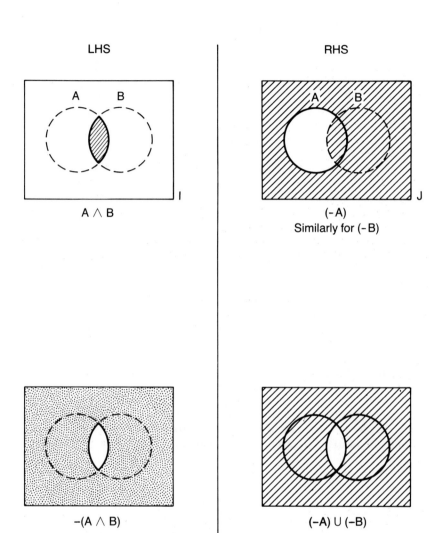

Fig. 2.4
THEOREM: $-(A \wedge B) = (-A) \cup (-B)$
VENN VERIFICATION

In this context we shall write

$$A \xrightarrow{f} B \text{ to indicate the mapping, whereas alternatives are}$$

f (a) = b

f (A) = B

f: a -->b

Mappings are quite fundamental to digital systems. A system of gates, for example, is said to map the set of input messages to a set of output messages.   Consider the system of gates shown in Fig. 2.5(a). Let the input be a set I = $\{i_0, i_1 .....i_8\}$ and the output be a set

$$Z = \{z_0, \quad z_1 ....z_8\}.$$

Say that the element of the set corresponds to the binary value of the subscript.   For example i_1 corresponds to input 001 at $x_1 x_2 x_3$ and z_0 is 110 at the output terminals.   The truth table for this system is shown in Fig. 2.5(b). The mapping $I \xrightarrow{m} Z$ is shown in Fig. 2.5(c).

A mapping from A to B is said to be ONTO, if every element of B is an object of the mapping.   For example if the mapping is one of adding a unit, say, modulo 3, one can say that:

0 maps to 1

1   "   to 2

3   "   to 3

3   "   to 0

If the lefthand is set A and the right hand is B then we note that the mapping is ONTO.   This is not the case with Fig. 2.5(c) where in Z, Z_1, Z_4, and Z_5 are not covered.   This is called an INTO mapping.   Indeed since the modulo 3 mapping above has only one element of A associated with each element of B, it is said to be a ONE-TO-ONE mapping.

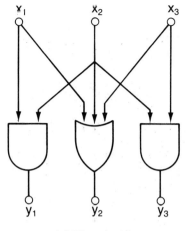

(a) The circuit

x_1	x_2	x_3		y_1	y_2	y_3	
0	0	0		0	0	0	0
0	0	1		0	1	0	2
0	1	0		0	1	0	2
0	1	1		0	1	1	3
1	0	0		0	1	0	2
1	0	1		0	1	0	2
1	1	0		1	1	0	6
1	1	1		1	1	1	7

(b) The truth table

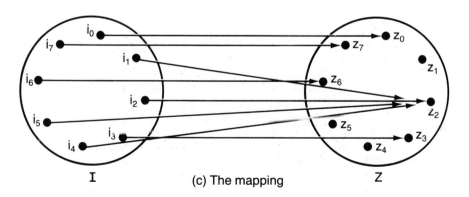

(c) The mapping

Fig. 2.5

2.6.3 Relations

A relation refers to pairs of elements in a set.   For
example, we can define a relation R to be such that, given
the set of integers

$$I = \{i_j / \text{where } i_j \text{ is an integer}\}$$

i_j R i_k (which reads i_j <u>stands in relation</u> to i_k)

$$\text{iff } i_j - i_k = 2.$$

Then we have   3 R 1

but   4 R 3   (i.e. does <u>not</u> stand in relation)

Relations are usually examined for special properties, in
particular, given a relation R and a set $A = \{a_1 \cdot a_2 \ldots\}$

R is <u>reflexive</u> iff a_j R a_j $\forall a_j \in A$,

R is <u>symmetric</u> iff a_j R a_k implies a_k R a_j $\forall a_j$, $a_k \in A$,

R is <u>transitive</u> iff given a_j R a_k and a_k R a_l implies a_j R a_l
$\forall a_j$, a_k, and $a_l \in A$.

A relation that has all three of these properties is called
an <u>equivalence relation</u> for the following reason.   Take a
set $A\{a_1 \ldots a_n\}$.   Take any element say a_1 and add to it
another element a_j if a_1 R a_j.   Then add to the set that is
being formed a_k such that a_l R a_k.   Due to the <u>transitive</u>
nature of R we know that a_j R a_k while due to the <u>symmetric</u>
nature of R, a_k R a_1, a_k R a_j and a_j R a_k.   Also a_1 R a_1 due
to <u>reflexivity</u> etc.   We continue adding elements of A to this
set until we no longer find any that stand in relation to any
that are already in the set.   By this process we have
isolated all the elements that stand in relation to one
another, <u>none</u> of which are so related to the rest of the set.
If one does this for an element outside the collection one
generates another set of related elements.   Carrying on like
this one divides (technical language: partitions) the entire
set into separate such sets (blocks) where all the elements
within each are related to one another with none related to
those of the other blocks.

TEXT EXERCISE 7: Taking the set of 12 integers $\{1, 2, 3...12\}$
show that R defined by
i_i R i_j iff $/i_j - i_n/ = 0, 3, 6$ or 9
is an equivalence relation.   Find the
equivalence classes (note $/x/$ is the
notation used for the absolute value of x).

2.6.4 Lattices

An interesting set of mathematical systems arises if one
merely alters one of the properties of relations on the
elements of a set, and that is the property of symmetry.
One replaces it by the <u>anti-symmetric property</u> which states
that:

$$a_j \; R_A \; a_k = a_k \; R_A \; a_j \quad \text{iff} \; a_k = a_j.$$

(R_A reads: anti-symmetric relation)

Consider the set of integers $I = \{1, 2....10\}$ and define R_A
as

$$i_1 \; R_A \; i_2 \quad \text{iff} \; i_1 \leq i_2.$$

It is noted that

R_A is <u>reflexive</u> as $i_j \leq i_j$ (it would not be if the relation
were defined merely as $<$),

R_A is <u>anti-symmetric</u> as $i_j \leq i_k$ $\langle\text{--}\rangle$ $i_k \leq i_j$ only if $i_j = i_k$;

R_A is <u>transitive</u> as <u>if</u> $i_j \leq i_k$ and $i_k \leq i_1$ then $i_j \leq i_1$.

This kind of system is known as an <u>ordering</u> and because the
relation $<$ applies to <u>all</u> pairs of elements in the set the
above system is a <u>total ordering</u>.   There are sets in which
the relation does not apply to <u>all</u> pairs of elements, and
such systems are called <u>partial orderings</u>. For example if,
for set I again, R_A were defined as

$$i_j R_A i_k \quad \text{iff} \; i_k - i_i = 0,2,4,6 \text{ or } 8$$

then the set has two subsets which may be drawn as in Fig. 2.6.

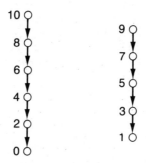

Fig. 2.6 A partial ordering

Fig. 2.7 Another partial ordering: every pair has a
                                    lowest upper bound

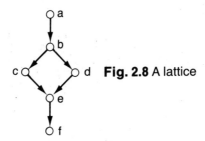

Fig. 2.8 A lattice

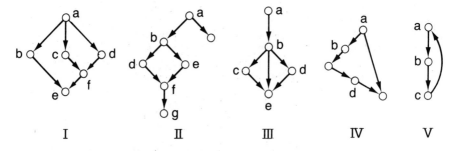

I   II   III   IV   V

Fig. 2.9 Which are lattices?

In a diagram of this kind there is a meaning to 'upness' and 'downness' in the sense that any two elements connected by a 'directed path' of downward arrows stand in relation to one another with the upper one on the right of the relation and the lower one on the left. The relation does not hold for disconnected elements. What if one were to draw a diagram such as Fig. 2.7? This too is a partial ordering as c and d do not stand in relation to one another (note, we no longer need to define the precise nature of the relation: we just draw its picture).

Consider the pair c, d. They have precisely two elements to which they stand in relation: a and b. These are called upper bounds of the set {c, d}. However, there is one lowest element of set {a, b} and, in this case, that is b, which is called the <u>least upper bound</u> (lub). Now consider Fig. 2.8, By a similar process a <u>greatest lower bound</u> may be defined, which for {c, d} is e ({e, f} being the set of lower bounds of {c, d}).

Taking this concept even further we note that every pair of elements in Fig. 2.8 has a (l u b) <u>and</u> a (g l b) because, for example for pair {e, f} the common upper bounds are {a, b, c, d, e} <u>e</u> being the least of these. It can be concluded that for any pair where $x \, R_A \, y$, y is the (l u b) and x the (g l b) of the pair.

TEXT EXERCISE 8: Draw a table showing the <u>least upper bound and greatest lower bounds</u> of all pairs in Fig. 2.8.

<u>Partial orderings for which all pairs of elements have a (l u b) and a (g l b) are called lattices.</u>

TEXT EXERCISE 9: Which of the figures in Fig. 2.9 are lattices and which are not? Give reasons.

In digital systems work it is sometimes convenient to express ideas regarding circuit minimization in terms of lattice algebra. Some search programs in computing are also often expressed as lattices.

2.7 SEMIGROUPS AND FINITE STATE MACHINES

2.7.1 Semigroups

So far, we have seen examples of algebraic systems such as algebra A which has a large number of embodiments. Here we begin to enquire into the nature of algebras themselves. What combinations of operations and properties make up mathematical systems that are in some way interesting and useful?

Probably the simplest system with useful properties is the semigroup defined as a system with:

one binary operation on a set S for which closure and associativity hold.

As seen previously, this means that, given an operation o

$$s_i \circ s_j = s_k \quad \text{where } s_i, s_j \text{ and } s_k \in S \text{ (closure)}$$

and $\qquad s_i \circ (s_j \circ s_k) = (s_i \circ s_j) \circ s_k \text{ (associativity)}$

If as an additional property, the system has an identity element s_I such that

$$s_h \circ s_I = s_I \circ s_k = s_k \qquad \forall s_k \in S$$

Then the system is called a monoid.

For example, it is easy to ascertain that the system of positive integers with the operation of addition is a semigroup without a zero and a monoid with it.

2.7.2 Free Semigroups

In informational systems one often deals with semigroups in two particular ways. The first of these is that sequences of symbols are related to a special kind of semigroup: the free semigroup, which is developed as follows.

Let the operation in the system be 'followed by' (the mathematical name for this is concatenation).

For example

reads:

$$\begin{array}{l} a\ b \\ a,\ \text{followed by } b. \end{array}$$

$$\text{If}\quad S = \{a,b,c,\ldots\}$$

it is clear that   a b $\in$ S

which means that <u>closure</u> does not hold, and the system, so far, is not a semigroup.

Nevertheless it is possible to <u>generate</u> a related set S^+ which is the infinite set of all <u>sequences</u> of symbols from S, that is

$$S^+ = \{\underbrace{a,b,c\ldots,}_{\substack{\text{all length} - 1 \\ \text{sequences}}}\quad \underbrace{aa,\ ab,\ldots ba,\ bb,\ldots \text{etc.}}_{\substack{\text{all length} - 2 \\ \text{sequences}}}\}$$

It now becomes possible to say that for the system

$$(S^+,\ \text{concatenation})$$

there is <u>closure</u>, on any sequence followed by another sequence merely generating another sequence.

Association clearly holds as

$$s_a\ (s_b\ s_c) = (s_a\ s_b)\ s_c$$

where s_a, s_b, $s_c \in S^+$

The above system is an infinite semigroup (or a <u>free</u> semigroup as it is sometimes called).

Equally, if one adds the <u>zero length</u> sequence z to S^+ that is

$$S^* = S^+\ \cup\ z$$

then (S^*, concatenation) is an infinite (or free) monoid.

2.7.3 Finite State Machines

The technicalities of finite state machines are very much the concern of Chapter 3 of this book. Here we provide a mathematical introduction to them and show that their behavior may be described by a semigroup.

A finite state machine is a system that relates three sets

$I = \{i_1, i_2 \ldots\ldots i_A\}$ a finite set of <u>inputs</u>

$Q = \{q_1, q_2 \ldots\ldots q_B\}$ a finite set of <u>internal</u> states

$Z = \{z_1, z_2 \ldots\ldots z_c\}$ a finite set of <u>output</u> states

Essentially the machine receives sequences of inputs from the input set and generates output from the output set, through the intermediary of <u>internal</u> states as follows.

$$I \times Q \xrightarrow{\ d\ } Q$$
$$Q \xrightarrow{\ w\ } Z$$

This means that every (i_j, q_B) pair maps into (that is, implies the next value of) the internal state, while each internal state maps into a particular output. Clearly, the latter is necessary in situations where internal states can change without affecting the output.

An example of such a system is a divider circuit, which, as may be the case in a digital watch, receives an input pulse from a quartz oscillator and outputs a visible pulse every second, while the oscillator may be pulsating at, say, 1,000 pulses per second.

Then only the 1,000th step in the divider (or counter) creates an output which all the others do not. However all the other states of the counter have a defined and distinct existence. In the present argument we shall only look at the

$$Q \times I \xrightarrow{\ d\ } Q \qquad\qquad \text{mapping.}$$

The input set defines a free semigroup:

$$(I^+, \text{concatenation})$$

The object now is to show that Q turns this into a finite semigroup.

First define a state vector as a distinct ordering of precisely B state. Further define the base state vector as

$$V_0 = \begin{bmatrix} q_1 \\ q_2 \\ . \\ . \\ . \\ q_B \end{bmatrix}$$

The number of possible state vectors is finite and precisely equal to B^B.

Now, take any sequence $J_a \in I^+$, apply it to each state in the base state vector. The end result of this procedure is a new state vector, each element of which is the end state of the system after the application of J_a to the corresponding state in the base vector. For example, if J_a is applied to the system states in q_1 and q_3 is the resulting state, then q_3 is the first element of the resulting vector.

All this may be written as

$$V_0 \xrightarrow{J_a} V_a$$

Clearly since the number of end vectors resulting from the application of sequences is finite, one can define a relation that J_a and J_b stand in relation iff

$$V_0 \xrightarrow{J_a} V_a \quad \text{and} \quad V_0 \xrightarrow{J_b} V_b,$$

$$V_a = V_b$$

It may be shown (easily) that this is an <u>equivalence relation</u> which partitions I^+ into at most B^B blocks.

We label these

$$P^Q{}_J = \{W_1, W_2, \ldots W_B B\}$$

Clearly, each W_a is infinite.

It is easy to show that the system

$(P^Q{}_J$, concatenation) is a finite semigroup if one understands that

$$W_a \, W_b$$

means ´any sequence from W_a followed by any sequence from W_b´.

Closure is evident as is association, hence the semigroup.

Indeed if one lets z be the zero length sequence so that

$$V_0 \xrightarrow{z} V_0$$

then the system becomes a <u>finite monoid</u>, with z as the identity element.

An example may clarify this issue.

Consider the machine with

$$I = \{a, b\}$$
$$Q = \{A, B, C\}$$

A ´state table´ shows the way in which these sets are related:

next state ___

$$
\begin{array}{c|cc}
& \multicolumn{2}{c}{I} \\
& a & b \\
\hline
(\ A & A & B \\
Q\ (\ B & B & C \\
(\ C & C & A \\
\end{array}
$$

We carry out a search to discover the existing partition of P^Q_J.

First note the <u>length one</u> input sequences

$$J_1 = a, \ J_2 = b$$

Let $V_0 = [A\ B\ C]^T$ (T, as usual means

'transpose')

then $V_0 \overset{J_1}{\dashrightarrow} V_0$

and $V_0 \overset{J_2}{\dashrightarrow} V_1$

where $V_1 = [B\ C\ A]^T$

Now note <u>length two</u> input sequences

$$J_3 = aa, \quad J_4 = ab, \quad J_5 = ba, \quad J_6 = bb$$

Also let the simple length sequences belong to clocks P^Q_J

$$J_1 \in W_1$$

$$J_2 \in W_2$$

Now $V_0 \overset{J_3}{\dashrightarrow} V_0\ \cdot\cdot\ J_3 \in W_1$

$\ \ \ V_0 \overset{J_4}{\dashrightarrow} V_1\ \cdot\cdot\ J_4 \in W_2$

$\ \ \ V_0 \overset{J_5}{\dashrightarrow} V_1\ \cdot\cdot\ J_5 \in W_2$

$\ \ \ V_0 \overset{J_6}{\dashrightarrow} V_2 = [C\ A\ B]^T$

Let $J_6 \in W_3$

It is noted that all <u>length two</u> sequences are equivalent to <u>length one</u> sequences except for J_6, hence for any <u>length three</u> sequences not to be equivalent to <u>length two</u> sequences, they must begin with J_6. There are only two more length three sequences

$$J_7 = bba \text{ and } J_8 = bbb$$

Now note that

$$V_0 \xrightarrow{J_7} V_2$$

$$V_0 \xrightarrow{J_8} V_1$$

Hence <u>all</u> length three sequences are equivalent to (i.e. in the same blocks of P^Q_J) as some <u>length two</u> sequences, and this means that all the blocks of P^Q_J have now been found. Note that this statement is justified by noticing that any sequence length n can be seen to be equivalent to a sequence length n-1 and so on until one establishes equivalence with J_1 J_2 or J_6. The entire semigroup may now be shown as a truth table

Concatenation	W_1	W_2	W_3
W_1	W_1	W_2	W_3
W_2	W_2	W_3	W_1
W_3	W_3	W_1	W_2

2.8 OTHER MATHEMATICAL SYSTEMS

A detailed discussion of abstract algebra is clearly beyond the scope of this book.   In this last section we simply provide a summary and refer the reader to a detailed reference on the subject (e.g. Clapham, 1969).

We have dealt with

Semigroups and Free Semigroups

and shall now briefly consider others.

A GROUP is a semigroup for which every element has an inverse.

An ABELIAN GROUP is a group for which the binary operation is commutative.

The most interesting mathematical systems occur when there are two binary operations in the system. The simplest of these is a RING. A RING is a group to which a second associative operation has been added.

A FIELD is a ring whose set of elements, with the group identity element removed, forms an abelian group under the second operation. We note that conventional arithmetic on real numbers with addition as the first operation, and multiplication as the second, forms a field.

Finally, a field defined on a finite set of elements is called a Galois field. This is of particular interest in communications where linear digital systems may be defined that have only two elements. They are AND and EXCLUSIVE OR as the two operations. Details of this are beyond the scope of this book, but may be found in Peterson (1961).

ANSWERS

1) s_k operating through o on s_j yields s_i where s_i, s_j and
    s_k all belong to set S for all values of i, j and k.

2) No, because no non-zero integer added to itself yields
    itself.

3) A x 1 = A for all A
    A   1 = A for all A
    A - 0 = A for all A
                                    etc.

4) If s_2 = r, A(11) yields s_1 # s_2 = r for s_1 = r and s_1
    = b , filling 3 boxes in the truth table.   A(9) yields
    the remaining box.

5) L $(s_1$ # $s_2)$ = Ls_1 o Ls_2

    let s_2 = r, the statement becomes

    Lr = Ls_1 o b   by A(11) and A(1)

    i.e. b = b by A(1) and A(10)
                which is true irrespective of the value s_1

    Now let s_2 = b

        $L(s_1$#b) = Ls_1 o r

        Ls_1 = Ls_1 by A(9) and A(12)
                    completing the proof.

6) Saying ´It is not true that either Harry is dead or John
   is dead´ is the same as saying

   ´It is true that Harry is not dead and John is not dead´

7) $/i_i$ - $i_j/$ = 0   hence <u>reflexivity</u> holds

   $/i_i$ - $i_j/$ = $/i_j$ - $i_i/$ hence <u>symmetry</u> holds

   since $/i_i$ - $i_j/$ is 0 or a multiple of 3

   aa / i_j - $i_k/$ is 0 or a multiple of 3

   $/i_i$ - $i_k/$ must be 0 or a multiple of 3 3,
                hence the relation is <u>transitive</u>

The resulting equivalence classes are

$$(1,4,7,10)$$

$$(2,5,8,11)$$

$$(3,6,9,12)$$

8)

	a	b	c	d	e	f
a	a / a	a / b	a / c	a / d	a / e	a / f
b		b / b	b / c	b / d	b / e	b / f
c			c / c	b / e	c / e	c / f
d				d / d	d / e	d / f
e					e / e	e / f
f						f / f

lub
glb

9) I   is a lattice

II   is not as c has no (g l b) with any of {b,d,e,f,g}

III   is a lattice

IV   is a lattice

V   is not – it is not even an ordering as a R c and c R a but a f̸ hence R is not antisymmetric for all elements.

REFERENCES

Boole, G. (1947) ´The Mathematicial Analysis of Logic´, Macmillan, Cambridge.

Clapham, C.R.J. (1969) ´Introduction to Abstract Algebra´, Routledge Kegan and Paul, London.

Godel, K. (1938) (English Translation) ´On Formally Undecidable Propositions´, Basic Books, New York, 1962.

Hilbert, D. (1900) ´The Foundations of Geometry´,Open Court Publications, London.

Meschkowski, H. (1968) ´Introduction to Modern Mathematics´, Harrap and Co., London.

Peterson, W.W. (1961) ´Error-Correcting Codes´ MIT Press, Cambridge, Mass.

Plato, ´The Republic´, Comford Translation (1941), Oxford.

Chapter 3

Automata theory

I Aleksander

3.1 WHAT IS AN AUTOMATON?

Clearly, one can answer that question by looking in a dictionary (Concise Oxford):

> ʹThing endued with spontaneous motion, living being
> viewed materially, piece of mechanism with
> concealed motive power, living being whose actions
> are involuntary or without active intelligenceʹ.

However, within the context of digital systems the word ʹautomatonʹ has been used in a much more precise, technical fashion. Nevertheless, there are points of similarity. First, one notes that ʹa machineʹ in technical history was thought of as being something that moves. Computer-like devices have changed all that, and it is perfectly clear that there exists a vast class of machines in which ʹmotionʹ is of very little importance, information being the life-blood of such machines as opposed to energy. Indeed, if one introduced ʹinformation processingʹ as being some kind of motion into the dictionary definition, the reason that the word ʹautomataʹ was appended to a formal class of information processing machines becomes fairly clear. Looking back at this definition, one notes that the important words are

ʹspontaneousʹ

ʹconcealedʹ

ʹinvoluntaryʹ

In other words, automata are devices which surprise us in some way as a result of some hidden inner machinery. We are now in a position to understand the technical definition of an ʹautomatonʹ centering, as it does, on this hidden inner machinery called an ʹinternal stateʹ.

In automata theory one tries to relate the input/output behavior of an automaton to this internal state. In the context of digital systems one normally assumes that messages are discrete and distinct. That is, an automatonʹs input can receive discrete messages, its output generates discrete messages and, in the same way, one assumes that the internal state is one of a set of discrete inner messages.

So, in answer to the original question, ´what is an automaton?´ we can now give a definition.

An automaton is defined by the set of five items (called a 5-tuple):

$$\langle\ I,\ Z,\ Q,\ d,\ w,\rangle$$

where

I is a finite set of discrete input messages;

Z is a finite set of discrete output messages;

Q is a set of internal state messages or just called internal states;

d is a rule which, by taking a pair made up of an element of I and the element of Q currently in force in the automaton, tells one which the next element of Q is going to occur in the machine;

w is another rule which relates the current input to the state to one of the elements of Z. That is, it tells us the value of the output at any point in time.

An example might be useful at this point. Imagine a combination lock which operates on the basis of a thumb wheel, with the numbers 0 to 9 on it, one number showing at one time and a push-button C which merely tells the automaton at what point in time it is to take cognizance of the digit on the thumbwheel (see Fig. 3.1 for a sketch of the system). It is intended that only the sequence of 1937 should open the safe. What, then, are the essential requirements for the inner state mechanism of the automaton? Assuming that it starts in some neutral state, i_0, it should remain in that neutral state until the combination 1C is received (we shall refer to pressing button C as input signal C). Should this happen, and in order to remember that it has happened, the automaton should change its internal state to, say i_1. This state indicates (as one would on a memo pad) that the first correct input has occurred.

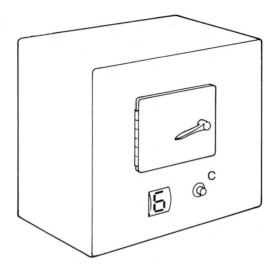

Fig. 3.1 A digital safe

Now, three events have to be taken care of: first, the release of button C should not cancel a record of the fact that 1 has occurred properly (that is, the state remains i_1), second, the combination 9C could occur, which should be noted by a change of state to, say, i_2, which is a note on the internal memo pad that <u>two</u> proper inputs have occurred. The third event covers all other possibilities, and would require that the note on the memo pad (about being one step forward) be scrapped – that is, a return to i_0. This procedure could now be described further using words similar to the above. However, the automata theoretician has a better way of describing such events. This is a graphical method known as a <u>state diagram</u>. The diagram that fits the above task is shown in Fig. 3.2.

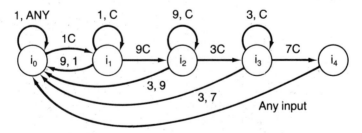

Fig. 3.2 Automaton representation of the safe

In this kind of diagram, circles are used to indicate
internal states, while arrows show transitions between
states. The symbol C is used to indicate that C is <u>not</u>
pressed and,similarly, 3 means any number except 3. On this
diagram we have also managed to indicate effects not
discussed so far. First, we show that i_4 is the state in
which the catch for the (spring loaded) safe door is
unlatched. Also one sees that the automaton returns to the
neutral starting state i_0 as soon as the C-button is released
after the safe opens: which means that once the safe door is
shut by the user it will not open again until the correct
sequence is input.

It is now possible to sharpen the 5-tuple definition of an
automaton mentioned earler, by fitting it to the above
example. For this example

$$I \quad = \quad \{0C, \ 1C, \ 2C, \ 3C, \ 4C, \ 5C, \ 6C, \ 7C, \ 8C, \ 9C$$

$$0\overline{C}, \ 1\overline{C}, \ 2\overline{C}, \ 3\overline{C} \ \ 4\overline{C}, \ 5\overline{C}, \ 6\overline{C}, \ 7\overline{C}, \ 8\overline{C}, \ 9\overline{C}\}$$

$$Q \quad = \quad \{i_0, \ i_1, \ i_2, \ i_3, \ i_4\}$$

is given by (see Fig. 3.2):

This property enables one to discuss in some depth the potentials and limitations of information processing machinery at a level which gets closer to fundamentals than to technological arguments.

However, before considering variations on the simple 5-tuple automaton definition and its embodiment in hardware, let us look at the history of automata concepts.

3.2 THE BIRTH PANGS OF AUTOMATA

It is an interesting exercise to follow the history of automata as a separate concept from digital computing. The fact which makes this possible is the property of an automaton that it is an abstract concept: a way of describing machinery without reference to the technology of the machine - a way of getting at the 'ghost in the machine'.

Indeed, this history may be seen as starting in 1937, ten years before the birth of the digital computer as we know it now (Burks, Goldstine and Von Neumann, 1946). This 'conception' took place in the mind of British mathematician Alan Turing, as a fertilization between two ideas: he had an interest in computing machinery and was well aware of the potential of electronics. Also, as a pure mathematician he was interested in the question of 'computable' functions, a function being a translation between one set of data and another. A typical function whose 'computability' may be questioned is the following. For input data N compute in a general manner the Nth prime number, starting with 1 as the first. If one allows exhaustive searches through numbers this is no problem, but if one looks for a function that can be directly evaluated the computability of the problem becomes suspect.

In order to decide whether certain functions were computable or not, Alan Turing invented an abstract machine now known as a Turing machine. The manner in which he used (in the abstract, of course) this machine to resolve computability problems is beyond our scope at the moment, but later in this chapter we will see that a Turing machine is a very simple

State	Input	Next state
i_0	1C	i_1
i_0	All others	i_0
i_1	$\overline{C}$	i_1
i_1	$\overline{9}C$	i_0
i_1	9C	i_2
.	.	.
.	.	.
.	.	.
.	.	.
i_4	$\overline{C}$	i_0

while W is given by

State	Output
i_0	safe not open
i_1	" " "
i_2	" " "
i_2	" " "
i_3	" " "
i_4	safe open

The major point one wishes to stress here is that both the above symbolic statements and the state diagram of Fig. 3.2 provide a complete statement of what the safe mechanism is doing. Note the lack of reference to any technology such as transistors or relays. In fact we shall, later in this chapter, show how the abstract description can be turned into a piece of hardware, but at this stage we merely stress the absence of technology from these descriptions.

automaton of the kind already defined, to which has been
added a rather long (possibly infinite) recording tape which
the machine can read and modify.

The gestation period lasted twenty-one years and saw
supporting developments take place, such as Shannon's
theories of switching logic (1938) and statistical
communication (1948). Indeed, the period saw the coming of
Wiener's book on Cybernetics where, although he shows
awareness of Alan Turing[*] ('I spent a total of three weeks in
England...I had an excellent chance...to talk over the
fundamental ideas of Cybernetics with Mr. Turing'), there is
no further mention of Turing's ideas on abstract automata in
the rest of that book. The major events of this period,
however, were still to come. Indeed, in 1951 John Von
Neumann first suggested models similar to the 5-tuple
presented earlier in this chapter, and indeed covered a great
number of applications of such models in learning machines,
the increase of reliability and processing using cellular
arrays. The latter includes the notion of the self-
reproduction of automata, which is a source of fascination to
many cyberneticians still today. The concept was given a
pre-natal recognition at a symposium in Princeton in 1956 and
which was originated by Claude Shannon and John McCarty. The
former is no stranger in this history, while the latter will
appear again in our consideration of Artificial Intelligence.
The title of the Princeton symposium was 'Automata Studies'
and contained much of the classical work in this field, some
of which will be discussed in this chapter.

However, the birth point of the subject surely came in 1957,
with the publication of Chomsky's influential analysis of
language called 'Syntactic Structures'. This showed that
the syntax of a 'language' could be expressed as a set of
production rules for surface and 'deep' symbols. Although
Chomsky aimed at providing a rigorous background to an
understanding of natural language, his influence on automata
theory was different. It pointed to the fact that one could
define artificial languages, and these in turn defined
automata which accept such languages. Indeed, this is
probably much more fundamental in automata theory than in
psycholinguistics, mainly because in the latter one needs to
take a rigorous view of meaning (semantics) in order to have
a full view of the subject.

---

[*]   Wiener (1948), p.32.

In automata theory, however, Chomsky's description of
grammars led to a classification of automata in terms of the
complexities of the language which they accept. This will be
pursued further in later parts of this chapter.

3.3 AUTOMATA TYPES:

DEALING WITH CONTINUITY AND UNCERTAINTY

The 5-tuple model presented earlier in this chapter has
tacitly been presented, laden with the following properties.

First, all the quantities it processes (including its own
internal states) are finite in number. The model is
therefore known as a finite state machine or FSM. When
looking at these restrictions it is reasonable to ask the
question:

'Do the restrictions limit the FSM model in its applications
at all?' It can be argued convincingly that the FSM is
fundamental and may be used to describe less restricted
phenomena, albeit by approximation in some cases.

The non-restricted types are

        a) continuous-state automata,
        b) probabilistic automata, and
        c) non-deterministic automata.

We shall consider them in turn.

To understand the concept of a continuous state automaton,
consider the example in Fig. 3.3. This is a circuit
characteristically used in electronics. There is no doubt
that, at least in part, this is a continuous device. It
works as follows (neglecting some of the practical details of
its components, e.g. base-emitter voltage on the transistor).
If the input switch is initially in the zero-volts position
and then switched to the 10-volt position, the capacitor will
start charging up according to the equation:

$$V = 10 \ (1-e^{-t/CR}) \ \text{volts.}$$

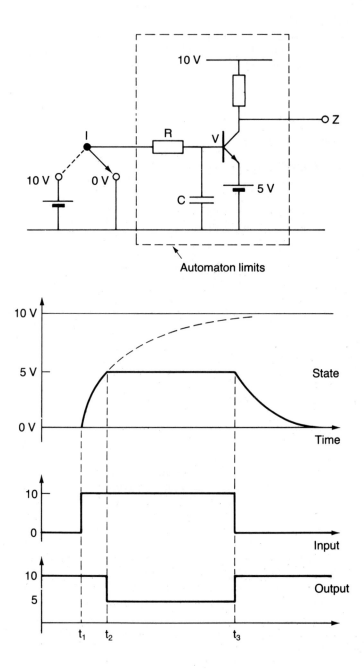

Fig. 3.3 An analog automaton

However, when V gets to 5 volts, the transistor switches ON, dragging the output down from 10 volts to 5 (at t_2). However, if the input is then switched back to 0, the voltage at V will start discharging, and the transistor will switch off, returning the output to 10 volts (at t_3).

Now, imagine that we have a FSM; clearly the input set I could be

$$\{0 \text{ volts}, 10 \text{ volts}\}$$

the output set Z could be

$$\{10 \text{ volts}, 5 \text{ volts}\}$$

the internal states are clearly needed to represent the action of the capacitor. In fact, as we have described the system, the capacitor and the resistor merely determine the difference between t_2 and t_1. (This is known as a delay circuit.) Now, assume that in our abstract automaton, state changes can occur only with some monotonous regularity. It is as if the C button on our safe example were pushed regularly by an in-built clock. Indeed, such automata are called <u>synchronous</u>. (As an exercise the reader could re-draw the diagram of Fig. 3.2 so that C did not appear in it, and the states are assumed to change at regular intervals.) Then all one needs is $Q = \{q_1, q_2 \ldots q_{100} \text{ (say)}\}$ and we assume that a state change takes place every 1/10 seconds. If $t_2 - t_1$ should be, say, 3 seconds, then one could get most of the way by having

$$q_1 \dashrightarrow q_2$$

$$q_2 \dashrightarrow q_3$$

$$\cdot$$
$$\cdot$$
$$\cdot$$

etc.

and   w, $\{q_1 \ldots q_{30}\} \dashrightarrow 10 \text{ volts}$

$$\{q_{30} - q_{100}\} \dashrightarrow 5 \text{ volts}$$

The reader will soon be able to see that one can use a large number of states to <u>approximate</u> continuous action. Indeed, if necessary one could even use the discrete state sequence to simulate the exponential variation in the continuous state.

What one is saying is that the 5-tuple model may be used to approximate a system where the state variations are continuous. To devotees of modern control theory this must be of some interest, since it sets up a relation between the FSM and the state-space representation of continuous control systems.[*]

A probabilistic automaton is one in which the transitions between states are specified as probabilities. Clearly these form an important class, since one is unlikely to find totally deterministic (or non-probabilistic) phenomena in nature. So, probabilistic automata are a vital tool in the modelling of natural phenomena, which could, of course, include human beings. A typical probabilistic automaton is shown in Fig. 3.4. Here we see that there are two states as usual, but now when one indicates that i_1 (say) causes a transition between state A and state B we say additionally that it does so with a probability of 0.5 (written in brackets next to the transition-causing input label).[**]

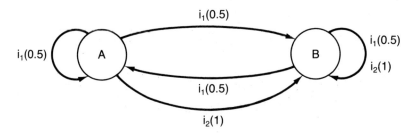

Fig. 3.4 A probabilistic automaton

So a probabilistic automaton may be defined as one which must state the probabilities of transitions to the next states for all possible inputs. Central here, however, is the relationship of this concept to the finite state machine.

---

[*]   Ref. Elgerd (1967)

[**] Footnote: Readers familiar with statistics will recognize this as being a description of a Markov chain.

A clue to this relationship is given in Fig. 3.5, where we see an FSM with four states and the same input parameters i_1 and i_2 as the probabilistic automaton. The additional features are an input marked C and the grouping of the pair of states A_1, A_2 and B_1, B_2. If one imagines that C is an input which is applied very often, but in a way uncorrelated with inputs i_1 and i_2, we see that this introduces an uncertainty regarding which pair of states is the current one. In fact, the first figure may then be a very good way of describing the second.

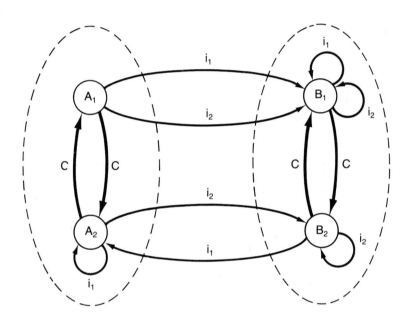

Fig. 3.5 FSM version of the probabilistic automaton

One could say, therefore, the second is a simulation or approximation of the first. One sees that as with the continuous case it is possible to approximate a probabilistic automaton with an FSM with a much larger number of states.

In fact, were the division of probability from A in our probabilistic automaton not 0.5, 0.5 but 0.01, 0.99, we would need 100 states in the FSM to represent one state in the probabilistic automaton.

Turning finally to the <u>non-deterministic</u> (ND) automaton, it is vital to dispel the confusion that arises between it and probabilistic devices. The confusion arises from the fact that in everyday language <u>both</u> words seem as if they mean <u>not deterministic</u>. But when used in a technical sense ND has a distinct and well-defined character.

Given an ND machine in state A and input i_1, we can express the idea that a transition to either state B <u>or</u> state C is quite legitimate under some circumstances or other. One does <u>not</u> need to state what the probability of doing either of these things is – it is merely a statement that both are allowed. An example should clarify why this type of artefact is required.

A testing system is required for strings of 0s and 1s such that it will pass all strings starting with an 0 and followed by any number (but at least one) of 1s. A desirable way of describing this task is shown in Fig. 3.6. This is called a <u>non-deterministic machine</u> (NDM). The states are labeled as S for Start state, I for Intermediate state, P for Pass state, X for fail state. (R stands for a resetting input.) The way that this diagram is interpreted is subtly different from the way that one looks at a state diagram for a FSM, and it is this:

> ´Suppose the system is reset to state S and a sequence of inputs has occurred. Can one find a path through the NDM which follows the inputs and ends in state P? If one can, the string is accepted.´

We note that strings that are not accepted end in state X.

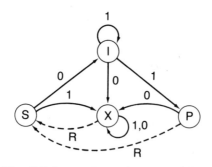

Fig. 3.6 A non-deterministic machine

So, for example, we have

Accepted strings.
01
011111
011111111111

Not accepted strings
101
01111110
010

We shall see later that this is a very convenient way of describing the necessary action of some machines which check computer languages. We shall also see that every NDM may be transformed into an FSM by means of a simple algorithm. In fact, the application of this algorithm brings about only a slight transformation to the NDM giving the FSM in Fig. 3.7. The reader can check for himself that the latter does a job equivalent to that of the former.

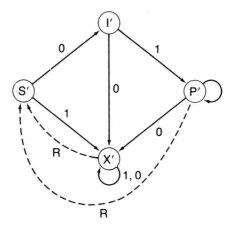

Fig. 3.7 FSM version of the non-deterministic automaton

We have seen in this section, therefore, that the FSM is a fundamental, but so far abstract, model for a vast range of information processing mechanisms, both natural and man made. Next, we shall do some engineering.

We shall demonstrate that the FSM is an artefact that may be used not only for experimentation and modeling, but also as a real, concrete building brick for information processing systems. Those not interested in hardware can skip the next section without loss of thread.

3.4 MAKING AUTOMATA

Recalling the 5-tuple abstract statement of the FSM $\langle I, Z, Q,$
$d, w\rangle$, it becomes clear that the first step in making an
automaton is to encode I, Z and Q into some palpable form.
This is no problem if one assumes some form of digital,
indeed binary, implementation. One imagines that at any
moment in time the current elements of these sets are held in
binary registers.

Therefore we define three registers labeled I, Z and Q, each
register containing at least $\lfloor \log_2 n \rfloor$ bits, where n is the
number of messages in the set in question (I, Z or Q) and [X]
is the least integer greater than X. The automaton is ´made´
by setting up a logical transformation circuit (see Chapter 1
p.19), which first relates the present content of 1 and Q to
the next content of Q according to d and the value of Z
according to w. The arrangement is shown in Fig. 3.8. If
the automaton were made by an electronics engineer, he would
use either logic gates (AND, OR, NAND), etc. to implement d
and w, or fixed memory circuits acting as look-up tables
where I and Q together act as an address, and the values of Z
and ´next´ Q are found at the desired address.

A computer scientist might do things a little differently.
The following is an example of a BASIC program which
implements a general automaton.

Program	Comment
10 DIM Q (K,L)	Dimension the d array
20 DIM Z (K,L)	Dimension the w array
30 FOR X = 1 TO K :FOR Y = 1 TO L	Set up loops
40 INPUT Q (X,Y) :INPUT Z (X,Y)	Input d and w
50 NEXT X: NEXT Y	Closure of loops

The above program builds d and w from data supplied by the
programmer. To use the automaton the program goes on as
follows:

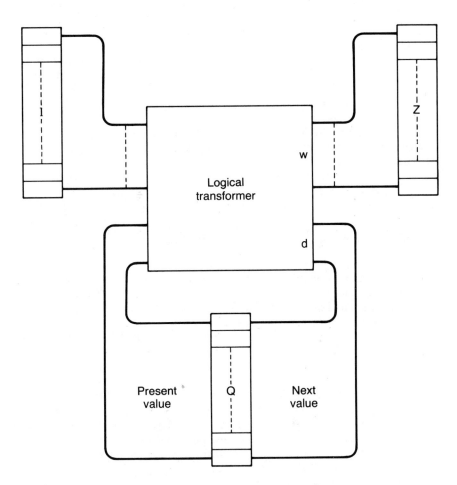

Fig. 3.8 The making of an automaton

```
 60    INPUT Q                 Input initial state

 70    INPUT I                 Input input message

 80    PRINT Z (I,Q)           Output output message

 90    Q=Q(I,Q)                Calculate next state

100    GOTO 70                 Start again with new input
```

Clearly, in both these examples there is some kind of
clocking arrangement implied. In the latter this is clearly
determined by the synchronicity of the program, while the
former would require clocking arrangements on the Q register,
at least.

3.5 SIMILARITIES AND DIFFERENCES BETWEEN FSMs

Some important questions one might ask, both from the point
of view of theory and that of engineering, are ́Given two 5-
tuple descriptions of FSMs, to what extent can identical
descriptions lead to different machines? ́ and also ́In what
way can different 5-tuple descriptions lead to identical
input-output behavior? ́

From the point of view of general theory the importance of
these questions lies at the very center of discovering
whether the FSM is a powerful tool for modeling general
systems or not. On the engineering side, these questions
have a bearing on whether the machine has been efficiently
made. For example, in this context a corollary to the second
question is:

        ́Does a machine exist which has the same input-
        output description as the machine I have designed,
        but which is in some way cheaper? ́

By ́cheaper ́ one usually refers to fewer states or fewer
circuit blocks.

One sad fact that becomes clear right from the start is that

no amount of input-output experimentation will guarantee the
revelation of details of the state-structure. Consider the
two FSMs in Fig. 3.9 (a) and (b).

Recalling that the labels on the transitions are of the form
X/Y, where X is the input causing the transition and Y the
output resulting from it, the reader can verify that, if only
measurements of such inputs and outputs are available there
is no experiment that will distinguish between the (a)
automaton and the one in (b). One needs a can opener to look
at the machinery inside in order to get at the real state
structures.

What, then can be achieved by means of input/output
measurements on an automaton?

Before answering that question one must become aware of yet
another factor that does not come to light through
input/output experiments. Consider Fig. 3.9(c). Say the
automaton starts in state A. Note that during an
input/output experiment it could enter state B and then state
C. Alas, no manner of further experimentation will lead the
system back to B or A, and the only information that further
experimentation can yield can only regard the state structure
involving states C and D. Such an FSM is said not to be
strongly connected. A strongly connected FSM is one in which
there exists at least one input sequence that enables the
system to go from an arbitrarily chosen state to another
arbitrarily chosen state.

Therefore, in answer to the quesion regarding what can be
achieved by input/output experiments, the automaton theorist
would give the following answer:

An in/out experiment can lead to a minimal state model of the
strongly connected part of an automaton. The model is as
accurate as the experimental data permits.

While the concept of strong connection has already been
partly explored, the two further key factors in the above
statement that require further elaboration are:

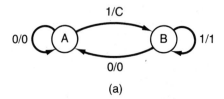

(a)

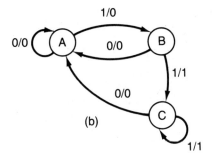

(b)

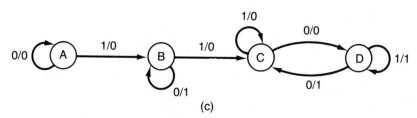

(c)

Fig. 3.9 Difficulties in input/output measurements

                                    the minimal-state concept,
                                    the question of accuracy.

Of all the FSMs that have the same input/output behavior (of
which there is an infinity for each behavioral pattern) some
have fewer states than others. Consequently there is a set
(with possibly just one member) which has the fewest states.
One the question of accuracy, one notes that the number of
input/output measurements determines the <u>amount</u> of state
structure that has been explored, and therefore determines
the model.

To illustrate these points, consider the following
progression of an input/output experiment for a machine with
an unknown number of states:

$$\begin{array}{llll} \text{Input} & 1 & 1 & 1 \\ \text{Output} & 0 & 0 & 0 \end{array}$$

The possible configurations for this experiment are shown in
Fig. 3.10(a). (The symbol * indicates the state at the end of
the experiment.)

We now continue with:

$$\begin{array}{llll} \text{Input} & 0 & 1 & 0 \\ & 0 & 0 & 1 \end{array}$$

This yields possibilities, some of which are shown in Fig.
3.10(b).

If the experiment were to stop here, all these models would
be valid. If one insisted that the machine were strongly
connected, models such as $\alpha\ \delta$ or $\beta\ \delta$ would remain valid.

If one were looking for <u>complete</u> models, only models such as
$\alpha\ \delta$ or $\beta\ \alpha$ would remain suitable candidates.
Clearly, however, a simple test input 1 would make α β
complete (why?).

Clearly the question ´which model is right?´ has no real
answer. To give it such an answer, our example indicates
that, besides knowing that the machine is strongly connected,

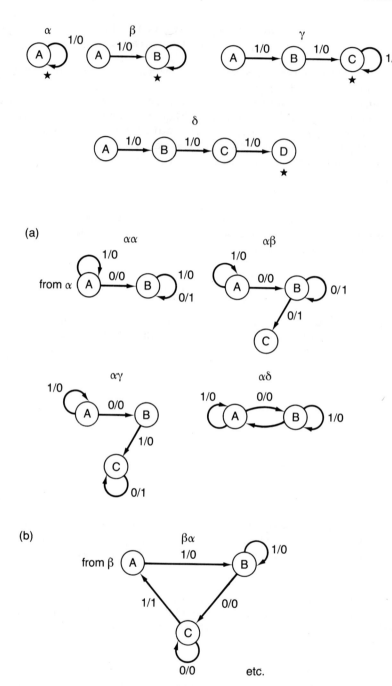

Fig. 3.10 Building feasible machines from test results

one must also know how many states it has! Then the complete
models that emerge with the right number of states become
highly suitable candidates for being ´the right´ model.   One
must realize that if at any time several such candidates
appear, experimentation must continue until all but one are
eliminated or the remaining models are equivalent, minimal-
state sets. We shall consider this question of equivalent
machines or states a little more closely.

3.6 WHAT HAPPENS NEXT?

Before we can consider equivalence between machines we look
at a most useful weapon in the automaton theoretician´s
armory: the concept of the ´next state vector´ or NSV.

This is simply described by means of the following example.
Consider the FSM in Fig. 3.11. It is generally clear that
the complete description of this machine can be given by
means of the following two tables, one for d and one for w:

The Table d

input

d		i_1	i_2
	A	D	A
	B	C	B
Present			
state	C	C	D
	D	D	A

next
state

The Table w

input

w		i_1	i_2
	A	z_1	z1
	B	z_1	z1
PS	C	z_2	z2
	D	z_2	z1

output

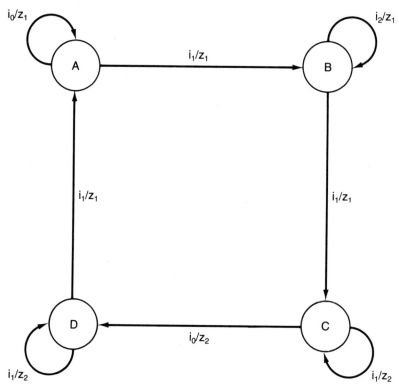

Fig. 3.11 Example for the study of next state-vectors

The NSV concept applies to the d table.   In fact, the NSV for i_1 is

$$\begin{bmatrix} B \\ C \\ C \\ D \end{bmatrix}$$

and for i_2

$$\begin{bmatrix} A \\ B \\ D \\ A \end{bmatrix}$$

The left-hand side of the table (that is, the list of all the states) is said to <u>map</u> into the appropriate SV <u>under</u> either i_1 or i_2, etc.

Now consider the following set of states and corresponding NSV (written horizontally to save space):

Set of States: A B C D E F = S

NSV (under i_1, say):   D E F A B C A.

Here we intoduce yet another tool: <u>a partition</u> of a set of states.   This means the breaking up of the set of states into blocks.

For example, we could break up S_1 into, say, three blocks:

Partition 1:   (A B)   (C D)   (E F G)

                      Block 1   Block 2   Block 3

or into two blocks as follows:

Partition 2:   (A B C)   (D E F G)

                      Block 1   Block 2

To discover equivalence between and within machines, the concept of a partition is used together with that of an NSV as follows:

Taking partition 1 first, see how the partition breaks up in the NSV - (we label the NSV in terms of the partition blocks).

	Block 1 (b1)	Block 2 (b2)	Block 3 (b3)
Partition 1:	(A B)	(C D)	(E F G)
NSV:	(D E)	(F A)	(B C A)
	b_1 b_3	b_3 b_1	b_1 b_2 b_1

We repeat this exercise for partition 2.

	b_1	b_2
Partition 2:	(A B C)	(D E F G)
NSV:	(D E F)	(A B C A)

The most noticeable difference is that for partition 2, the blocks in the NSV have mapped into <u>single blocks</u>, which is not the case for partition 1.

Finally we can see how this is useful. Consider an example where A B C all give output 1 and D E F G give output 0. Then for i_1, say, we have the NSV: D E F A B C A as above, while for i_2 we have the NSV: A B A F D G G.

We note that for partition 2 now block 1 maps into block 1 and block 2 into block 2:

	<--b_1-->	<--b_2-->
$P_1 2$:	(A B C)	(D E F G)
NSV	(A B A)	(F D G G)
	$b_1 b_1 b_1$	$b_2 b_2 b_2 b_2$

In doing an input-output experiment, it becomes clear that no amount of experimentation will distinguish between states (A B C) on one hand or (D E F G) on the other. In fact, the experimenter would report a simple two-state machine with the following mappings:

d	i_1	i_2
X	Y	X
Y	X	Y

w	i_1	i_2
X	0	1
Y	1	0

So, all in all the business of finding a partitions that map into themselves in the NSV turns out to be a technique for finding groups of states that behave equally in some way. In the above example it has been seen that, since these groups also have equal outputs, they lead to a way of computing the minimal-state version of a given machine.

In fact, techniques exist whereby this grouping of states (which in the literature is called the Substitution Property) may actually be used to engineer or design FSMs for which the state structure is given. We allude briefly to how this is done, leaving the curious reader to pursue greater detail elsewhere.[*]

First we note that a major problem in the translation between an abstract FSM into a real digital machine is the choice of coding for the internal states into suitable patterns of 0s and 1s. This is called the state assignment problem, and is seen to be a 'problem' because some choices of coding lead to very different circuit structures from others. Indeed, the cost of the circuit depends on this assignment. Knowing about the substitution property helps, since one can spot groups of states (blocks) which may only depend on other groups and lead to assignments that simplify the circuitry. Again, an example might help to clarify the matter.

Consider the automaton in Fig. 3.12. This is not a strongly connected machine, but one of a kind often used in satellite communications as a checking scheme. The input comes from an earth-generated signal, and the output is broadcast back to earth. It is assumed to start off in state Z on switch-on.

---

[*] Aleksander and Hanna (1978).

State Table

	0	I
W	Z	X
X	Y	Y
Y	X	Z
Z	W	Z

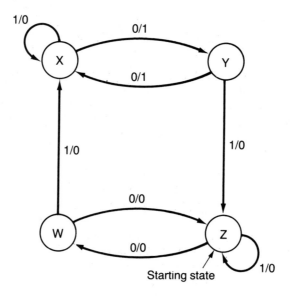

Fig. 3.12 Example of state assignment

It then looks for a trigger sequence which contains an odd
number of 0s. Note that any other sequence with an even
number of 0s separated by any number of 1s leaves the machine
in state Z.

Any odd sequence of 0s puts the machine into states X and Y,
where it broadcasts a 1 for all sequence of 0s. It returns
to Z if the sequence of 0s has an odd number of 0s in it,
when the sequence returns to Z and starts again.

We now wish to build this device, and to do so we must assign
binary codes to the states. There are four states, so two
binary variables will do. This means that the states W, X, Y
and Z must somehow be associated with the messages 00, 01,
11, 10: but how? That is the state assignment problem as
stated earlier.

To see how these tie in to NSVs and partitions, note that any
assignment implies a 2-block partition on the states with two
states in each, one block being coded 0 and the other 1.

In fact, we can look at all (three) of the possible
partitions for this machine (it´s small enough!):

$$ (W\ X\ ) \qquad (Y\ Z),\ ---> P_1 $$

$$ (W\ Y) \qquad (X\ Z),\ ---> P_2 $$

$$ (W\ Z) \qquad (X\ Y),\ ---> P_3 $$

Looking at the two NSVs, we note that only P_1 and P_2 have the
substitution property as defined earlier. P_3 fails since,
although (WZ) maps into (WZ) under 0, it maps into XZ under
1, which is not a block of the partition (WZ) (XY). Now let
us do the assignment twice, once using the two partitions
with substitution property (P_1 and P_2) and once involving a
partition which does not (P_1 and P_3).

To heighten the effect of the demonstration we start with the
second first. So we have:

for P_1 (W X)--> 0, (Y Z)--> 1 as the code for the first
digit (clearly, 0 and 1 could be reversed, without,
as we shall see, affecting our argument).

for P_3 (W Z)--> 0, (X Y)--> 1 as the code for the second
digit.

Thus the coding of the states is

$$W = 00, \quad X = 01, \quad Y = 11, \quad Z = 10.$$

So, the encoded next state table reads (labeling the left-
hand state digit q_1, and the right-hand one q_2, the input
being 1 and the output irrelevant for the time being):

Present

$q_1\ q_2$	$i = 0$	$i = 1$
0 0 (W)	1 0 (Z)	0 1 (X)
0 1 (X)	1 1 (Y)	0 1 (X)
1 1 (Y)	0 1 (X)	1 0 (Z)
1 0 (Z)	0 0 (W)	1 0 (Z)

next $q_1\ q_2$

The circuit designer must find the <u>logic expression</u> for q_1
and q_2 (next) (say $q_{\prime 1}$, $q_{\prime 2}$) in terms of their <u>present</u> values
and the value of i. He would be able to show that (and the
reader is encouraged to verify this):

$$q'_1 = \overline{i}\ \overline{q}_1 + i\ q_1$$

$$q'_2 = \overline{q}_2 + i \qquad *$$

We see now that even though q'_1 depends only on i and its own
previous value, one needs the value of i and <u>both q_2 and q_1</u>
in order to compute q'_2.

---

*   Note on notation

$q'_1 = \overline{i}\ \overline{q}_1 + i\ q_1$ reads $q'1$ is 1 if, and only if,(i is <u>not</u>
1 <u>and</u> q_1 is <u>not</u> 1) <u>or</u> (i is 1 <u>and</u> q_1 is 1), etc.

However, if one takes P_1 and P_2, it may be shown that for the coding

$$P_1: \quad (W\ X) \longrightarrow 0, (Y\ Z) \longrightarrow 1 \text{ for the first digit}$$
$$P_2: \quad (W\ Y) \longrightarrow 0, (X\ Z) \longrightarrow 1 \text{ for the second digit}$$

we have:

$$q_1{}' = \overline{i}\ \overline{q}_1 + i\ q_1$$

$$q_2{}' = \overline{q}_2 + i$$

We now note that to compute p_1 we only need know q'_1 (and i), and for q'_2 we only need to know q_2.

The crux of all this is that this effect was predictable from the very fact that P_1 and P_2 have the substitution property. That is, the next value of a group of states (coded in the same way) depends only on its present value and not of that of other states!

Unfortunately, such demonstrations are fraught with detail. All that the reader need absorb here, however, is that an analysis of the partitioning of states of an FSM leads to some understanding of its possible internal structure. In passing, it may be mentioned that engineers have found this helpful not only in assigning states to FSMs, but also in studying how large machines may be broken down into smaller ones, an art known as ´decomposition´.[*]

3.7 ARE FSMs LIMITED?

The obvious limitation of a finite state machine is, indeed, the finitenesss of its states. This is a realistic, practical limitation, since any man-made machine must have a finite number of states. However, the question can be asked in a more meaningful and subtle way.

---

[*] Aleksander and Hanna (1978).

Take a simple home computer. It is likely to provide its
user with, at least, 16,000 words of typically 8 bits each.
The entire computer might cost less than a bicycle. However,
the number of states provided by this amount of fast, local
storage is of the order of

$$S \;=\; 2^{16,000 \times 8}$$

This turns out to be approximately

$$S \;=\; 10^{43,000}$$

which, indeed, is an astronomical figure. If one adds to
this the amout of backing store that disk and tapes may add,
one finds that even simple machines are much more akin to
infinite state machines, for which the FSM model is not so
much inadequate as inappropriate. The answer, therefore, to
the question of whether FSMs are limited, is centered on the
fact that in no way could one handle FSM concepts such as
NSVs and state diagrams because of their enormity. And yet
machines exist and people work with them despite the enormity
of the number of states. The rest of this chapter,
therefore, looks at automata models better suited to modeling
such systems.

The central theme of such models is that they are concerned
with the nature of language. Computer languages provide the
means for communication with machines, and as a result
provide a rather special type of input. ´Special´ refers to
the contrast with FSMs where the input is assumed to be
totally unrestricted. We shall therefore look at the nature
of this restriction next.

3.8 WHAT IS A LANGUAGE?

In every-day conversation this question may be answered in
familiar terms, by referring to well-known languages shared
by many people. However, the automata theorist would like to
define it a little more closely than, say, ´a conventional
use of words placed in phrases and sentences whose meaning is
shared by many people´.

The need for this closer definition stems from a curiosity in the fact that people (and, for that matter, people and machines) do not only communicate by means of well-defined languages of words and phrases, but are also capable of using abstract symbols and formulae. For example one can, within the BASIC language, sit at a machine and type

$$A = 3 \text{ (return)}$$

$$B = 6 \text{ (return)}$$

$$\text{PRINT } "(A * B) + A = "; \ (A * B) + A$$

and the computer will type

$$(A * B) + A = 21$$

all of which seems a reasonable informational transaction.

So we can define a <u>language</u> in a way that will satisfy the digital systems engineer. The essentials are:

a) An <u>alphabet</u> or <u>vocabulary</u>: these are the basic units which constitute the symbols of the language. For example, the alphabet of a computer language might contain symbols such as +, -, LET, GOTO, END, etc. Indeed, it becomes necessary to see <u>words</u> as the basic units of natural language, although it would not be impossible to think of letters as such symbols. It will become clear later that this would be somewhat counterproductive.

b) A <u>set of rules</u> which enables one to check whether combinations of symbols do or do not belong to a language.

c) In general, it is assumed that a language consists of sequences or <u>strings</u> of symbols rather than other (say 2-dimensional) arrangements.

These definitions appear free and easy, so let us see whether we can construct some arbitrary languages.

Language L_1 consists of the following <u>vocabulary</u> symbols:

X meaning scissors

[]   "   paper

0   "   stone

The rule of the language is such that a symbol can follow
another as long as it does not <u>dominate</u>. (The reader might
recall the children's game where two participants make signs
with their hands representing these symbols: scissors
dominate paper by cutting it, paper dominates the stone by
wrapping it, and the stone dominates the scissors by breaking
them. The player presenting the <u>dominating</u> sign wins.) So a
sequence of L_1 beginning with X could be

$$X \; X \; [\;] \; O \; O \; X \; [\;] \; O \; X \; [\;] \; [\;] \; [\;] \; [\;] \; \text{etc.}$$

On discovering sequences containing

$$X \quad O \quad [\;]$$

one could come to the conclusion that they do not belong to
L_1. Although it is quite feasible to imagine the design of an
FSM which, at the end of a given sequence, will signal
whether the sequence belongs to a given language or not, it
is also easy to see that slight modifications to the <u>rules</u>
would make this less easy.

For example, if we define the rules as requiring that at the
end of a sequence the majority (or some other proportion) of
the consecutive pairs should not have a dominant second
symbol, then the FSM design would depend on the length of
sequence one expects. However, it is quite possible to
specify the rules of the language without reference to the
length of sequences (as was done in the previous sentence),
so this creates a disparity between the language
specification and an FSM checking model, making the FSM model
inappropriate due to its finiteness.

The checking model for a language has a specific name:
<u>an acceptor.</u> That is, it accepts a sequence if it belongs to
a given language, or rejects it, otherwise.

We shall look next at the classification of languages largely
in terms of the implications they have on such acceptors.
Before doing this, however, it may be important to clarify a
major point. All the formal work done on languages in
automata theory relates to <u>syntax</u> - that is, the grammatical
structure of the language. Very little of this relates to
meaning or <u>semantics,</u> which is a difficult question that will

not be ignored, but rather left for discussion in the chapter on Artificial Intelligence. To illustrate these terms very briefly, ´The cheese ate the mouse´ has the correct syntax, but its semantic content is incorrect. Automata theory, in general, does not get to grips with the latter.

3.9 GRAMMATICAL DIFFERENCES BETWEEN LANGUAGES

When one tries to find the difference between languages, one does this principally by looking at differences between the rules. By doing this one can categorize rules into classes, and, consequently, languages into corresponding classes. To understand this we need a framework in which to cast language rules: this is called Grammar (alluding to the way of specifying the rules of natural languages such as English or French).

Formally a Grammar consists of the following:

a) Vocabulary (as before), but this time split into two kinds of symbols:

$$\text{Terminal symbols } (V_T), \text{ and}$$

$$\text{Non-terminal symbols } (V_N)$$

Terminal symbols are symbols that actually appear in the strings of the language, while non-terminal symbols are there only as an aid to generating sequences. This will be clarified in an example which follows soon.

b) Production rules (P), which state how one group of symbols may be replaced by another.

c) A starting symbol (S) (usually one of the V_N).

Consider the following example (language L_2)

$$V_N = a$$

$$V_T = (,) \quad \text{(the comma is not a symbol)}$$

P : a --> ( ) (rule 1) | The arrow reads

   a --> (a) (rule 2) | ´may be replaced by´

Starting with a we apply rule 2 and get:

(a)

Then, applying rule 2 a further two times, we get:

(((a)))

Then, applying rule 1 we get:

(((( ))))

One notes that the last production contains only terminal symbols, and therefore is a legitimate sequence of language L_2. Indeed, it is easy to realize that all the sequences in L_2 consist of a number of left-hand brackets followed by an equal number of right-hand ones.

This is known as the set of ´well-nested´ brackets. It is fun to see how easily the production rule can be varied in order to create language L_3 (say) which allows sequences and combinations of well-nested brackets. One simply takes the production rules of L_2 and adds the production

a --> aa (Rule 3) to P

Now we can have a production process as follows:

(a)
(aa)
(aaa)
(( ) ( ) (a))
(( ) ( ) (()))

Also note that a sequence such as

(( )) (( )( )

could never be generated by the production rules of L_3.

It is precisely the nature of the production rules which has been used to classify languages and pinpoint the differences between them. The classification runs from the most restricted (and easiest to check) to the least restricted (and hardest to check) as follows:

      i)   finite state languages

      ii)   context free languages

     iii)   context sensitive languages

      iv)   phrase structured languages

      v)   all languages

The classification is of a kind where the more restricted language is always in the less restricted. For example, all finite state languages are also context free, but not all context free languages are finite state. Thus all languages from i) to iv) are phrase structured in the sense that they have production rules, while the class of all languages (v) contains some which are not characterized by production rules.

We shall now work our way down this list and consider the ever-lessening restrictions on production rules, and the implications this has on the mechanisms of acceptance.

3.10 FINITE STATE LANGUAGES

The restriction on the production rules of a finite state language is that they are always of the form:

$$a \quad\quad > Kb$$
$$\text{or} \quad a \quad \text{---}> K$$

    where a and b are non-terminal symbols,
    while K is the terminal symbol;

(an alternative is a --> b K, a -->K, which is no different in kind).

Consider the following example: L_4 is the language of all sequences of the form

4.5 or 7.9, that is of the form

<decimal digit> .   <decimal digit>

This language may be defined as follows:

$$V_N = S, A, B$$

$$V_T = \{0,1,2,3,4,5,6,7,8,9, . \}$$

that is
$$= \{\{\text{decimal digits}\}, .\}$$

Starting symbol = S.

P = S --> 0 A or 1 A or 2 A, etc.

that is   S --> <decimal digit> A

A --> .B

B --> <decimal digit>

Clearly, working through replacements from S, we get the desired form as follows:

S --> <decimal digit>   A

--> <decimal digit> . B

--> <decimal digit> . <decimal digit>

Now, the 'finite stateness' of this language can be seen as a result of the fact that a state diagram may be drawn to represent the above situation. This is shown in Fig. 3.13 where it is seen that the only additional element over and above those found in the definition of the production rules, is a state marked END. This signifies that the production process is finished, and occurs whenever a production of the type a --> K is encountered.

It is interesting that the resulting state diagram is in fact
the direct design for an acceptor for the language of the
kind shown in Fig. 3.14. The only modification to the state
diagram which is needed is that it must be logically
completed. That is, one must lead undesirable steps into a
'fail' state. This is shown in Fig. 3.15, where the output
labeling for the states is also shown, and resetting
arrangements are indicated. The diagram now contains all the
information needed to actually build an acceptor (except for
decisions about coding of inputs and states), and the reader
can soon check that the only sequence that the system accepts
are those in the language itself.

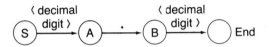

Fig. 3.13 A finite state language

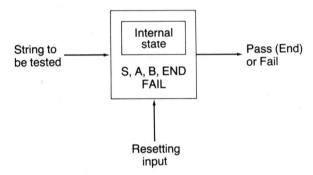

Fig. 3.14 Box diagram for an acceptor of the finite state language

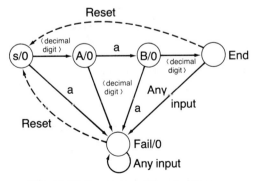

Fig. 3.15 Acceptor state structure

Now for a slight snag - but one that can easily be overcome.
Consider language L_5 with the following properties:

$$V_N = S,A,B \text{ (as before)}$$

$$V_T = \{<\text{decimal digits}> .\} \text{ (as before)}$$

$$P : S \longrightarrow <\text{decimal digit}> A \text{ (as before)}$$

$$A \longrightarrow .B \text{ (as before)}$$

$$B \longrightarrow <\text{decimal digit}> B$$

$$B \longrightarrow <\text{decimal digit}>$$

Starting symbol   : s = S

We note that now legitimate sequences are 4.67 or 7.45128,
etc.

This harmless looking addition to the production rules is
well within the definition of the characteristics of a finite
state language.   Its partial state diagram is shown in Fig.
3.16, and this shows up the difficulty. Clearly, state B has
an exit both to itself and to the end state.   This merely
means that the definition of a finite state language allows
for non-deterministic acceptor designs (as we defined them
earlier).   A standard way of transforming non-deterministic
machines into deterministic ones involves transformations
such as from Fig. 3.16 to Fig. 3.17 for the example in hand.

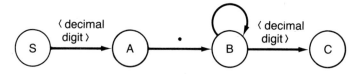

Fig. 3.16 A non-deterministic language

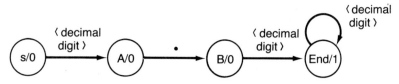

Fig. 3.17 Deterministic version of Fig. 3.16

It is noted that the latter will accept all legitimate
sequences in L_5 provided that the output signal (0 for
not accepted, 1 for accepted) is taken into account and the
whole of the sequence to be tested is presented to the
machine.

Again, for completeness, the completed machine is presented
in Fig. 3.18, and the details of the method for carrying out
these transformations is tackled in the next section.
Readers who are not interested in the design of such machines
can skip this section without losing the thread of the
development of the subject matter.

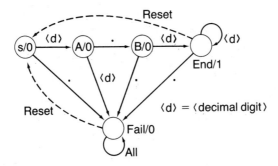

Fig. 3.18 Complete acceptor state structure

3.11 FROM NON-DETERMINISTIC TO DETERMINISTIC

The complete non-deterministic machine in Fig. 3.19 is used
as an example to illustrate the translation procedure. We
call this ND and the transformed machine M.

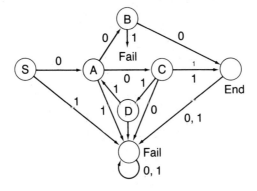

Fig. 3.19 A non-deterministic automaton

Step 1.   From   the   starting   state   (S)   find   all   the   next
           states   for   all   inputs.   In   M   allow   one   state   for
           (S)   and   <u>one</u>   following   state   for   each   input.   If   ND
           goes   from   (S)   to   <u>more   than   one</u>   state   for   any   input,
           label   that   state   in   M   by   the   names   of   all   these
           states   in   ND   (this   does   not   happen   in   the   example).

Step 2.   Repeat   step   1   for   all   (but   only)   new   states   that
           have   been   added   to   M   in   step   1.

Step 3.   Go   back   to   step   2   and   repeat   the   procedure   of   step
           1   for   all   new   states,   and   so   on   until   no   new   states
           can   be   added   to   M.

The   progressive   way   in   which   M   builds   up   to   completion   is
shown   in   Fig.   3.20.   Several   factors   which   remain   to   be
explained   are   the   following.

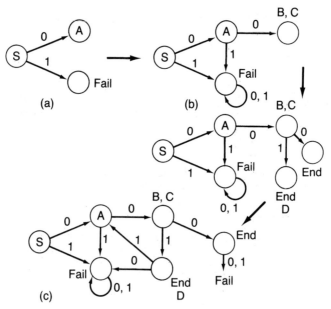

Fig. 3.20 Tranformation to a deterministic automaton

First, if the procedure is applied to a new composite state
(such as B, C) the next state is computed as follows. If,
say, state X_1 under input i goes to set of states N_1, N_2, N_3,
N_4, N_5, so, in our example B under 1 goes to (end). C under
1 goes to D so B, C under one goes to (end, D).

Secondly, if a composite state in M contains (fail) in its
label, one simply ignores it by omitting it. This is
justified by the fact that one is interested in those
sequences that have a possibility of passing.

For example, sequence 0, 0, 0 must find a path to (end) since
it is a legitimate sequence of the language, even though if
the wrong path is taken in N D it could lead to (fail).
Finally, there is one more rather obvious step:

Step 4.   Label <u>all</u> states in M that <u>contain</u> end with the
           output that indicates a pass.

3.12 CONTEXT FREE LANGUAGES

Consider the following simple grammar:

$$V_n = \{s\}$$

$$V_t = \{(,)\}$$

P . {s --> s , ...(rule 1)

s --> () ...(rule 2)

s --> (s)}...(rule 3)

Starting symbol = s.

First, note that this is not a finite state language, since
the productions do not obey the rules.

Secondly, consider the nature of strings implied by the
productions.

A typical production might go as follows:

    Start with   ....s

    Apply rule 1 ....ss

    Apply rule 3 twice ....(s)(s)

    Apply rule 3 and rule 1 ....((s))(ss)

    Apply rule 2 to all <u>s</u> symbols ....((()))((()())

One notes that this is the language of well-formed brackets, and some such language is, indeed, embedded in much computing machinery. The characteristic which makes this language different from finite state language (outside of theoretical considerations about production rules, which we shall come to later) is best seen if one actually tries to design an acceptor for this language.

We might notice that a <u>finite state</u> acceptor is capable of accepting even very long recurring strings (by continuous recycling over a closed loop in the state structure of its non-deterministic automation) a context free language demands a bit more. For example, the acceptance of a string ((((...(can only occur if, at some state, a similar number of))...) brackets occurs. This is, the acceptor must <u>keep track</u> of the number of times the one symbol has occurred and compare it with the <u>number of times</u> another has occurred. This notion of <u>number</u> does not enter directly into the range of ability of a re-entrant group of states in a non-deterministic finite state automaton. The reason is that such automata do not readily lend themselves to demands for a large memory capacity. However, later we shall consider, in some depth, a device known as a ´stack automaton´ which, indeed, does have this property of an easily extensible set of demands on memory. For the time being we return to a formal definition of a context free language.

A language is said to be context free if all its productions are of the form

$$n \longrightarrow B$$

where n is a <u>non-terminal</u> symbol and B is a string of any symbols from the language (clearly, the empty string must be excluded from B so as to prevent some production from disappearing in smoke).

Here one notices the way in which the class of context free languages <u>includes</u> that of <u>finite state</u> ones. Clearly the finite state production rule format

$$n \longrightarrow Tm \text{ or } n \longrightarrow T$$

(n and m being non-terminal, and T a terminal) is more restricted than, and included in, the

$$n \longrightarrow B \text{ rule demanded above.}$$

3.13 STACK AUTOMATA

The secret of a stack automaton is that it can call upon a large memory which is organized a bit like a stack of plates (see Fig. 3.21).

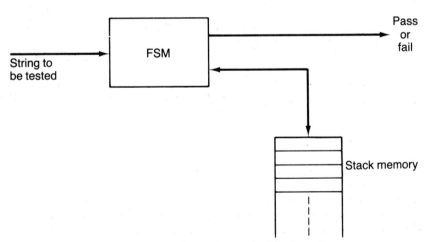

Fig. 3.21 A push-down stack automaton

The finite state machine considers input symbols and is
capable of placing them on top of the stack. When a new
symbol is placed on top of the stack, all the other symbols
move one place down. When the stack is empty, a special
symbol 0 is said to be at the top of the stack. To
illustrate such a machine let us consider the language of
well-formed brackets described in the last section. Clearly,
the ploy is to place all opening brackets on the stack as
they occur and remove them as the closing brackets occur.

That is, for example

$$((()))(()())$$

the stack develops as the input is accepted as follows (the
stack is shown left to right, left being topmost).

Input	Stack content
	0
(	(
(	((
(	(((
)	((
)	(
)	0
(	(
(	((
)	(
(	((
)	(
)	0

We note that when an acceptable string has been seen at the
input the stack is at 0. The specification for the FSM of
Fig. 3.21 is:

I (the set of input messages) = {[(, 0], [), 0], [(, (]
                                         [), (], [),)]}

where the left-hand symbol of a pair is the incoming symbol,
and the right-hand one is the top-of-stack symbol.

One could label these combinations

$I = \{i_1, i_2, i_3, i_4, i_5, i_6\}$ respectively.

The output of the FSM both affects the stack and signals pass or fail, according the the following recipe.

Input	next stack action	pass/fail (if end of string)
i_1 : [(,0]	add (	f
i_2 : [),0]	–	p
i_3 : [(,(]	add (	f
i_4 : [),(]	take off (	f
i_5 : [(,)]	impossible	–
i_6 : [),)]	impossible	–

Inputs i_5 and i_6 turn out to be impossible because symbol) can never get to the top of the stack. In this case, the FSM that drives the stack turns out to be a simple combinational circuit demanding only one internal state.

Clearly, in practice one cannot have infinite memory in the stack so that such practical machines usually issue a ´stack overflow´ error if the demand is too great.

An important point regarding context free languages is that their production rules may be represented in the form of a graph.

For example, the production rules for the well-formed bracket language is shown in Fig. 3.22. As a result, any particular string of the language may be represented as a set of trajectories through this graph, or a tree as shown for the ((())) (()()) example in Fig. 3.23. This is known as a parsing tree.

It is now necessary to look at a slightly more complex language, in order to appreciate some of the difficulties of designing stack automata. This is a kind of subset of the sort of thing one finds in real languages, and has to do with some particular statements.

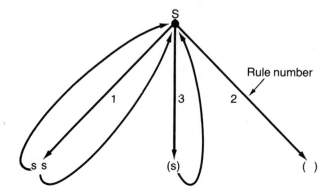

Fig. 3.22 Production rules for the well-formed bracket language

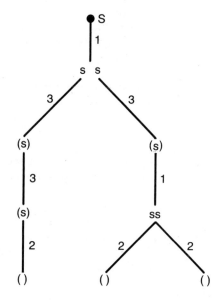

Fig. 3.23 Parsing tree for ((()))(()())

We have non-terminal symbols:

                <statement>,   <assignment>,   <expression>

                <variable>,   <integer>.

In shorthand the same symbols respectively are:

$$\{s,\ a,\ e,\ r,\ i\}.)$$

We also have terminal symbols:

$$\{A,\ B,\ C\ ....Z,\ 1,\ 2\ ....9,\ 0,\ =\ ,\ +,\ -\ \}$$

The production rules of the languages are

    <statement> --->   <assignment>   /   <expression>

(note that the slash / indicates an alternative production).

    <assignment --->   <variable>   =   <variable>
                    / <variable>   =   <expression>

    <expression>--->   <integer>
                    / <expression> + <expression>
                    / <expression> - <expression>

    <integer>   --->   1/2/....../9/0
    <variable> --->   A/B/C......Y/Z

Working through these production rules, one notes that strings such as the following can be produced:

$$A = B + C$$
$$A = C + D - E + F$$
$$A$$
$$A + B - Z - X$$

Examples of the parsing trees of A = B + C and A + B - Z - X are shown in Fig. 3.24 and Fig. 3.25 respectively. The assumption made earlier is that the FSM in the stack automaton accepts one symbol at a time. In the case of the example just quoted, it should be noticed that precisely the same symbol can precede two differently structured statements.

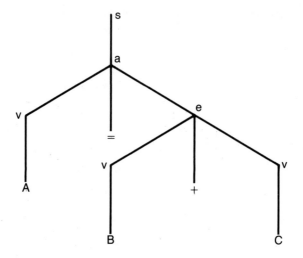

Fig. 3.24 Parsing tree for A = B + C

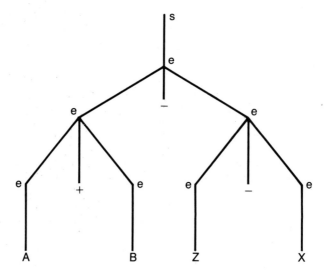

Fig. 3.25 Parsing tree for A + B − Z − X

It is not merely a question of counting as in the brackets example. The stack is used to <u>anticipate</u> possible developments of the incoming sequence and remove such anticipations as they occur. For example, to accept the two examples of Fig. 3.24 and Fig. 3.25 the stack development may be the following:

a) For A = B + C we have:

Step	Stack content	Comment
1.	s	the starting symbol is always top of stack to start.
2.	a	this is called an ´autonomous´ move according to the production s --> a.
3.	v = e	again an autonomous move according to the prod. a --> v = e.
4.	= e	the first symbol A has been <u>accepted</u>, clearing v from the top of the stack.
5.	e	= has been accepted and cleared.
6.	v + v	autonomous move.
7.	+ v	B accepted
8.	v	+ accepted
9.	empty	C accepted (whole string accepted)

b) Similarly for A + B - Z - X we have:

Step	Stack content	Comment
1.	s	
2.	e	auto
3.	e-e	auto
4.	e+e-e	auto
5.	+e-e	A accepted
6.	e-e	+ accepted
7.	-e	B accepted
8.	e	- accepted
9.	e-e	autonomous
10.	-e	Z accepted
11.	e	- accepted
12.	empty	C accepted - whole string accepted.

Clearly, the above examples only show the stack automaton taking the __correct__ action.   Since the actions are defined by the production rules, things could go as follows for the __first__ sequence (A = B + C):

Step	Stack content	Comment
1.	s	
2.	e	(going the wrong way)
3.	e+e	still wrong
4.	+e	A accepted
5.	Clash!	+ expected, = found.

The procedure must <u>not</u> fail at this stage, but simply back-track along the tree and try an alternative path in what is, after all, a set of non-deterministic possibilities. Only when all the possibilities have been exhausted does the FSM allow a failure. This is a problem which comes under the 'tree-searching category' and will be considered in much more detail in the next chapter.

3.14 OTHER LANGUAGES

Next on the scale (that is, with even fewer restrictions) is the context sensitive language. Despite the restrictive-sounding name, these languages are less restricted than context free ones. Consider the restriction on the production rules:

all production must be of the form

$$k \; X \; e \; \longrightarrow \; k \; m \; e$$

where k, e and m are strings of language alphabet, while X is a single, non-terminal symbol. The reason that such languages are <u>less</u> constrained than context free ones may be seen from the following example:

$$\text{let} \quad V_t = Y, Z$$
$$V_n = s, c$$

$$\begin{aligned} P: \quad s \;\; &\longrightarrow\; c \; Y \\ c \;\; &\longrightarrow\; c \; Y \\ cY \;\; &\longrightarrow\; Yc \\ YcY \;\; &\longrightarrow\; YZY \end{aligned}$$

Starting symbol = s

Now, consider some sequences

$$s \longrightarrow cY \longrightarrow cYY \longrightarrow YcY \longrightarrow YZY$$
or $s \longrightarrow cY \longrightarrow cYY \longrightarrow cYYY \longrightarrow YcYY \longrightarrow YZYY$ or YYcY
$$\longrightarrow YYZY$$

In other words, the scheme generates sequences of the kind Y^n Z Y^m where m and n are non-zero integers. It will be noted

that it is precisely the contextual productions such as cY-->
Yc and YcY --> YZY which makes this possible.

Thus, being able to specify production in context allows
greater flexibility in the creation of languages hence is a
lesser constraint. Again one can use parsing techniques,
although searching may be even more laborious.

Turning now to phrase structured languages in general, that
is those that do not qualify as being context dependent, we
shall show that they cannot be parsed.

First, a well-known result must be quoted. If the production
rules contain a production of the kind

$$a ----> b$$

(both a and b being any string from the paper vocabulary)

where a is <u>longer</u> than b, <u>then</u> the language is <u>not</u> context
sensitive or lower in the restriction ladder. In other
words, another test for a context sensitive grammar is

<u>a should be equal to or shorter than b.</u>

The effect of this is that context sensitive (or more
restricted) languages have ever-increasing length as more and
more productions are used. Therefore a given string provides
some information regarding the length and parsing procedure.
That is, the parsing must shorten the string length in
heading for the starting symbol. Without this safeguard, one
does not know how many backward steps are needed to be taken
in parsing before abandoning the search. This simply means
that languages other than context sensitive are more
restricted and cannot be parsed with certainty that the
procedure will terminate.

The above class of languages is phrase structured and very
little else. One now asks whether there are languages that do
not have phrase structuring, that is, cannot be derived from
production rules. The answer is obviously that there are. For
example one could define a language with sequences of the
kind

$$aa^R \text{ where } a^R \text{ is the reverse of sequence a, etc.}$$

In fact there is an infinity of such languages, but the diversity of their specifying rule does not allow us to study them as a coherent whole.

3.15 TURING MACHINES

As a final topic in this brief survey of automata, we refer to a machine which has access to an infinite memory in the same style as the stack automaton, but is much more powerful.

A Turing machine is a simple FSM that interacts with an infinite tape on which information may be written, or from which it may be read. The machine can also move left and right over the tape. An illustration of the concept is shown in Fig. 3.26.

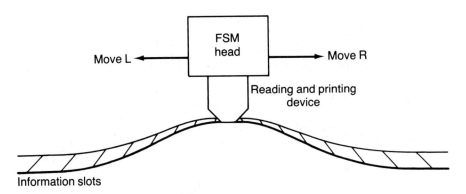

Fig. 3.26 A Turing machine

In answering the question ´What can a Turing machine do?´ Turing himself formulated an answer which has become known as the ´Turing hypothesis´. In essence, the Turing hypothesis holds that ´anything that can be explicitly stated can be computed on a Turing machine.´   This is hard to prove, but here we can put it to the test by investigating whether a Turing machine can check sequences of the general language mentioned in the last section. I refer to the language where

$$aa^r ......(sequence\ a\ followed\ by\ a\ reverse\ version)$$
where a is a sequence from the set {S, T}

This is not even a phrase structured rule and we therefore
have no way of checking it with a state automaton. The
difficulty lies in not knowing when a is finished.

The Turing machine would operate on this problem in the
following way. One assumes that the sequence to be checked in
written in adjacent locations on the Turing tape. One also
assumes that a special symbol b may be used to indicate blank
space. So, the desired sequence is embedded on the tape in
the midst of blank locations. For example we may have

                ...b b b S T T S S S S T T S b b b ...

The machine is assumed to start with its reading head over a
blank section of tape to the left of the string to be
checked.

The recipe for doing this might be (in shorthand form)

1) move right until a non-b character is reached
2) read the character, remember it and replace it by a blank
3) move on until a blank slot has been reached
4) move one to the left
5) read the character and compare with the stored one
   (if different fail, if the same, replace it by a b)
6) move one to the left, if b end, else go to step 7
7) move left until b is reached.
8) return to step 1

This can quite simply be turned into the block diagram for
the operation of the FSM. This is shown in Fig. 3.27. Here
one merely need realize that this is a Moore model where the
states have been labeled solely in terms of their output : L
for move and step to the left; R for move and step to the
right; b for print a blank; PASS and FAIL. Information read
by the head is shown on the transitions. The reader can
check the correctness of the diagram for himself.

Although this demonstrates the power of Turing machines with
respect to language checking, one should note that the Turing
hypothesis implies a greater power, that is universality in
respect to any well-stated problem.

However, one should be aware of the fact that this well-
statedness does not refer to the statement of the task, but
the ´algorithm´ whereby the task is carried out.

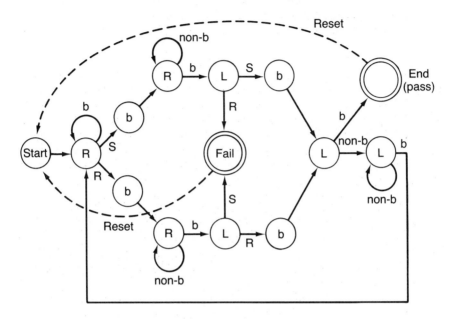

Fig. 3.27 A Turing machine for pass aa´

3.16 SUMMARY

Having worked through the nature of known classes of automata
ranging from the finite state machine to the Turing machine,
a word needs to be said about the ´use´ of such knowledge.

Automata theory is often criticized for not having sufficient
direct application. It is said that there is nothing in
automata theory that helps one to design machines with a
large number of variables, because the methods that arise
from finite state machine theory imply an exponential growth
of required computational effort as a function of complexity.
Mathematical linguistics comes under fire because, again, it
does not define a clear set of algorithms for the design of
syntax checkers (it gives no clues to the solution of
optional parsing problems).

Turing machines are criticized for being impractical. Although these criticisms may be true, they are badly founded. It is hoped that this chapter has provided sufficent evidence that the _use_ of automata theory lies in providing insight into complex informational situations.

For example, it is worth knowing that for FSMs the assignment of binary states is not arbitrary and is sensitive to the way that state vectors compare with one another, or that the _type_ of syntax checker one designs depends on whether the rules of a grammar pass certain tests. Turing machines were never meant to be _built_, they are merely a conceptual crutch whereby the theoretician can _express_ ideas regarding things that can and things that cannot be computed.

Indeed that leads to a second ´use´ of automata theory. It provides a means of expression whereby when discussing complex informational machinery people in different disciplines can understand one another. This fact alone makes automata theory a central focusing agent for digital systems design.

QUESTIONS

These are typical examination questions set on this subject, and should serve as a guide for the reader to review some of the topics covered in the chapter.

1. Distinguish between a probabilistic and a deterministic automaton and justify the statement: ´a probabilistic automaton can always be built by designing an appropriate deterministic automaton´.

2. What is a partition on a set of states in a finite state machine (FSM)?

    Discuss the following, giving examples, and defining all terms and justifying your main statements:

    a) a perfect state assignment for a FSM,

b) a reduction in the number of states in a FSM,
c) a parallel decomposition into two FSMs,
d) a serial decomposition into two FSMs.

3. Keep your answers brief but accurate.

a) Argue convincingly that the set of finite state
    languages is a subset of context free languages.

b) Why can one not use a finite state machine to check
    the syntax of a context free language?   What must be
    used to do this and how?

c) Why is a syntax checker of a context free language
    usually said to be non-deterministic?

d) Why can a practical syntax checker for a context free
    language never be perfect?   How does one deal with
    this?

e) Why is it not guaranteed that a Turing machine will
    automatically check the syntax of any phrase
    structured language?

4. a) Define the following language classes:

            context free;
            finite state.

b) A finite state grammar is defined by

$$G = \langle V_n, V_t, P, s \rangle$$

$$V_n = \{K, L, M\}$$

$$V_t = \{0, 1\}$$

$$P = \{K\text{->}1K, K\text{->}1L, L\text{->}0K$$

$$L\text{->}0M, M\text{->}1L, M\text{->}1\}$$

$$s = a$$

Design a finite state automaton which accepts this
language.

5. Distinguish between a context free and a context
    sensitive language.

    Why are computer languages usually context free?

    A language has the following set of termimal symbols

    $$a \quad b \quad + \quad (\quad)$$

    Define a grammer that generates well-bracketed
    expressions of this form:

    i) a + (b + a)

    ii) a(b + a)(a + (a + b))

    Demonstrate the validity of this grammar by showing
    parsing trees for the two expressions.

    Briefly describe a push-down stack automaton that may be
    used to accept such languages and illustrate its
    operation as a syntax checker for expression (i) above.

6. What sort of strings does the following context sensitive
    language generate?

    $$V_t = \{A, B, C\}$$

    $$V_n = \{s, \beta, \gamma\}$$

    $$P: s \longrightarrow B\ C$$
    $$\beta \longrightarrow A/A\ \beta\ \gamma$$
    $$\gamma B \longrightarrow B\ \gamma$$
    $$\gamma C \longrightarrow BCC$$

    s is the starting symbol

    Design an acceptor for this language remembering that
    finite length tapes are allowed whereas infinite counters
    are not. (Hint, this last statement points to a Turing
    machine solution.)

REFERENCES

Aleksander, I., and Hanna, F.K. (1978) ˊAutomata Theory: An Engineering Approachˊ, Ed. Arnold.

Burks, A.N., Goldstine, H.H., and Von Neumann, J. (1947) ˊA Preliminary Discussion of the Logical Design of an Electronic Computing Instrumentsˊ, Princeton Institute of Advanced Study.

Chomsky, N. (1957), ˊSyntactic Structuresˊ, Mouton.

Chomsky, N. (1965), ˊAspects of the Theory of Syntaxˊ, Mouton.

Elgerd, O.I. (1967), ˊControl Systems Theoryˊ, McGraw Hill, New York.

Shannon, C.E. (1938), ˊA Symbolic Analysis of Relay and Switching Circuitsˊ, Trans AIEE 57.

Shannon, C.E., and McCarty, J. (1956), ˊAutomata Studiesˊ, Annals of Mathematical Studies No. 34, Princeton University Press, Princeton.

Shannon, E.C., and Weaver, W. (1949), ˊThe Mathematical Theory of Communicationˊ, University of Illinois Press.

Wiener, N. (1948) ˊCyberneticsˊ, MIT Press, Boston.

Chapter 4

Programming languages and abstraction

C M P Reade and L Johnson

This chapter is intended as an overview of some programming language concepts that have been developed over the last two decades, and emphasizes the progressive abstractions they have introduced. Principally we discuss abstract data types, concurrency and functional programming languages.

We start with two short sections on the nature of programming languages and the nature of abstraction. The third section is a long one covering abstraction facilities in programming languages, viz. data abstraction, storage abstraction and control abstraction. The fourth section is shorter and deals with functional programming languages.

The notes contain only a few technical details but references to the literature are given throughout. In particular, formal treatments of the topics covered here may be found in Bauer and Wossner (1982), Tennent (1976, 1981), Bjorner and Jones (1978), Gordon (1979). The more pragmatic aspects of the topics covered are treated in Ghezzi and Jazayeri (1982).

4.1   THE NATURE OF ABSTRACTION

The main problem facing designers of both hardware and software in computing is how to handle complexity and there are, in general, two classes of tools which facilitate design. The first class of tools relates to combination, that is means of combining objects from a given collection to form new objects, and these may be used to construct more complex designs as combinations of simpler designs. The second class of tools relates to abstraction; there are tools for abstracting to more general situations from particular situations by supressing irrelevant detail and tools for the reverse process of particularization of general situations. Both these classes of tools are used along with a collection of 'primitive objects' or 'basic building blocks' appropriate to the particular design area.

In this chapter we are primarily concerned with how abstraction integrates with the other tools. We must make it clear, however, that by 'abstraction' we mean to cover all the senses described in ADJ (1976):

> 'There seems to have been some confusion about the meaning of the term "abstraction" in computer science. It has been

used in at least three ways which are distinct but related. First, there is the meaning common to most of science: "abstraction" occurs whenever one creates a mathematical model or description of something. In particular, one speaks in computer science of an "abstract machine" as opposed to real hardware, when referring to a mathematical model of a machine; similarly, one speaks of an "abstract implementation" when one uses sets, sequences, or other mathematical entities to model some computational process or structure.

A second meaning, closely related to the first, refers to the process (or result) of generalizing, so that certain detailed features can be ignored. There are many examples in computer science, since one of the main advantages of mathematicization is to "abstract" some details out of view. In particular, finite state machine models of hardware, and fix-point models of software, permit us to ignore many details of how processes are actually carried out.

However, a somewhat different sense of "abstraction" has gradually come to play a more specific role, particularly in the theory of programming languages, for the several important cases where one wishes to consider a concept independent of its representation.

For example, "abstract syntax" considers syntactic structure, independently of whether it is represented by derivation trees, parenthesized expressions, indented program text, canonical parses, or whatever. This notion of abstract syntax is useful, for example, in specifying the semantics of a programming language in a manner independent of how it is implemented. '

4.2   THE NATURE OF PROGRAMMING LANGUAGES

Programming languages have evolved as abstract levels of description for the computational processes (algorithmic behavior) of machines.

It is through this abstraction that high level languages have become sufficiently machine-independent to be used for describing solutions to problems and methods for solving problems generally (i.e. for many different types of machine). To quote L.A.Rowe:

> 'All languages provide an abstraction of a machine. Control abstractions are provided to specify the sequencing between statements in a program (e.g. conditional branches) and data abstractions are provided to specify the entities and their operations used in the algorithm (e.g. arrays with selection and assignment of individual elements).
>
> Low level languages, such as assembly languages, provide abstractions which are essentially equivalent to the instruction set of a machine. High-level languages, such as Pascal (Jensen and Wirth 1975), provide abstractions which highlight the algorithm, or computation, and suppress the implementation detail.' (Rowe, 1981)

A further abstraction to what are sometimes referred to as very high level languages, suppresses the details of sequence control in computations and accidental properties of the data. There has been a recent resurgence of interest in this area (Backus, 1978), (Henderson, 1980), (Darlington et al., 1982) partly because of a desire to make programming languages mathematically more tractable and partly because the removal of sequencing control details has allowed parallel evaluation mechanisms to be explored, and this coincides with the development of new hardware architectures which provide for a high degree of parallel computation enabling totally new methods of language implementation to be tried. (This is discussed further in Section 4.4.)

At an even higher level of abstraction we have pure specification languages which are completely independent of any machine or computational restrictions (non-algorithmic languages). Using such languages, we can express problems without having to simultaneously solve the problem or describe a mechanical means of solving the problem.

There is much current research involved with closing the gap between pure specification languages and high level or very high level programming languages and with finding general purpose specification languages which encompass the whole spectrum of abstraction levels between machines and problems (see e.g. Bauer et al., (1981), Bauer and Wossner (1982), Bjorner and Jones (1982)). Transformations from specifications to efficient programs can then be done with machine assistance and the correctness of such transformations can be established formally.

In the above paragraphs we emphasized the development of programming languages as abstractions away from machine details. Current thinking about the nature of software and the software development process gives more emphasis to methodologies for solving problems and to how abstraction can be used to break down problems in order to specify software solutions. From this more contemporary point of view, the programming language is a particular design tool to be used in conjunction with a variety of other tools such as tools for specifying software requirements, certifying software (that is testing and proving it correct), maintenance of software, transporting software,etc. The nature of the programming language can help or hinder the construction and use of these other tools, hence the wider concept of the language as an integral part of the software development environment (see, for example, Ghezzi and Jazayeri,1982).

If a programming language is to be used as a software development tool, one of the main programming language design objectives is to choose high level primitives and expressive and flexible forms for combination of these primitives. These primitives and combining forms should be of sufficient generality to be used for many purposes by many people.

The programming language designer is designing an interface between the implementor (who undertakes the implementation of the primitives and combining forms using low level machine abstractions) and the user (who will be forced to work through this interface and cannot directly use the low level details to gain efficiency). The implementor is similarly limited by the interface because he cannot predict the many ways in which the primitives will be used in combination, and so cannot guarantee the best possible use of the machine for each program.

One possible solution to these programming language design problems is to make the language very large by incorporating many different facilities but then it becomes very difficult to learn how to use as well as implement (PL/1 (ANSI, 1976) is often criticized as a programming language on these grounds). A better solution is to provide a small number of highly flexible primitives with minimal restrictions on how they may be combined. This is called orthogonality of design (Algol 68 (van Wijngaarden et al.,1976) is a good example). In addition to this design objective the programming language designer needs to provide the user (programmer) with means of expressing further levels of abstraction suitable for his specific problem. The programmer then has the responsibility for implementing these abstractions in terms of the language primitives.

For a programming language to be a good tool it should enable
the easy construction of further tools.

4.3   ABSTRACTION FACILITIES IN PROGRAMMING LANGUAGES

Both historically and conceptually, assembly languages provided
the first level of abstraction from machine code using mnemonics for the machine operations and storage cell addresses
rather than their bit pattern code.

In the late 1950s and early 1960s Fortran was developed for
scientific purposes concentrating on abstractions from the
control of Von Neumann machines, and Cobol was developed for
commercial data processing concentrating on abstractions from
the storage of data on Von Neumann machines. The control
abstractions developed in Algol 60 (Naur, 1963) were a great
improvement over those of Fortran and have formed the basis of
control abstractions in many subsequent programming languages
(e.g. Pascal, Algol 68, Simula, Clu, Modula, Ada).

In Section 4.3.3 we look at some of the developments of control
abstraction since Algol 60. Before that, however, in Section
4.3.1, we look at how data types have developed and how the
concept of data, i.e. the values manipulated in programs, has
led to another form of abstraction, viz. data abstraction. In
Section 4.3.2 we mention how data and control combine in the
intermediate area which is concerned with the control of data
storage.

4.3.1 Data Abstraction

At a very low level of abstraction, machines manipulate bits (0s
and 1s) but we may perceive certain combinations of bits as
representing characters or integers or other values at higher
levels of abstraction. We might expect a programming language
to provide data types such as integer or character as 'built in'
so that the (bit pattern) representation details need no longer
concern users. Having introduced the concept of data types into
languages, the provision of some sort of automatic checking of
programs becomes possible. A certain degree of protection from
accidental misinterpretation can then be guaranteed so that,
for example, a character cannot be added to an integer.

Nowadays, a data type is generally considered to mean a class of objects such as integers along with, and inseparable from, a collection of operations appropriate for these objects (see Morris, 1973 and Dahl et al, 1972). For example, in the case of integers the 'allowable' operations are addition, subtraction, multiplication, comparison ($<$, $=$,$>$), etc.

In the following we classify programming language data types as being **Primitive**, **Structured** or **Abstract** reflecting the historical development of the use of data types as programming languages have evolved and then consider some of the important issues surrounding the concept of abstract data type and its use as a major tool for large scale software development.

Primitive data types

Most programming languages provide 'built-in' data types such as **integers**, **booleans**, **characters** along with their appropriate operations. These types are considered as primitives of the language, but need not be primitives of the machine on which the language is implemented (for example integers may be represented as fixed length sequences of bits, with additions performed by bit pattern manipulations). An important aspect of primitive data types is that they cannot be misused through by-passing the language interface and accessing the details of the implementation. For example one should be prevented from dividing a number by two by deleting the last bit of its representation in binary form. This protection from misuse is not in practice guaranteed by all languages, but if the language uses the principles of **strong-typing**, which means that semantically incorrect use of types in programs can be found syntactically, such guarantees can be made.

Structured data types

Structured data types provide a means for dealing with specific groupings of data objects which may be of the same type or different types. By such groupings we may deal with one compound object which has the original objects as components. For example we may consider a complex number which is composed of a real part and an imaginary part (both of which are real numbers) as a single entity. Similarly, information about an aircraft flight may comprise a flight number, an arrival time, a departure time, arrival and departure points, date, number of seats available, etc. and all this could be combined to form a single object of type **flight info**. The component's arrival and departure time, would be objects of type **time** which are themselves comprised of hours and minutes where hours are 'integers from 0 to 23', minutes are 'integers from 0 to 59'.

From this example, we see that the grouping of objects to form structured objects can be <u>nested</u> by many levels and this nesting is what makes such types so useful in modelling information which is conceptually hierarchical in nature.

The set of values of a compound type can be taken as the cartesian cross-product of the constituent types.

> e.g.   **type complex = real x real**
> **type time   = hours x minutes**

The operators to be associated with any structured type will include <u>selectors</u> which decompose a compound object into its constituents and <u>constructors</u> which combine components into one object. The selectors actually correspond to projection functions from the cartesian product onto component types, but we can give them meaningful names like 're', 'imag', 'hrs', 'mins'. One way of introducing these names might be to incorporate them in the type definition as in the following (pseudo) notation where the components are annotated:

> **type complex** = (**real** re, **real** imag)
> **type time**   = (**hours** hrs, **minutes** mins)

Thus type <u>complex</u> has two components selected by 're' and 'imag'. Notations such as 're(x)' or 're of x' or 'x.re' may be used to indicate the first component of a complex value x.

Other notations abound for defining structured types. For example, in Pascal:

> **type complex** =   **record**
>   re   : **real** ;
>   imag : **real**
>   **end**

The constructors may be given a name as well. For example, we might call the constructor which makes a complex value from two real values 'mk_complex' thus:

mk_complex(x,y)   or we may simply write:

complex:(x,y)   where x and y denote values of type **real**.

Sometimes integers, or other enumerations, may be used for selectors as in the case of arrays where a[i] or a_i or a(i) would denote the ith component of an array a, and selector i is called an <u>index.</u>

It is more convenient to regard such types not as simple cartesian products, but as finite mappings from the set of indices to the component type. That is:

$$a \text{ is a mapping from } [1,2,....,n] \rightarrow T$$

where n is the number of components and T is the type of the components, and the suggested notation a(i) coincides with the usual notation for function application. If the number of components is variable and unbounded (i.e. there is no upper bound for the entire class - although there is a fixed number for each member of the class) we call them 'sequences' and write T* to denote the type of 'sequences of T objects'.

e.g.   **type string = character***

The selectors for such types would (normally) be integers,˙ but sequences can also be treated as a special case of recursive types (see below).

Another common way of combining types is to take the disjoint (discriminated) union which includes values from each of the constituent types separately. Actually this type constructor is sometimes only used indirectly in a programming language (for example <u>variants</u> in Pascal records) but it may be used directly (for example <u>union</u> modes in Algol 68). We will use the symbol '±' (read as <u>'or'</u>) to separate the alternatives in a union:

e.g.   **type** T = T1 **+** T2

If T1 and T2 have values in common, these values will be <u>distinguishable</u> in the union type T. This means that we can always ask if a T value comes from T1 or from T2, with <u>predicates</u> (operators with boolean results) such as 'is_T1', 'is_T2'. Selectors, constructors and predicates form the three classes of operators to be used with any structured type.

Product (**x**), Union (**+**) and Sequence (*****) form three of the principle data type combining operators described by C.A.R. Hoare in Dahl et al (1972) (see also Hoare, 1972, 1975). Another one is Functions (**→**) which we only mention briefly in Section 4.4.2 and there is also Powersets (which we do not discuss here).

In the sequel, we will assume 'x' has higher precedence than '+' but lower precedence than '*', and we will also make use of a special type empty which has a unique value usually called 'nil' and the predicate 'is_empty' (also called 'null') when empty is used as an alternative in a union.

Recursive types and objects

As well as combining previously defined types to form a compound type, we can recursively define a type in terms of itself. For example we may say that a tree can be composed of some basic item along with a number of sub-trees. This means that some of the components of an object of type tree are also objects of type tree so that the nesting can continue without bound. It is, however, also convenient to consider the degenerate case of 'empty' trees with no subcomponents as an alternative and then we may consider only finitely nested objects ultimately composed of empty trees and items (see Fig. 4.1).

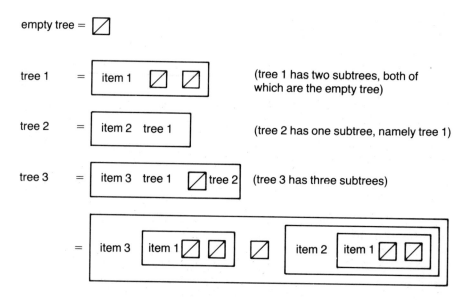

Fig. 4.1 Trees as nested objects

We may describe such recursive types by listing the components
and alternatives as usual, but allowing self reference as well.
For example we may define a type <u>bintreechar</u> - a special form
of tree with characters for items and always two subtrees (hence
'bintreechar' - binary trees with characters) as follows:

type bintreechar = empty + character
x bintreechar
x bintreechar

or, using the notation mentioned in Section 4.3.1 which defines
selectors:

type bintreechar = empty + (character label,
bintreechar left,
bintreechar right)

This may be read as 'A bintreechar object is either empty or it
is structured in which case it has three components: a character
selected by "label" and two further bintreechar objects
selected by "left" and "right"'. Figure 4.2 shows (i) A
pictorial representation of a <u>bintreechar</u> object t defined as:


```
t =  mk_tree('A',
          mk_tree('B',
                mk_tree('D',
                     mk_tree('F',nil,nil),
                     nil),
                mk_tree('E',nil,nil)),
          mk_tree('C',nil,nil))
```


showing the tree-like structure. (ii) Another representation of
t showing how subtrees are components of trees. (iii) A third
representation of t which shows the nesting more clearly. (iv) A
representation of the left subtree of t, selected as 't.left' or
'left of t' or 'left(t)'.

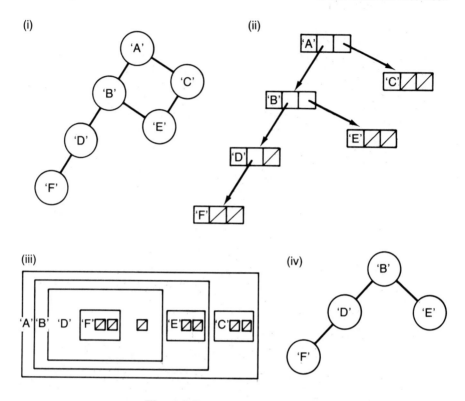

Fig. 4.2 Representations of trees

Another useful example of a recursive type is that of LISTS, defined by:

type list = empty + (item head, list tail)

where we have several possible choices for the type <u>item</u>. For simple <u>linear</u> lists we just take items to be some basic <u>atomic</u> type (say <u>integer</u>) and usually use the notation [1,2,3,4,5] to represent a list whose head is 1 and whose tail is [2,3,4,5]. ([ ] will denote the empty list also referred to as 'nil' and is the tail of e.g. [5]). Actually this notation is more in keeping with the treatment of lists as sequences:

type list = item*

The usual constructor for the recursive definition is 'cons', and we should write [1,2,3,4,5] as :

cons(1,cons(2,cons(3,cons(4,cons(5,nil)))))

or possibly using an infix notation ':' for 'cons':

1:2:3:4:5:nil

For lists of mixed objects such as integers and characters we would have to define <u>item</u> as a union (e.g. **type item = integer + character**).

More interesting is the class of hierarchically nested lists which we obtain by taking

type item   = atom + list

which means that we include lists of items which are either atomic or further lists. Atoms may then be defined as integers or characters, etc. An example with integers as atoms is

[1,[2,3,4],0,[[6],[7,1],[8]],9]

Note that the two definitions

type list = empty + (item head, list tail)
type item = atom + list

should be read together as mutually recursive since they refer to each other.

We may represent this sort of list pictorially rather like trees by indicating the two components 'head' and 'tail' which make up each list (see Fig.4.3).

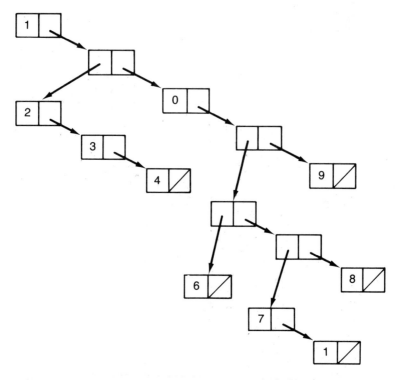

Fig. 4.3 A tree-like representation for a list. (A diagonal bar is used to denote the empty lists)

Closely related to such lists are LISP-type S-expressions (McCarthy et al., 1965) which could be defined by :

type lisp = empty + atom + (lisp car, lisp cdr)

This type has predicates 'is_atom' and 'null' as well as the constructor 'cons'.

Usually a recursive type includes all the finitely nested objects with the given structure, but if no restriction is put on the finite nesting we can describe infinite objects of recursive types by giving recursive (i.e. circular) definitions which can be represented with a cyclic diagram (see Fig. 4.4).

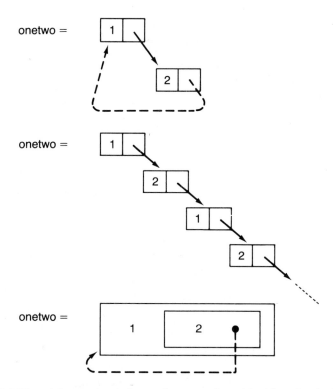

Fig. 4.4 Pictorial representations of a recursive object 'onetwo' which is defined by onetwo = cons(1,cons(2,onetwo))

Abstract data types

One of the problems of using structured data types, which does not arise with primitive data types, is that the operations that can be performed on the data include all the structuring and indexing operations (i.e. constructors and selectors) along with operations defined for components, and these cannot be restricted even if they are conceptually inappropriate for the intended use of the type (cf. accessing bits of integer representations with primitive data types).

As an example, suppose we wish to store lists as pairs of type:

int x list

where the integer component gives the length of the list given as the second component. (This might be useful if we frequently need to check the length and do not wish to compute it each time.)

We must then make sure that whenever such an object is constructed, that the length of the list is correctly given by the integer and this may not be easy if the programmer defining the type is not the programmer using the type.

Just as the language implementor may have ´protection´ for the primitive types, the programmer should be able to protect his (user-defined) types so that they may be used in interfaces between parts of programs and hence between programmers working as a team.

By hiding the representational information (that is the structure of a type) but at the same time providing operations which are appropriate for the type along with their properties, the programmer can produce types with the same protection and security that primitive types enjoy. The user of such types may then treat them as primitive, and need not be in any-way concerned if the representation is changed at any time, provided that the properties ascribed to the type remain true in the new implementation. Such changes to the representation should only require modifications to the implemented operations and not programs using them, thus localising their effect (see Figs. 4.8 and 4.9).

The rationale for hiding structure in this way is that it allows data objects to be classified according to their abstract behaviour rather than according to their representations. This is the essence of the concept of abstract data type which is ´representation independent´ (see Liskov and Zilles, 1974, Guttag, 1976).

Primitive types such as integer, boolean, etc. mentioned earlier were of course abstract data types; they were only distinguished by the fact that the language implementor/ designer defined them and not the language user (programmer). In general abstract data types which are not primitive must be implemented (simulated) by the programmer using structured data types. Values of the abstract data type must be represented by values of some structured data type, and the operations of the abstract data type must be simulated using (combinations of) operations on the representing values.

It is clearly important that that the programming language supports the abstraction (e.g. by providing an encapsulation mechanism for information hiding) in order to gain the advantages of protection for these types (see Section 4.3.1).

Example: Stacks

Stacks are a useful abstraction which arise frequently in programming. For the moment we consider only stacks of integers, but the generalization to handle stacks of any type is quite straightforward. The principle of the stack is that a number of objects (integers in this case) may be accessed by adding and removing in such a way that the last one added (thought of as being at the top) must be the first removed (LIFO – Last In First Out). Integer stacks may be introduced by providing the following operators with indicated functionality

push:	**integer**	**x**	**intstack**	**→**	**intstack**
pop:	**intstack**	**→**	**intstack**		
top:	**intstack**	**→**	**integer**		
is_new:	**intstack**	**→**	**bool**		

along with the constant newstack

newstack: **→ intstack**

(Note that constants can be treated as operators which take no arguments and therefore produce a fixed value.)

Push is the operation which adds a new integer to a stack, top produces the top integer of a non–empty stack and pop removes the top of a non–empty stack. Newstack is the empty stack (or rather the nullary operation which produces the empty stack) and is_new is a predicate which asks if a stack is the empty stack.

One possible implementation of type intstack uses type lisp (defined in Section 4.3.1) for representing stacks. (We assume for convenience that type atom = integer.) The stack operations may then be implemented using lisp operations as follows:

push	is implemented as	cons
pop	is implemented as	cdr
top	is implemented as	car
isnew	is implemented as	null
newstack	is implemented as	nil

This is a very direct implementation because there is a simple lisp operation corresponding to each intstack operation, but note that cons(3,4) for example, does not represent any intstack object although it is a lisp object.

Specification of abstract data types

In the previous example, the type <u>intstack</u> was only described informally. In general it is necessary to give a much more precise description or specification of the type and we need to be able to do this in a representation-independent way if possible. The same problem of specification faces the language implementor/designer with primitive types. Most primitive types are familiar and need little explanation in the language manual, but for an unfamiliar type, an informal description in English should be supplemented with a more precise (mathematical) description which preferably does not refer to the actual implementation in case this changes (e.g. between implementations on different machines). The description should only pick out relevant properties of the type.

One approach to solving this problem might be to give a mathematical model of the type (i.e. using familiar mathematical representations of sequences, sets, functions, etc.) but this has the drawback that although the description could be relatively abstract (undetailed) it may <u>not</u> be representation-independent. Another approach focuses on the relationships between operations defined for the type. The reason for this is that: (i) all we need to know about is the 'abstract behavior' of the objects which we can observe, and (ii) we may only observe objects (and create them or decompose them) using the operations provided with the type. Thus if the type can be uniquely determined by the relationships between operations (given in the form of axioms and without further specifying the operations), the need to mention representations can be avoided.

For example we can describe stacks by identifying some properties of the operators

pop(push (x,y))	=y	where x range over
top(push (x,y))	=x	all <u>integers</u>
isnew(push (x,y))	=false	y ranges over all
isnew(newstack)	=true	<u>intstacks</u>

and top (newstack) and pop (newstack) are undefined.

This approach is exemplified by the <u>Algebraic</u> <u>Method</u> (Zilles, 1975, Guttag, 1975, ADJ, 1975, 1976, 1980).

In mathematical terminology, a (one sorted) algebra is a set called the 'carrier' along with a collection of operations defined on the set, and so the concept seems to coincide with that of data type.

More generally, a many-sorted algebra is a collection of 'sorts' with a carrier for each sort and operations on or between the carriers. For example, the operations associated with integer stacks involved sorts integer and boolean as well as intstack. (The word 'sort' is used to avoid over-using the word 'type' which can then be reserved for the whole collection of the sorts with their carriers and operations.)

A great deal of mathematics concerning algebras and mappings between them (homomorphisms) has proved very useful in studying data types and tools for specifying them. For example, the use of equational axioms involving only the operator names and variables (as used above for intstack) gives a very powerful way of specifying the abstract data type. Also the concept of abstract algebra (that is, the class of all algebras with the same structure where algebras have the same structure if and only if they are isomorphic) captures very well the idea of abstract data type since it ignores representational differences. Any actual algebra in the isomorphism class can be seen as a representative (i.e. an implementation) of the abstract data type. (It is common algebraic practice to treat an abstract algebra as a single algebra by using isomorphism for equality; thus one often finds, for example, 'X is unique (up to isomorphism)'.)

There are many important issues in this area which we can only briefly mention here, but see for example ADJ (1975, 1976, 1980), Guttag and Horning (1978) for more details. One issue is how 'errors' should be handled. We stated above that top (newstack) was not defined in the axioms for intstack, but this should be more carefully explained as implying either the use of partial functions or that error values are included as objects of the type (see ADJ, 1976, Bauer and Wossner, 1982).

Other important issues concern the problem of establishing for a given abstract data type specification its consistency (non-contradictory properties) and its completeness (non-ambiguity) which are in general unsolvable problems, although methods which can be used for most practical examples have been found.

For consistency, one generally provides an example type constructed mathematically since an inconsistent specification can have no models. The more difficult problem of completeness concerns ambiguity of the specification in that there may be many non-isomorphic models, and thus a unique abstract algebra has not been completely specified. In general, there will

always be an 'initial' model in which no two expressions are
taken to denote the same object unless required by axioms, and a
'terminal' model in which expressions do denote the same object
unless required not to by axioms. These models may not
coincide and there may be many other models between these
extremes. However, under certain conditions (not described
here) one can ensure that the specification is <u>sufficiently
complete</u> (Guttag and Horning, 1978) that no two models will give
different behaviors for the user.

The importance of the algebraic approach to the specification
of abstract data types can be seen in the powerful techniques it
provides for proving properties of types. For example, establishing that an implementation of a type is correct merely
requires checking that the implementation satisfies the axioms
(and is therefore an algebra in the isomorphism class defined by
the axioms). Properties may be established using the usual
rules for equality and substitution. For example, from the
properties of integer stacks we can easily derive that

> push(1, pop(push(2, push(3, newstack)))) and
> pop(push(6, push(1, push(3, newstack))))

describe the same stack value. Quite often, to prove a
property of abstract data type objects, or to define additional
functions which operate on objects of the type, we need to use
'structural induction' which for the case of <u>intstacks</u> means
that it is sufficient to prove the property (define the
function) for:

> i)   newstack
> ii)   push (x,y) where we may assume it is true
>   (defined) for y

in order to prove it is true (defined) for all objects of the
type (this assumes we only include objects which are finitely
generated from the operators). For example, we could define
height: **intstack** → **integer** (giving the number of elements in
the stack) by:

> height(newstack) = 0
> height(push(x,y)) = 1 + height(y)

and similarly prove that height(x) $\geqslant$ 0 for all x in **intstack.**

<u>Further Examples</u>:

LISTS

We give an <u>abstract</u> specification of integer lists using equations, so that the structured type defined using cartesian product notation can be seen as a particular model.

<u>abstype</u> <u>intlist</u>

<u>operators</u> and <u>their</u> <u>sorts</u>:

```
cons    :integer x  intlist  →intlist
head    :intlist →integer
tail    :intlist →intlist
null    :intlist →boolean
nil     :          →intlist
```

equations: (for all x in **integer**,
                for all y in **intlist**)

```
head (cons (x,y)) = x
tail (cons (x,y)) = y
null (cons (x,y)) = false
null (nil)        = true
```

head (nil) and tail (nil) are undefined

SETS

For a slightly more complex example we show how finite sets of integers with the usual set operations may be described with equations. The special operator 'if_then_else' of sort <u>boolean</u> x intset x intset → intset is used in the equations with its obvious meaning.

<u>abstype</u> <u>intset</u>

<u>operators</u> <u>and</u> <u>their</u> <u>sorts</u>:

```
union :          intset x intset  →intset
intersection:    intset x intset  →intset
difference:      intset x intset  →intset
remove:          integer x intset →intset

insert:          integer x intset →intset
nullset:                          →intset
```

```
delete1(n,x)    = if null(x) then nil else
                  if is_atom(x) then nil else
                  if car(x) = n then cdr(x) else
                            cons(car(x), delete1(n,cdr(x)))

deleteall(n,x) = if null(x) then nil else
                  if is_atom(x) then nil else
                  if car(x) = n
                  then
                            deleteall(n,cdr(x))
                  else
                            cons(car(x), deleteall(n,cdr(x)))
```

```
Implementation 1 :   nullset    is implemented as   nil
                     insert      is implemented as   cons
                     remove      is implemented as   deleteall
                     ....

Implementation 2 :   nullset    is implemented as   nil
                     insert      is implemented as   addnumber
                     remove      is implemented as   delete1
                     ....
```

(Note that the difference between these implementations is
essentially whether or not repetitions are kept in the **lisp**
object representating a set. It is fairly easy to check that
both implementations are correct using substitution and induction.)

The equations defining **intset** look very similar to the
'equations' used in the recursive definitions of contains,
addnumber, etc. One might well ask why the type-defining
equations cannot be used directly as an implementation and
indeed this is possible under certain conditions. This is
another big bonus we get from the algebraic approach: the
equations can be treated as rewrite rules by a system which
reduces terms to their simplest form and this means that
specifications can be run. Usually this direct implementation
will be highly inefficient, but it is potentially very useful as
a running prototype when defining large systems.

Parameterized abstract data types

From the examples **intlist**, **intstack**, it seems clear that an
abstraction by means of parameterization to allow **stack**(X) and
list(X) where X is an (arbitrary) type parameter should be
considered. For the example of **intstack,** no use was made of the

fact that items where integers other than to record that, for
example, push was expected to have an integer as first argument.
Thus we could simply replace such occurrences of 'integer' by
'X' - a parameter - and replace 'intstack' by 'stack(X)'.
Intstack can then be obtained as **stack(integer)**. That is, by
applying the parameterized type stack to argument integer (thus
we consider types as objects which may be used as arguments).

Such a facility for parameterizing in this way gives a very
powerful design tool. For example, consider the simplicity of
a description of 'stacks of queues of integer-character-pair-
lists' as

stack (queue (list (pair (integer, character))))

which comes free along with all the appropriate operations for
such objects, once each of the parameterized types have been
specified and/or implemented.

In general, however, arguments for parameterized types will
need to be not just arbitrary (in the sense that any type will
do) but restricted to specific forms. For example, a type
which includes **list**(X) objects and operations and in addition a
sorting operator which produces sorted lists from arbitrary
lists of X-objects, would only be defined for types X having a
total ordering operation defined on them.

Thus we may define:

listsort(X)   (**provided** X $\equiv$ **ord**(Y) for some type Y)

where **ord**(Y) contains objects of Y, along with an ordering
operation.

The complex theory involved in such mechanisms is still under
active research, and is beyond the scope of these notes (but see
ADJ, 1980, Burstall and Goguen, 1977, 1980, Ehrig, 1982,
Ganzinger, 1983).

Some programming language support for abstract data types

Simula 67 (Dahl et al., 1970) introduced 'classes' for encap-
sulating data, but did not give automatic protection. Later
Clu (Liskov et al., 1977) introduced 'clusters' for defining
abstract data types specifically, and modules were used in
Modula (Wirth, 1977), Mesa (Mitchell et al., 1979) and Euclid
(Popek et al., 1977). More recently Ada (Ichbiah et al., 1979),

which uses packages for a modularizing mechanism, enables abstract data types to be declared and also separates the implementation from the interface declaration (called a specification in Ada, although it does not require properties (axioms) to be given only operator names). Ada also provides a limited mechanism for passing types as parameters to procedures and packages termed 'generics'.

Of the functional languages (see Section 4.4) ML (Gordon et al, 1979) provides a mechanism for encapsulating operators for abstract data types, but requires an implementation to be given and fixed at the same time. ML also makes use of polymorphic type checking (Milner, 1978) which allows a form of implicit type parameterization. The language HOPE (Burstall et al, 1980) extends the use of abstract types and polymorphism in combination with modules.

Also there exist pure specification languages such as CLEAR (Burstall and Goguen, 1980) and OBJ (Goguen and Tardo, 1979) which are entirely based on abstract data type specification thus providing a tool to be used in conjunction with other software tools such as programming languages.

4.3.2 Variables and Storage

So far the objects of each type have been considered as mathematical objects which are neither created nor changed nor destroyed, but just exist. At a lower level of abstraction, the mechanisms for storing such objects in memory cells of a computer may be described. For very high level languages, it is unnecessary and indeed undesirable for programmers to provide this description, especially if alternatives to Von Neumann architectures are to be used in implementations, but most current programming languages include the concept of a variable (program variable) which is an abstraction of the memory-cell. Similarly the control abstraction of assignment corresponds to the destructive updating of contents of cells.

It is important to distinguish the data objects which are values from variables which refer to storage in which values may be placed, and to note that by means of directly referring to storage, its use can be economized, reusing cells to store different objects as they arise in a computation.

This is particularly significant when structured objects are stored, because it allows the possibility of treating a structured object variable as a structured variable. That is,

the storage of structured objects can be achieved using
structured storage enabling individual components of the stored
object to be changed by an assignment without having to restore
the entire new object. This is what makes arrays, for example,
particularly efficient - arrays as data objects are just
structured objects which are homogeneous (all components have
the same type) and have computable indices such as integers (so
that indices are treated as objects). However, arrays as
storage structures (also called displays) closely correspond to
contiguous blocks of memory with indices being used to provide
offsets from the base address of the block for fast location of
components, which can be changed one at a time during
computations without copying the whole array object.

Another storage technique for representing structured objects
is to use indirection for components, which means that a
location is stored as a component of a stored object, and not
the actual value (the value is then stored at the given
address). This is called 'using pointers' and enables each
type to be given a fixed amount of storage for the compound
object as well as being necessary for recursively defined
objects (infinite objects). In most programming languages such
use of pointers must be explicitly given by the programmer.

So we find for the type <u>bintreechar</u> a definition such as:

```
type bintreechar = record item : integer
                          left: ↑ bintreechar;
                          right: ↑ bintreechar
                   end
```

where

     ' ↑ bintreechar' means 'pointers to **bintreechar** objects'.

When we come to implement an abstract data type in terms of a
structured data type, we can of course, ignore the fact that
structured type variables may be considered as structured
variables when using assignments. However, for reasons of
efficiency we may well wish to update parts of the stored
structure representing an abstract value and this causes a
conflict in the use of abstractions. For example, if stacks
are represented as arrays with a pointer to indicate the top
position, then the storage operation

```
X := push ( X , 5)
{where X is a stack program variable)
```

could be carried out very efficiently by inplace updating of the structure stored in X. If A and N are array and integer variables respectively which together represent X we could carry out the operation by changing A and N as follows:

    N := N+1 ; A(N) := 5

Thus we would like to implement X := push (X , a) rather than just the operation, push (X , a). To do this we could create a module (package) which contained procedures with side effects such as

    PUSH (X , a) with the same effect as X := push (X , a)

and implement these using storage structures, rather than trying to implement the abstract type itself in terms of other types. The concept of the abstract type would still be needed to explain the properties of these procedures. For example, we might claim:

        If the stack-value stored in X is x before calling
        the procedure PUSH (X , a) then the value stored
        in X is push (x,a) afterwards.

The module then encapsulates the combination of the abstract type along with the storage of values in program variables and the hiding of implementation details from the user can still be achieved.

4.3.3 Control Abstraction

It was mentioned in the last section that most machines on which current languages are implemented are based on the Von Neumann architecture where values are stored in cells and updated destructively by basic operations of the machine. This has given rise to the abstractions of variable for storage-cell and assignment statements for updating. In addition, the automatic updating of the program counter to fetch the next instruction, gives us the abstraction of statement sequences (usually separated by ';' in most languages) and the possibility of updating the program counter allows jumps (either uncon- ditionally or according to the result of some test) to new points (abandoning the remaining sequence). From all the possible control path patterns which these jumps allow, the two fundamental patterns of selection (if statements) and repet- ition (loop statements) were considered as more comprehensible and sufficient for programming in most cases. Other uses of jumps and bizarre uses of the program counter were seen as causing too much complexity and theoretically unnecessary for describing algorithms (Bohm and Jacopini, 1966). Thus the restriction to working purely with the abstractions of selection, repetition and sequence provided the first step in structured design of control.

(Note, however, that direct abstractions of the jump in the form of ´goto´ statements still appear in many high level languages alongside the structured control. Jumps are analogous to the bit pattern level of abstraction in data types and their use should be compared with for example the use of operations which alter the bits representing an integer value.)

The next step was to provide a mechanism for treating as single named units, entire patterns of control built from primitive control abstractions. These units are referred to as procedures or routines and the mechanism of procedural abstraction provides for an improved design methodology with economy of use of control patterns. The procedure is implemented as a stored copy of the control pattern and its invocation (call) is implemented by automatic jumping to and returning from the pattern. Of course procedures may be called from other procedures so that control patterns may be nested and it was shown in Samelson and Bauer (1960) how a simple stack mechanism could be used to allow recursive and mutually recursive calls (giving unbounded nestings).

Since Algol 60, the control primitives of most languages have been based on the use of if statements, do loops, sequencing and procedures. (Blocks can be seen as a special case of procedures which are unnamed and used once at the point of declaration). However new abstractions have been provided by the use of mechanisms for encapsulation and parallel processing.

In the following sub-sections we concentrate on procedural abstraction and these new mechanisms and do not consider further variations on the primitive control abstractions such as case statements, loop iterators, exception handling jumps, etc.

Parameterised procedures

An issue which has led to a variety of different mechanisms and deserves careful study, is that of procedure parameterisation. The references to variables occurring in a procedure may be abstracted out (functional abstraction) to give a more general purpose parameterized procedure which can then be applied to different variables to give different instances.

    e.g. **procedure** p   = **begin** ....x ....x .... **end**

becomes when x is 'parameterized'

    procedure p(x)   = **begin** ....x ....x .... **end**

and calls of p must now be replaced by call of p(V) for different variables V.

This is an important conceptual simplification, for if we wish to consider procedures in isolation from the program in which they are used, then all the variables referred to in the body of the procedure should be parameterized.

However, there is a serious problem with parameterization of variables in procedures which arises from the fact that variables are related to both values <u>and</u> storage. We have to ask <u>what</u> is being abstracted from – is it just the value of the variable or is it the storage address or <u>both</u>? The different possibilities give rise to different parameter passing mechanisms and different calling mechanism for procedures and since different results can be produced, the mechanisms used are a crucial part of the language semantics. Some classic examples for parameter passing are:-

(i) BY VALUE (only the value of the actual argument is passed for use in the procedure).

ii) BY REFERENCE (the address of a storage cell is passed and thus the contents can be updated in the procedure).

iii) BY NAME (the parameter in the procedure body again refers to a storage address but this is computed from the actual argument each time the parameter appears in the body and can give different results each time).

iv) BY VALUE-RESULT (both the value and the storage address are passed, but a local storage variable is initialized with the value and used as the parameter in the body. The address of the actual argument is then used to store the final value of this variable when returning from the call).

Subtle differences between these mechanisms can be observed, for example, with calls like

```
p ( X , X )
```

where the program variable X has been given 'aliases' by appearing as two of the parameters. Note also that it is the changing of stored values in the body of procedures which gives rise to different results.

Modules and binding

Modules are not an abstraction from machine details, but are a device for controlling the scope of definitions; they are a tool or aid in the description of software.

Early programming languages had restricted means for defining variables, etc. Algol 60 provided a nested structure for programs which allowed definitions (and declarations) to have local scope at the level of nesting in which they appeared. The declarations were also automatically imported into inner levels of nesting unless this caused a clash. Thus, for example, in the following program segment:

```
begin integer x,y ;
      x := 0 ; y := 0 ;
      begin integer x ;
            x := 1 ; y := 1

      end ;
      print(x,y)
end
```

the variable y to which 1 is assigned in the inner block (fourth line) is imported as the y declared in the outer block on the first line. On the other hand the x declared on the first line is not imported as it would clash with the x declared in the third line. The print statement is in the scope of the variables declared in the first line, so the values 0 and 1 are printed.

This mechanism for associating scopes with variables and occurrences of variables with their defining occurrence is called static binding, and is used in most programming languages. There are some languages (e.g. SNOBOL and LISP) which use dynamic binding. With dynamic binding the runtime stack determines the binding of variables and this is not always compatible with the natural (textually nearest) association of variables given by static binding.

For languages with static binding it is possible to introduce the mechanism of _modules_ which are essentially packages of declarations which may be textually isolated. Rather than relying on nested program structure to give scope to definitions and declarations, modules may allow the explicit naming of other modules on which there definitions depend (_imported modules_) and also restrictions on which definitions in the module may be used elsewhere (_exported_). This provides both an encapsulation mechanism as well as a means for breaking up large programs into separate units which may not just be simply nested. The possibilities for separately compiling these units without jeopardizing the integrity of their interfaces can then be exploited. Different forms of the module concept occur in several current languages (as was mentioned in Section 4.3.1).

Towards concurrency

The idea of coroutines (co-operating routines) was introduced by Conway (1963) and appeared in Simula 1 (1966) and Simula 1967. These provided a mechanism for jumping back and forth between two (or more) control patterns (routines) thus extending the less symmetrical concept of one procedure called from within another 'enclosing' procedure, which only allowed a jump to the beginning and return from the end of the pattern representing the called procedure (see Fig. 4.10). A simple extension of the single stack to a stack for each coroutine or a 'cactus stack' provided an implementation.

Coroutines were a first step towards multi-programming (concurrent programming). They allowed the programmer to split up computations into separate units of control which were _not_ hierarchically nested but which may nevertheless have interdependencies, provided that the control jumping between the components were also specified so that a single machine could 'follow' the control. In effect, the jumping between coroutines gave an explicit interweaving of the otherwise independent patterns resulting in a single control path.

Later developments allowed the programmer to omit such information and regard the separate computations as running in parallel on different machines but with communications between them specifiable by the programmer.

This communication between processes (concurrent units) only forced a _partial_ ordering on control patterns, and the problem of further interweaving them to obtain a _single_ total ordering of the control sequence was the responsibility of the language

implementor. Actually, there may be many acceptable inter-
weavings for a given partial ordering, so the detail of a
particular choice had been abstracted away from in the
language. Furthermore, the possibility of running the processes
on many processors is neither ruled out nor forced on the
implementor using such an abstraction. The extra interweaving
is only necessary when the number of actual processors
available is less than the number of concurrent processes used
by the program, and the exact choice of interleaving can be left
until run time in order to make use of actual running times of
processes (see Figs. 4.11 and 4.12).

4.3.3 Communication (between concurrent processes)

If there were no communication between the component processes
of a concurrent program, then they could be conceptually and
practically dealt with as independent programs with little
advantage in considering them together. More likely, the
components interact with each other, either by message passing
('loosely coupled processes') or sharing stored data ('tightly
coupled processes'), so at the center of concurrent programming
is the mechanisms for communication between processes.

Example

Consider the two concurrent processes:

    A: i:=0 ; i:=i+1   and   B: i:=2

which share the variable i. If these are interleaved, we may get
different results depending on the interleaving:

    1) i:-0;   i:=2;   i:=i+1   (result i=3)
    2) i:=0;   i:=i+1;   i:=2   (result i=2)
    3) 1:=2;   i:=0;   i:=i+1   (result i=1)

Worse still, the statements themselves may not be considered
atomic and so interleaving at a lower level may allow even more
non-determinism of results (see Fig. 4.5).

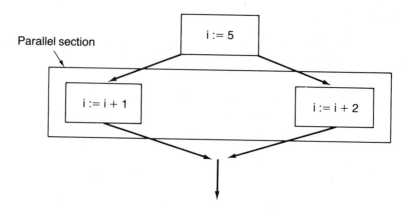

Fig. 4.5 Parallel statements

The parallel section shown in the diagram may be decomposed as:

        evaluate(i+1) ; assign result to i
        evaluate(i+2) ; assign result to i

which may then be interleaved in several ways, such as:

        evaluate(i+1) producing result1;
        evaluate(i+2) producing result2;
        assign result1 to i;
        assign result2 to i

with possible results i=8, i=6 or i=7 at the end.

Such non-determinism seems too dangerous as it may not be intended by the programmer, and clearly <u>protection</u> is needed to control sharing of data.

The first abstraction was to use <u>signals</u> and later Dijkstra's <u>semaphores</u> (Dijkstra, 1968a,b) (which appeared as primitives in Algol 68) for communication so that processes could 'hold each other up' while they entered 'critical sections' which were not to be interrupted by an interleaving.

Analogously to structured data types, accidental misuse of semaphores could cause many problems, so a later abstraction of monitors (Brinch-Hansen, 1973, Hoare, 1974) provided a means of encapsulating the shared data with controlled use rather like abstract data-types, but this time it was the multi-access by several processes which was controlled. Thus monitors are an essentially passive encapsulation of shared data for safe access by many active processes. They were introduced into

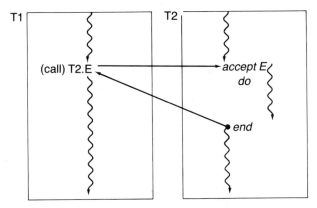

Fig. 4.6 Task T1 calls T2 (Entry E), but T2 may be busy.
The call is queued (by the implementation) until
T2 reaches an appropriate accept point.
Conversely if T2 reaches the accept point before
a call arrives, it waits at this control point for a call
(from any task). Note the forking to two control
paths at the end of the accept statement ('end')
as well as the existence of two control paths at
the beginning of T1 and T2.

Task T1 calls T2 (entry E), but T2 may be busy. The call is
queued (by the implementation) until T2 reaches an appropriate
accept point. Conversely if T2 reaches the accept point before a
call arrives, it waits at this control point for a call (from
any task). Note the forking to two control paths at the end of
the 'accept' statement ('end'), as well as the existence of two
control paths at the beginning of T1 and T2.

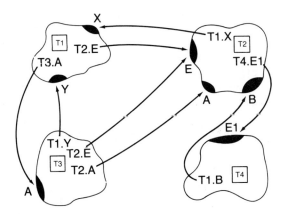

Fig. 4.7 Tasks communicate on different entries

Concurrent Pascal (Brinch-Hansen, 1975, 1977) and into Modula
(Wirth, 1977). More recently, with Ada (Ichbiah et al.1979) the
concepts of task and rendezvous have been introduced for
communication, enabling both processes and monitors to be
subsumed as active tasks. Tasks are separate processes which
run concurrently and they may call each other rather like
procedures. However, (unlike procedures) the called task is
active, and may only 'accept' the call at appropriate points in
its control (see Fig. 4.6); there may be several different ways
of calling a task; these are called different entries of the
task (see Fig. 4.7).

Once a calling task and accept statement have been synchron-
ized, the two tasks 'rendezvous' - input parameter values are
passed from caller to called; the control following the accept-
statement between 'do' and 'end' is obeyed while the tasks are
locked together, output parameters are passed back, and the
tasks separate again. This fairly simple principle becomes much
more sophisticated, when several tasks call a single task, and
mechanisms for choosing which one to accept are added (see Pyle,
1981, Barnes, 1982).

It is important to note that all these high level mechanisms for
controlling concurrency only protect programmers from certain
classes of error. Important problems such as deadlock (where
processes wait ad infinitum for each other to release a
resource) are still the concern of the programmer and not just
the language implementor. Many theoretical tools for studying
concurrency have been proposed (too numerous to mention) and
some have recently led to new language designs, see e.g. Hoare
(1978).

4.3.4 A More Abstract View of Control

The previous section (4.3.3) considered control abstraction at
the statement level. Within statements there can be expressions
- e.g. on the right-hand side of assignment statements or as
arguments in procedure calls. In some programming languages
(for example Algol 68) expressions are allowed to contain inner
statements and so the distinction between expressions and
statements is blurred. When only pure expressions are used, the
control of evaluation is only given implicitly by the structure
of the expression.

To be more precise, in pure expressions we make no direct
reference to storage, but rather use variables to denote the
values stored. The administration of storage for intermediate

results during evaluation and the linearization of an expression to a sequence of operator applications is done automatically (i.e. dealt with by the language implementation not by the programmer).

Example: Consider the evaluation of the expression:

f(x+3) - g(x*f(y))

Usually this is translated into a linear sequence of actions which cause operations to be applied to a stack of intermediate values. We may thus get as a control sequence (informally):

1) put the value of x (stored in x) on the stack
2) put the value 3 on the stack
3) execute 'add' (using the top two elements of the stack as arguments replacing them with the result)
4) execute f (using the stack for argument and result)
5) put the value of x on the stack
6) put the value of y on the stack
7) execute f
8) execute 'multiply'
9) execute g
10) execute 'subtract' (subtracting the top element from the second element on the stack)

But this is by no means the only possible implementation, and indeed there is room for <u>parallel evaluation</u> of subexpressions like f(x+3) and g(x*f(g)) which, with pure expressions (i.e. where there are no explicit references to storage from side effects such as from inner assignments), are independent of each other.

This removal (abstraction) from control details thus provides a much more machine-independent view of computations paving the way to the very high level languages which we consider next.

4.4 FUNCTIONAL (APPLICATIVE) PROGRAMMING LANGUAGES

Functional languages are essentially very high level languages based on pure expressions without side-effects or references to storage details and explicit control flow. The two main reasons why such an abstraction away from these machine-oriented details is seen as advantageous are:

1) The resulting languages have a clean and mathe-
    matically much simpler semantics and the algebraic
    properties of expressions are uncluttered by imple-
    mentation details. This makes programs easier to
    reason about and leads to better possibilities for
    correctness proofs, transformations, automatic opti-
    mizations, etc. (i.e. more and simpler tools for
    programming as a whole).

2) The freedom to use non-conventional implementations
    (specifically on highly parallel machines where the
    implementor may take advantage of the available
    parallelism) is not restricted unnecessarily by the
    programmer over-specifying the problem or solution
    (e.g. by giving details appropriate only to restricted
    forms of implementation).

4.4.1   Referring Directly to Data

Identifiers used in applicative languages refer directly to
values and not cells in which values may be placed as was the
case with program variables. So for example the use of x in the
phrase:

$$\textbf{let } x = g(2,3) \textbf{ in } f(x,x)$$

does not dictate any particular evaluation order or storage of
the value resulting from evaluation of g(2,3). (Although an
obvious implementation strategy would be to evaluate g(2,3) and
store the result in a cell, then evaluate f(x,x), ensuring that
references to x are associated with the value in the above-
mentioned cell.)

The process of evaluation is constructive in the sense that
values are obtained ('described') as results of applying
functions to other values, but there is no concept of
'destroying' a value. (The number 5 is not 'destroyed' by adding
it to 2 but continues to exist independently of the result 7.)

To solve problems, it seems much simpler to work directly with
values and abstract from machine details, and this allows us to
consider software in a new light. The changing view is described
in Dijkstra (1976)

'...(There was a time) when it was the general opinion that
it was our program's purpose to instruct our machines, in
contrast to the situation of today in which more and more

people are leaning towards the opinion that it is our
machine´s purpose to execute our programs.´

At first sight, the abandonment of assignment statements might
seem to be a great loss for the expressibility of algorithms but
there are other ways of making expressions more expressive and
readable to describe large computations (<u>without</u> compromising
their properties by embedding them in Von-Neuman control and
storage oriented concepts). In fact this approach can give much
more powerful means of expression leading to far greater
efficiencies in the long run.

4.4.2 Higher Order Functions

Apart from syntactic niceties which allow very readable forms of
definitions and expressions, one of the most significant
additions to ´powers of expression´ comes from treating
<u>functions</u> as data objects to be manipulated and used by other
<u>functions</u> just as other data is.

This means that we allow higher-order functions in expressions,
which can take other functions as arguments and produce
functions as results.

<u>Example</u>

For any function (of one argument) f and list x of
appropriate arguments for f

(each f) x

means ´apply f to each element of x individually forming a list
of results´. Thus

$$\text{(each f) } [a_1, a_2, a_3, \ldots a_r] = [f(a_1), f(a_2), \ldots f(a_r)]$$

The operator ´each´ is a higher order function taking f as its
argument.

As another example, we define the function ´compare´ as:

compare a b = a $\leq$ b

(that is, compare a b gives the result ´true´ if a $\leq$ b and ´false´
otherwise). Here ´compare´ is not just a two argument function
but a higher order function which can be given its arguments one
at a time. The result of applying compare to 5 is a

function which may take one argument and compares it with 5. This means that it makes sense to apply 'each' to 'compare 5':

each (compare 5) [6, 5, 1, 8, 2, 2]

=   [true, true, false, true, false, false]

If we write T1→T2 for the (structured) type of functions with arguments in T1 and results in T2, then 'each' will have a type of the form

$$(T1 \rightarrow T2) \rightarrow (list(T1) \rightarrow list(T2))$$

and 'compare' will have type

integer → (**integer** → **boolean**)

(Note that we have written 'g x y' for '(g x) y' in the examples and that juxtaposition 'g x' means 'apply g to x', so '(g x) y' means 'apply g to x and apply the result of this to y'.)

There are limited possibilities for defining higher order functions in some traditional languages (Ada, Pascal, Algol 60 allow arguments to be functions but not results, Pascal allows only up to second order) but when mixed with <u>imperative</u> features (assignments) rather inefficient implementations result and this deters people from using them.

Once the importance of higher order functions is recognized, one can view functions as the main building blocks for software.

4.4.3 Manipulating Programs

The important task of combining programs to form new programs and especially of using programs to create programs have often been neglected in language design. With functional programs, we have a great advantage in that programs describe functions, and functions may be considered as data for other functions (programs).

Thus to describe a single program p which has the effect of running program p_2 on the data resulting from p_1 we merely write:

$p = p_2 \circ p_1$ (function composition).

Similarly if p_1 is to be run on data d_1 to produce a <u>program</u> which is then to be run on data d_2, we merely write $(p_1\ d_1)\ d_2$.

It is this straightforward and fundamental ability to combine functions and manipulate them with other functions in various ways which makes software construction quicker, easier and more reliable with functional programming languages.

4.4.4 Lazy Evaluation

Another useful but non-essential feature of some functional languages allows the possibility of defining infinite objects (such as the list of all even integers) without necessarily requiring them to be fully evaluated (and hence causing non-terminating computations).

When this is allowed, certain computations can be described much more succinctly and clearly - in fact this facility is already present in the use of functions as data, since a function can be associated with an infinite set of argument-/result pairs.

Lazy evaluation (Henderson and Morris, 1976, Friedman and Wise, 1976) is a particular way of evaluating expressions which ensures that infinite computations are not 'blindly' started unnecessarily (by not evaluating arguments to functions until they are required), and that argument evaluation is not repeated unnecessarily. It is one of a variety of methods (and a particularly efficient one) for dealing with 'non-strict' functions which may produce results even for undefined arguments.

The conditional expression:

> if e_1 then e_2 else e_3

usually has to be treated as a **special form** requiring e_1 to be evaluated before e_2 and e_3 in case one of these is undefined.

> e.g. if x=0 then 1 else y/x

('y/x' is not defined if x=0), but in fact the if_then_else_ construct is just an example of a non-strict function.

Only with such non-strict possibilities for the semantics of functions could we freely define functions such as:

cond (x,y,z) = **if** $x=0$ **then** y **else** z

(Note, however, that FP (Backus, 1978) is based on strict functions and the conditional is treated as a higher order non-strict combining form to avoid the above problem.)

4.4.5 Logic Programming

Yet a further abstraction towards programming with values is to regard the program as describing a relationship between values. This has the great advantage that the same program can be used in different ways depending on which values in the relationship are taken as known (input arguments) and which are to be deduced (output arguments). For example:

Sum(x,y,z) may describe the relationship

'the value of z is the sum of the values of x and y'

allowing the deduction $z = 8$ from Sum$(3,5,z)$ but also allowing the deduction $x = 3$ from Sum$(x,5,8)$. (This use of identifiers x,y,z as 'unknown values' is in keeping with a mathematical use of variables and they are often refered to as logical variables to indicate that they are not the same as traditional program variables.)

Computations can be viewed as <u>deductions</u> and they rely on <u>unification</u> (a powerful form of pattern matching combined with logical variables) to direct them along with a mechanism for <u>backtracking</u> from failed computation paths. These techniques come under the heading of <u>logic programming</u> (Clark and Tarnland, 1982, Kowalski, 1979, Clocksin and Mellish, 1981).

The use of higher orders with relations is not quite so straightforward and easy to understand as it is with functional programs, and so compromises are being sought between the two approaches, sometimes collectively referred to as applicative or declarative programming.

4.5 CONCLUSIONS

With the removal of implementation details from a programming language, the distinction between the formal specification of a problem, and a program to solve the problem becomes more blurred. Instead of a sharp distinction between the two, there is now only a degree of 'efficient implementability' distinguishing them. Most of the formalism used for describing problems can be directly implemented to provide automatic deduction of solutions, but such direct implementation is often very inefficient, and the purpose of constructing a program is to improve the efficiency of implementation.

Rather than write a specification and a program separately and go through the difficult task of showing one correctly implements the other, it is seen as perspicuous to use essentially one language for programs and specifications and develop means of transforming specifications into more ef- ficiently implementable forms where necessary, but preserving the meaning (i.e. correctness).

Sometimes a language has such expressive power that the specification is efficiently implementable without change, for example consider the text (program/specification) of a function to compute factorial of non negative integers in the language KRC (see Turner, 1982):

    fac n = multiply [1..n]

where multiply describes a function which multiplies together the elements of a list and [1..n] produces a list of the numbers from 1 to n. (Both multiply and [1..n] are already implemented relatively efficiently in KRC.)

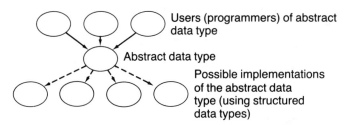

Fig. 4.8 Abstract data types may be seen as interfaces

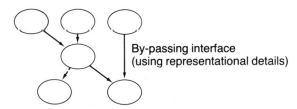

Fig. 4.9 By-passing an interface prevents simple changes of implementation

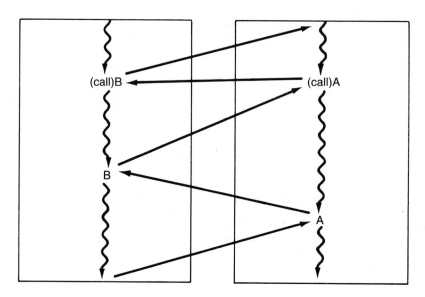

Fig. 4.10 Co-routines

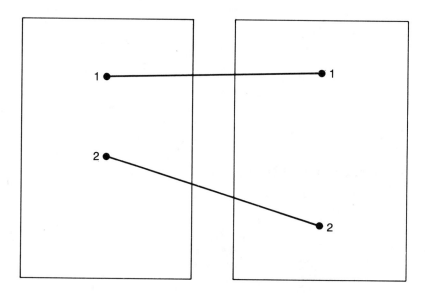

Fig. 4.11 Communication points for two otherwise
independent processes

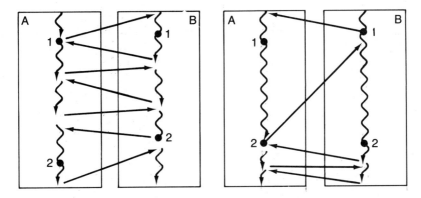

Fig. 4.12 The communication points (1,2) only restrict the control(s) to ensure that
B cannot proceed beyond B.1 until A has reached A.1
A cannot proceed beyond A.1 until B has reached B.1
B cannot proceed beyond B.2 until A has reached A.2
A cannot proceed beyond A.2 until B has reached B.2

REFERENCES

ADJ (1975) ´Abstract Data Types as Initial Algebras and Correctness of Data Representations´ Goguen, J.A., Thatcher, J.W., Wagner, E.G., Wright, J.B., Proc. Conf. on Computer Graphics, Pattern Recognition and Data Structure, May 1975.

ADJ (1976) ´An Initial Algebra Approach to the Specification, Correctness and Implementation of Abstract Data Types´, (Goguen, J.A., Thatcher, J.W., Wagner, E.G.) IBM report RC6487 Oct. 1976 (also in ´Current Trends in Programming Methodology, IV:Data Structuring´ (ed. Yeh, R.), Prentice-Hall, New Jersey (1978).

ADJ (1980) ´Parameterized Data Types in Algebraic Specification Languages´ (short version), (Ehrig, H., Krowski, H.-J., Thatcher, J.W., Wagner, E.G., Wright, J.B.,), Proc. 7th ICALP, Nordwijkerhout, July 1980. ´Lecture Notes in Computer Science´, Vol.85, Springer.

ANSI (1976) American National Standard Programming Language PL/1 (ANS X3.53-1976) New York, American National Standards Institute.

Backus, J. (1978) ´Can Programming be Liberated from the Von Neumann Style? A Functional Style and its Algebra of Programs´, Comm. ACM 21 (8) Aug. 1978.

Barnes, J.G.P. (1982) ´Programming in Ada´, Addison Wesley International Computer Science Series.

Bauer, F.L., Broy, M., Dosch, W., Gnatz, R., Krieg-Bruckner B., Laut, A., Luckham, M., Matzner, T., Moller, B., Partsch, H.,Pepper, P., Samelson, K., Steinbrugger, R., Wirsing, M., and Wossner, H. (1981) ´Programming in a Wide Spectrum Language: A Collection of Examples´, Sci. Comp. Program. 1 (p.73-114).

Bauer, F.L., and Wossner, H. (1982) ´Algorithmic Language and Program Development´, Springer Texts and Monographs in Computer Science.

Bjorner, D. (ed.) (1980) ´Abstract Software Specification´, 1979 Copenhagen Winter School Proceedings, Lecture Notes in Computer Science Vol. 86, Springer.

Bjorner, D., and Jones, C.B. (eds) (1978) ´The Vienna Development Method: The Meta Language´ Lecture Notes in Computer Science Vol. 61, Springer.

Bjorner, D., and Jones, C.B. (1982) ´Formal Specification and Software Development´, Prentice-Hall International Series in Computer Science.

Bohm, C., and Jacopini, G. (1966) ´Flow-Diagrams, Turing Machines, and Languages with only Two Formation Rules´, Comm. ACM 9 (5) May 1966.

Brinch-Hansen, P. (1973) ´Operating Systems Principles´, Prentice-Hall, Englewood Cliffs, NJ.

Brinch-Hansen, P. (1975) ´The Programming Language Concurrent Pascal´, IEEE Transactions on Software Engineering SE 1 (2) June 1975.

Brinch-Hansen, P. (1977) ´The Architecture of Concurrent Programs´, Prentice-Hall, Englewood Cliffs, NJ.

Brodie, M.L., and Zilles, S.N. (eds) (1981) ´Proceedings of the Workshop on Data Abstraction, Databases and Conceptual Modelling´, Pingree Park, Colorado June 1980, ACM Sigplan Notices, Vol. 16 No. 1 Jan. 1981.

Burstall, R.M., MacQueen, D.B., and Sanella, D.T. (1980) ´Hope: An Experimental Applicative Language´, Proc Lisp Conference, Stanford, Ca., August 1980.

Burstall, R.M., and Goguen, J.A. (1977) ´Putting Theories Together To Make Specifications´, Proc. 5th Int. Joint Conf on AI, Cambridge, Mass., Aug. 1977.

Burstall, R.M., and Goguen, J.A. (1980) ´The Semantics of CLEAR, a Specification Language´, in Bjorner (1980).

Clark, K.L., and Tarnland, S.A. (eds) (1982) ´Logic Programming´, Academic Press.

Clocksin, W.F., and Mellish, C.S. (1981) ´Programming in Prolog´, Springer.

Conway, M.E. (1963) ´Design of a Seperable Transition-Diagram Compiler´, Comm. ACM 6 (7) July 1963.

Dahl, O.J., Myhraug, B., and Nygaard, K. (1970) ´The Simula 67 Common Base Language´, Publication S22 Norwegian Computing Centre, Oslo.

Dahl, O.J., Dijkstra, E.W., and Hoare, C.A.R. (1972) ´Structured Programming´, Academic Press, New York.

Darlington, J., Henderson, P., Turner, D. (eds) (1982) ´Functional Programming and its Applications: An Advanced Course´, Cambridge University Press.

Dijkstra, E.W. (1968a) ´Cooperating Sequential Processes´, in ´Programming Languages´, ed. F. Genuys, Academic Press, New York.

Dijkstra, E.W. (1968b) ´The Structure of the Multiprogramming System´, Comm. ACM 11(5) May 1968.

Dijkstra, E.W. (1976) ´A Discipline of Programming´, Prentice-Hall, Englewood Cliffs, NJ.

Ehrig, H. (1982) ´On the Theory of Specification, Implementation and Parameterisation of Abstract Data Types´, JACM 29 (1) Jan 1982.

Friedman, D.P., and Wise, D.S. (1976) ´CONS Should Not Evaluate
Its Arguments´, in ´Automata, Languages and Programming´ (eds
Michaelson and Milner) Edinburgh University Press.

Ganzinger, H. (1983) ´Parameterised Specifications: Parameter
Passing and Implementation with Respect to Observability´, ACM
Toplas 5(3) July 1983.

Gerstmann, and Olengren, (1980) ´Abstract Objects as Abstract
Data Types´ in Bjorner (1980).

Ghezzi, C., and Jazayeri, M. (1982) ´Programming Language
Concepts´, Wiley & Sons.

Goguen, J.A., and Tardo, J.J. (1979) ´An Introduction to OBJ : A
Language for Writing and Testing Formal Algebraic Program
Specifications´, Proc. Conf. on Specifications of Reliable
Software, Cambridge, Mass., April 1979.

Gordon, M.E. (1979) ´The Denotational Description of
Programming Languages´, Springer, New York.

Gordon, M.E., Milner, R., and Wadsworth, C. (1979) ´Edinburgh
LCF´, Lecture Notes in Computer Science Vol. 78, Springer.

Guttag, J.V. (1975) ´The Specification and Application to
Programming of Abstract Data Types´, University of Toronto,
Computer Systems Research Group, Technical Report CSRG-59,
Sept. 1975.

Guttag, J.V. (1976) ´Abstract Data Types and the Development of
Data Structures´, Supplement to Proc. Conf. on Data
Abstraction, Definition and Structure, ACM Sigplan Notices 8(3)
March 1976. (Also in Comm. ACM 20(6) June 1977.)

Guttag, J.V. (1980) ´Notes on Type Abstraction (version 2)´,
IEEE Transactions on Software Eng. Vol SE-6 1, Jan. 1980.

Guttag, J.V., and Horning, J.J. (1978) ´The Algebraic
Specification of Abstract Data Types´, Acta Informatica 10 (1).

Henderson, P. (1980) ´Functional Programming: Application and
Implementation´, Prentice-Hall, Englewood Cliffs.

Henderson, P., and Morris, J.H. (1976) ´A Lazy Evaluator´, 3rd
annual ACM SIGACT-SIGPLAN Symp. on Princ. of Prog. Langs.,
Atlanta.

Hoare, C.A.R. (1969) ´An Axiomatic Basis of Computer Programming´, Comm. ACM 12 (10) October 1969.

Hoare, C.A.R. (1972) ´Proof of Correctness of Data Representations´, Acta Informatica 1.

Hoare, C.A.R. (1974) ´Monitors: An Operating System Structuring Concept´, Comm. ACM 17(10) Oct. 1974.

Hoare, C.A.R. (1975) ´Data Reliability´, Proc. International Conf. on Reliable Software, Los Angeles, Cal.

Hoare, C.A.R. (1978) ´Communicating Sequential Processes´, Comm. ACM 21(8), August, 1978.

Ichbiah, J.D., Heliard, J.C., Roubine, O., Barnes, J.G.P., Krieg-Bruckner, B., and Wichman, B.A. (1979) ´Preliminary Ada Reference Manual´ and ´Rationale for the design of the Ada Programming Language´, ACM Sigplan Notices 14(6) parts A and B, June 1976.

Jensen, K., and Wirth, N. (1975) ´PASCAL User Manual and Report´, Lecture Notes in Computer, Science Vol. 18, Springer 1975.

Kowalski, R.A. (1979) ´Logic for Problem Solving´, Artificial Intelligence Series, North-Holland.

Liskov, B.H., Snyder, A., Atkinson, R., and Schaffert, C. (1977) ´Abstraction Mechanisms in CLU´, Comm. ACM 20(8) Aug. 19⁻7.

Liskov, B.H., and Zilles, S.N. (1974) ´Programming with Abstract Data Types´, Sigplan Symposium on Very High Level Languages, Sigplan Notices 9(4) April 1974.

McCarthy, J., Abrahams, P.W., Edwards, D.J., Hart, T.P., and Levin, M.I. (1965) ´Lisp 1.5 Programmers Manual´, 2nd Ed. MIT Press, Cambridge, Mass.

Milner, R. (1978) ´A Theory of Type Polymorphism in Programming´, Journal of Computer and System Sciences 17, 348-375.

Mitchell, J.G., Maybury, W., Sweet, R. (1979) ´Mesa Language Manual (Version 5.0)´, Xerox Research Center, Palo Alto Cal., CSL- 79-3 April 1979.

Morris, J.H. Jr. (1973) ´Types are Not Sets´, ACM Symp. on Principles of Programming Languages, Boston.

Naur, P. (ed.) (1963) ´Revised Report on the Algorithmic Language Algol 60´, Comm. ACM 6(1) Jan. 1963.

Popek, E.J., Horning , E.E., Lampson, B.W., Mitchell, J.E., and London, R.L. (1977) ´Notes on the Design of Euclid´, Proc. ACM Conf. on Language Design for Reliable Software, Sigplan Notices 12(3) March 1977.

Pyle, I.C. (1981) ´The Ada Programming Language´, Prentice-Hall International.

Rowe, L.A. (1981) ´Data Abstraction from a Programming Language Viewpoint´ in Brodie and Zilles (1981).

Samelson, K. and Baur, F.L. (1960) ´Sequential Formula Translation´, Comm. AM 3(2).

Tennent, R.D. (1976) ´The Denotional Semantics of Programming Languages´, Comm. ACM 19(8) August 1976.

Tennent, R.D. (1981) ´Principles of Programming Languages´, Prentice-Hall International Series in Computer Science.

Turner, D.A. (1982) ´Recursion Equations as a Programming Language´, in Darlington et al. (1982).

van Wijngaarden, A., Mailloux, B.J., Peck, J.E.L., Koster, C.H.A., Sintzoff, M., Lindsay, C.H., Meertens, L.G.L.T., and Fisher, R.G. (1976) ´Revised Report on the Algorithmic Language ALGOL 68´, Springer, New York.

Wirth, N. (1977) ´Modula: A Language for Modular Multi-Programming´, Software - Practice and Experience 7.

Wulf, W.A., London, R.L., and Shaw, M. (1976) ´An Introduction to the Construction and Verification of Alphard Programs´, IEEE Trans on Software Engineering SE-2, Dec. 1976.

Zilles, S.N. (1975) ´An Introduction to Data Algebras´, working draft paper IBM Research, San Jose, Sept. 1975.

Chapter 5

Artificial intelligence and digital systems

I Aleksander

5.1 INTRODUCTION

There is little doubt that the digital computer has come
closer to being the uncomplaining slave than any other
machine in history. Although originally conceived by Van
Neumann as an image of man in combination with a calculating
machine, it soon fired the imagination of scientists, and
engineers as a possible replacement for man in an industrial
setting. Writers of textbooks on information (e.g. Gordon
Pask, 1961) forsaw the completely automatic factory with
machines doing as diverse things as the sampling of candy to
maintain its quality, and controlling the parameters of
machine tools. (Indeed, to put this work into a realistic
perspective, we shall retain the theme of automation as one
against which we can measure the effectiveness of digital
systems for AI.)

One is not trading in unemployment for all factory workers.
Automation should be an extension of man and not his
replacement. From this standpoint, the industrial world
presents endless tasks either at present done by humans or
not, but which are dehumanizing or, at best, just deadly
boring. As such, they are best done by machines. Most such
tasks occur on production lines where every piecepart needs
inspecting or manipulating, or in dangerous situations where
life might be at risk. The inspection of oil pipelines might
be such a job.

So it is not difficult to establish a need for an
uncomplaining slave in the world of automation. However it
has turned out to be quite insufficient merely to point at
the omnipotence of the digital computer. Here are some of the
reasons.

When one talks of 'the extension of man', one is really
referring to the extension of some of man's faculties.
Indeed the digital computer extends man's calculational
faculties by several orders of magnitude both in speed and
accuracy.

However, probably the last thing one actually does when doing
a boring industrial job is calculating. Most tasks involve a
mixture of perceptual acuity and problem solving.

Just think of a production line assembly worker who is trying to assemble electrical appliances. The parts generally present themselves ´in parallel´ so that the human asembler can use his judgement in finding fast assembly methods which he as an individual finds suit him best. Clearly extensions of this faculty involve the mechanization of some form of problem-solving judgement.

One could surmise that artificial intelligence grew out of boredom with the sheer calculatory powers of digital computers. It was John McCarthy in the late 1950s who coined the phrase ´Artificial Intelligence´ arguing that the calculational power of a digital computer could be harnessed in order to work one´s way rapidly down a ´tree´ of choices so as to optimize one´s actions in a problem-solving situation. This, he argued would give the machine a semblance of ´common sense´.

So it is the intention here to examine progress in artificial intelligence particularly with respect to application. This means that McCarthy´s claims will come under scrutiny, central being the question:

> ´to what an extent does the methodology of AI meet notions of automation being an extension of man?´

First, a historical perspective will be taken to appreciate a maturing process that has taken place in this field. Then questions of problem solving and artificial vision will be scrutinized a little more closely.

A point that should be made at this stage is that AI has not only been concerned with artificial vision and problem solving. Indeed, one of its major areas of concern has been the business of handling natural language. This is by no means outside the interest of the automation engineer for the following reason. It is quite clear that the uncomplaining servant-computer should be capable of being used by non-specialists, that is, people who have not been specially trained in computer programming. To this end it would be useful for anyone from a factory floor manager to a shift worker to be able to communicate with the machine. Indeed, some of the most useful work on the understanding of natural language by computer was done in the context of instructing a robot arm (albeit hypothetical) driven through a computer armed with an artificial 'eye'. This too therefore will be discussed.

Finally, a little more will be said regarding deeper modeling techniques which stem for a psychological or even physiological understanding of man. It is felt that this is a necessary step in order to maintain some semblance of completeness in the fact of the fact that AI has, with the passage of time, become dominated by the need to exploit the conventional digital computer in the pursuit of non-numerical tasks. It may be that the freedom afforded by new machine structures inspired by silicon chip technology, allow one to revisit some of the earlier man-modeling aspirations of AI.

5.2 THE COLD LIGHT OF HISTORY

In October 1968 the British publication 'Science Journal' devoted a special issue to the topic 'Machines Like Men'. A clear degree of optimism may be discerned from the statements made in this publication by those deeply committed to the emergence of the new AI paradigm. For example, Charles Rosen (1968) then manager of the Applied Physics Laboratory at the Stanford Research Institute (a laboratory charged with the task of developing an intelligent machine in the shape of a mainframe-driven mobile robot) wrote:

> 'Exciting possibilities exist for the use of both completely mancontrolled autonomous robots which can operate in manmade environments where it is either difficult or impossible to maintain humans for protracted periods of time. Fabrication processes exist which require either very high or low temperatures or an oxygen-free atmosphere or high vacuum...'

No one can deny the desirability for such machines and, indeed Rosen's notion is synonymous with the extension of man idea. The problem arises from Rosen's contention in the article that mainframe-driven machines could already be found in American Laboratories which '...can manipulate objects, move around laboratory environments autonomously, explore, learn and plan'. On close investigation, however, it transpired that the environments were restricted to a trivially small set of polyhedra, the learning was mainly a matter of memorizing and the planning was slow and laborious. So this opened a credibility crevasse in AI which still persists at the time of writing. Can prowess shown in trivial situations be transported into real life? Some still argue that there is a qualitative barrier between the two, while others, even more damningly, point out that it is only the latter that requires <u>intelligence</u> while the former may be based on mechanical techniques where intelligence is replaced by calculational speed.

It may be prudent, however, to keep away from this type of argument altogether and, at the end of the day, assess the AI paradigm by the usefulness or otherwise of the techniques it has generated. McCarthy's use of the word <u>Intelligence</u> in the coining of this field's name may be at fault rather than the work generated by its practitioners.

In Great Britain, during the late 1960s and early 1970s most of the control effort in AI was occurring at the University of Edinburgh under the guidance of Donald Michie, Professor of Machine Intelligence in the Department of Experimental Programming. Central to this work was the design and construction of a hand-and-eye arrangement called FREDDY, which was intended to control the assembly of a very simple toy car, amongst other things (see Ambler et al., 1975).

At about the same time, an event took place in Great Britain which was to have a major effect on the development of AI not only in the UK, but throughout the world. Sir James Lighthill, a mathematician of some repute and a generalist, was asked by the UK Science Research Council to examine the very question of translation between trivial and non-trivial environments of the results found in AI. His findings (albeit later highly criticized by the AI community) were quite damning. He coined what is now a commonly used phrase in AI: the combinatorial explosion. This scourge is one that can be found in many programming examples and relates to the fact that computing time could be an exponential function of the complexity of a problem. That meant that in the translation between toy and real worlds, some AI programs would demand computing powers in excess of what was available at reasonable cost, not only then but also in the foreseeable future. Lighthill (1973) argued that even some of the more sophisticated methods of pruning computation times (such as heuristic searches, to be described later), were insufficient to fight the scourge of the combinatorial explosion.

Lighthill's criticisms developed further than merely pointing at exploding computing times. He argued that if the aims of AI were the improvement of automated proceses, they were likely to find little acceptance on cost grounds alone. Secondly, he drew the simple conclusion that, had it ever been the intention of AI practitioners to shed light on human processes, they had patently failed since humans do not seem to suffer from the combinatorial explosion. Thirdly, he questioned whether there was an intrinsic value in the techniques being developed within the AI paradigm.

Looking back on Lighthill, it turns out that he had been unduly pessimistic about the ingenuity of AI scientists. But of course it is hard to assess how much current development has beeen triggered off by his criticisms and how much would have happened anyway.

Putting aside the rights or wrongs of Lighthill's criticism, one can distinguish a clear post-Lighthill era in the development of the AI paradigm. This is largely coincident with a swing in AI towards a concern with efficent storage of 'knowledge' and has underpinned the emergence of concepts such as 'knowledge engineering' and 'expert systems' (see Michie, 1980). It is interesting that this trend has occurred at the same time as the rise of the microcomputer and has given the work a certain commercial character. Indeed, expert system programs are becoming available for quite small 'personal' computing systems at minimal cost.

5.3 WHAT IS ARTIFICIAL INTELLIGENCE?

Even the most ardent followers of the paradigm answer this question in different ways. For example, Margaret Boden (1977) sees AI as providing some sort of a theoretical background to 'humanist psychology', and defines her own understanding of the term as:

'...the use of computer programs and programming techniques to cast light on the principles of intelligence in general and human thought in particular'.

Boden also finds it difficult to align herself with utilitarian attitudes in AI:

'People working in a technological context sometimes describe AI as an "engineering discipline", a description hardly calculated to appeal to those with primarily psychological interests'.

Clearly, here we shall be primarily interested in matters of a technological nature, and so find the attitute expressed by Nils Nielsson in his second book on the subject (1980), more relevant to our chosen direction:

'If...a <u>science of intelligence</u> could be developed it could guide the design of intelligent machines as well as explicate intelligent behaviour as it occurs in humans and other animals. Since the development of such a theory is still very much a goal rather than an accomplishment of AI, we limit our attention here to those principles that are relevant to the engineering goal of building intelligent machines'.

In the paragraphs that follow we shall see AI as a pursuit of the following questions:

'How can one make a computer acquire <u>knowledge?</u>'
'How can one store this knowledge efficiently?'
'How can one access this knowledge rapidly?'
'How does an intelligent machine create confidence in its own function?'

At the same time we shall resolve that such questions are to be answered in the context of automation. So one refers to classical application areas of AI, namely problem solving, artificial vision, and interaction in a natural language. But we shall start with a somewhat unexpected area: game-playing. This needs some justification.

5.4 WHY PLAY GAMES ON COMPUTERS?

Referring again to the 1968 issue of the Science Journal, one finds a somewhat eloquent justification for interest in game-playing. Donald Michie wrote in rousing style:

> ˜Machine Intelligence is what can be generalised. Into this category fall various tree-searching techniques initially developed in mechanized game-playing. Although the first explorations of these designs were made in attempts to program computers to play games, the nascent playing abilities of intelligent machines will increasingly be devoted to playing the game against nature´.

Although automation can, in some far-fetched way be seen as ˜playing the game against nature´ this now seems an unnecessarily flamboyant statement. It is the first part of Michie´s justification which makes game-playing a necessary field of study in the context of automation. After all, most tasks in automation boil down to decision making. Games concentrate one´s mind to the fundamentals of the mechanization of decision-making processess, situations where the rules are explicit and well understood. The information that needs to be sorted in order to take decisions may be represented in terms of predictive trees of events, and it is by referring to the playing of games that one can express with some degree of fluency, the strategies and programs that can be used to search through such trees and combat as far as possible that scourge of intelligent machinery: the combinatorial explosion!

5.5 SAMUEL´S PRINCIPLES

An interesting characteristic of several strands of work in AI is that the major principles were discovered very early on, and much subsequent work only represents minor advances over such principles. So it is with game-playing. Claude Shannon first took the game of chess in 1950 and discussed way of pruning pathways through astronomically dimensioned choice trees.

Shannon's searching techniques go under the headings of MINIMAXING and ALPHA-BETA processes. We shall return to these later.

It was A.L. Samuel who, armed with Shannon's searching techniques provided a complete look at the mechanization of game-playing, in 1959. His principles may be set out as follows: First, one must realize that the 'state' of a game such as chess or draughts (checkers in the USA), and hence the nodes of a search tree, are related to board configurations. For example, the board with draughts pieces in the three back rows for each player is the starting state or tree node for every game. So the starting player can take one of seven moves, each of which will change the state of the game. This can clearly be represented as one node in a graph leading to seven others. Central to the mechanization process is a way of placing a value on moves so that decisions about optimal choices can be made. Samuel's first principle is that due to the very large number of possible board states it would be foolish to assign a value to each. So he recommends that the features of a move such as the piece pattern in the immediate locality of the moved piece be assessed. This greatly reduces the computational needs, simplifies the mechanism and brings the mechanized system closer to the human player's way of doing things.

Samuel's second principle centers on the fact that values of the patterns found above should be assigned by a process of 'learning' which can be abstracted from 'watching' a good opponent (of the machine, that is) or by a processes of correcting bad moves. We shall illustrate these principles by following through in some detail, the design of a modernized version of the game Fox and Hounds. We call the updated version of this 'Trap the Invader'.

5.6 TRAP THE INVADER

This game is played on 16 playing positions as shown below.
There are four ´patrol´ members numbered 1 to 4 and one
invader marked I. The starting positions are shown below:


```
Home Row ---   X(1)X(2)X(3)X(4)
               ( )X( )X( )X( )X
               X( )X( )X( )X( )
               ( )X( )X( )X( )X          ( ): legitimate playing
               X( )X( )X( )X( )               position.
               ( )X( )X( )X( )X
               X( )X( )X( )X( )
               ( )X( )X(I)X( )X
```


The invader can move to any empty, adjoining playing
position, in any direction, while the patrol can only move
downward, but again to adjoining positions either to the left
or to the right. The object of the game for the patrol is to
immobilize the invader either by pinning it against the edge
of the board, or surrounding it. The invader on the other
hand, wins if it breaks through the ranks of the patrol and
reaches the home row. In the mechanized game it is assumed
that the machine plays the invader´s role and that a human
opponent takes charge of the patrol. We also introduce a
slightly more compact notation to indicate the board state:


```
                    +1+2+3+4
                     + + + +
                    + + + +
                     + + + +
                    + + + +
                     + + + +
                    + + + +
                     + +I+ +
```


In passing, we note that there are 4368 such board states,
which is an evaluation of the expression: 16!(5!(16-5)!).

5.7 HEURISTICS

The word <u>heuristic</u> often appears in classical work in AI.
Unfortunately it does so only in loose resonance with its
meaning as defined by (say) Chamber's dictionary. In the
latter ´heuristic´ is said to mean something based on past
personal experience or self-learning, based on the Greek
<u>Heuriskein</u>: to find. In AI, on the other hand, a heuristic
search is defined as one that takes paths most likely to lead
to a goal, less promising avenues being left unexplored.

Here we can use our Trap The Invader game (TTI, from now on)
to illustrate some of the pros and cons of heuristic
programming methods in mechanized game-playing.

Every heuristic may be specified by some simple form of a
rule. An example of an everyday heuristic may be: ´If going
from London to Brighton, whenever at a junction take the fork
which points most in a Southerly direction´. It is clear
that this kind of rule will get you somewhere near Brighton,
but could just as easily miss by several miles. In TTI one
of the simplest heuristics is to assign high values to
invader moves that take the invader nearest to the home row.

An evaluation procedure which flows from this principle is to
assign a value of 7 to the home row, 6 to the one below, and
so on, leaving 0 for the starting row of the invader.
Consider the following example:

```
        -  -  -  -
        -  -4-  -
        -  -2-  -
        -3-  -  -
        -  -  -a-
        -  -I-  -
        -  -c-b-
        -  -  -  -
```

It is seen that three legal moves are available to the
invader: a, b and c. According to our heuristic these score
3, 1 and 1 respectively. The tree-search situation may be
represented simply as follows:

```
                    *
                a   b   c
                *   *   *
                3   1   1
```

Clearly it would make sense here for the invader to take the
move giving the highest score. This, however, is not always
true. Consider the following states:

```
                - - - -
                 - - - -
            -I- -3-4
            a-2- - -
            -1- - -
            b-c- - -
                - - - -
                 - - - -
```

Here again the invader has three possibilities a, b and c,
with respective values 3, 2 and 2. However, here it would be
most foolish for the invader to take the move with the
highest value since the patrol would move piece 2 into the
slot vacated by the invader, pinning it against the left edge
and winning. This does not, at this stage devalue the
concept of a heuristic rule, but merely points to the need of
looking further ahead before the rule should be applied.
Ways of doing this will now be discussed.

5.8 MINIMAX PROGRAMMING

Taking the last state above, we now look not only at the
immediate moves that the invader can take, but also at the
patrol moves that might follow, and, indeed the invader moves
that might follow the patrol. This ´tree´ is shown in Fig.
5.1, where one notes the following. The first three invader
moves are given the label ´level 1´, the following patrol
moves are at level 2, then the invader moves after that are
at level 3, and so on. At this point we note that our
heuristic does not tell us how to evaluate the patrol moves.
We choose to do this in the simplest possible way, namely we
see all moves as neutral except those which give the patrol
an outright win. Remembering that we are still looking at
the game from the point of view of the invader, we assign a

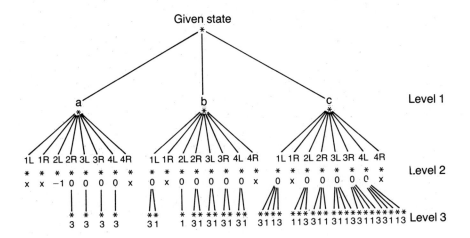

Fig. 5.1 Three-level lookahead minimax evaluation

negative value −1 (say) to a patrol win and a value of 0 to
all other patrol moves. This evaluation is shown in Fig.
5.1, where the patrol moves have been labeled XL or XR, X
being the number of the patrol member involved in the move.
Also illegal moves have been shown as ´x´.

We now look further to the next invader move, and evaluate
the possible move according to our stated heuristic. This too
is shown at level 3 in Fig. 5.1. The minimax procedure
operates as follows: (looking ahead only three levels for
purposes of illustration, the number of levels is usually
determined by how long one is prepared to wait for the
machine to make a move). Imagining that the invader is at
level 3, the player would clearly choose the move that gives
him the highest score, wherever at that level the invader
might be. This is noted by writing a new set of playing
values for each of the patrol moves, and these are precisely
the maximum values found at level 3. We show these new values
(or backup values as they are called) in the table below.

GROUP   PATROL MOVE

	1L	1R	2L	2R	3L	3R	4L	4R	
a	x	x	−1	3	3	3	3	x	
b	3	x	1	3	3	3	3	x	backup values
c	3	x	3	3	3	3	3	x	

It is noted that only those values originally assigned to 0
are replaced by backup values, since these are the only moves
from which play can proceed. Particularly one should note
that the winning move retains its negative value which is in
concord with its signification of disadvantage to the
invader.

We now repeat this procedure in looking ahead from level 1 to
level 2, but this time there is one slight difference. The
invader player must assume that the patrol player will take
the move that gives the invader least advantage. In other
words it will take the move that has the minimum backed-up
value from the next level. Clearly if the game state is a, it
is likely that the patrol player will choose move 2L which
has the winning evaluation (i.e. absolute minimum) of −1. If,
however, the state of the game is b the patrol player would,
by the same taken be expected to take move 2L which is valued
at 1. Any other would give the invader a greater advantage as

evidenced by the fact that all other backup values are 3. If
we now consider c as being the state of the game, we note
that whatever legitimate move the patrol player may take, it
will allow a value 3 move to the invader.

In this way we can develop backup values for level 1 moves
simply by choosing the minimum of the backup values at level
2.

Hence the following backup values for level 1 moves are
obtained:

MOVE	BACKUP VALUE
a	-1
b	1
c	3

Now, of course, it becomes an easy matter for the invader
player to choose the move which will, at level 3, give him
the greatest advangage, i.e. the highest backup value. That
is move c. Note how the process of choosing maxima and
minima at alternative levels gives the method its name.

5.9 ALPHA-BETA SHORT CUTS

The trouble with the minimaxing procedure just described is
that it requires full evaluation of the furthest level that
has been choosen. However this is often not necessary and
the waste in computing time may be avoided. This is done by
evaluating intermediate nodes in the tree as their backup
values become available.

The essence of the method may be gleaned by referring again
to Fig. 5.1. If we assume that the search is carried out
from left to right, at level 2 one very soon notes the
winning patrol move at 2L. This means that node ´a´ can be
given the value of -1 at that point in the search, since it
is unlikely that the patrol player will choose a less
damaging move. Not only does this avoid further search at
level 2, but also a vast amount of searching at further
levels subtended by node ´a´ is no longer necessary.

Formally, the alpha-beta procedure can be expressed as follows:

First, we define a MAX node as 'one's own node' from which one would choose a maximum decision, and similarly, a MIN node is an opponent's evaluation point from which one would choose a minimum decision. We now define as ALPHA the variable value of a MAX node obtained from depth-first searches below that node and BETA the variable value of a MIN node. One should note that ALPHA and BETA values are NOT the same as the backed-up value found during a breadth-first search. ALPHA and BETA values are altered as follows.

The ALPHA value is set to be the same as the current largest backed-up value of its direct successors, while BETA is the smallest current backed-up value of its immediate successors.

Finally, one defines search termination rules. First, one discontinues a search below a MIN node whose BETA value has fallen below (or becomes equal to) the ALPHA value of any of its MAX ancestors. Second, one discontinues the search below any MAX node whose ALPHA value has risen above (or becomes equal to) the BETA value of any of its MIN ancestors. The elegance of the procedure is due to the fact that ALPHA values of the MAX node can never decrease, while the BETA values of MIN nodes can never increase.

This all sounds a bit intertwined, so an example might help.

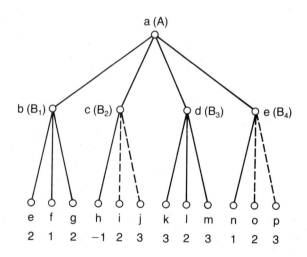

In the above search tree (a fictional one chosen for purposes of illustration only), A are the ALPHA values, while B_j are the BETA values of the nodes as shown. The dynamic evaluation process may be tabulated as below:

SEARCH   RESULT
ROUTE
----

b e
b f
b g B_1 becomes 1 as does A.

c h B_2 goes to at most -1 evoking the termination
             rule causing further searches from c to be
             abandoned.
d k
d l B_3 and A go to 2.

e n B_4 goes to 1 (less than A), further search from
             e discontinued.

It is seen that 4 out of the possible 12 third level calculations have been avoided. In deeper searches this can clearly have quite a marked effect. However, the somewhat haphazard nature of this saving ought to be noted, it depends on the order of the search. The reader can verify that the result in the above example is less impressive if the search is carried out from right to left.

5.10 LEARNING TO PLAY GAMES

So far, we have only used a heuristic to evaluate the nodes of the search tree. Samuel's first principle is satisfied (that is, that one ought to extract the features of a board state), we need however to look at the second and that is the principle of learning. That is one ought to be able to improve the evaluation strategy itself during the course of 'training the machine to play games'.

Before looking at some of the details of this, it is important to ask one very telling question: 'where does the

machine get its information?´   There are three   major
alternatives. First, the machine can be made to take note of
board states that lead to a win, etc. It would then give a
higher evaluation to states that are on a path to victory
rather than others.   This, however, means that the machine
must play a vast variety of games before a large enough set
of board states receives a sensible evaluation.

Secondly, one could design a system that effectively contains
two players, and the above procedure could be made to run at
machine speed, without human intervention.   The difficulty
here is that the two machines must somehow have built into
them a ´desire to win´, or a goal-seeking rule otherwise they
could reach stability just by playing a bad game, but
satisfying some weaker criterion such as ´the starting player
must win or draw´.   The goal-seeking rule unfortunately
reverts the machine back to playing according to   a
heuristic, and any learning that might take place would
merely shift around information already given to the machine.

The third method is one where a human player acts as a
collaborative teacher.   The interaction could take several
forms.   Either the ´teacher´ merely plays the game while the
machine updates values of board states that are selected,
devaluing those that are not, or the same value
incrementation could be achieved by a process of ´reward´ and
´punishment´ enacted by the teacher. We shall expand on this
third method so as to clarify some of the computational
issues involved.

Clearly, there are too many board states to evaluate, so,
taking Samuel´s first principle seriously and using ´Trap the
Invader´ as an example, we look for feature attributes of a
board position of which there is not an astronomical number.
The ploy adopted here is to look around five nearby positions
after the invader has taken a move.   This is illustrated
below.   Consider the immediate surrounding of an invader,
plus one extra position as shown:

                    X (c) X
                    (b) X (d)
                    X (I) X
                    (a) X (e)

The relative positions a, b, c, d, e can each have one of three values, say: 0 for an empty position, 1 for a position containing a patrol token and 2 if the position is off the board. Thus the total number of the patterns that can be found in this surround is, at most, $3^5 = 243$. Of course some of these patterns can never occur (e.g. c and a, or e, can never take up the value 2 simultaneously). In any case, the programmer need only set aside 243 variables which even in the most modest of machines, is not frightening. These variables are assigned values as the interaction with the teacher proceeds, these values representing move evaluations which can later be used in a tree searching program, instead of heuristically defined values, as discussed earlier.

Consider the following board state:

```
+ + + +
 +2+3+ +
+ + +4+
1+I+ + +
+ + + +
 + + + +
+ + + +
 + + + +
```

Clearly there are four possible ways in which the invader (whose turn it is) can go: up to left (UL), up right (UR) down left (DL) and down right (DR). We use a five digit tertiary code to indicate which 'surround variable' is found. These are of the form V_{abcde} where abcde have values from (0,1,2) as explained before. We can tabulate which variables are found for the four possible moves:

(UL): V_{100010}

(UR): V_{01010}

(DL): V_{01000}

(DR): V_{00000}

Assuming that training has just begun, we assume that all these variables are set to zero. Under such conditions, further assume that the system is merely observing the

teacher at play.   The simple learing algorithm is that   the
selected   move surround variable is incremented by one.   Or,
in a punishment-reward scheme if the machine takes the   wrong
move,   this wrong surround variable is decremented, while the
right one is incremented.   In this way,   through playing the
game in a cooperative fashion the surround variables build up
importance   values   which   are   more   pertinent   than those
obtained through a heuristic.   For example, one would expect
to   end up with V_{d222d} valued very highly (this is a   winning
move, $\underline{d}$ meaning $\acute{}$don$\acute{}$t care$\acute{}$)while V_{22d10} would have a   very
low value due to the possibility of remaining trapped.

Clearly, $\acute{}$Trap the Invader$\acute{}$ is a highly localized game,   but
the   reduction   of   large   numbers of   board   states   to   the
existence or otherwise of playing features can be extended to
most games,   as evidenced by Samuel$\acute{}$s work in respect of the
game of checkers.   Now let us turn to the business of playing
games in a broader context,   and that is the issue of general
solutions to problems.

5.11 PROBLEM SOLVING

It is interesting that the classical problem-solving scenario
is set in the context of a robot with a stated task.   Let us
say that the problem is simplified down to a world consisting
of two equally sized blocks A and B, and a robot arm which is
capable   of picking up and putting down one block at a   time.
The task is,   say,   one of getting from a state where block B
is on top of block A to a state where this is reversed,   that
is, A on B.

A very simple way of arranging this problem in   computational
terms,   is   to concentrate on two entities,   the state of the
scene and the rules whereby this state can be changed.   Take
the state first.

There are two kinds of object in the problem,   blocks and the
hand.   The   former   can be associated   with   either   nothing
(denoted by 0) when its top is clear,   or another block which
may   be   resting directly above.   A state may   include   such
conditions in the form of statements such as:

ON (B,A) or, perhaps ON (A,0)

meaning that B has A above it or that A has nothing above it respectively. Similarly one can include the state of the hand:

HOLD (H,A) or, perhaps HOLD (H,0)

meaning that the hand (H) is holding A or is empty, respectively.

One can now specify the complete state of the scene as the conjunction (using AND) of all these conditions. For example the following ´formula´ indicates the starting state for the above problem:

ON (A,B) AND ON (B,0) AND HOLD (H,0).

In a complete program one could assign truth values to arrays called ON and HOLD in order to establish the above, and the state of the problem would then merely be the content of such arrays. Clearly the target state could be expressed as:

ON (B,A) AND ON (A,0) AND HOLD (H,0).

Developments of this type of formulation are referred to as PREDICATE formulae, and manipulations of these are possible which are called PREDICATE CALCULUS. An example of such manipulation is the second of our important entities, that is the set of rules whereby that state may be changed.

Typically such rules have the following form. First there are rules that test the state of the problem in order to see what is the possible set of actions that may ensue. For example, if ON (P,0) implies PICKUP(P), where the latter is a subroutine that in the actual problem world would cause the machine to find and pick up block P. Indeed, to be more precise, this rule would have to be formulated as

ON (P,0) AND HOLD (H,0) implies PICKUP(P),

in order to make sure that the hand is empty before it attempts to do any picking up.

To complete that change of state, having selected one possible action, one needs to make reference to further

rules.   For example, PICKUP (P) <u>implies</u> HOLD (H,P) where the
latter is a variable of the next state.   Also PUTDOWN   (P,Q)
could be seen as a rule <u>implied by</u> part of a state HOLD (H,P)
AND ON (Q,O).   These   rules   are   given   the   name   FORWARD
PRODUCTIONS in predicate calculus formulations.

Clearly,   every state does not imply only one action, so that
the   states and their choices of actions form a tree such   as
found   in   game – playing.   The tree has to be searched   for
arriving at the target state.   Before asking whether one can
take short cuts in this tree-searching application similar to
those   taken   in game-playing,   we shall follow   through   the
above 2-block example.

State 1:
          ON (A,B) AND ON (B,O) AND HOLD (H,O)

Possible Actions:
          PICKUP (B)

States at level 2: (there is only one)
          ON (A,O) AND HOLD (H,B)

Possible Actions:
          PUTDOWN (B,A) or PUTDOWN (B,O)
          (latter refers to the table)
Resulting states at level 3:
          ON (A,B) AND ON (B,O) AND HOLD (H,O)....state 3.1
          ON (A,O) AND ON (B,O) AND HOLD (H,O)....state 3.2

Clearly   state   3.1 is merely a repetition of what   has   gone
before,   and need not be pursued.   Then a brief inspection of
further development of the tree shows that actions PICKUP (A)
and PUTDOWN (A,B) achieve the desired target.

In this case the searching is not too taxing an affair, while
in more complicated robot worlds the search tree could become
quite   immense.   So,   in this kind of problem   solving   too,
there have been attempts to short-cut the search procedure.

We shall briefly refer to two such methodologies.

The first of these rests in the realization that BACKWARD productions could be defined with as much ease as the forward ones seen earlier. In fact, in this particular example, due to the reversible nature of the robot-arm operations, the backward productions are identical to the forward ones. So, in theory, one can grow trees both from the current state and the goal state simultaneously and find a path between these two where the trees meet. Clearly this reduces the ´breadth´ to which such trees could grow. The use of combined forward and backward deduction is central to the well-known robot-planning program STRIPS, described by Fikes and Nielsson (1971).

The second short-cut is a bit like the now-familiar heuristic. A means is found for measuring the ´distance´ between a state and the goal. For example, in a block-heaping exercise such as the one in the example seen in this section, one can count the number of blocks that have been heaped from the table upwards in the correct order. Then one has an evaluation measure to guide the tree search. Again this can be done in both a backward and forward fashion, that is, the backward action acting as a set of sub-goals for the task. This method may be found in the fundamental paper by Newell, Shaw and Simon (1960) on what they called the General Problem Solver (GPS).

To sum up the significance of game-playing and problem solving in the context of automation, it is worth realizing that in automated processes of the future there will come a point where the state of a process will be available through a set of measurements and this will have to be compared to a production target. Getting from one to the other will be a matter of strategy, and the short cut techniques discovered by computer scientists while playing games may well come into play.

We now continue the discussion of the relevance of artificial intelligence to automation by taking a closer look at the difficult question of the measurement of a process. Particularly problematic is the situation where this measurement has to be of a kind that extends human vision.

5.12 ARTIFICIAL VISION (IN SIMPLIFIED WORLDS)

Skipping directly to the truth of the matter, one finds that
many years of effort in artificial intelligence have not come
up with a system that is adequately capable of describing
even as simple a scene as a handful of nuts and bolts. In a
later discussion we shall look at some methodologies that go
under the head of ´pattern recognition´ where greater success
have been obtained on the <u>classification</u> of scenes into
categories. This work was able to stretch into the world of
reality, while the aims of artificial intelligence for vision
go a little beyond the need for classification. The aim is
to observe a scene, perhaps through the eye of a TV camera,
feed the digitized result to a computer which then describes
the scene in terms of it component parts. Ideally, one would
wish an output such as:

        Size 6 nut flat, orientation 5deg. position 34,897 mm.
        Size 4 nut 40% threaded on 1" bolt orientation.

Although, as has been said, such a performance may not be
entirely within grasp, a great deal of effort has gone into
moving towards this position, and again many worthwhile
techniques have emerged which are sure to have a place in
computing for automation in the future.

5.13 REAL TO STYLIZED WORLDS

In every real scene analysis situation the scene must be
conveyed to the computer by means of some kind of optical
transducer. Although one can imagine several sophisticated
arrangements of laser and light-stripe range-finding methods,
probably the most cost-effective way of looking at a real
scene is by means of a simple Vidicon line-scan camera or its
solid-state equivalent. A coding device is usually employed
to turn the real image into a series of numbers, each
representing the light intensity of a dot in the image (such
dots are called pixels).

So, even if the real scene contains highly simplified objects
in it (say simple rectangular blocks) much of the real

straightness of lines may have been destroyed if not by the
quantized nature of the computer image, then possibly by the
presence of camera ´noise´. Most of the ´intelligence´ work
done in vision has been based on the fact that some skillful
image processing has already been done on the raw image made
of numbers.

Such processing usually takes the form of sequential phases,
for example, the first phase might find the edges of objects
and the second might realign them so as to form sensible
objects. It is noted that the second of these phases assumes
some knowledge of the nature of the objects.

For example, if blocks are known to be in the scene, one can
reorientate lines so that three would meet to form a true
corner rather than a disembodied group of lines.

5.14 A STORED KNOWLEDGE OF GEOMETRY

Amongst the early attempts at the design of programs that
describe visual scenes is that of Roberts (1965).   This
relied very heavily on storing the rules of projective
geometry in the machine, in order to describe the objects in
view. To illustrate this consider the wedge-and-block images
shown in Fig. 5.2. Roberts´ program was entirely limited to
such shapes, and relied heavily on the existence of a line-
finding and corner-adjusting program, such as described
earlier, in order to provide near-perfect line-drawing
representations of the objects.

The first step is to identify the corners of the line drawing
by looking either for line direction changes, or specific
line meeting points (e.g. 1 and 3 in Fig. 5.2(a),
respectively). One then notes the connections between the
corners, and stores the result in (say) matrix form.   For
example, all the information regarding the image in Fig.
5.2(a) can be indicated on a suitable matrix.   In such a
matrix the rows and columns are labeled with corner numbers,
and a 1 is entered in the matrix if the two corresponding
corners are connected.

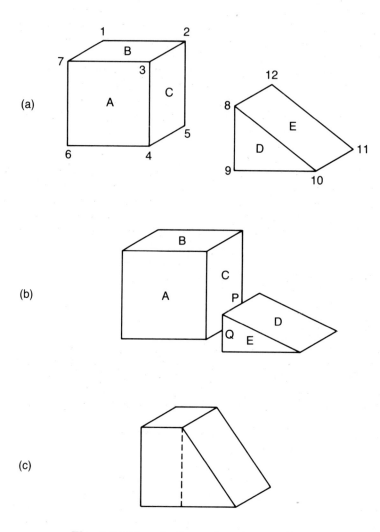

Fig. 5.2 2-D projections of wedges and boxes

For Fig. 5.2 we have:

	1	2	3	4	5	6	7	8	9	10	11	12
1	1	1	0	0	0	0	1	0	0	0	0	0
2	1	1	1	0	1	0	0	0	0	0	0	0
3	0	1	1	1	0	0	1	0	0	0	0	0
4	0	0	1	1	1	1	0	0	0	0	0	0
5	0	1	0	1	1	0	0	0	0	0	0	0
6	0	0	0	1	0	1	1	0	0	0	0	0
7	1	0	1	0	0	1	1	0	0	0	0	0
8	0	0	0	0	0	0	0	1	1	1	0	1
9	0	0	0	0	0	0	0	1	1	1	0	0
10	0	0	0	0	0	0	0	1	1	1	1	0
11	0	0	0	0	0	0	0	0	0	1	1	1
12	0	0	0	0	0	0	0	1	0	0	1	1

Several things can be noted from this matrix. First, any decomposition of the matrix will show that the group 8, 9, 10 11 and 12 is independent of the rest, indicating a separate object. Also, given that dead-on viewing is unlikely, all box-like shapes will result in the same 7x7 matrix under relabeling of the corners. Clearly, wedges too will result in either the same 5x5 matrix, or an alternative 6x6 one (the reader might care to work out the reason for the latter personally).

The method is powerful enough to deal with some degree of covering by one object of another. For example, in Fig. 5.2(b), provided that the system is programmed to ignore 'T' junctions such as Q and P, all that occurs in the 12x12 matrix is that row and column 5 disappear. However, the true meaning of the scene could still be retrieved if one were to allow 'near miss' matching methods in the comparison of matrices.

Finally, it is worth noting the Roberts' paper suggests ways in which one can introduce further properties of projections of 3-D objects into two dimensions. For example, notions of parallelism of lines would cause the system to realize that the shape in Fig. 5.2(c) was not a box, but could be thought of as a composition of a box and a wedge, as indicated by the dotted line.

5.15 A BETTER USE OF CUES

It was realized by several workers in the artificial vision
field that a heavy reliance on projective geometry was likely
to lead to a heavy computational overhead (remembering the
need for making permutation matches, and near-miss matches on
large connectivity matrices). Thus several projects sought
to make a better use of visual clues and their direct
implication on what can be concluded from viewing a scene.
After all, people make such assessments with no conscious
reference to projective geometry at all.

The pioneering work was started at MIT by Adolfo Guzman
(1969) and later elaborated by Max Clowes (1971) at the
University of Sussex in the UK. Here we report only on some
of the main principles involved leaving the reader to follow
up the details in the literature quoted above.

The central idea in this work is that local cues such as 3
etc. in Fig. 5.2(a) and P in Fig. 5.2(b) provide relations
between the surfaces of a line drawing. Thus a first step in
the right direction is to identify surfaces and distinguish
them from background. This is done by labeling all surfaces
which are completely enclosed by the lines found through
line-finding programs. In the example of Fig. 5.2(a) the
program would find areas A, B, C, D and E as shown.

The ´forks´ and ´T-junctions´ are then given a meaning which
indicates whether the feature relates surfaces in the same
object, or separates objects. For example, the ´star´
feature 3 relates surfaces A, B and C to one another and as
belonging to the same object. On the other hand, a feature
such as P (a ´T-junction´) separates C and D out as belonging
to different objects. The end point of this computation is
in the form of a graph where the verticals are the surfaces
and the edges are the corner feature. One notes that there
is a certain degree of redundancy in this representation as
the features support each other´s evidence. This can be used
in dealing with obscured features. Indeed, one notes in the
resulting graph below, that the P and Q features merely act
in a supporting role, the graphs resulting from (a) and (b)
being otherwise identical.

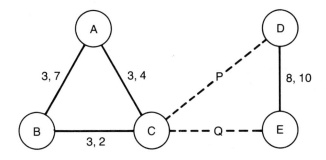

Fig. 5.3 Graph representation of Figs. 5.2(a) and 5.2(b)

This type of approach has proven itself to be quite
fundamental and has been extended into areas of images that
contain curved objects and shadows (see Turner, 1974). On
the negative side, however, this method relies heavily on a
careful study of the problem area, and the intelligence is
achieved through a human spotting of relationships between
cues and image items, rather than a subsequent computer run.

5.16 COMPOSITE STRUCTURES: SEMANTIC NETWORKS

P.H. Winston (1975) took the concept of a representational
graph such as the one shown in Fig. 5.3, further into the
realm of representations of composite objects. For example,
a typical composite object is the group in Fig. 5.4(a). The
aim of Winston's methodology is to create a graph, called a
semantic network in which the nodes represent single objects
and the edges represent the relationships between these
objects.

A typical semantic network is shown in Fig. 5.4(c). It is
intended that such a network structure be stored (perhaps as
a database) so that if an unknown image were turned into a

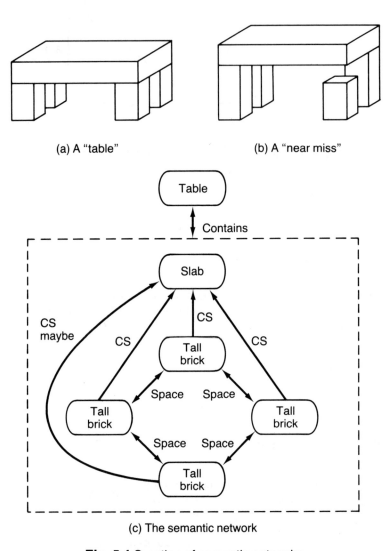

(a) A "table"   (b) A "near miss"

(c) The semantic network

Fig. 5.4 Creation of semantic networks

similar network, one could initiate a search procedure which would hopefully terminate in a match. The search network would differ from the target one only in terms of the lack of labeling of the top node. We note that it is this top node which carries the identification of the composite object, so that the search match can enable the computer to exclaim 'this is a table'.

The way in which such networks are built relies on an element of 'training'. Winston recommends using not only actual examples of the composite objects in question, but also 'near misses' which would serve to define the relationship between parts, by showing which relationships lead to NOT-objects. For example, the near-miss in Fig. 5.4(b) would strengthen the relationship between the legs of the table and the top slab, in the sense that the relationship must be one of support rather than overhang. Also showing 'near-misses' where the legs are badly placed under the table would refine the relationship to one of 'corner support' (CS).

It is interesting that the fourth leg may or may not be seen, and the 'maybe' relationship takes care of this degree of freedom.

The structural representations introduced by Winston and his semantic networks, may, in fact, be seen as just one step in database structures for the representation of knowledge in general. The reader is advised to follow up his interest in this field by reading Minsky's work on frames (1975).

5.17 ARTIFICIAL VISION IN REAL WORLDS AND ROBOTS

In the context of real automation it is vital to raise that central question: 'Can one transfer what has been learned from artificial vision, in the over-simplified worlds above, into the real world of the needs of the production engineer?' First, however, one must ask the supplementary question as to where such needs might arise.

A new buzzword has recently entered the vocabulary of the
production engineer: ROBOTICS. This usually refers to
situations where a mechanical arm is used to carry out
repetitive production tasks. The level of ´intelligence´ of
such devices has been rather low in the sense that they are
´taught´ tasks such as picking an object placed in a well-
defined position and placing it onto another well-defined
place. The original moves are made with the aid of a human
operator, stored as instructions for a series of stepping
motors at the joints of the arm, and repeated as long as
required.

A defined need exists for artificial vision in this context,
as one could then relax considerably the need for perfect
placing of objects. One could also envisage robot arms
operating in confusing environments where parts of many kinds
would be presented to the robot and it, having analyzed the
scene, could pursue an assembly task unaided (by a human
being, that is).

Using the artificial vision techniques discussed earlier, the
central worry lies in the area of whether methods developed
for stylized objects such as boxes and wedges placed in ideal
lighting conditions can be applied to highly variable and
ill-defined set of shapes found in industrial assembly tasks.
Unfortunately there is not one single answer to these
questions. On the one hand, where scenes consist solely of
hexagonal nuts and standard bolts, it is conceivable that
Guzman/Clowes methods could cope. Indeed, at the Stanford
Research Institute, scenes containing the parts of an engine
(crankshafts, connecting rods, castings, etc.) have been
analyzed using a related methodology. However, this does not
apply in other areas, where the number of parts is very large
and alters as part of the natural developments of the
product. An example of such an industry is the toy car model
manufacturer. Toy designers bring out new models by the
week, and Guzman/Clowes methods would require not only a
redrafting of the basic algorithms, but also Winston-type
semantic nets would grow enormously with the need to
recognize subtle differences between parts. It will be
argued in a later chapter that good vision systems in such
realistic applications are best served by techniques that go
under the heading of ´pattern recognition´ rather than
artificial intelligence.

There remains, however, a very important area of work which
is related, in AI, to robotic situations, and that is the
need to communicate with such machines in a simple but
relatively natural language. This need is quite powerful in
the sense that the need to learn a special language to
operate a computer is an imposition on the human being
anyway. In the context of a factory operative it becomes
more that that, it turns out to be a total lack of reality.
We look at such efforts next.

5.18 TALKING TO ROBOTS

The foundational step in this area is due to Terry Winograd
(1972) and stems from the need to extend the processes of
checking the syntactic correctness of a language to
extracting meaning, that is, formally attacking the question
of semantics.

A classical example of a syntactically correct statement is:

'little green ideas sleep furiously'.

Clearly, there is a need to check such statements in the real
world in order to discover whether they make sense or not.
Particularly in the realm of robotics, it is vital that the
machine should be able to extract the meaning of statements
relating to its field of view, and react to them accordingly.

To illustrate the process, we refer to a highly simplified
world of shadows of nuts and bolts such as shown in Fig. 5.5.

One can imagine that these are going past a camera and that
the machine is capable of recognizing the items. We assume
that only two sizes of each item are available and that the
system is equipped with a robot arm. The first step is to
develop a grammar with which sentences relating to this
simple world can be created:

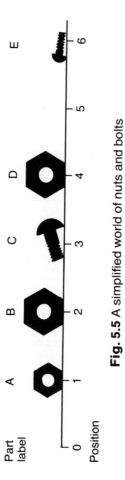

Fig. 5.5 A simplified world of nuts and bolts

```
(sentence)  := (question)/(assertion)/(command)*
(question)  := Is (nounphrase)(relation)(nounphrase)?
(assertion) := (nouph) is (relation) (nouph)
(command)   := Pick (nouph)
               /Pick (nouph)(relation)(nounphrase)
               /Place(nouph)(relation)(nounphrase)
(nouph)     := (article)(adjective)(noun)(article)(noun)
(relation)  := to the left of/to the right of
(article)   := the/a
(noun)      := nut/bolt
(adjective) := big/small
```

This indicates that there are three types of sentences one
can use in the language: questions, assertions and commands.

Examples of these are:

assertion: a small nut is to the left of the large bolt;

question: is a large nut to the left of the small bolt?

command: pick a large bolt to the right of the small nut.

These sentences are seen as being input by a human user of
the machine. So the first step is for the machine to be able
to check the grammatical validity of the sentences. This is
done using conventional parsing techniques as shown below.


```
        IS A LARGE NUT TO LEFT OF THE SMALL BOLT?

        art  adj  nou -----rel----- art  adj  nou

        nounphr----                 ----nouph----

        ------------------question------------------
```

---

* Notation: non-terminals are placed in brackets,
   := reads ´becomes´, / means ´or´ (as in Chapter 3)

In order to translate the above procedure one starts by
defining a four-heading database.

LABEL	NAME	SIZE	POSITION
A	nut	small	1
B	nut	large	2
C	bolt	large	3
D	nut	large	4
E	bolt	small	6

One then creates sets and set operations that are related to
the symbols and production rules of the language.   Examples
are given below:

$$
\begin{aligned}
\text{(noun)} &:- \{ABCDE\} \\
\text{nut} &:- \{ABD\} \\
\text{bolt} &:- \{CE\} \\
\text{large} &:- \{BCD\} \\
\text{small} &:- \{AE\}
\end{aligned}
$$

(relation): the conjunction of all sets of objects that stand
in the given relation in a translated set.

An example, this is the case where, if the translated set is,
say, {CD}, and the relation 'to the left of' the result of
the relation operation is to yield

$$\{AB\} \; U \; \{ABC\} = \{ABC\}$$

(adjective)(noun): this translates as the conjunction of the
sets involved. For example, (small)(bolt) yields

$$\{AE\} \; \& \; \{CE\} = \{E\}$$

Where the system has parsed out a question, it either returns
the contents of a set, or answers in the negative.   For
example if the question were:

IS THERE A SMALL NUT TO THE LEFT OF THE LARGE BOLT?

it should answer   YES, A.

While the answer to the question:

IS THERE A SMALL BOLT TO THE LEFT OF THE LARGE NUT?

should simply be:

NO.

Similarly a statement would return either TRUE or FALSE, while a command would complain if the instruction is impossible or ambiguous, or proceed with planning its execution if the command is clear. Let us follow through the procedure as it occurs for the input IS A LARGE NUT TO THE LEFT OF THE SMALL BOLT?, as before.

The step-by-step translation of this takes the following form:

IS A {BCD}&{ABD} TO THE LEFT OF THE {AE}&{CE} ?

IS A   {BD}   TO THE LEFT OF THE   {E}   ?

IS A   {BD} &   {ABCD}   ?

IS A   {BD}   ?

At this point the parser recognizes the question and notes the answer set, replying: YES, BD.

5.19 THE AUTOMATED EXPERT

Much of the effort in artificial intelligence has, in the early 1980s focused in an area known as ´expert systems´. The central quest here is to effect a transfer of knowledge between an expert in a particular field and a computer program. The latter could then be interrogated by a non-expert who would be able to access the stored knowledge. Part of this interaction would be devoted to the ability of the machine to answer questions about the advice it was offering.

In the context of automation, the expert system could be seen
as an aid for the production engineer. One can imagine a
conversation between the computer and the production engineer
which may go a little like this:

PE: The yield in line B is 18% low. Product throughput
      at checkpoint 3 is normal.

CO: Is the workforce distribution normal?

PE: Yes. Why?

CO: Area 3.6 is sensitive to workforce reduction
      because of production pileups. Check material
      supplies at area 3.2.

PE: Wait.

CO: OK.

PE: Material 90% of normal at area 3.2

CO: Likely cause of problem: material shortage at area
      3.2.

PE: Why?

CO: Point 3.2 is sensitive to material shortage because
      operator efficiency drops as a result of the need
      to place forward flow items in a buffer.

      etc.

Michie (1980) has written a brief but useful overview of the
nature of expert systems. Here we touch only briefly on some
of the broadest characteristics of such systems. Primarily
an expert system must consist of two well-matched parts: a
flexible database, and a programming system capable of
coping with problems of inference and deduction.

Databases in expert systems are generally known as 'knowledge
bases'. They consist mainly of rules which are addressed by
looking for a match with the requirements of the problem in
hand. In the context of the above example, rules may
be stored in the knowledge base as:

Field 1	Field 2	Field 3
Rule 1		
Poor workforce distribution	Low yield	Pileups
Rule 2		
Material shortage	Low yield in specific areas given by table X	Efficiency drop due to operators placing forward flow in buffer

In such an arrangement, field 1 holds the cause, field 2 the
result and field 3 the explanatory reason. The request for
help with a given problem causes a search for a match in
field 2.

In this case, the first match for a 'low yield' request is
satisfied by rule 1 suggesting its probable cause in the
computer output. On discounting cause, the system goes on
to discover the next cause (and location by lookup table) as
shown. Explanations are read out from field 3 if and when
required. Clearly, this is a much simplified view of what
could amount to be an enormously complex database. More
sophisticated examples may be found in abundancy in the
literature referenced by Michie (1980).

On the side of the required program, a development of a
language called PROLOG has been hailed by many as being the
ideal communication medium for expert systems (Kowalski,
1974). This language is based entirely on principles of
predicate calculus, and programs in it are written as a
sequence of facts and rules, the rules being mainly
implications as in the example above.

A program (i.e. the search for a cause or an explanation in
an expert system) is 'called' by some result whose
implications have to be found. Thus PROLOG directly operates
at the level of 'backward deduction' required by an expert
system. This facility not only makes it easy to deduce
causes from phenomena by implicative rules, but also makes

the job of creating the database a simple matter of making
implicative statements, which to PROLOG are merely part of
its language.

5.20 CONCLUSION

There is no doubt that AI has provided programming methods
which are usable in machines of any size. This means that,
in the context of digital systems AI programs could become
part of a larger system and become the components of a
system.

On a grander scale, the question of whether such programs can
be pushed up the 'intelligence' scale remains with us.
Further ideas along these lines will be discussed in Chapter
6.

QUESTIONS

1. Explain and illustrate the use of the following concepts
    in artificial intelligence:

    > Minimaxing
    > Alpha-beta assessment
    > Forward/backword productions
    > Heuristic searches

2. a) Discuss briefly the steps that have to be taken to
    cause a computer, connected to a TV camera, to analyze
    and describe a simple polyhedral scene.

    b) Explain the role of 'translation' in the context of an
    interaction in 'natural language' with a computer
    operating on a simplified world containing only
    colored blocks.

3. Distinguish between the following approaches to problem
    solving:

                    General Problem Solver
                    Robot Plan Formation
                    Logical Statement Proofs

Given the initial and final states of a simple robot
task, discuss the way in which one might find sequences
that solve the problem on a computer.

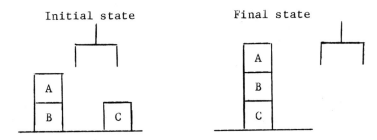

In your answer illustrate the terms:

                    Predicate Calculus State Descriptions
                    Forward and Backward Production Rules

4. Think of applications of expert systems which are
    feasible and write them down. Now think of areas where
    the expert system approach would not work. Explain the
    reasons for creating the distinction.

REFERENCES

Ambler, A.P., et al. (1975) ´A Versatile System for Computer-controlled Assembly´, Artificial Intelligence 6, 129-156.

Boden, M. (1977) ´Artificial Intelligence and Natural Man´, Harvester Press.

Clowes, M.B. (1971) ´On Seeing Things´, Artificial Intelligence 2, 79-116.

Fikes, R.E., and Nielsson, N.J. (1971) ´STRIPS: A New Approach to the Application of Theorem Proving to Problem Solving´, Artificial Intelligence 2 (3/4), 189-208.

Guzman, A. (1969) ´Decomposition of a Visual Field into 3-D Objects´ in ´Automatic Interpretation and Clarification of Images´ ed. A. Grasselli pp.243-276, Academic Press.

Kowlaski, R. (1974) ´Predicate Logic as a Programming Language, Information Processing, North-Holland, Amsterdam, pp. 569-574.

Lighthill, J. (1973) ´A Report on Artificial Intelligence´, UK Science Research Council, London.

Michie, D. (1980) ´Expert Systems´, Computer Journal 23 and 24.

Minsky, M. (1975) ´A Framework for Representing Knowledge´, in ´The Psychology of Computer Vision´, Ed. P.H. Winston, McGraw-Hill, New York, pp. 211-277.

Newell, A., Shaw, J., and Simon, H. (1960) ´Report on a General Problem Solving Program for a Computer´, Information Processing: Doc. International Conference at IP UNESCO PARIS, pp. 256-264.

Nielson, N.J. (1980) ´Principles of Artificial Intelligence´ Tioga Press, Palo Alto, California.

Pask, G., (1981) ´Principles of Cybernetics´, Hutchinsons.

Roberts, L.G. (1965) ´Machine Perception of 3-D Solids´, in ´Optical and Electro-Optical Information Processing´, eds. J.T. Tippett et al., pp. 159-198, MIT Press, Cambridge, Mass.

Rosen, C.A. (1968) ´Machines that Act Intelligently´, Science Journal 4 (10), 109-114.

Samuel, A.L. (1959) ´Some Studies in Machine Learning Using the Game of Checkers´, IBM Journal of R&D 3, 211-229.

Shannon, C.E. (1950) ´Programming a Computer for Playing Chess´, Philosophical Magazine (Series 7) 41, 256-275.

Turner, K.S. (1974) ´Computer Perception of Curved Objects´, Proc. AISB Conference, University of Sussex, pp. 238-246.

Winograd, T. (1972) ´Understanding Natural Languages´, Edinburgh University Press.

Winston, P.H. (1975) ´Learning Structured Descriptions from Examples´ in ´The Psychology of Computer Vision´, ed. P.H. Winston, McGraw-Hill, pp. 157-210.

Chapter 6

Practical pattern recognition

T J Stonham

6.1 IS IT DIFFICULT FOR COMPUTERS TO RECOGNIZE PATTERNS?

As we scan over the words of this page and translate the symbols into meaning, our eyes and brain are busy doing an intricate data processing task. This happens to be called 'pattern recognition'.

When human beings recognize patterns it seems easy and natural. Maybe that is because we do it almost all the time, not only when reading or looking at pictures, but when driving a car, playing tennis, saying hello to the cat or assembling a watch. All these tasks involve an element of pattern recognition.

So, it is hardly surprising that in the automation of production processes there is a need for mechanized, or computerized, pattern recognition schemes. This is not a new revelation, indeed, attempts at computer-based pattern recognition date almost as far back in technological history as the computer itself.

As a result of this, it appears curious that pattern recognition should be seen as a difficult problem in an age when microprocessors are seen to be doing <u>everything</u> from playing Beethoven's Fifth Symphony on a wristwatch (in a key to suit one's mood) to cooking steak to tender perfection in an automated microwave oven. However, the difficulties are considerable and over the years have, at times, appeared insurmountable.

The problem is almost always underestimated by the potential user. This is perhaps because of the natural ability and skill we as humans display when recognizing patterns. We are able to read the print on this page and do not have to define a set of rules and conditions in order to interpret the letters, words and syntax. Any machine which attempts to emulate this process must be supplied with the rules or have some method of evolving them.

A conventional computer requires rules, in the form of a program, in order to interpret data. The final performance, leaving aside any operating speed constraints, will depend on

the validity of these rules. In situations where rules are
not available or not used by the human, and he relies on
intuition or some natural ability to recognize speech or
faces or the like, we have an insuperable problem, as far as
programming a computer to do the task is concerned.

An alternative approach is where the system is self-evolving
and forms its own rules. However this necessitates a
suitable processing structure The performance of this system
will be limited both by the data available to formulate the
rules and also the adequacy of the processing structure.

In view of the human's undeniable expertise in pattern
recognition, it is not surprising that researchers have
looked towards the brain and neural models, in order to find
clues as to how pattern recognition can best be implemented.
After all, the brain is processing binary information in the
form of the firing of cells and operating on data which can
be represented in a digital form either via the eyes or other
sensory organs.

On looking very superficially at brain structures, it is
obvious that we are not dealing with a serial Von Neumann
machine, we do not have a memory and a processor with
information being continually transferred to the processor,
where it is operated on according to a stored set of rules
and then returned to the memory. The brain is clearly a
much more parallel cellular processor than a conventional
computer. Here lies the first clue to the structure of our
pattern recognizer – a parallel processor is essential.

Electronic hardware and data transmission systems already
operate several orders of magnitude faster than neurons.
Information propagation speeds are of the order of 10^8 m/s
in electronic systems as opposed to a 10^2 m/s transmission
speed in nerves. Hence an electronic processor is not likely
to be limited by speed at the cell level. If a suitable
structure could be specified for a pattern recognizer, it is
likely that current technology would allow operating speeds
far in excess of pattern recognition by humans. The machine
approach would also overcome the human failings due to tedium
and inconsistency arising from distraction, boredom and
general lack of concentration that we all suffer from when
performing a repetitive task over long periods.

In order to obtain a more precise idea of the structure of
the brain, one could attempt to explore it. Apart from the
moral and ethical objections to this approach, it is unlikely
that we should make very much progress because of the
complexity of the system. A typical human brain has about
10^{10} cells, and each cell can have up to 5,000 inputs. We
can compare the problem of discovering how it works with that
of unraveling the detailed structure of a large computer
without having any knowledge of computers or the relevant
circuit diagrams or operating manuals. We would be unlikely
to get beyond finding the on/off switch.

At the brain cell level, however, we have a much more
detailed knowledge of the processes which take place. The
McCulloch and Pitts model of the neuron was proposed in 1946,
and this in itself provides a structure for pattern
recognition in the form of a linear discriminant function
which can be implemented as an analog circuit or simulated
on a general purpose computer. Furthermore, if a threshold
is applied to the weighted inputs of this neuron model, the
processing performed by the cell can be regarded as a Boolean
function of its inputs, and this can be implemented as a
logic function in a random access memory. Both these
implementations will be examined later in this chapter.

6.2 WHO NEEDS PATTERN RECOGNITION?

Since the late 1950s the driving force for automatic pattern
recognition was not commercial but military. Could one
process a picture of the jungle taken from a helicopter
hovering over Korea and work out whether there were any
hidden tanks or anti-aircraft guns in the image? Then, in
the early 1960s, postal engineers all over the world thought
it would be nice to have automatic reading machines which
would decipher postal codes even if written in an untidy
scrawl. Strangly enough, neither of these applications had
enough force to bring pattern recognition to life in a
commercial sense, perhaps because most methodologies just did
not work fast enough nor have a commercially acceptable cost
using the technology of the day.

It now seems clear that there are two major areas where a

sophisticated electronic eye and a silicon-chip brain are needed: the first of these being the automatic production line. The sorting of pieceparts and the control of their quality is central to the automation process. The second broad area is simply that of automatic reading: postal codes if needs be, but more pertinently, data on checks, census forms, supermarket labels, VAT forms, library tickets, passports, banker´s cards and so on. On the whole, it seem as if wherever one finds human drudgery, there is a requirement for automatic pattern recognition.

It should be said that here one is <u>not</u> trading in redundancy for all production-line workers and clerks. As in the case with all really worthwhile instances of automation, the cost-effectiveness comes from the fact that all new techology promises an extension and development of what has up till now been done with human effort alone. As an example, some manufacturers of roller bearings can only afford to examine their products on a sample basis. However, it has been shown that serious failures do not always happen as a result of faults distributed in a neat statistical way that can be spotted in a sample. It´s the crack in the odd item that can be disastrous. But still, the quality control engineer has to weigh up this low probability against the cost (and operator boredom) of inspecting every part.

The Public Records Officer (as an example of the second broad area of automation) has lorry loads of documents on which the writing is slowly fading away. It would take a vast army of typists to enter the information they contain into computers. This is a clear case for automatic reading, where the eventual pay-off has a human rather than a direct, commercial advantage. In a similar vein the reading of print in all fonts as an aid <u>for the blind</u> has undeniable human value. This <u>has</u> to be cheap if it is to be purchased by the blind.

In medicine as a whole, there is a vast set of needs for automatic vision systems ranging from screening (e.g. cervical smears, X-ray plates) to the simple problem of sorting medicament packages through reading codes that are also readable by humans. (At present color coding or bar coding is machine readable, but this leaves a possible credibility gap since the machine and the human read <u>different</u> data.)

On the other hand the <u>automatic verification of signatures</u> on
checks   is   a   highly   cost-effective   machine-reading
application. Most clearing banks need to refer checks to the
originating   branch   for a verification of the fact that   the
signature   bears some resemblance to that of   their   client.
The   major   source of fraud which necessitates these   massive
transfers   of paper is the instance where,   after stealing   a
check book,   the thief signs the customer's name on the check
in   his   own   handwriting - given that the   owner's   name   is
clearly written in the bottom right-hand corner of the check.
Expert   forgers   who can sign at speed are few,   and   do   not
cause   much concern.   Thus an automatic verification   system
which   relates the signature to a set of check digits on   the
check would save the vast sums which are at present   spent on
just moving bits of paper between banks.

Also,   in security appplications the recognition of   personal
characteristics   other   than signatures   is   pertinent.   For
example,   it would be useful to check faces,   or fingerprints
as a means of personal identification.   Indeed, still in the
security area,   the state of occupation of an entire building
could   be checked by an effective vision system shared   among
many television cameras.

Under   the   buzzword 'robotics' there is the obvious area   of
vision   for industrial automation processes, including giving
sight to manipulator-arm robots.   These find their way   into
production   processes   ranging from welding of car bodies   to
the   grading   of   apples.   In   fact,   wherever   there   is   a
conveyor-belt   type   of   production   process there   is   an
application   for a vision system,   comprising a   good   vision
transducer backed by a fast and reliable pattern classifier.

The input transducer is,   after the processor structure,   the
most important element of the pattern recognition system.   In
a   general system the specification must be adequate to cover
a   range of applications and the resolution sufficient to   be
able   to detect pattern characteristics.   In practice   it   is
preferable   to optimize and refine,   and perhaps simplify,   a
system in terms of cost or complexity,   than to find that   it
is incapable of dealing with a problem when confronted with a
real   working situation,   because of a lack of resolution or
information   regarding the range of data to   be   encountered.
This   has   been   the case with so   many   pattern   recognition
systems in the past.

6.3 WHAT THE AUTOMATIC EYE NEEDS TO SEE

Probably the cheapest and most reliable vision transducer is the television camera. Also, since some of the tasks for vision automation fall into the category of those distinguishable by the human eye on a TV screen, the resolution and accuracy of a TV image appears reasonable for a general-purpose machine. This would clearly include not only Vidicon systems as used at present in TV, but also solid state devices such as photodiode arrays and charge-coupled devices.

However, the point of this discussion is to calculate the amount of data that one should aim to process in a general-purpose vision system. Working with the nearest power of 2, and square, black-white images one takes 512 vertical and horizontal samples (which is 2^9 the nearest value to the 625 lines resolved by a household TV set) and converts the image into 512x512 dots called 'pixels'.

The number of intensity levels between black and white needed at each pixel to give a visually smooth image is typically 16 (i.e. 2^4). This can be represented by 4 bits of information and one says that such a system has 16 'grey levels'.

In any picture processing task using a TV image, we must store at least one frame of the data (a TV camera produces 25 such frames in one second). Each frame contains

$$512 \times 512 \times 4 = 1,048,576 \text{ bits}$$

In conventional computer jargon, since information is stored in words (i.e. packets of bits) this requires

        131,072 words in a small 8-bit computer
        such as a PET or APPLE

or   32,768 words in a larger 32-bit computer
        such as a DEC VAX 11/750

Clearly this is a heavy demand (impossible for the Apple or Pet) before any intelligent processing takes place.

6.4 HOW FAST DOES IT NEED TO SEE?

The operating speed of a pattern recognizer is vitally important. In practice we may wish to recognize pieceparts on a conveyor belt. The parts have to be physically moved, and if unconstrained cannot travel faster than about 1 metre per second, or they will fly off the surface. A typical throughput is about four parts per second. However, even at electronic speeds, the time taken to handle a TV image stored in a conventional computer could amount to hundreds of milliseconds, and the desired throughput of four parts per second begins to look doubtful due to the time required to manipulate the data itself, before any recognition processing takes place.

6.5 WHAT THE PATTERN RECOGNIZER NEEDS TO COMPUTE, AND HOW

There is a wealth of literature, produced over the past thirty years, on the theory and practice of pattern recognition, and many publications (Ullmann, 1973, Fu, 1976 and Batchelor, 1978) provide in-depth consideration of pattern recognition methodology. This level of research was triggered and sustained by the rapid development of fast gigantic serial digital computers, and the assumptions about the speed at which these devices could process real world data, such as pictures, scenes and patterns, which are essentially parallel, were unrealistic.

One of the prime concerns of a pattern recognition user is the technological feasibility of this method, and whilst claims are constantly being made regarding performance of various techniques, it is the adequacy of the hardware that is paramount to the user. A performance of 99.99% correct identification for a piecepart recognizer is not acceptable if the processing time per part is 30 minutes. A 95% performance may be more acceptable if the processing time is 3 milliseconds, especially if the patterns the system does not recognize are rejected rather than misclassified.

Before discussing some of these methodologies we shall define some terms:

Pattern: An array of numerical intensity values representing an image ´seen´ by the transducer.

Current Pattern: The pattern currently ´seen´ by the system and assumed to be stored in readiness for processing.

Pattern Class: The set of patterns that is to be recognized as being the same. For example, the recognition of hand printed letters involves 26 pattern classes.

Learning System: A system which has the flexibility to form part of its own recognition strategy, from being given patterns whose originating pattern class is known and also given to the system.

Training Set: That set of patterns whose classification is known, which is given to a learning system during the strategy formulation phase of its operation.

Learning Phase: The strategy formulation period in a learning system.

Test Phase: That operational period during which a learnt strategy is being tested.

Features: A pre-supposed set of defining characteristics of a pattern class. For example, the hand printed letter A may be described as three features consisting of two almost upright lines meeting towards the top of the picture and an almost horizontal line joining the two near their middles.

Preprocessing: An information reduction operation on an image which standardizes the image in some way. Examples are ´thinning´ or ´skeletonizing´ of line-like images or the extraction of major radii from blob-like images. This is a vast subject and beyond the terms of reference of this book. Nevertheless it should be realized that preprocessing is highly problem-dependent.

It is for this reason that no
preprocessing is included in the WISARD[*]
system. However, general-purpose parallel
machines exist which could be used as pre-
processors (see Wilson, 1980, and Duff,
1978).

The major methodologies we shall discuss here go under the
names:

(a)   Mask or Template Matching

(b)   Discriminant Function Analysis

(c)   Logical n-tuple methods

Although this leaves out many other trends and strands, it is
felt that the computational properties of those omitted are
similar to the ones mentioned. The thrust of the discussion
is aimed to show that (c) is best suited to novel silicon-
chip architectures.

6.5.1 Mask or Template Matching

This scheme relies on storing a set of representative
prototypes from each pattern class. If, for example, well-
printed and carefully positioned letters are to be
recognized, early schemes would store one prototype for each
of the 26 pattern classes. Assuming that only black-white
images are considered, an unknown image is compared point-by-
point with each of the stored prototypes. The unknown pattern
is assigned to the class with whose prototype it has most in
common.

Extensions of the scheme can operate with grey-level images
and masks built up by learning, where probabilities of
occurrence of data at each point bases on the training set,
are stored. Statistical methods which use such probabilities
are widely reported in the literature. Many other

---

[*]   WISARD: Mnemonic for WILKIE, STONHAM AND ALEKSANDER'S
RECOGNITION DEVICE - a computer with a novel architecture,
built at Brunel University with the support of the UK
Science and Engineering Research Council, to whom thanks
are due.

methodologies have been developed on the basis of mask
matching, the best known perhaps being the ´nearest neighbor´
method, where it is usual to store many patterns from the
training set and, during the test phase, to measure the
difference (or ´distance´) of the unknown pattern from all
the stored patterns, assigning its classification according
to what is its ´nearest neighbor´.

Computationally this scheme may be taxing on storage, while
being fairly light on calculation requirements. The storage
demands grow with the diversity of patterns within each
pattern class. For example, using a 512x512 binary image to
distinguish horizontal lines from vertical lines of, say 12
pixels in width, the system would have the following
specification:

Storage: Two sets of templates are required, each
                    containing about 500 templates (one for
                    each position of the line).
                    That is,
                    $2 \times 500 \times 512 \times 512 \simeq 25 \times 10^6$ bits.

                    This would defeat most computer
                    installations if the storage were to be
                    directly accessed.

Calculation Time: For each new pattern that has to be
                    recognized one has to carry out

                    n x 512 x 512 simple comparisons of the
                    type (n is the number of templates):

                    *   load a word from the image into the
                        accumulator

                    *   ´exclusive or´ it with a word from the
                        template

                    *   right shift K times and count the
                        number of 1s in the accumulator (K is
                        the number of bits in the word).

                    So, to a rough approximation, the decision
                    time for an unknown pattern is:

$$\frac{n \times 512 \times 512 \ (1 + K)}{K} \simeq n \times 512 \times 512$$
computation cycles.

This for a computing cycle of, say (optimistically) 1 µs would take seven or eight minutes to recognize an image, given a conventional machine architecture.

If grey levels are used, then the comparison becomes more complex. A perfect match between a prototype mask and an input pattern becomes less likely, and one can resort to a ´nearest neighbor´ approach in order to find the closest match between the input pattern and the reference masks or training set. A ´pattern space´ model can be used to represent the problem. All the patterns can be represented as unique points in d-dimensional space where d is the dimensionality of the data and is equivalent to the total number of pixels or measurements per pattern. The co-ordinates of each pattern point are numerically equal to the grey levels of the pixels.

Given a mask represented by $\underline{A}$ and an unknown pattern $\underline{X}$, a measure of their similarity is the Euclidean distance between $\underline{X}$ and $\underline{A}$ in pattern space, which can be calculated as follows:

$$D_{XA} = \sqrt{(x_1-a_1)^2+(x_2-a_2)^2 +...+ (x_d-a_d)^2}$$

The storage requirements for a grey level masking system will be increased by a factor of 4 if 16 grey levels are used, or more generally $\log_2 N$ for N grey levels. The increase in the calculation time needed to obtain a similarity measurement based on Euclidean distance, will be more substantial for the grey level problem, as the processing will have to be carried out pixel by pixel as opposed to processing words representing x pixels in the black/white image match. For each pixel, a subtraction has to be performed together with a multiplication. An accumulation of the output of each pixel process followed by a square root operation completes the distance calculation.

The processing time is increased by at least an order of magnitude. The precise figure will depend on the word length and the instruction time of the particular computer being used.

The distance measurement can be simplified. One could use the square of the Euclidean distance, but the savings would only amount to one operation per distance calculation (that of the square root). Other distance measurements depart from the Euclidean formula. Two common distances used are the city block distance where:

$$D_{CB} = \sum_{i=1}^{d} |A_i - X_i|$$

and the square distance, where

$$D_S = \max_{i=1 \text{ to } d} |A_i - X_i|$$

(The latter is so named because its equidistant contours are square in two-dimensional space.)

Both these distances are faster to calculate than the Euclidean measure, but do not offer any speed advantages over the binary masking scheme. Furthermore, both the city block and square distances are, under certain conditions, unstable. The decision hyperplane in pattern space, which is the locus of points equidistant from two training patterns, can become a hypervolume in which test patterns cannot be classified.

Mask matching is not, however, confined to computer implementation. Primitive pattern recognition schemes patented before the advent of the general purpose computer, relied on optical masking, where an image was matched to a negative photographic plate and the degree of matching measured by the amount of transmitted light. Whilst the calculation of the matching factor could be carried out in real time by a photocell system, the need to physically move and accurately position photographic masks made the system totally impractical for most applications. Furthermore, this optical system is not capable of detecting all mismatch

conditions. A white area on an image can be masked by a
black areas on a negative mask.   This is a match condition,
and no light will be transmitted through the mask.   Now, if
the same area on the image was black, there would be a
mismatch condition, but again no light would be transmitted.
The optical system cannot resolve a mismatch on the black
area of an image.

The photographic mask can be replaced by an analog electronic
system comprising for each input pixel a detector having
complementary outputs, one giving maximum output for an all
black input and the other giving maximum for an all white
input. The mask can then be defined by the connections taken
from the detectors.   If a given pixel is black for a
particular class, the black output would be taken in order to
measure the maximum match, or the white output could be used
to measure the minimum mismatch.

In practice, even if parallel hardware is devised to perform
the matching, the problem of holding the masks makes severe
demands on storage, and the operating speed will still be
dependent on the number of categories and templates within
each category.   The technique only finds practical
application with low resolution data which has minimal
diversity within each pattern class.

6.5.2 Discriminant Function Analysis

In order to overcome the need to store a vast number of
templates within a recognition system, the discriminant
function approach attempts to define a weight vector which,
when operating on patterns, will give an identifiable
response with one class and a distinctly different response
to another pattern category. The device in its simplest form
can only partition data into two categories, and a tree of
these dichotomizers must be employed if multicategory
recognition is required.   The principles behind discriminant
function analysis can readily be seen if a pattern space
model is used.   Consider a set of patterns which are
described by two measurements: for example, the perimeter and
the area of sheet metal pressing.   These two measurements
describe the shape of the parts, and can be represented as
vectors and consequently points in a two-dimensional pattern
space.   In Fig. 6.1 the points marked X represent one type of
part and the Ys represent a different part.   A partitioning

vector, known as a weight vector $\underline{W}$, is required which will separate the Xs from the Ys.

By weighting each of the patterns with $\underline{W}$, a response can be obtained thus:

$$R = W_1 X_1 + W_2 X_2$$

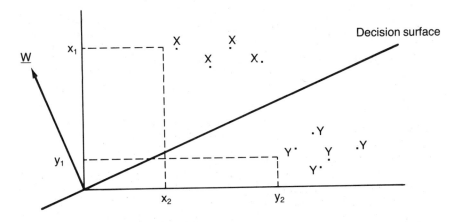

Fig. 6.1 A decision surface defined by $\underline{W}$ in two-dimensional pattern space

This calculation is in fact the scalar product $\underline{W}.\underline{X}$ and is equal to

$$|W| . |X| \cos \theta$$

where θ is the angle between $\underline{W}$ and $\underline{X}$.

It can be seen in this two-dimensional example that the set **X** can be distinguished from the set **Y** by a weight vector that gives a positive scalar product with **X** ($\theta < 90°$) and a negative scalar product ($\theta > 90°$) with **Y**. The weight vector defines a decision surface which is linear and perpendicular to $\underline{W}$ and separates the data into set **X** and set **Y**.

This method provides an attractive solution to some pattern recognition problems. There are a large number of two class problems associated with inspection and quality assurance

where the decision categories are ´accept´ and ´reject´ or
´pass´ and ´fail´, and the data within those classes can be
very diverse. Here the linear discrimination approach would
appear to be an appropriate methodology, providing a suitable
weight vector can be found.

Computationally the system ostensibly needs less storage than
mask-matching, since only the weights need be stored.
However, the product and addition calculations take
considerably longer than a simple comparison. Also, the
training phase may be extremely long and unproductive.
Therefore, given that weights can be found, the specification
for the TV-compatible system would be:

Storage: 512 x 512 bytes (for integer arithmetic)
                      per class pair, which, for one class-pair
                      and eight-bit bytes, comes to
                      approximately 2×10^6 bits.

                      This compares favorably with mask-
                      matching.

Calculation Time: Allowing 10 µs for multiplication and 3 µs
                      per addition and temporary storage
                      overheads, the TV system ought to be
                      capable of providing a decision in

                      $13 \times 10^{-6} \times 512 \times 512 \simeq 3$ seconds

                      Although this compares favorably with mask
                      matching, it falls short of most
                      industrial robotics tasks where four
                      images per second is a standard. Clearly,
                      recognizing images at TV frame speeds
                      (25/second) seems even further out of
                      reach.

The major drawback with the discriminant function method lies
in the training phase, in which the weight vector is
established. In any real problem we are likely to encounter
many more than two dimensions and a weight vector cannot be
obtained simply by examining the distribution of vectors in
pattern space. A weight vector can only classify data in

which a linear decision hyperplane will separate the pattern points into two distinct and meaningful classes and there is, unfortunately, no simple test that can be applied to training data in order to assess its linear separability.

Consider the horizontal and vertical line problem discussed in the previous section. Let the resolution be reduced to 2 pixels by 2 pixels giving 4-dimensional binary vectors. The patterns are:

$$\begin{array}{cccc} 1\ 1 & \text{and} & 0\ 0 & \\ 0\ 0 & & 1\ 1 & \text{horizontal lines} \end{array}$$

and
$$\begin{array}{cccc} 1\ 0 & \text{and} & 0\ 1 & \text{vertical lines} \\ 1\ 0 & & 0\ 1 & \end{array}$$

Let the image be numbered

$$i_1 \quad i_2$$

$$i_3 \quad i_4$$

and let $\underline{W}$ be the weight vector which will classify the horizontal patterns as being positive and the vertical as being negative. The scalar product with the horizontal images gives:

$$W_1 + W_2 > 0 \qquad (1)$$

and
$$W_3 + W_4 > 0 \qquad (2)$$

and for the vertical patterns

$$W_1 + W_3 < 0 \qquad (3)$$

$$W_2 + W_4 < 0 \qquad (4)$$

Summing equations (1) and (2) gives

$$\sum_{i=1}^{4} W_i > 0$$

and (3) and (4) gives

$$\sum_{i=1}^{4} W_i < 0$$

These conditions cannot be satisfied with real weights; therefore the data cannot be partitioned with a linear decision hyperplane although the two data categories are quite distinct.

In practice, one attempts to find a suitable weight vector
with respect to a training set of patterns using an error
correcting feedback procedure. If the data is linearly
inseparable no weight vector will emerge, and the process is
terminated after a specified time. The data must then be
processed using a more sophisticated partitioning procedure,
or alternatively the best weight vector with respect to the
training set can be used and the accuracy of the system based
on the best error performance, obtained during the training.

A further requirement for the linear discriminator which
severely limits its practicability is the number of training
patterns needed to be processed before a weight vector can be
regarded as being valid. The number of training patterns T
must exceed the dimensionality d of the patterns. (A
generally accepted rule of thumb is T = 3xd.) If this
condition is not fulfilled and there are numerically fewer
patterns than the dimensionality, a weight vector can always
be found which will partition the training patterns even if
they belong to linearly inseparable categories. This can
readily be seen by considering two points in a three-
dimensional box. They can always be separated by a plane,
regardless of their locations. In the case of the vertical
and horizontal lines, a four-dimensional problem, if we only
use one of each for training, the following conditions must
be satisfied.

$$W_1 + W_2 > 0$$

$$W_1 + W_3 < 0$$

By inspection, a solution would be $\underline{W}$ = 1,2,-2,0 and the data
as represented by the two training patterns appears to be
linearly separable. However, both the horizontal and
vertical lines which were not used for training are
incorrectly classified with this weight vector.

When dealing with high resolution images the vector
dimensionality can be reduced by several orders of magnitude
by preprocessing. However, this may severely reduce
operating speeds. In the case of a sheet metal piecepart a
digitized picture can be obtained at 512 x 512 bit resolution
via a TV camera in approximately 40 milliseconds. Using a 20
MHz linear array, the data capture time reduces to 12
milliseconds. However, the data in this form is a binary

vector of 2^{18} dimensions. The information can be reduced to 2^3 dimensions by calculating the centroid of the shape (x,y), the longest radius r_1 and the radii at 60° intervals from r_1 in a clockwise direction giving a pattern vector

$$\underline{X} = (x, y, r_1, r_2, r_3, r_4, r_5\ r_6).$$

This form is sufficiently accurate to represent parts machined to a tolerance of + 0.2%. However, the amount of preprocessing required to create the eight dimension vector form, which has to be carried out on each and every training and test pattern, can take tens of seconds on a serial digital computer.

If the data is known to be linearly inseparable a dichotomy can be made using piece-wise linear functions or non-linear functions. The piece-wise linear approach requires several linear discriminators per decision which operate in different regions of pattern space. The training problems are exacerbated, and in the limit the system would degenerate to having one template per pattern.

In the case of non-linear functions, one is seeking to create a curved hypersurface which will separate the categories. A non-linear surface in two dimensions is shown in Fig. 6.2.

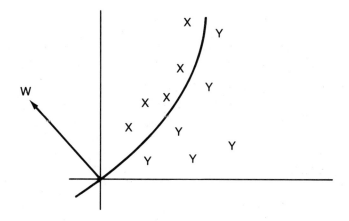

Fig. 6.2 A non-linear decision surface

A non-linear surface can best be implemented in pattern space
by applying a non-linear transform to the patterns and
attempting to linearly partition the transformed pattern
space. This approach creates new problems, not least of
which is the specification of the transform. As there is no
simple way of deciding on a suitable transform one might
resort to an exhaustive approach. This is, in the case of a
second order system, a quadric discriminator. Transformed
pattern $\underline{Y}$ can be expressed as:

$$\underline{Y} = x_1{}^2 + x_2{}^2 + ... + x_d{}^2 + x_1 x_2 + x_1 x_3 + ... + x_{d-1} x_d + x_1 + x_2 + ... + x_d$$

Hence a d dimensional pattern $\underline{X}$ is transformed into pattern $\underline{Y}$
having

$$d + \frac{d(d-1)}{2} + d \text{ dimensions.}$$

This means a relatively modest 100 pixel pattern is
transformed into 5,150 dimensions, making it difficult, if
not impossible, to assess the validity of any weight vector
in transformed pattern space for all but the lowest
resolution pictures.

One does not, of course, have to use an exhaustive transform,
and limited transform systems (ϕ processors) have been
proposed. In such schemes the choice of transform does
become somewhat arbitrary and these devices are of little
practical use.

A further practical restriction of the use of higher order
functions is imposed by the input transducer. The simplest
and most desirable input format in terms of hardware and
processing time is binary pixel encoding. If the elements of
the pattern vectors are taken as pixels and limited to binary
values 0 and 1, higher order transforms are of little value.
In the case of the quadric discriminator, the squared terms
are identical in value to the individual pixels $x^2{}_i = x_i$ and
product terms are zero unless all elements are at logical 1.
The effectiveness of the non-linear transform is reduced
significantly and linear separability remains a very real
problem.

Although discriminant functions appear to solve some of the storage and timing problems found in mask matching, the uncertainty as to whether the method will work at all with any particular problem has limited the practical applicability of the technique. If it is adopted, the storage and computational overheads involved in the training phase and data preprocessing are significant. However, if a set of weight vectors can be established for a particular problem and the efficacy demonstrated, then the implementation of the method does not present any major difficulties. It is the generation of the weight vectors which, in most cases, presents insuperable problems.

6.5.3 Logical n-tuple Methods

In higher order discriminant analysis one is endeavouring to collect and operate on information in the form of a product series of pixel measurements. When applied to binary pixels, a product series is most likely to become zero, and if the pixels are in grey levels, identical values can be obtained for different patterns. Suppose $\underline{X} = 4, 3$ and $\underline{Y} = 2, 6$, then transform term $i_1 \, i_2$ would have the value 12 and no weight exists which would distinguish between them.

Joint occurrences among pixels define the shape of an image as far as human pattern recognition is concerned. This is particularly true in industrial robotic applications where one is generally dealing with solid state objects which can be defined by their shape. It is the joint occurrence at the pixel level which defines the features of the shape and enables us to identify them. They are clearly of great importance when recognizing patterns, but in terms of machine recognition a product series is not the most appropriate way of representing the data. In the logical n-tuple method Boolean functions are generated, during a training phase, which give a desired reaction to patterns of a particular class. The use of logical operators has a distinct advantage over arithmetical operations - it overcomes the ambiguities associated with higher order discriminant functions.

Consider the 2x2 bit horizontal and vertical line problem again. Taking the pixels on the top row, let i_1 and i_2 be binary inputs to a logic function which will respond with a logical 1 at its output when the data on $i_1 \, i_2$ is part of a vertical line.

For the first vertical line

$$F_{V_{\text{row } 1}} = i_1 \wedge \overline{i}_2$$

Now for the second vertical line, the function must respond to

$$i_1 = 0 \text{ and } i_2 = 1$$

and the logic function becomes

$$F_{V_{\text{row } 1}}{}^1 = (i_1 \wedge \overline{i}_2) \vee (\overline{i}_1 \wedge i_2)$$

$$= i_1 \oplus i_2$$

Similarly, at the same sampling points, a function to detect horizontal lines is

$$F_{H_{\text{row } 1}} = (i_1 \wedge i_2) \vee (\overline{i}_1 \wedge \overline{i}_2)$$

$$= (\overline{i_1 \oplus i_2})$$

One can readily see that the logical functions can distinguish between inputs from different classes of patterns when the sample of n pixels (the n-tuples) contains zero valued cells. Furthermore, as the training of the function proceeds, the response to previously trained patterns is not changed. Thus two of the major objections to the discriminant function method are overcome. The logic function can readily be set up within memory elements, either random access memories or read only memories, and the system can be organized as a parallel processor.

6.6 THE RANDOM ACCESS MEMORY AS A LEARNING PATTERN RECOGNIZER

The essential elements of a random access memory (RAM) are shown in Fig. 6.3. (This is not a complete circuit diagram: it is just intended to aid the description that follows.) The RAM as a learning pattern recognizer operates in the following way: There are 2^n possible distinct address patterns which can occur at the n address terminals.

Each of these patterns selects a different two-state (0/1) device causing the value of its state to appear at the data-out terminal. The above is known as the read or use mode.

Another mode, the write or teach mode, is entered by energizing the write-enable control line. In this mode the contents of the addressed flip-flop may be set to a value determined by the logical value of the data-in terminal.

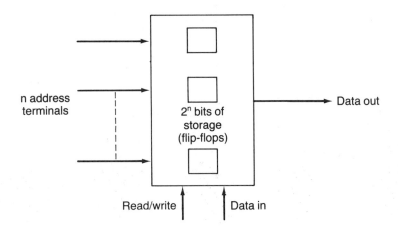

Fig. 6.3 Random-access memory

A RAM on its own can act as a rather trivial pattern recognizer in the following way. Assume that the pattern is applied at the n binary address terminals. The memory will recognize one class of pattern by outputting a 1 when a member of this class is present at the input.

Assume that all the flip-flops are initially at zero. That is, no pattern is identified. Suppose now, that the all-1s patterns and the n patterns with only one 0 are taught to the RAM by presenting them in turn to the adddress terminals with the write-enable wire energized and a 1 at the data-input terminal. During a subsequent 'use' phase, the RAM will recognize the n + 1 patterns it was taught during the previous 'teach' phase, but no others. Hence, it acts as a learning pattern recognizer, but one with no generalization. It is because of this latter point that the scheme was labeled as being 'trivial'. It will now be shown that very simple networks of RAMs are not trivial in the same way.

6.7 GENERALIZATION

Generalization – the ability to classify patterns other than those in the training set – is the central, most important property of a pattern recognizer. The simple mask matching scheme does not have any generalization, neither does the single RAM system. Generality can be introduced by considering distances from training patterns or masks, however this does not provide a solution in all pattern recognition problems. Unfortunately all possible versions of, say, the letter A, cannot be defined as being within 5% variation, based on a pixel by pixel comparison, of a prototype.

The linear discriminant functions have very wide ranging generalization properties – all possible patterns are partitioned into one of two classes for each function, and this over-generalization can be undesirable, especially where multicategory recognition has to be achieved. A typical generalization situation is shown in Fig. 6.4.

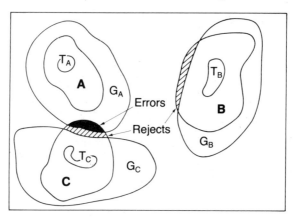

Fig. 6.4 Generalization sets

In this 3 class problem, T_A, T_B and T_C represent the training data and sets **A**, **B** and **C** represent the totality of patterns for those classes, and any data category will not necessarily be linearly related to its training sets. G_A, G_B and G_C represent the generalization sets based on T_A, T_B and T_C respectively. In an ideal situation G_A, G_B and G_C would correspond exactly with **A**, **B** and **C**. However, in a practical situation, some patterns within a class may fall outside the generalization sets, giving rejects, or errors if they fall within the generalization set of another category (see Fig. 6.4). In general, a rejection is more desirable than a misclassification. It is equivalent to the system saying "I don't know" rather than making the wrong decision. In the recognition of postal codes, for example, the rejected item could be salvaged and classified by a human, whereas the incorrect machine decision would cause it to be sent to the wrong address.

6.8 SOME SIMPLE LOGICAL n-TUPLE NETWORKS AND THEIR

GENERALIZATION PROPERTIES

In Fig. 6.5 a simple arrangement is shown where a 3 x 3 binary matrix is connected to three RAMs. The "data in" terminals of the RAMs are connected together and an AND gate receives the "data output" terminals. In this way, the RAMs are taught to respond with 1s for the patterns in the training set, and only those patterns causing all three RAMs to output 1s would be classified in the same way as the training set.

It is assumed that all stores are at 0 before training commences. A specific training set T_A is shown in Fig. 6.5(b) and it is represented as a subset of the universal set **U** in Fig. 6.5(c). Note that **U** contains $2^{3 \times 3} = 512$ patterns. The generalization set G_A may be computed as follows:

Looking at the way the RAMs are connected, one notes that during the entire training session each RAM "sees" precisely two addressing subpatterns. The set G_A is then clearly made up of all combinations of such addressing subpatterns.

In general, the size of G_A (denoted by $|G_A|$) is given by

$$|G_A| = k_1 \times k_2 \times k_3 \cdots\cdots k_e$$

$$\Phi = \prod_e k_j$$

where k_j is the number of subpatterns seen by jth RAM during training.

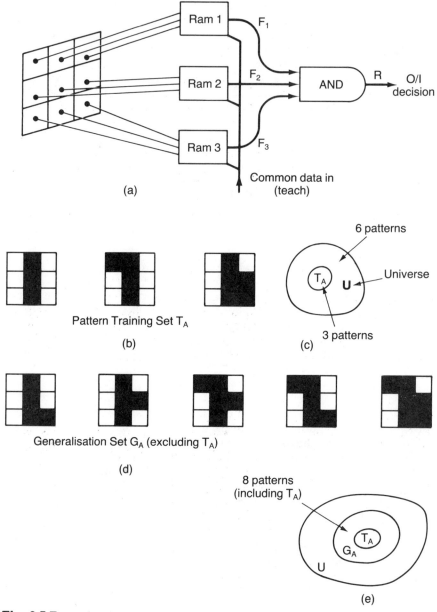

Fig. 6.5 Example of training and generalization in a simple single-layer net.
- a 3 x 3 binary matrix
- b Specific training set
- c Subset of U
- d 'Seen' subpatterns
- e Set diagram

In this example

$$|G_A| = 2 \times 2 \times 2 = 8$$

Subtracting from this number those patterns in T_A, G_A must contain another 5 combinations of 'seen' subpatterns. These are shown in Fig. 6.5(d) and the set diagram is given in Fig. 6.5(e).

The network is based on memory elements, but it must be emphasized that at no time during the operation is any pattern or subpattern stored. The pattern n-tuples form addresses to the memories, and it is the desired response (0 or 1) which is entered into the memory. In the above example the RAMs are performing the following logic functions:

$$F_1 = i_2 \cap \overline{i}_3$$

$$F_2 = \overline{i}_4 \cap i_5$$

$$F_3 = \overline{i}_7 \cap i_8$$

and the classification function is

$$R = F_1 \cap F_2 \cap F_3.$$

Consider now what would happen if the AND gate were replaced by an OR gate, the rest of the system remaining exactly the same. In this case, a pattern will be classified as being in G_A provided at least one of the RAMs sees an input which has occurred during training. One can show that G_A is now much larger and, in fact, contains 296 patterns. This large number includes patterns as diverse as those shown in Fig. 6.6(a).

Clearly, one gets a feel for the fact that the more restricted decision at the output (AND) causes G_A to include patterns that are more directly related, that is, similar to the training set.

There is another way of affecting G_A by means of network changes. Suppose the connections to the input patterns are as shown in Fig. 6.6(b). It is assumed that the training set is the same as in Fig. 6.5(b). This time, however, we note that the first and third RAMs see two subpatterns, whereas the second sees only one.

(a)

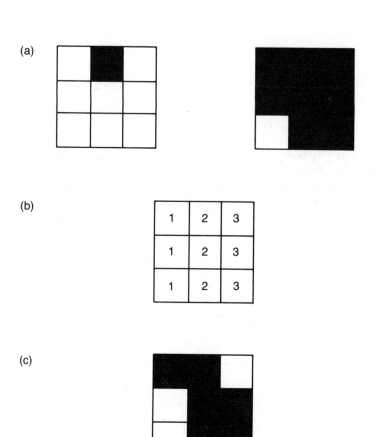

(b)

(c)

Fig. 6.6 a Examples of generalization using an OR gate at the output of Fig. 6.5.

  b Reconnection pattern; this differs from Fig. 6.5(a) in the sense that the cells marked 1s are connected to RAM 1, etc.

  c Reduced generalization set with AND output function and input connections as in Fig. 6.6(b).

Hence the total number of patterns in G_A is

$$|G_A| = 2 \times 1 \times 2 = 4$$

Hence, outside the training set there is just one pattern in G_A, and this is shown in Fig. 6.6(c). This connection has, in fact, picked out a very important common feature of the training set: the central vertical bar.

The networks discussed here have a particular name: single-layer nets, or SLNs. They always have the following physical characteristics:

(i)   Given a binary matrix of R points, an SLN contains R/n n-input RAMs connected (often at random) so that each RAM input (i.e. address terminal) ´sees´ one, and only one, matrix point.

(ii)   A simple decision such as AND, OR, MAJORITY or GREATER-THAN-X, is made at the output of the RAMs.

(iii) From the examples in this section of this chapter one learns that:

    (a) Generalization is affected first by the diversity of the patterns in the training set; that is, the more diverse the patterns in the training set, the greater will be the number of subpatterns seen by each RAM, resulting in a larger generalization set.

    (b) Secondly, the output decision, based mainly on the value of a threshold, placed on the number of RAMs that respond with a 1, strongly affects the size of the generalization set. The smallest set is achieved with an AND decision (i.e. threshold between R/n and R/n −1), and the greatest with an OR decision (i.e. a threshold between 0 and 1).

    (c) Thirdly, the connection of RAMs to common features in the training set reduces the generalization set.

6.9 MULTICATEGORY PATTERN RECOGNITION

A single-layer net tends to divide a universal set into two categories. those paterns in G_A and those that are not. Clearly, most pattern recognition problems require classification into more categories (for example 26 for the letters of the alphabet).

This is achieved by using several SLNs. In theory, one could use $\log_2 K$ SLNs for a K-class problem. For example, two nets (Fig. 6.7(a)) could be used to recognize, say, three classes **A**, **B**, **C**, as shown in Fig. 6.7(b). This requires that for training set T_A, only SLN α is taught to output a 1, for T_B, both α and β are taught to output a 1, while for T_C only β is taught to output a 1. When neither net responds, this is taken to be a ´reject´ or ´don´t know´ condition.

There is a major difficulty with this kind of scheme. The nets have to be trained to respond in the same way to patterns that are clearly in different classes. Consequently it is likely that the patterns on which the SLNs are trained will have a great diversity, leading to inappropriate generalization.

Consider the problem in which **A** is the set of three vertical patterns, of which Fig. 6.7(c) is an example, **B** is the set of three horizontal patterns of which Fig. 6.7(d) is an example and **C** is the set of three diagonal patterns (or negative slope) shown in Fig. 6.7(e). If the nets are connected as in Fig. 6.5, it may be seen that if α is trained on **A** and **B** and on **B** and **C**, all the patterns in **A** and **C** will give a **B** response. (i.e. both α and β will output 1).

One imagines that the problem could be solved by altering the connections and the training. For example, one could let net β be connected as in Fig. 6.6(b) and the horizontals be A, the verticals C with the diagonal as B. The intent here is to tailor the matrix connections to the features of the patterns. However, the scheme does not work one because one notes that, as the diagonals are used to teach both nets, α cannot distinguish between diagonals and verticals, whereas β cannot distinguish between diagonals and horizontals. Hence, any pattern will give the B response.

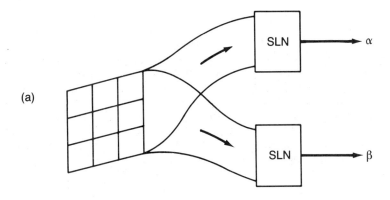

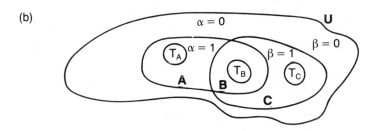

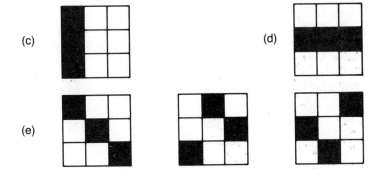

Fig. 6.7 Multinet systems
    a   Two nets of a 2-class problem
    b   Coding of net output
    c   Example of vertical pattern
    d   Example of horizontal pattern
    e   Diagonal patterns

A more usual way of dealing with the multicategory problem is to assign one modified SLN per class. The modification entails not having an output decision circuit for each net, but leaving the output decision to a circuit called a maximum-response detector which receives responses from all the nets. Such a system is shown in Fig. 6.8(a) for a 3-class problem. The maximum-response detector assigns (to the test pattern) the classification of the discriminator which has the strongest response. The resulting generalization sets are shown in Fig. 6.8(b). All multiple responses (in the sense that two or more SLNs respond in the same way) are classed as ´don´t knows´.

The major advantage of this scheme is that each network, now known as a discriminator will be trained on a set of patterns which are in some sense similar. Also, one can tailor the discriminator connections to suit an individual class of patterns. Returning to the example of the horizontal, vertical and diagonal lines, one would require three discriminators. Say that the first, H, is to distinguish horizontals and has its RAMs horizontally connected, the second, V, has it RAMs vertically connected, and the third, D, has them diagonally connected. During training each discriminator is taught on one and only one class of pattern. For the vertical pattern discriminator one RAM will be taught to output a 1 for the all-1 address and the other two RAMs output a 1 for the all 0 address. Consequently, when any pattern in a training set is presented to the system, each of the three RAMs will fire in its own discriminator, and no RAMs will fire in the other two. This provides perfect recognition of the training set. Now, consider a pattern which is a distortion of a vertical training pattern, say

$$0 \quad 1 \quad 0$$

$$1 \quad 1 \quad 0$$

$$0 \quad 1 \quad 0$$

Clearly, two RAMs in the V discriminator will fire and none in the others, still giving the correct decision. Indeed, all single-bit distortions of the training sets will be correctly classified.

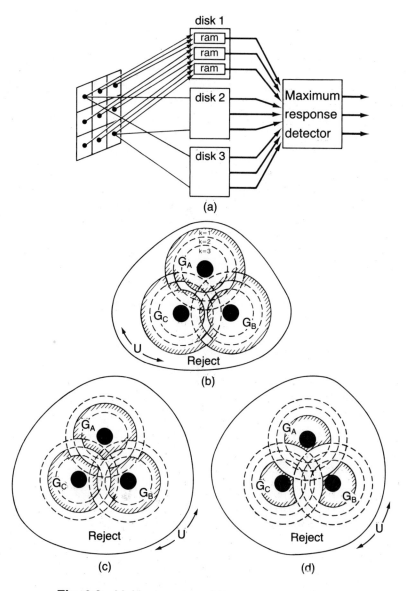

Fig. 6.8 Multicategory problem
- a 3-category system
- b Strongest-response discrimination
- c Difference threshold of 2 between the second highest response.
- d Difference threshold of 3

A further point of interest in this kind of discriminator system is that one can obtain control over the generalization by insisting that there will be a minimum difference (threshold) between the highest and the second responses. If this difference is not exceeded then the input pattern is rejected. Figure 6.8(b) shows the generalization set with no minimum difference threshold. In Fig. 6.8(c) the generalization set is shown with a difference threshold of 2 and in Fig. 6.8(d) the threshold is 3.

In summary, the K-discriminator system for a K-class problem has the following advantages:

(a)   The discriminators are not required to accept a greater diversity of patterns than contained in a single class. This avoids exaggerated generalization.

(b)   Connections can, in certain cases, be tailored to suit individual classes.

(c)   Predetermination of output decision thresholds (fixed-output decisions) is avoided.

(d)   Differential thresholds between discriminators may be used to control the ´reject´ class size.

6.10 THE PARAMETERS OF THE LOGICAL n-TUPLE METHOD

AND THEIR OPTIMIZATION

The logical n-tuple pattern recognition parameters can be divided into two broad groups – those relating to the data categories and those to the system. The data parameters are the input resolution, number of categories, number of training patterns and the diversity and population of the data categories. Clearly, the number of categories which can be processed using one discriminator per class scheme, developed in the previous section, will be hardware limited. The WISARD system which utilizes the n-tuple method is capable of partitioning 8,000 data categories at low resolution (16 x 16) bits or 8 categories at 512x512 bit resolution using a recognition logic store of 2Mbits.

The diversity of the data also has a direct bearing on the hardware architecture of a logical n-tuple recognizer. If, for example, one was attempting to recognize constrained pieceparts where very little variation occurs between different images of the same part, one can attempt to implement the ´log$_2$ K discriminators for K categories´ hardware. A practical compromise which has proved to be satisfactory is the ´2 in N´ scheme, in which the category detection is as follows: each of N discriminators is trained on N-1 categories, but no two discriminators are trained on more than one common category. In this approach the generalization sets are very much larger than the data sets, and may overlap. However, the data sets remain small and distinct because of the uniformity of the categories. A 2-in-N training scheme allows N discriminators to recognize

$$\frac{N^2 - N}{2}$$

categories, and a specimen training scheme for a 4-discriminator system is shown in Table 6.1 where 6 data categories can be recognized.

TRAINING SPECIFICATION				
Discriminator	1	2	3	4
Training Categories	A B C	A E D	F B D	F E C
CATEGORY/DISCRIMINATOR ASSIGNMENT				
Category	Detected by Discriminators			
A	1 and 2			
B	1 and 3			
C	1 and 4			
D	2 and 3			
E	2 and 4			
F	3 and 4			

Table 6.1 Training specification for a 4-discriminator 2 in N classifier

Unconstrained and highly diverse classes of data can be solved by assigning one or more dedicated discriminators to each data category. Face recognition has been demonstrated using WISARD, and the system could be applied to a small organization of, say, 20 persons, recognizing faces in order to monitor security. However face recognition applied to a much larger population becomes impossible due to the hardware requirements (one discriminator per person) but verification of faces is feasible on a vastly increased data set, without requiring a proportional increase in the number of discriminators required.

It is important to distinguish carefully between recognition and verification. In recognition one is applying data to a system and in the case of faces asking the question ´Who am I?´ In verification you tell the recognizer who you are − ´I am Joe Smith´ − and ask the question − ´Do you agree?´

The recognizer in the verification mode will have discriminators which will not necessarily respond highly to Joe Smith´s face, but they will respond in a consistent way. Joe will cause a recognizer to output a reproducible response profile, and this becomes his personal identification which is initially input to the system when he is to be verified. The recognizer generates its own response profile, which must correspond with the personal identifier for a positive verification.

Such a system will depend on the consistency of the response profile and its embodiment in a personal code. It is, however, potentially very powerful. If, for example, the response profiles are encoded as the order of discriminators giving highest to lowest responses, one has the potential to verify $N!$ categories with an N discriminator system. A 10 discriminator system could at its upper bound verify 3,628,000 categories. (In a practical system the number will usually be significantly lower than this, but nevertheless still substantial.)

Now consider the system parameters. The principal ones are the n-tuple sample size and the connection mapping which determines the way the n-tuple are formed.

The n-tuple size has a major bearing on the hardware requirements, as an increase of 1 in the value of n doubles the storage required to implement each n-tuple logic function.

The advantage of increasing the value of n lies in the ability to make more decisions at the n-tuple level. A 3-tuple has a maximum decision potential of 1 in 8 categories, whereas increasing the sample size to 4 allows a maximum of 16 different responses at a given sampling site. In general, a larger n-tuple is required if the pattern categories are very similar, or the data is susceptible to noise or if there is a wide diversity of patterns within each category. In practice, n=8 has proved to be more than adequate for most applications.

The sampling of the patterns in order to form the n-tuples can be based on knowledge of any specific features within a pattern category. If detailed knowledge of the data is not available, one usually randomly selects the pixels for each sample in the first instance. If required,the connections can be optimized after an initial training phase, by comparing corresponding functions in different discriminators, which operate on the same sampling points. If the functions are identical, then the n-tuple sample cannot contribute any information to the recognition process, and the connections can be removed from the input retina without adversely affecting the classification characteristics.

6.11 n-TUPLE HARDWARE

Taking a 512x512 bit pattern and an n-tuple size 4, there are 65,536 n-tuple samples in each image. The storage required to implement the logic in each discriminator is

$$65536 \times 2^4 = 1 \text{ Mbit.}$$

This amounts to 4 integrated circuit packages (256k-bit RAMs) and is equivalent to the amount of storage required to hold 4 templates. Therefore, in terms of storage alone, if more than 4 templates per class are necessary the logical 4-tuple

system requires less storage. The more significant
advantages of the n-tuple scheme are that the method needs
virtually no calculation overheads and it is ideally suited
to a parallel or semi-parallel hardware organization.

The system could, theoretically, operate at speeds of the
order of the access time of a memory element (10^{-7} s) and
be independent of the number of data categories. At 512x512
bit resolution this is somewhat academic, as the internal
interconnection problem would be insuperable. The WISARD
scheme which operates at this resolution has a semi-parallel
architecture where the processing within the discriminators
is serial but all the discriminators themselves are operating
in parallel. This gives a minimum operating time of

$$65536 \times 10^{-7} \simeq 70 \text{ milliseconds}$$

and once again this figure is independent of the number of
data categories the system can recognize.

6.12 SPECIAL ARCHITECTURES FOR PATTERN RECOGNITION

A cursory glance at the three pattern recognition methods
categories will show that they could all be made more
efficient by means of special architectures. Mask-matching,
for example, could be based on a parallel system of registers
and comparators. However, it may be shown that the
performance of a mask-matching system is equivalent to an n-
tuple system, with n-1, and therefore not only limited, but
lacking in generality. Therefore it would appear unwise to
launch into the design of such special architecture with
mask-matching methodology in mind.

Discriminant function methods rely heavily on calculation,
and one could envisage an array system where each cell
performs the necessary weight - multiplication calculation.
In fact, such architectures exist (Gostick, 1979, and Duff,
1978) which could be adapted for this application and the
research may be worth doing. However, the performance
uncertainties of the scheme mitigate against optimism. The
n-tuple method, however, is viable within a conventional
computer scheme and is also a good candidate for special

architectures. To achieve speed, one arranges for the n-
tuples to be addressed in a semi-parallel way, where the
degree of parallelism and other characteristics such as
window size, value of n, etc. are under operator control.
WISARD was constructed with these advantages in mind, and
details of design decisions will be published in due course.

So far, the main concern here has been the structure of
learning systems which improve their performance by being
'shown' a suitable training set. However, there are many
applications where a fixed pattern recognition task has to be
carried out over and over again. The n-tuple method lends
itself to a process of reduction which implements the
essential parts of the <u>learnt</u> logic in a learning
system either as logic gates, programmed logic arrays or
read only memories.

This is not the place to dwell on details of this type of
procedure, except to realize that it is purely a mechanical
and easily computable procedure. For example, if the 512x512
horizontal/vertical line problem had been solved with
horizontal 2-tuples, with the two elements of each 2-tuple,
13 pixels apart, then it can be shown that for the
'horizontal' pattern class the memories could be replaced by
AND gates, whereas for the 'verticals' these could be
replaced by 'exclusive OR' gates. In fact, the design of
such logic is based on the realization that the contents of
the store associated with each n-tuple is merely a 'truth
table' derived during a learning process. For details of
this see Aleksander (1978).

6.13 ESSENTIAL FEATURES OF A PRACTICAL PATTERN RECOGNITION SYSTEM

Over the past 30 years, pattern recognition literature has
highlighted the performance of systems and methodologies, but
very little practical implementation has been achieved. It
may well be that this emphasis has been misplaced, and
greater effort should be concentrated on the practicalities
of the techniques. It is quite possible that, given
sufficient time and hardware, any of the three basic methods
which have been examined in this chapter would produce

equally good results. The ultimate performance does seem to
depend more on data than methodolgy. The desire for
automation provides a strong stimulus for practical pattern
recognition, and the benchmarks which are of paramount
importance in any system concern:

1) <u>Operating speed</u>   a pattern recognition system must not
retard any system in which it is
integrated.

2) <u>Flexibility</u>   a pattern recognition system should be
capable of being adapted to perform a
range of tasks as products and
operations are changed.

3) <u>Ease of use</u>   the interface with the operator should
be as simple as possible and not
require sophisticated programming, at
hardware or software level.

4) <u>Cost</u>   must be acceptable. A central
characteristic of the silicon chip
'age' is the remarkable reduction in
costs of information storage. Even in
the last 15 years the cost of storage
has dropped by a monetary factor of
over 300. In real terms the WISARD
recognition store would have cost the
equivalent of ten 4-bedroom houses in
London 15 years ago; it now costs as
much as one domestic color television
set.

The logical n-tuple method satisfies all of the practical
requirements, not least of which is the means of exploiting
the silicon chip economic revolution. Practical pattern
recognition is, however, only the start of the story. There
is much one can do to improve the 'intelligence' of pattern
recognition machines such as WISARD and the like. In
particular, one notes the possibility of closing the loop
between the recognition signals in these systems and their
input, producing an interesting dynamism. This would enable
the system to recognize sequences of events and generate
sequences of recognition signals effectively bringing closer
the sequential but powerful way in which humans recognize
patterns.

The theory of such schemes was pursued before experimentation became economically feasible, therefore it is expected that the practical economic advantages brought about by silicon chips and machines such as WISARD will make interesting experiments possible. This may bring about a novel race of computing machines, more flexible than the conventional computer and better adapted to communicate with human beings.

REFERENCES

Aleksander, I. (1978) ´Pattern Recognition with Memory Networks´, in Batchelor (1978).

Aleksander, I., and Stonham, T.J. (1979) ´A Guide to Pattern Recognition using RAMs´, IEE Journal Computers and Digital Techniques (1), 29-40.

Batchelor, B. (1978) ´Pattern Recognition: Ideas in Practice´, Plenum.

Duff, K.J.B. (1978) ´Parallel Processing Techniques´ in Batchelor (1978).

Fu, K.S. (1976) ´Digital Pattern Recognition´, Springer Verlag.

Gostick, R.W. (1979) ICL Tech Fair 1 (2), 116-135.

Rutovitz, D. (1966) ´Pattern Recognition´, J. R. Stat. Soc. Series B/4, 504.

Ullman, J.R. (1973) ´Pattern Recognition Techniques´, Butterworth.

Wilson, M.J.D. (1980) ´Artificial Perception in Adaptive Arrays´ IEEE Trans. Systems Man and Cybernetics X (1), 25-32.

Chapter 7

Intelligent digital systems

I Aleksander

7.1 INTRODUCTION

Despite the considerable feats displayed by the artificial
intelligence programs as seen in Chapter 5, and the ability
of digital systems to acquire discriminatory visual powers as
seen in Chapter 6, one is left with the feeling that there is
still a long way to go before a machine might acquire
intelligence that approaches the human definition. One might
argue that this sort of approach may not be necessary, that
the achievements of AI are sufficient to deliver as much
programming excellence as required. There is one serious flaw
in this. Truly intelligent programs and systems should make
virtually no programming demand on their users, obey their
every (natural language) request, and instantly understand
the significance of what they see through their TV eye. The
automation industry, if no other, would soon turn this
´sixth´ or ´seventh´ generation of computing to advantage.

But even to the most ardent supporter of AI, this sounds on
the borderlines of science fiction. This chapter does not
provide recipes for generating the super-intelligent machine,
it merely points to a couple of methodologies that one might
scrutinize more closely. It also suggests that the way one
interprets theories about intelligence should be
investigated, because both of these avenues are rooted in
psychological theory.

As has already been broached in Chapter 5, some AI workers
maintain that since an AI program runs and produces roughly
the desired simulation of intelligent actions, the program is
a theory of intelligence. Hence we take strong exception to
this way of thinking and substitute it by another. In order
to have an intelligent system, one needs a theory about
intelligent behavior first.

The next part of the chapter looks more closely at the
relationship between theory and instantiation of a program,
particularly surrounding the question ´can man-made systems
exhibit Understanding and Intentionality?´ This leads first
to a consideration of a theory known as ´Personal Construct
Theory´ which claims to capture man´s acquisition of
understanding and intentionality. Secondly we shall switch to
the opposite extreme: the level of neurophysiology. Here we
discuss ways in which the computational level of systems such

as those in Chapter 6 may be enhanced by adding feedback to pattern recognition nets. It is almost certain that natural systems themselves would not be able to function without this artifact, and therefore there may be a double-edged advantage in investigations of this sort, that not only could result in more sophisticated computing machinery, but also may throw more light on the relationship between structure and fuction in neurophysiological problems.

Clearly much research in both these areas remains to be done, this chapter should be seen as an introduction to such research possibilities.

7.2 A LACK OF UNDERSTANDING

Still raging fiercely in the rarefied atmosphere between AI and philosophy, is the argument as to whether a story understanding program can be said to have understood anything at all. Worse still may be the claim that a story understanding program is ´a theory of understanding´.

The central opponent to this notion is John Searle (1980), who sees an implication that a computer must possess intentionality in order to understand the story. Thus any theory of understanding must have intentionality as one of its axioms. Searle comes under heavy fire from the ´strong AI´ community that subscribes to Daniel Dennett´s influence. They define intentionality as something that may be attributed to a machine or an AI program should its level of competence be high enough.

The interesting question here is not so much who is right, but why it appears to be so difficult to reconcile these two views. Clarity at the level of what is and what is not a theory, and when a theory is about something and when it is not, is helpful in reconciling such divergent views.

Possibly the most positive outcome of this discussion will be that, provided some basic rules of mathematical procedure are followed, it is possible to find properly framed systems of

axioms that could encompass intentionality (in the Searle
sense) as one of the emergent theorems. Indeed, it may be
possible to show that intentionality is a deep and
fundamental property of some systems that can either be built
or programmed.

7.3 THE APPROPRIATENESS OF A THEORY

In Chapter 2 we have seen that since the turn of the century,
pure mathematics has taught us to cope with the existence of
non-Euclidean theories. That is, David Hilbert freed
mathematicians to seek their theories in abstract ways. The
test of a good theory is the consistency of its axioms and
the logic of its theorems.

This has also clarified the way in which the theory can be
about something. The axioms of the theory are seen as being
related to the events of the real world by a hypothesis. The
theorems of the theory may then be translated into the real
world framework by means of the same hypothesis. If these
translated theorems then turn out to be predictive of new
events in reality, the theory can be said to be about this
reality.

A typical example of this kind of relationship working well,
is the hypothesis that a real-world dynamical system (such as
a pendulum) may be represented by systems of differential
equations containing time derivatives (the axioms). The
theorems are the solutions of these equations which predict
the time behavior of the system in the real world.

It is interesting that this notion of theory can extend even
to totally non-mathematical concepts. For example, ´Freud´s
theory´ may have among its theorems something like:

> ´The suppression of X in early childhood may lead
> to behavior Y in adult life´

This is a typical explicative theory, which generally answers
the question ´why do we observe Y?´ As such it is perfectly
acceptable, provided that the abstractions used to get from X

to Y are logical enough to be convincing. The mapping to and from observed events forms a hypothesis. The theory will remain valid if this hypothesis is shown to be false. The getting from X to Y is a separate issue which may remain valid even in the face of a contradicted hypothesis.

Looking at AI programming styles, a theory appears to consist of structural axioms (such as model states related by production rules) and behavioral theorems, that is, the performance of the program at run time. For example, the actual stories generated by James Meehan's programs (1975) may be seen as theorems resulting from sets of facts and production rules that organize facts into story states. Broadly speaking, the latter is an axiomatic structure.

Several criticisms may be leveled at this interpretation of a theory. First, it may be argued that the theorems are not emergent from the axioms, but were there almost as a goal before the axioms were thought of. The second, is that some writers in AI extend the notion of the theory to saying it is about something. For example, Robert Wilensky (1983) refers to his story understanding algorithms as a

'theory of understanding through explanation'.

The algorithms are excellent, relating as they do, a new input to a story to the state of the story so far. This is done by forward productions, while the 'explanation' is carried out through backward tracking through the selected forward path. The program runs and answers questions about stories and new inputs. But implied in the statement 'theory of understanding' is the fact that the theory is about understanding in general, including human understanding.

This is clearly a category mistake. For example, a similar mistake would be made were one to say that a higher order differential equation constituted a theory of human being's ability to remain upright on his feet in a balanced position. True, human balance may be described and indeed, simulated by a system of differential equations, but it would be useless to teach differential equations to someone whose legs had just been amputated!

Finally, it is necessary to drive home the inappropriateness

of Daniel Dennett's point that a program which is attributed
by a human as having human property X, is indeed a theory
about property X. A lesson may be learned in this respect
from some experiments carried out by John Andreae in the late
1960s. He built a box containing three pushbutton switches
marked A, B and C, and one light. The experimenter was asked
to develop a 'theory' of button-pushing strategies that made
the lamp switch. The real 'theory' was that the machine was
probabilistic. Switch A had a probability of lighting the
lamp of 1/4, switch B, 2/4 and switch C, 3/4. That is, there
was no meaning in the order in which the switches were
pressed. Most experimenters produced complicated theories of
sequence that lit the light. Only the most persevering
experimenters noticed the probabilistic effect and reported
it, while some attributed to the machine the ultimate human
property: 'It's got a will of its own!' The lesson learned
here is that attribution can be arbitrary, and its value
should be treated with suspicion. Those who attributed the
wrong theory to the machine, although probably right within
their span of experimentation, were not in a position to
predict future behavior. Equally Dennett followers, although
they produce accurate programs about their own attribution,
cannot be in a position to be fairly judged, if attribution
be the only criterion. Their theories are not predictive of
human performance except in an arbitrary way.

7.4 SPECIFICATION FOR A PROGRAM WITH INTENTIONALITY

The main message so far, is that an intelligent program that
might carry the attribute of having intentionality must be
based on a theory that has intentionality as one of its
emergent theorems. The key ingredient of such a theory must
be a set of axioms that allow for a build-up of experience.
Translated into programming terms, it appears necessary that
a program that captures intentionality must be of a learning
kind. Clearly, this is an intuitive judgement.

As a further intuition, it seems clear that the sort of
program where knowledge is acquired mainly from input
generated by a user, would be inadequate. Typical of this
class are the learning programs of Winston (1975), or
classical expert system schemes. The unsatisfactory part of
of these theories lies in the fact that the program has no

control over its teaching data.   That is, <u>need</u> for data is
not one of the theorems of the theory.   Without having such
needs how can a program <u>know</u> what it wants?   In fact, how can
it know anything as a result?

Thus,   if intentionality is defined as the ability to direct
mental events at existing real-world objects (Brentano, 1874)
the following theoretical definition might follow:

> ´Intentionality is   a   theorem in a   system   whose
> axioms   contain   actions   directed   at   resolving
> mental ambiguities´

It is only once this mechanism of enquiry has been properly
established,   that   the   object-directedness   of   the   system
might   map into what we understand to be   object-directedness
in humans.   In psychology,   there happens to be a   properly
stated theory that has ´man-the-scientist´ or ´enquiring man´
as its main theme.   This is a Personal Construct Theory,   a
theory of   personality,   first   developed   by   a   clinical
psychologist,   George Kelly,   in 1955.   Although this may be
only one example of useful theories of this kind, the rest of
this paper will be devoted to the sketching out of a
hypothesis that maps this theory into a computing framework.
A full treatment of the subject is found in MacDonald (1983).

7.5 PERSONAL CONSTRUCT THEORY AND PROGRAMS: A SKETCH

This remarkable theory, although not entirely embraced by the
whole psychology community,   has developed a large following.
It is used by clinicians as an orientation for therapy and by
industrial psychologists as a way of getting people to
explain their feelings about,   say,   products of their
organizations.

Kelly was concerned with rigor,   and attempted to state his
theory formally as a single axiom and eleven   corollaries.
The driving force was to banish the notion of ´man-the-
biological-organism´ or ´man-the-lucky-guy´ which he saw
inherent in the psychological theories of the day.   To him
(although he did not explicitly say so) such theories did not
capture man´s intentionality.   He was a Searle to the

psychologists' attempts to see man as an automaton. His
theory is about 'man-the-scientist', that is, man with a
developing individual personality who goes about predicting
and controlling his own destiny in the world. This
constitutes an understanding of the world itself. If this
does not embrace intentionality as part of the apparatus,
what does?

A programme of research has been centered around this theory
at Brunel University. There are two targets. First, despite
its apparent clarity, Kelly's theory is not easy to
interpret. It was interpreted by Kelly himself over three
large volumes, and in the last 25 years there have been over
300 interpretive papers written on the subject.[*] Therefore,
subjecting the theory to computational accuracy has required
a thorough investigation of the coherence of the theory in
itself. Second, a hypothesis has to be developed that
translates the theory into computational terms. It is the
latter activity that is outlined here.

7.5.1 The Fundamental Axiom

'A person's processes are psychologically
channelized by ways in which he anticipates
events'.

The translation into a computational form starts with a
program which may be called 'The Intentional Program' (or
IP). This is the translation of a 'a person's processes'. A
list of such translations is given below.

Kelly	Algorithm
Person's processes	Intentional Program (IP).
Psychologically	Defines the range of convenience of the IP to 'thoughts and actions' as being the state labels of the IP program (as opposed to , say, digestion or skin texture).

---

[*] See Adams-Webber (1979) for a list of these papers.

Channelized	The IP has a structure (flow chart or state transition diagram or a tree, etc.).
Ways	Points to a possible non-determinism in the structure, there being more than one way to progress through the structure.
Anticipates	States in the IP structure are related to previously experienced inputs.
Events	Input to the IP related to world realities.

7.5.2 Intentional Program Fundamental Axiom

An Intelligent Program **about** human thought and action has a non-deterministic structure that is predictive of its own input.

7.5.3 Kelly's Construction Corollary

´A person anticipates events by construing their replications´.

Kelly explains that by ´construing´ he means ´placing an interpretation´. Man could not survive were he not able to package the stream of data he faces into meaningful events.

He must be endowed with a mechanism for doing this, so this is an important part of the specification for the IP. Kelly suggests that similarities and differences in this stream are to be noticed by the human machine.

7.5.4 IP Construction Corollary

The IP **becomes** predictive of input by assigning interpretation labels to similarity groupings in the input stream.

7.5.5 Kelly's Individuality Corollary

´Persons differ from each other in their construction of events´.

This gives man his right to individuality, and allows that no two instantiations of the IP need necessarily to be the same.

7.5.6 IP Individuality Corollary

Different instantiations of the IP may assign interpretation labels to input streams of different ways.

7.5.7 Kelly's Dichotomy Corollary

´A person's construction system is composed of a finite number of dichotomous constructs´.

This is a crucial corollary, as it defines the process of assigning interpretation labels. It implies a double associative relationship between input events and their interpretations. The first part of this is that input-related events or elements address a construct. The construct itself consists of a pair of further elements that act in contrast. For example, the input element may be ´Mozart's Clarinet Concerto´ which addresses a ´CLASSICAL-JAZZ´ construct.

The second assignment is one that states how far the element lies along a one-dimensional scale between the two poles. For the above example most people would assign the element to 100% CLASSICAL and 0% JAZZ. Whereas, were the construct GOOD-BAD, then the placing might be anywhere along the scale depending on personal preference.

7.5.8 IP Dichotomy Corollary

Interpretation labels in the IP are called constructs. They are organized as an associative database so that input-related elements address a construct and obtain an applicability value between two further elements that make up the construct.

7.5.9 Kelly's Organization Corollary

'Each person characteristically evolves, for his
convenience in anticipating events, a construction
system embracing ordinal relationships between
constructs'.

This suggests that the construct database does not consist of
a set of unrelated items, but that the constructs are linked
by non-symmetrical relations. Kelly notes that there are two
ways in which this could happen. First the poles of one
construct could include those of another. For example, in
some people's opinion GOOD-BAD could include CLASSICAL-JAZZ,
because GOOD includes CLASSICAL and BAD includes JAZZ. on
the other hand, one pole of a construct could include an
entire construct. For example, the YOUNG pole of a YOUNG-OLD
construct might include the BABY-CHILD construct.

Another important aspect of the corollary is the word
'evolves'. This suggests that the relations are not set once
and for all, but change in an evolutionary fashion with
proper anticipation of events as the criterion for change.

7.5.10 IP Organization Corollary

IPs will update and structure the construct database so as to
include non-symmetric relations between constructs and thus
aid the anticipation of inputs.

7.5.11 Kelly's Choice Corollary

'A person chooses for himself that alternative in a
dichotomized construct through which he
anticipates the greater possibility for extension
and definition of his system'.

Kelly's theory totally banishes notions such as 'goal-
seeking' or 'motivation' as parts of the human apparatus.
This corollary is about <u>drive</u>. It suggests that new
elements are assigned to constructs so as to allow as much
flexibility as possible for the future. For example, faced
with a new human acquaintance, a person who assumes it to be
FRIENDLY in a FRIENDLY-HOSTILE construct anticipates that he

will learn more about that person than were he to assume the
opposite pole. Thus, the fundamental drive in Personal
Construct Theory is <u>curiosity</u>. Clearly the organization
corollary allows ´a change of mind´ were the first assignment
to lead to erroneous anticipations.

7.5.12 IP Choice Corollary

New elements are assigned by the IP to constructs so as to
minimize the potential growth of the database.

<u>Note</u>: the implication here is that the IP continually tries
to anticipate events while a new element is added to
the database, and that no evaluative mechanism need be
built in, as part of the anticipation lies in
addressing the GROWTH-NO GROWTH construct. It is this
construct that appears to be required right at the
start of the life of the program.

7.5.13 Kelly´s Range Corollary

´A construct is convenient for the anticipation of
a finite range of events only´.

This is self-evident and may be translated directly.

7.5.14 IP Range Corollary

A construct in the IP database may be addressed by a finite
range of elements only.

<u>Note</u>: another way of seeing this is that a particular event,
during the process of anticipation, would extract a
subset of the database in which all the constructs had
that event in their range of convenience.

7.5.15 Kelly´s Experience Corollary

´A person´s construction system varies as he
successively construes the replication of events´.

This stresses Kelly´s belief that man´s view of the world is
constantly changing. The word <u>successively</u> indicates that

changes are made one by one: the system needs time to adapt to and evaluate changes as they occur.

7.5.16 IP Experience Corollary

The IP varies its construct database step by step, in response to its ability to interpret and predict events.

7.5.17 Kelly's Modulation Corollary

'The variation in a person's construction system is limited by the permeability of the constructs within whose range of convenience the variants lie'.

PERMEABILITY-NONPERMEABILITY is a construct in itself that a person uses to evaluate other constructs in respect of their ability to accept a wide (permeable) or narrow (nonpermeable) set of elements. In programming terms this could be measured as the number of elements that address a particular construct.

7.5.18 IP Modulation Corollary

The amount by which the IP can vary its construct database is limited by size of the element sets addressing each construct.

Note: the practical point of interest that arises from this corollary is that there is a self-limiting growth of the construct database that depends on the flexibility of the constructs themselves. Whatever this may be, it is clear that such databases will be open to attributes such as 'narrow minded' or 'broad minded' depending on the permeability question.

7.5.19 Kelly's Fragmentation Corollary

'A person may successively employ a variety of construction sub-systems which are internally incompatible with each other'.

This is an important corollary as it basically states that the construct database need not be logic-tight. This would be a clear departure for some AI approaches in which knowledge stores are continually scanned for logical consistency. However, we know that people do not construe their world with impeccable logic. It may be that the ability to withstand logically incompatible subsystems is part of being able to possess true intentionality. Typical may be the situation where a person's acts of kindness are construed by another with suspicion, while the same act, if performed by someone else may be accepted without question.

7.5.20 IP Fragmentation Corollary

The IP may address, in turn, parts of its construct database that are logically incompatible with each other.

7.5.21 Kelly's Commonality Corollary

'To the extent that a person employs a construction of experience which is similar to that employed by another, his processes are similar to those of another person'.

The last two corollaries allow Kelly to express ideas relating to interpersonal relationships. There is not much point in seeking computational meaning in the phrase Inter-Program Relationships. Instead, it seems important to ask the question 'what kind of relationship can a human build up with a machine endowed with an IP?'

Probably the best known product of these theories is the Repertory Grid. This is a grid that can express a person's elements and constructs almost as a truth table. It is as a result of this grid that Personal Construct Theory has found clinical and industrial application. After all, it is a way of measuring what a person thinks about people and objects. Ways of eliciting such grids are interesting but beyond the scope of this paper (see Bannister and Mair, 1968). The similarity mentioned in the commonality corollary may therefore refer to similar sections of the repertory grid.

7.5.22 IP Commonality Corollary

To the extent that a person employs a construction of experience which is similar to that employed by the IP (as measured by a repertory grid), his processes are similar to those of the IP.

A remarkable feature of this translation is that the theory itself grapples with the man-machine relation. This is not commonly a feature of other AI schemes in which the man-machine relationship is mainly seen as one of programmer and memory.

7.5.23 Kelly's Sociality Corollary

'To the extent that one person construes the construction process of another he may play a role in a social process involving the other person'

Again this can be related to the man-machine question.

7.5.24 IP Sociality Corollary

To the extent that the IP construes the construction processes of a person, it may play a role in a social process involving this person.

This is obviously a controversial issue and some may care to ask whether the word 'extent' points to anything except a trivial extent. However, taking this point seriously, it is clear that there are important practical implications for an IP structured on Personal Construct Theory lines. The main one is its readiness to act as an expert system which 'knows what it wants'.

7.6 A SUMMARY OF THE PERSONAL CONSTRUCT INTENTIONAL PROGRAM

The excitement in this approach lies in the fact that it suggests a simple intentional program that not only is capable of intelligent responses to data, but has an acquisition mechanism that depends on its 'needs'. This need

is a part of the program itself and seems to be central in
establishing an intentional relationship with the objects of
the real world. The obvious question that arises here is
whether, outside of having intentionality, the program would
be of any use.

As already mentioned, this sort of approach may lead
computing into areas of expert system in which human
judgement has as great a part to play as stored logic and
data. Advances in computer-aided design may benefit from
this approach, not only because a Construct IP would be
receptive to esthetic as well as functional information, but
also, if used as an aid, through the sociality corollary, it
would have a capacity for understanding the needs of
individual users. A similar effect would be beneficial in the
medical world too, where the possibility of a two-way
transaction during a terminal session (as opposed to open-
loop one-way schemes currently being developed) would be
beneficial.

What effort is required to structure a realistic intentional
program? Unfortunately, the answer is: a great deal. First,
no mention at all has been made of the input and output
interfaces with which such a system would interact with its
world. Kelly's theory operates at the conceptual level and
assumes that the human actually sees objects and not
meaningless assemblages of pixels. Therefore any development
programme that heads in the direction of Construct IP, must
also look at ways in which low-level interactions in such
system may take place. Systems that, in fact, turn
assemblies of pixels into concepts. The rest of this chapter
will describe a programme of work that seeks to identify
important emergent properties in structures of distributed
memory networks.

7.7 ARTIFICIAL INTELLIGENCE AND NEURAL NETS

Artifical intelligence work in the seventies has displaced
earlier research into the mechanisms of intelligent behavior
of neural nets based on the 1943 McCulloch and Pitts model of
the neuron. The main reasons for this demise are understood
to be the following:

a)   The 'perceptron' limitations of neural nets were
     stressed   by Minsky and Papert in 1969. These largely
     centered on the inability of some nets to carry out
     simple objects counting operations.

b)   The writing of programs that have a surface behavior
     which, if attributed to humans, would be said to require
     intelligence, has become a well-developed and understood
     science (Boden, 1978).

c)   The generality of the conventional computer structure
     discourages a study of architectures incompatible with
     it.

d)   Neural nets are programmed through exposure to data and
     in this sense are 'learning machines'. It is argued
     that the age of the universe would be required to learn
     human-like intelligent behavior and this is best avoided
     by more direct programming.

Here it is argued that a) is invalid as it applies only to a
limited class of neural nets; b) is one of many methodologies
of studying mechanisms with an intelligent surface behavior,
another, the pattern recognition neural net, is being
proposed as have equal validity; c) has been invalidated by
the possibility of totally novel architectures being
facilitated by advancing VLSI techniques whereby
'intelligence' may be derived with great cost-effectiveness
than is offered by the conventional computer. The argument
in d) is appealing but extreme. In the same way as
algorithmic AI approaches provide a limited window view of
intelligent behavior, so can studies in learning neural
networks. It is the knowledge-gaining efficacy of the
research that is at stake. It is argued hence that this may
be greater through a study of neural-nets and that, indeed,
the vistas over mechanisms of intelligent behavior may be
wider. The central argument evolves around the conept of
'emergent intelligent properties' of a system, as will be
discussed in the next section.

7.8 WHAT ARE EMERGENT PROPERTIES?

The question of emergent properties of machines and their
relationship to parts of these machines has recently been
lucidly discussed by Gregory (1981). The architecture of the
brain, that is the parts of the brain machine and their
interconnections, is undeniably based on building blocks that
consist of neural tissue. Intelligent behavior is one
emergent property of such tissue. In AI any intelligent
behavior exhibited by the computer is not an
emergent property of the computer itself, but rather, of the
program. The latter however needs to be argued – it is not as
obvious as one would like it to be.

On the other hand, it could be argued that programming a
computer is like painting a canvas. No one would believe that
the image on the canvas is an emergent property of the canvas
and the paints. It is merely an expression of the artist's
intent. The fact that a computer pronounces: 'The black box
is in front of and slightly to the left of the green
pyramid', the canvas-and-oil school would argue, is merely a
confirmation of the programmer's (artist's) original
intention.

On the other hand, the AI fraternity would argue that the
statement issued by the machine is an emergent property of
the rules obeyed by the program, rules which the programmer
has chosen with great care. Are these rules just the spots of
a pointillist painter or the true atoms of a system whose
internal action creates an effect not contained in the atoms
themselves?

Here one does not seek to resolve this question. Alternative
technical structures are presented which are both
technologically interesting because of their advanced
performance and fundamentally attractive as intelligent
behavior is much less dependent on a highly directed choice
of programmed rules.

But what constitutes this 'fundamental attraction'? The
alternative structures are indeed neural-like while at the
same time being technologically feasible and properly adapted
to implementation. However the 'fundamental attraction'

comes from the fact that the emergent properties of these stuctures may be much more general than those ensuing from a carefully chosen set of rules. For example, the emergent properties of such a system may be the ability to append proper linguistic labels to <u>all</u> the examples shown in Fig. 7.1. Even to the most enthusiastic AI practitioner this appears as a difficult task due to the exploding multiplicity of rules that may be required. Clearly this chapter will not present a structure that meets this specification either. It will, however, examine to what extent artificial neural net structures are likely to have emergent properties that head in the stated direction without an exploding set of elements.

Fig. 7.1 A collection of vision tasks

7.9 LEVEL 0 STRUCTURES: IMAGE CLASSIFIERS

It will be shown that increased prowess in the emergent properties results from a progression of physically distinct structures, each level of complexity relying on an understanding of the previous level. At the lowest level (0), the nature of the simple artificial neuron is defined (much of this being available in the published literature) as is the nature of the simplest network structure; the single-layer net as shown in Fig. 7.2.

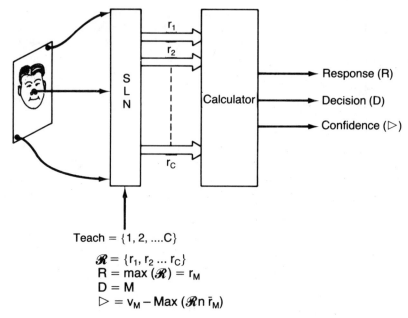

$$\mathcal{R} = \{r_1, r_2 \dots r_C\}$$
$$R = \max(\mathcal{R}) = r_M$$
$$D = M$$
$$\triangleright = v_M - \text{Max}(\mathcal{R} \, \text{n} \, \bar{r}_M)$$

Fig. 7.2 Level 0 structure

This, indeed is the structure of the WISARD system whose principles are discussed in Chapter 6, and which is used in practice for high performance image identification. The single-layer net is described here in terms convenient for the rest of the chapter the reader being referred to Chapter 6 for a technological and theoretical description of the principles involved.

The artificial neuron is defined as a bit-organized random access memory where the address terminals are the synaptic inputs (N in number), the data output terminal is the axonic output, while the data inptu terminal is the ´dominant synapse´ (in the terminology of Brindley, 1967). During a training phase the RAM stores the response (0,1) to the binary N-tuple at the synapses as required by the dominant synapse. During a ´usage´ period the last stored response or each occurring N-tuple is output at the axon. Clearly variants on this are possible: the neuron can be made to store and output a number, if word rather than bit-organized. Also a statistical function would be used to control the output (as in Uttley, 1959). However, these schemes may be shown to be variants of the ´canonical´ neuron discussed above.

Now the <u>single-layer net</u> itself may be defined as follows: A
single-layer net consists of C sets of K artificial   neurons
each.   Each set is call a <u>discriminator</u>.   Each neuron in a
discriminator receives the <u>same</u> data input bit.   It may be
helpful   to the reader to relate this   definition   to
discriminators as found in Chapter 6.   Each discriminator
thus has KN synaptic inputs assumed to   receive the   input
image.   The connection of the bits of an image to this vector
is   one-to-one but arbitrary.   Once such an arbitrary
connection has been determined it remains fixed for the net.

The same connection may be used for all discriminators
(coherent net) or not (incoherent net). Such coherence may be
shown to have little effect on behavior.

Training   involves   one   discriminator   per   class   to   be
distinguished.   For a representative set of images a logical
1   is   fed to all the elements of the   discriminator
corresponding to the known class of the current image.   When
an unknown pattern is present at the input, the number of 1s
at each discriminator output (out of a total of C) is
counted.   The <u>first properties</u>, proven and discussed in
Aleksander (1982), may now be stated for completeness.

7.9.1 Property 0.1: Recognition and Confidence Level

The system transforms an input binary vector $\underline{I}$ of magnitude
KN bits into an output vector of C numbers (responses),   each
such number being the number of 1s at the discriminator
output, expressed as a proportion of K.   The discriminator
with the highest response is said to classify the image.   The
classification has been shown to be predictable through a
somewhat awkward set of expressions that can be simplified to
the following.   The response of the jth discriminator r_j is
most likely to be

$$r_j - \simeq \frac{S_j}{(NK)} N \qquad \ldots\ldots(1)$$

where S_j is the overlap area between the   unknown   incoming
vector and the closest pattern in the training set for the
jth discriminator.   The fact that this is <u>not</u> a mere pattern
match and that performance depends on N is brought home by
the <u>confidence</u> with which a decision is made.

Confidence is defined as

$$CON \simeq \frac{r_1 - r_2}{r_1}$$ where r_1 is the strongest discriminator

response and r_2 that of the next one down. This becomes

$$CON \simeq 1 - (\frac{S_2}{S_1})^N \qquad \qquad \ldots\ldots(2)$$

where S_2 is the overlap of the unknown with the closest element in the second most strongly responding discriminator, and S_1 with the first. The confidence (and, as argued in Aleksander, 1982, avoidance of saturation of the system) increases with N. Against this, one must realize that the cost of the system grows exponentially with N. Two further particular emergent properties may be noted.

7.9.2 Property 0.2: Acceptance of Diversity

The training set for a particular discriminator can be highly diverse (examples may be found in papers already quoted: many orientations and expressions of a face, rotation and position of a piecepart). The system performs its classification without a search. The response vector may be generated after one pass through the storage system. This property is most rare in AI work in general.

7.9.3 Property 0.3: Sensitivity to Small Differences

The system can accept both to differentiate or group together images with small differences between them. For example, experiments on WISARD have demonstrated that a distinction may be obtained for smiling and unsmiling faces or, if required, faces may be recognized independently of their expression. This is achieved merely by task-definition through training, where the system accommodates the trainer's requirements as best it can. It would be most difficult to find an a priori set of rules which is guaranteed to differentiate between any two faces, which may subsequently be easily modified to react differently to different expressions. Finally, it should be noted that a single-layer network can distinguish the presence or absence of the dog in a 'Marr-Dalmation scene' probably with greater ease than a human being, as its action can be forcefully directed towards the task. The important fact is not that the system recognizes the dog but that it is <u>sensitive</u> to such complex data.

More interesting, perhaps, is a speculation on whether a SLN might be able to recognize the face of the politician in Fig. 7.1. The transfer from a grey-tone image to an outline is, apparently, not a learnt function. The classical approach to explaining this transfer phenomenon relies on the supposition of the existence of a neural system in the visual pathway that performs a differentiation operation. This would provide the similar output for both representations. Neural nets that are ´pre-programmed´ to perform the differentiation are well understood, and will not be discussed here.

7.10 LEVEL 1 STRUCTURES: DECISION FEEDBACK

The added ingredient of all structures from here on is the inclusion of feedback between the response vector and the input as shown in Fig. 7.3.

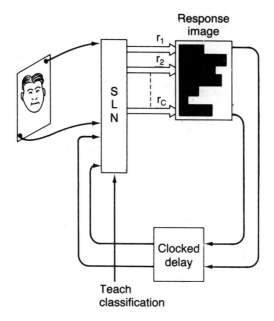

Fig. 7.3 Level 1 structure

In this case, one merely mixes the output vector bits in with
the input vector to create a new input vector. The latter is
then distrubuted among the N-tuple inputs as before. This
technique was first reported in Aleksander (1975), and has
more recently been investigated further using the WISARD
system and the following method.

Figure 7.4 shows the experimental arrangements. Two cameras
are used, one for input and the other for a display of the
discriminator responses. These two images are mixed to form
the input field to WISARD. A feedback clock is included in
the system allowing step by step recordings to be made. This
connection leads to the next emergent property.

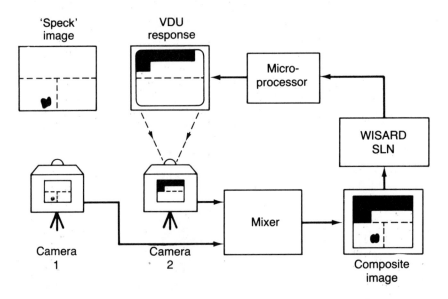

Fig. 7.4 Level 1 experiment

7.10.1 Property 1.1: The Amplification of Confidence

This is particularly useful in discriminating very small
differences between images. For example, the scheme can
distinguish with high confidence (after a few steps of
feedback) whether a small speck is on the left or the right
of the image. Clearly a single-layer net would have a
limited confidence since S_1 and S_2 in equation 2 would be
very close in this situation. The results obtained with

WISARD are shown in Fig. 7.5 where a ´speck´ consisting of
5% if the image is sought either on the right or to the left
of the image (N=6 for the experiment). It may be seen that
the maximum confidence without feedback would be about 30%
whereas the feedback system reaches over 90%.

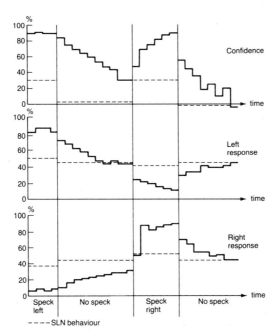

Fig. 7.5 Results in confidence amplification

7.10.2 Property 1.2: Short-term Memory of Last Response

The results also clearly show a second emergent property
common to many feedback structures: a short-term memory. In
this case this relates to the last-made positive decision
which persists even when the image is removed. In the
context of AI, the only importance of this structure is that
it overcomes one of the perceptron limitations brought to
light by Minsky and Papert (1969). It is clear that a neural
perceptron structure with no feedback would not be a suitable
´speck´ detector in the way discussed above. The
discontinuation of work on neural systems in the seventies
was due to the discovery of several limitations of this kind
which as partly shown here, only apply to some (mainly level
0) artificial neural structures.

7.11 LEVEL 2 STRUCTURES: A PREAMBLE

One property noticeably lacking in the structures described so far is the ability to regenerate or recreate learnt patterns. A structure whose emergent property is that, at any point in time, it has an inner <u>state image</u> in the following sense.

Let us suppose that the response vectors of a single-layer net are no longer trained on desired 1-in-C classification vectors, but that the training consists of applying another <u>**image**</u> vector to the C training terminals. The emergent property of a system of this kind is that it could respond with prototypes of patterns (having been trained on them) to variants of input images. For example, the input could be a square and a triangle in any position in the field of view while the output could be the prototype of each of the two classes. A typical result of this form of training is shown in Fig. 7.6.

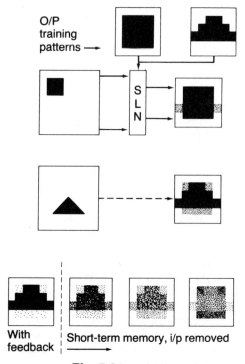

Fig. 7.6 Level 1/2

It has been shown theoretically in Aleksander (1982) that a
2-discriminator SLN operating on a 512 x 512 image with N =
10 and C = 2, may be expected to recognize squares and
triangles both having an area of 16,384 pixels as shown
appearing in any 'rest' position. Experiments have supported
this, but shown that the recognition takes place with a low
degree of confidence, in some cases. In practice, the dotted
areas in Fig. 7.6 would have about 80% intensity with the
black areas being 100% dense.

Note that in the proposed structure, the output can produce K
gray levels at each 'pixel' which my be excessive. In fact,
it is possible to reduce the size of the net right down to a
binary output pixel, in which case each output cell only
'sees' one N-tuple of the input image. This can lead to
interference by the last-seen pattern. It has been shown
that if one adds the property of 'forgetting' to the net
(note: not an emergent property, but a change in structure),
this effect may be compensated.

7.11.1 Property 2.1: Short-term Image Memory

So far, we have only pointed to 'lemmas' of a level 2
structure. The final item is the introduction of feedback
between the output and the input as for level 1 structures.
Clearly this has the property of increasing confidence, i.e.
increasing contrast in the output image. This, incidentally,
now becomes the state image, so that the short-term property
of the level 1 net translates into a short-term memory of the
prototype of the last seen image which fades with time as
shown in Fig. 7.6.

Finally, one can add a variant to the level 2 structure in
the way that the 'dominant synapse' or 'teach' terminals are
connected. This technique simply feeds image information
from the input to the teach terminals as in Fig. 7.7. This
gets around the rather unnatural situation of needing a
separate channel for training.

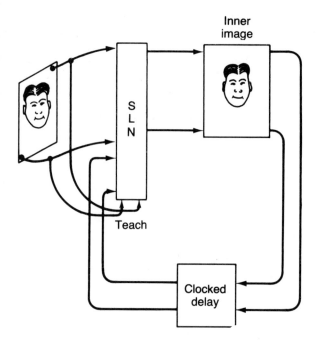

Fig. 7.7 Level 2 structure

7.12 LEVEL 2 STRUCTURES: EMERGENT PROPERTIES

7.12.1 Property 2.2: Artificial Perception

This property has been described by Wilson (1980) albeit in respect to an array network, where specific feedback connections (from a ´nearest neighbor´ arrangement) were used. The essence of this is that, starting from random states, the system rapidly enters state replicas of images seen during training. This link occurs <u>only</u> for ´learnt´ images, non-learnt ones leading to random state changes. This emergent property is thought to be the key to ´modeling-of-the-environment´ within neural nets.

7.12.2 Property 2.3: Sequence Sensitivity

The dynamic property relates to the <u>chaining</u> ability of the system which enables one to train the system to form associations between pairs of input images or longer sequences.

The training goes as follows. One starts with, say a blank state b, and input i_1. This, upon applying a training pulse transfers i_1 to the state. The input is then changed to i_2 and so on. The end of the sequence can again be identified with a blank. This training sequence can be summarized as

Step No.	input	state	next state
1	i_1	b	i_1
2	i_2	i_1	i_2
3	i_3	i_2	i_3
.			
.			
n	b	i_{n-1}	b

This results in a finite state machine approximately as shown in Fig. 7.8. The approximation comes from the interference effect. Experiments with simulated systems show that a version of the input sequence, with a degradation due to interference occurs if the same input sequence is presented a number of times.

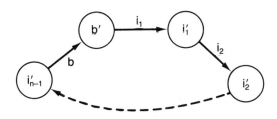

Fig. 7.8 Sequence sensitivity

7.12.3 Property 2.4: Lexical Acceptor

The chaining property may be extended further.

Assume that the two training sequences are:

$$* \ J \ O \ H \ N \ *$$

and $$* \ L \ O \ N \ D \ O \ N \ *$$

(* is another, more pictorial, representation of a blank.)

The resulting state diagram is as shown in Fig. 7.9.

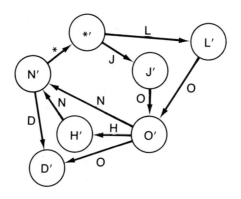

Fig. 7.9 A lexical acceptor

It should be stressed that such diagrams are incomplete and the departure from the ´taught´ sequence remains unspecified. ´Acceptance´ in terms of this kind is seen as a state sequence that is ´sympathetic´ to the input sequence. Clearly a departure from the ´stored´ sequence indicates non-acceptance.

7.12.4 Property 2.5: Image-Name Associations

If the input image were split so that an image part (constant) and a set of name symbols (time varying) were applied simultaneously to be input of the net, cross retrieval between the image and its corresponding name may be

achieved.   Let IM_1 be the (say) facial image of *JANE* and
IM_2 be the facial image of *JON* and the net training on the
two as before,   then the state diagram in Fig. 7.10 results.
The emergent property is clearly the concept that if IM_1 is
presented to the system, it will enter the JANE cycle, while
for IM_2 the JON cycle. Also given a repeated presentation of
JANE, IM_1 will be recreated as will IM_2 for JON.

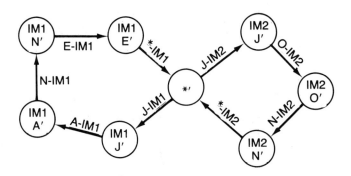

Fig. 7.10 Image-name associations

7.13 LEVEL 3 STRUCTURES: THE ATTENTION MECHANISM

This is shown in Fig. 7.11.   The SLN has two specific
outputs: the first deals with a decision based on the
incoming pattern in the usual way, while the other feeds back
to the input frame.   The input frame itself is somewhat
special: it contains an area of high resolution embedded in a
field of lower resolution.   The high resolution area may be
moved around through instructions fed to a window position-
controller as shown.

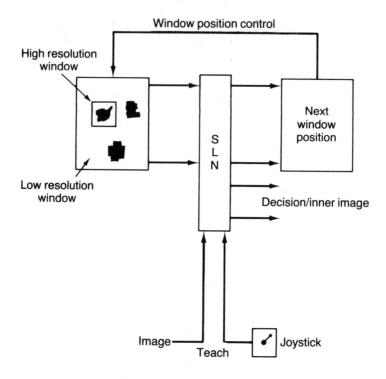

Fig. 7.11 Level 3 structure

7.13.1 Emergent Property 3.1: Blob Finding

A joystick input may be used to train the central window to move in the direction of a ´blob´ and stand still only when the latter is properly centered.

This is a far more efficient way of obtaining position-independent recognition than the scan training discussed in Aleksander (1982). All that is needed is that the ´decision´ output be trained once the blob has been found.

7.13.2 Emergent Property 3.2: Saccadic Jumps

Should there be several ´blobs´ in the field of view, it is clearly possible to teach the system to center on these one at a time, in some ´taught´ order, for example, clockwise, or in a scanning motion. A study of level 3 structures has received only scanty research attention in the past (Dawson, 1975) where it was shown that scenes consisting of several blob-like structures could be properly described by means of a level 3 system combined with conventional computing power. A deeper study is the subject of a current investigation. The aim of such study is to investigate an 'enhanced' level 3 structure in which the SLN is operating as part of both a level 2 loop, and a level 3 one. One can speculate on some emergent properties of such systems.

7.13.3 Speculative Emergent Property 3.3:

Feature Sequence Detection

The level 2/3 system may be taught to take saccadic jumps from feature to feature in an image. The level 2 part would be able to interpret this sequence as belonging to a single object or scene. For example, the system may be taught to label a sequence of saccadic jumps between the corners of any triangle as 'triangle', and, through the same process, distinguish it from a square.

7.13.4 Speculative Emergent Property 3.4: Disambiguation

The same scheme may be used to center the high resolution window on features that determine, say, whether one object is in front of another. This property may also unscramble some of the letter heaps shown in Fig. 7.1.

7.14 CONCLUSIONS ON NEURAL NETS

Clearly the progressive series described does not end at level 3. Interesting possibilities emerge as ever deeper nesting of the structures described takes place, and it is the objective of much current work to bring these to light.

In this final section it may be worth drawing attention to some important parallels or lack thereof, between the emergent properties of artificial neural nets and living systems.

a)   The parallels only begin to become interesting when
      feedback becomes part of the structure. The precise
      training of level 0 nets appears artificial and it is
      only at level 2 that one notes that particular exposures
      of the system to data through a single channel leads to
      association of the type one finds in living systems.

b)   Interesting feedback loops are being discovered by
      physiologists which appear to have some of   the
      characteristics of level 2/3 structures.   For example,
      loops controlling the eye muscles are well known and
      reminiscent of level 3, while recently Barlow (1982)
      has reported that feedback between area VI of the visual
      cortex and the lateral geniculate body is coming under
      greater scrutiny.   This is reminiscent of level 2
      structure and may play a parallel role.

c)   The ´Marr–Dalmatian´ experiment where once the dog is
      noticed it remains clearly perceived points to an
      interaction between the immediate discriminant (low
      level) process of the human visual system and a higher
      level of processing.   In terms of the structure
      discussed here, this would be equivalent in level 2 to
      an inability, at first, to find the appropriate
      classification (or feedback cycle).   Movement, or some
      knowledge of the presence of the dog is equivalent to an
      aided entry into the recognition cycle, which, once
      entered is easily entered again.

Clearly, much work remains to be done with structures at
level 3,   composite structures,   and beyond.   However,
referring back to Fig. 7.1, it is felt that the pattern
recognition neural net approach provides an interesting
alternative to the AI paradigm, where higher level structures
may have a range of emergent ´intelligent´ properties that
are wider than any single AI programming methodology.

REFERENCES

Adams-Webber, J.R. (1979) ´Personal Construct Theory Concepts and Applications´, Wiley and Sons, Toronto.

Aleksander, I. (1975) ´Action-Oriented Learning Networks´, Kybernetes 4, 39-44.

Aleksander, I. (1982) ´Memory Networks for Practical Vision Systems´, Proc. of the Rank Prize Fund International Symposium on the Physical and Bilogical Processing of Images, London.

Aleksander, I., Stonham, T.J., and Wilkie, R.A. (1982) ´Computer Vision Systems for Industry´, Digital Systems for Industrial Automation 1 (4), 305-320.

Bannister, D., and Mair, J.M.M. (1968) ´The Evaluation of Personal Constructs´, Academic Press, London.

Barlow, H.B. (1982) ´Understanding Natural Vision´, Proc. of the Rank Prize Fund International Symposium on the Physical and Biological Processing of Images, London.

Boden, M. (1978) ´Artificial Intelligence and Natural Man´, Harvester Press, Hassocks.

Brentano, F. (1974) ´Psychology from an Empirical Standpoint´, Felix Meiner, Hamburg.

Brindley, G.S. (1967) ´The Classification of Modifiable Synapses and Their Use in Models for Conditioning´, Proc. R. Soc. B 168, 361-376.

Dawson, G. (1975) ´Simple Scene Analysis Using Digital Learning Nets´, PhD Thesis, Faculty of Natural Science, University of Kent, Canterbury.

Dennett, D. (1978) ´Brainstorms´, Harvester Press, Hassocks.

Gregory, R. (1981) ´The Mind in Science´, Weidenfeld and Nicholson, London.

Kelly, G.A. (1955) ´The Psychology of Personal Constructs´, Norton, New York.

MacDonald, A. (1983) Brunel PhD Thesis (to be published).

McCulloch, W.S., and Pitts, W.H. (1943) ´A Logical Calculus Immanent in Nervous Activity´, Bull. Math. Biophys. 5, 115-133.

Meehan, J. (1975) ´Using Planning Structures to Generate Stories´, Am. J. Computational Linguistics, Microfiche 33, 77-93.

Minsky, M.L., and Papert, S. (1969) ´Perceptrons: An Introduction to Computational Geometry´, MIT Press, Cambridge, Mass.

Nielsson, N. (1981) ´Principles of Artificial Intelligence´, Tioga Press, Palo Alto, California.

Searle, J.R. (1980) ´Mind Brains and Programs´, The Behavioural and Brain Sciences, Vol. 13, Cambridge University Press.

Uttley, A.M. (1959) ´Conditional Computing in a Nervous System´, in ´Mechanisation of Thought Processes´, HMSO, London.

Wilensky, R. (1983) ´Planning and Understanding´, Addison Wesley, Reading, Mass.

Wilson, M.J.D. (1980) ´Artificial Perception in Adaptive Arrays´, IEEE Trans. Systems, Man and Cybernetics 10, 25-32.

Winston, P.H. (1975) ´Learning Structural Descriptions from Examples´, in ´The Psychology of Computer Vision´, ed. P.H. Winston, McGraw Hill, New York.

Chapter 8

Artificial intelligence approaches to concept learning

Robert C. Holte

8.A Introduction

Suppose we are told that each of the objects in Fig. 8.1 is
'grisbot' and are then set the task of classifying arbitrary
objects as being either grisbot or not grisbot. That is, we
are required to decide whether a given object is grisbot or
not on the basis of the objects which we have been told are
grisbot. To do this, we adopt some method for classifying
objects as grisbot or not grisbot which is based on the
objects which are definitely grisbot and which is applicable
to any object.

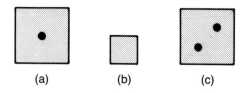

Fig. 8.1 Objects which are "grisbot"

Method 1: if the given object is one of the objects which
we have been told is grisbot, then classify it as
grisbot. Classify all other objects as not
grisbot.

Using method 1 we would classify the object in Fig. 8.2(a)
as grisbot and the objects in Figs 8.2(b), 8.2(c), and
8.2(d) as not grisbot.

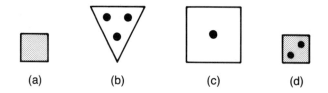

Fig. 8.2 Grisbot or not grisbot?

Alternatively, we may have noticed that all of the objects which we have been told are grisbot are square and adopted a method of classification based on this observation.

Method 2: if the given object is square, then classify it as grisbot. Classify all other objects as not grisbot.

Several objects are classified differently by method 2 than they were classified by method 1; for instance, method 1 classifies the objects in Figs 8.2(c) and 8.2(d) as not grisbot, whereas method 2 classifies these objects as grisbot.

Having adopted method 2, and perhaps used it on several occasions, we are suddenly told that the objects in Fig. 8.3 are not grisbot. To our dismay we discover that method 2 is not quite correct: it would have us classify the object in Fig. 8.3(a) as grisbot which is contrary to the known classification. Wishing to find a method which class-ifies all objects correctly, we abandon method 2 and re-examine all of the objects whose classification we have been told. We notice that all of the grisbot objects are not only square, but also gray. Furthermore, no object which we know to be not grisbot is both square and gray. Based on these observations we adopt the following method.

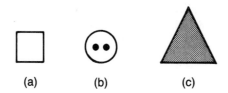

(a)   (b)   (c)

Fig. 8.3 Objects which are not grisbot

Method 3: if a given object is both square and gray, then
classify it as grisbot. Classify all other objects
as not grisbot.

This method correctly classifies all of the objects in Figs
8.1 and 8.3. Of the objects in Fig. 8.2, this method classifies those in 8.2(a) and 8.2(d) as grisbot and those in
8.2(b) and 8.2(c) as not grisbot.

In this example there are two distinct activities. First,
there is the activity of examining the objects whose classification is known and constructing a method of classification; and second, there is the activity of applying the
method of classification to any given object. The former
activity is called concept learning, and its automation is
the subject of this chapter. That is, we will be looking at
algorithms for concept learning, and systems which employ
such algorithms. For the purposes of this chapter, the
phrase 'learning system' will be used as an abbreviation for
'concept learning system'. The latter activity is concept
application or use: this activity will be considered in this
chapter only to the extent that it influences the concept
learning task.

8.A.1 THE CONCEPT LEARNING TASK

To have a concept (e.g. grisbot) is to have a method for
distinguishing objects which instantiate the concept (e.g.
those which are grisbot) from those which do not. Objects
which instantiate a concept are called 'members' of the
concept; objects which do not instantiate a concept are
called 'nonmembers'. Concept learning is the process of
constructing a method for distinguishing members of a
concept from nonmembers. Input to a concept learning process
consists of a set containing some objects which are known
to be members of the concept, and some objects (perhaps
none) which are known to be nonmembers of the concept.
Objects in this set which are known to be members of the
concept are called 'positive examples'; objects in this set
which are known to be nonmembers of the concept are called
'negative examples'.

An example of a concept learning algorithm is the algorithm which always constructs the method:

Classify a given object as a member if and only if it is a positive example. Otherwise classify it as a nonmember.

Method 1, above, is typical of the classification methods produced by this concept learning algorithm. An alternative, but equally simple concept learning algorithm is the algorithm which always constructs the method:

Classify a given object as a nonmember if and only if it is a negative example. Otherwise classify it as a member.

The first concept learning algorithm assumes that all members of the concept are positive examples. The second algorithm assumes that all of the nonmembers of the concept are negative examples. In general neither of these two assumptions is true. Nevertheless, variants of these two simple concept learning algorithms will recur in several places in the chapter.

8.A.2
CONCEPT LEARNING ALGORITHMS BASED ON PROPERTIES OF OBJECTS

In constructing methods 2 and 3 above, attention was paid to properties of the objects. To automate this kind of concept learning we will assume that a set of properties of objects is given, and that all objects which are presented to a concept learning system and a concept applying system are characterized in terms of these properties. The properties and the instances of these properties which shall be used in this chapter are shown in Fig. 8.4. Note that this is a small subset of the conceivable properties and instances which could have been used: properties such as the size and relative orientation of the spots, the position of the object on the page, and the average reflectance of the object have been omitted, and instances which would enable more precise characterizations of object size, color and shape have also been omitted.

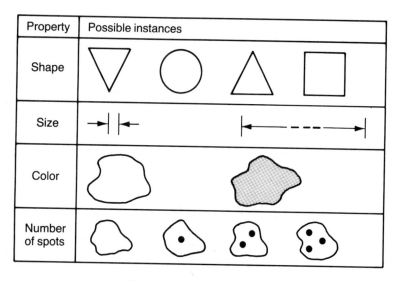

Fig. 8.4 Properties of objects

One should not overlook the significance of restricting the characterization of objects to a relatively small, fixed collection of properties and instances of properties. For instance, the objects in Fig. 8.5 are clearly distinct, but they do not differ in any of the properties which we shall use. Similarly, the objects in Fig. 8.6 are clearly distinct, but the instances of the shape, size and color properties which we shall use are not able to distinguish them. Should some of the objects in Fig. 8.5 (or 8.6) be members of a concept and others nonmembers, no method of classification based only on the properties and instances of properties in Fig. 8.4 could classify all objects correctly. A collection of properties and instances of properties is said to be 'inadequate' if it characterizes in an identical fashion an object which is a member of a concept and an object which is a nonmember of the same concept.*

---

* Quinlan (1979,1982,1983b) discusses the difficulty of constructing an adequate collection of properties and instances of properties.

Only 64 distinct entities can be characterized with the properties and instances of properties in Fig. 8.4. These are shown in Fig. 8.7. Each entity shown in this figure stands for a whole collection of objects which are distinct, but which cannot be distinguished on the basis of the properties and instances of properties which are being used. The set of all distinct entities is called the Universe, or simply U. Henceforth, the terms 'object', 'entity' and 'element of U' shall be used interchangeably to refer to entities.

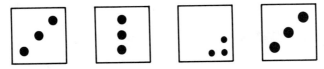

Fig. 8.5 Objects not distinguishable on the basis of the properties in Fig. 8.4. (All of these objects are characterized as square, large, white, 3 spots)

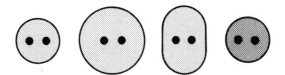

Fig.8.6 Objects not distinguishable on the basis of the instances of properties in Fig. 8.4. (All of these objects are characterized as circle, large, gray, 2 spots)

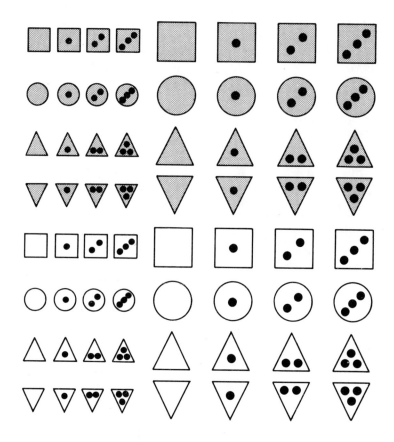

Fig. 8.7 The Universe of entities which are distinct given the properties and instances in Fig. 8.4.

Each property partitions U into a collection of subsets, with one subset for each instance of the property. For instance, the property color partitions U into the subset of gray objects and the subset of white objects. The conjunction of two instances of properties corresponds to the intersection of the corresponding sets: for instance, objects which are 'gray and square' are found in the intersection of the set of objects which are gray and the set of objects which are square.

8.A.3 REPRESENTING OBJECTS WITHIN LEARNING SYSTEMS

For the purposes of manipulation and comparison within a learning system, the properties and their possible instances must be encoded or represented. Each property can be represented as a category or predicate family, and each possible instance of a given property can be represented as a value of the appropriate category, or as a predicate in the appropriate predicate family. The representations of the properties and instances of properties in Fig. 8.4 are shown in Fig. 8.8. An object can be represented as a collection of the representations of the instances of properties which apply to, or are true of, that object.

Category	Possible Values
SHAPE	inverted triangle, circle, triangle, square
SIZE	small, large
COLOR	white, gray
#SPOTS	0, 1, 2, 3

Fig. 8.8 Representing the properties of objects in Fig. 8.4.

Four different ways of representing objects will be used in this chapter. These are demonstrated in Fig. 8.9 for the object in Fig. 8.1(c), and described in the following paragraphs.

Object
"Object1c"

(a) *Vector representation*
Assuming SHAPE   Corresponds to position 1
                SIZE   Corresponds to position 2
                COLOR   Corresponds to position 3
                #SPOTS Corresponds to position 4

<square, large, gray, 2>

(b) *Predicate representation*

Square (object1c) & large (object1c) & gray (object1c)
& 2 (object1c)

(c) *Relational representation*

SHAPE (object1c, square) & SIZE (object1c, large)
& COLOR (object1c, gray) & #SPOTS (object1c, 2)

(d) *Functional representation*

SHAPE(Object1c) = square & SIZE(object1c) = large
& COLOR (object1c) = gray & #SPOTS (object1c) = 2

Fig. 8.9 Four ways of representing objects
(see text for full discussion)

Vector representation (Fig. 8.9(a)):
Each category corresponds to a fixed position in the vector.
The value in position 'k' of a particular vector is drawn
from the possible values for the category assigned to
position 'k' as appropriate for the object which is being
represented.

Predicate representation (Fig. 8.9(b)):
In this representation the object being represented is
assigned an arbitrary name, and the predicates, which
represent instances of properties, take an object name as
their only argument. A predicate, P, in predicate family,
F, is true for argument (object name) N if and only if the
object named N instantiates the property represented by F in
the manner represented by P. For example,

GRAY(object1c) is true if and only if the object named
'object1c' is, in fact, the color gray.

An object is represented by the conjunction of all of the
predicates which are individually true of that object.

Relational representation (Fig. 8.9(c)):
Again, the object being represented is assigned an arbitrary
name. A category acts as a relational predicate whose first
argument is an object name and whose second argument is
drawn from the possible values for this category. The
relation $F(N,P)$ is true if and only if the corresponding
predicate, $P(N)$, is true. An object is represented by the
conjunction of all of the relations which are individually
true of that object.

Functional representation (Fig. 8.9(d)):
Again, the object being represented is assigned an arbitrary
name. A category acts as a function whose domain is the set
of possible objects (as represented by their object names)
and whose range is the set of possible values for this
category. Relational predicates (such as '=') whose first
argument is a category-function and whose second argument is
a value from that category are used to represent the manner
in which a particular object instantiates a property: $F(N)=P$
is true if and only if the corresponding relation $F(N,P)$ is
true. An object is represented by the conjunction of all
such '=' relations which are individually true of that
object.

8.A.4 REPRESENTING METHODS OF CLASSIFICATION

In the two concept learning algorithms which follow, the
representation of methods for distinguishing members of a
concept from nonmembers will be based on decision trees. A
decision tree is a tree in which each node is identified
with a particular test which is defined in terms of the
categories and values with which the objects are represented, and each branch leading from a node is identified
with one of the possible outcomes of the test identified
with that node. Each leaf of a decision tree contains a
decision value such as '+', '-', or '?'. An example of a
decision tree is given in Fig. 8.10. The use of a decision tree in classifying an object, O, as a member or nonmember of a concept involves three distinct activities: (1)
the application of the node tests to O; (2) the interpretation of the outcome of such tests as an indication of which
node to visit next; and (3) the interpretation of decision
values as indicators of concept membership or nonmembership.
The most natural interpretation of a decision tree is
demonstrated by the following algorithm.

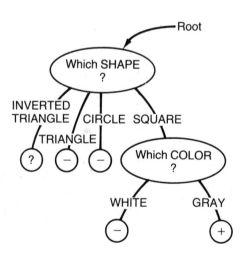

Fig. 8.10 Typical decision tree

8.A.4.1 Algorithm DT

dt1. Begin with the root of the decision tree.

dt2. Apply the test associated with the current node to O. Follow the branch which corresponds to the outcome of this test when applied to O.

dt3. IF this branch leads to a leaf THEN classify O by interpreting the decision value at this leaf according to the table in Fig. 8.11. Finished.

dt4. IF this branch leads to a non-leaf THEN repeat steps dt2 through dt4 for the node to which it leads.

Decision value	Interpretation
+	Member
−	Nonmember
?	No firm grounds exist on which to base a classification. Unknown.

Fig. 8.11 Natural interpretation of decision values

Individual decision trees, when used in conjunction with an interpretive algorithm such as DT, represent methods for classifying arbitrary objects. The method which is represented by the decision tree in Fig. 8.10 (as interpreted by algorithm DT) is

Method 4: classify a given object, O, as follows:
    if SHAPE(O)-circle or triangle then classify O as not grisbot.
    if SHAPE(O)=square and COLOR(O)=gray then classify O as grisbot.
    if SHAPE(O)=square and COLOR(O)=white then classify O as not grisbot.
(*) if SHAPE(O)=inverted triangle then classify O as unknown.

When applied to the object in Fig. 8.1(a), whose name shall be 'object1a', method 4, as represented by algorithm DT and the decision tree in Fig. 8.10, acts as follows

dt1. Begin with the test 'SHAPE(object1a) ?'

dt2. SHAPE(object1a)=square, so follow the branch labeled SQUARE.

dt3. The branch does not lead to a leaf.

dt4. The branch leads to the test 'COLOR(object1a) ?'

    dt2. COLOR(object1a)=gray, so follow the branch labeled GRAY.

    dt3. This branch leads to a leaf labeled '+'. Interpret this decision value according to Fig. 8.11. Conclude that the object in Fig. 8.1(a) is grisbot. Finished.

It must be emphasized that the decision tree alone does not represent a method for classifying objects. Method 4 results from the interpretation of the decision tree in Fig. 8.10 by algorithm DT. Other interpretations of a decision tree are possible. Most commonly, one finds alternative interpretations of the decision values. For instance, decision trees may contain the decision value '?'. It may be, however, that the interpretation of '?' as 'unknown', as in (*) in method 4, is not acceptable, i.e., that the method for classification must deliver a verdict of either grisbot or not grisbot. There are a number of ways of mapping '?' onto these two possible classifications: one method might interpret all occurrences of '?' as 'classify as grisbot'; another method might interpret them all as 'classify as not grisbot'; and a third method might interpret some occurrences of '?' as 'classify as grisbot' and others as 'classify as not grisbot'. Algorithm DTL below offers yet another interpretation of the decision value '?'. The decision values '+' and '-' may also be interpreted in more than one way: algorithm DTS below demonstrates an alternative interpretation of '-'. The method of classification is thus jointly determined by the decision tree and the algorithm which interprets the decision tree. This relationship is depicted in Fig. 8.12.

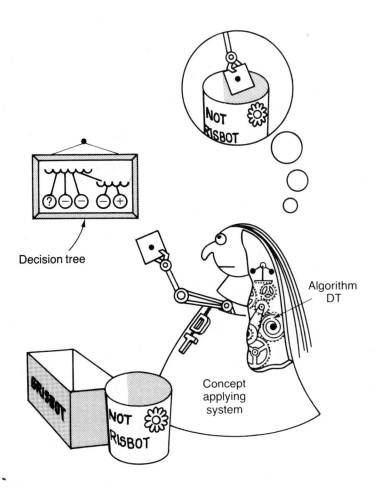

Fig. 8.12 A method for classification is jointly determined by a decision tree and an interpretive algorithm

Decision trees and the operation of algorithm DT can be
understood in terms of subsets of the universe U. Each test
in the decision tree is a partition of U, and each branch
is one of the subsets in the partition. Associated with
each such subset (branch) is either a decision value or a
partition (test) of the subset. Algorithm DT can be restated
in terms of subsets of U as follows:

dt1'. Let O be the object to be classified. Begin with the
      partition specified in the root of the decision tree.

dt2'. O will be in exactly one of the subsets of the current
      partition. Associated with this subset is either a
      decision value or another partition.

dt3'. IF a decision value is associated with the subset
      containing O, THEN classify O by interpreting this
      decision value according to the table in Fig. 8.11.
      Finished.

dt4'. IF a partition is associated with the subset contain-
      ing O, THEN repeat steps dt2' through dt4' for this
      partition (note that this is a partition of the subset
      containing O and not of all of U).

A method for classifying an arbitrary object as a member or
nonmember of a concept may be viewed as a partition of U
consisting of three sets. One set contains all elements of U
which the method classifies as members; one set contains all
elements of U which the method classifies as nonmembers;
and the third set contains all members of U which the method
classifies as unknown. The decision tree in Fig. 8.10, when
interpreted by algorithm DT, represents method 4 above.
Fig. 8.13 shows method 4 viewed as a partition of U. In this
figure, and all subsequent figures containing such partitions, circled decision values are used to indicate the
classification of the objects in each subset: the set of
members is indicated by a circled '+'; the set of nonmembers
is indicated by a circled '-'; and the set of objects which
are classified as unknown is indicated by a circled '?'.
Method 4 may be viewed as a partition in which the set of
members is the set of square, gray objects; the set of
nonmembers is the set of objects which are circular, triangular, or square and white; and the set of objects classified as unknown is the set of inverted triangular objects.

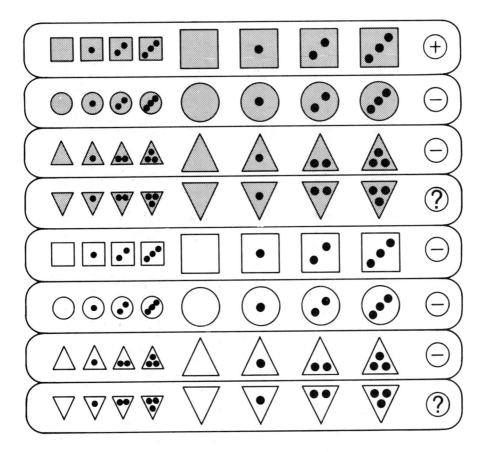

Fig. 8.13 Method 4 viewed as a partition of U.
 ⊕ indicates objects classified as members
 ⊖ indicates objects classified as nonmembers
 ⑦ indicates objects classified as unknown

8.A.4.2 Concept Learning Algorithm Q*

Having specified the properties and instances of properties
with which objects will be characterized, and having chosen
a representation for these, for objects, and for the method
of classifying objects, we can now specify a concept learning algorithm. The first concept learning algorithm which
we shall consider will be called algorithm Q. It assumes
that concept application will be done using algorithm DT.
It learns a concept by constructing a decision tree for the
concept which, in conjunction with algorithm DT, provides a
method for distinguishing members of the concept from
nonmembers. The relationship between algorithm Q and
algorithm DT is depicted in Fig. 8.14.

Under the assumption that the output of algorithm Q will be
interpreted by algorithm DT, the operation of algorithm Q
can be described in terms of the partitions of U which
correspond to the categories which are used to represent
the objects. Given the set of positive and negative
examples, Q chooses a partition of the universe, and in-
spects the contents of each subset in this partition. If a
subset contains none of the positive examples and none of
the negative examples, then Q associates with it the decision value '?'. If a subset contains some positive examples
and no negative examples, then Q associates with it the
decision value '+'. If a subset contains some negative
examples and no positive examples, then Q associates with
it the decision value '-'. Finally, if a subset contains
both positive and negative examples, then the algorithm is
applied recursively to this subset (i.e. a partition of this
subset is chosen and the contents of these subsets are
inspected and either have appropriate decision values
associated with them or are further partitioned). Stated
in terms of decision tree construction,

---

* similar in spirit to ID3 (Quinlan,1979,1982,1983b).

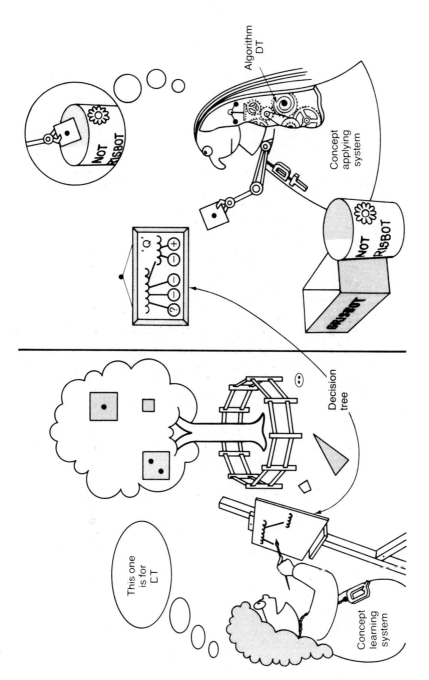

Fig. 8.14 The relationship between algorithm Q and algorithm DT

Algorithm Q

q1. Begin at the root of the decision tree with
    P = { positive examples }
    N = { negative examples }

q2. Choose a category, CAT, to act as the test for the
    current node. Create one branch leading from this node
    for each possible value of this category. Label the
    branches with the names of the possible values, say,
    v1, v2, etc. Each branch leads to a node whose content
    is determined by step q3.

q3. Have the branch labeled w (which may be any of v1, v2,
    etc.) lead as follows:

    q3(a). IF there is no object, O, in P or in N for which
            CAT(O)=w, THEN have the branch lead to a node
            containing the decision value '?'.

    q3(b). IF there is at least one object, O, in P for
            which CAT(O)=w, and there are no objects in N
            for which this is true, THEN have the branch lead
            to a node containing the decision value '+'.

    q3(c). IF there is at least one object, O, in N for
            which CAT(O)=w, and there are no objects in P
            for which this is true, THEN have the branch lead
            to a node containing the decision value '-'.

    q3(d). IF there are objects O1 in N and O2 in P for
            which CAT(O1)=w and CAT(O2)=w, THEN have the
            branch lead to the root of the decision tree
            built by applying step q2 to the revised sets:

            revised P = { all objects, O, in P for which
                                                   CAT(O)=w }
            revised N = { all objects, O, in N for which
                                                   CAT(O)=w }

The following is a step by step account of algorithm Q
constructing a decision tree assuming it was given the
objects in Fig. 8.1 as positive examples and the objects
in Fig. 8.3 as negative examples. Each step will be illustrated both in terms of the decision tree which is under
construction and in terms of the partition which corresponds
to the partially constructed decision tree as interpreted by

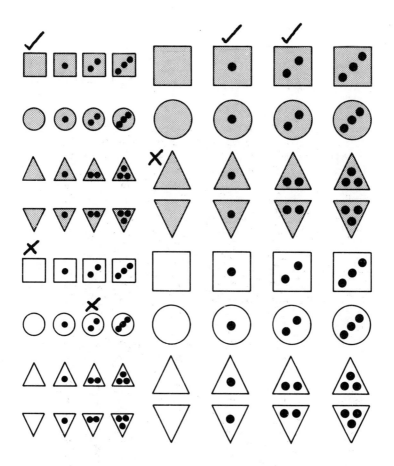

Fig. 8.15 The Universe
✓ indicates a positive example
✗ indicates a negative example

algorithm DT. Positive examples are indicated with a 'check' in the figures, and negative examples are marked with an 'X'. The set P (N) corresponds to the set of 'checked' ('X'ed) objects in the subset of U which is under consideration at any given point in the algorithm. In the text, names such as 'object1a' for the object in Fig. 8.1(a) will be used to indicate the contents of sets P and N.

q1. The initial set of objects under consideration is the entire Universe, as shown in Fig. 8.15.

P = { object1a, object1b, object1c }
N = { object3a, object3b, object3c }

q2. A category must be chosen to act as the test in the root of the decision tree under construction. Suppose that the category SHAPE is chosen. One branch leading from the root is created for each of the four values of SHAPE. The branches are labeled INVERTED TRIANGLE, TRIANGLE, CIRCLE, and SQUARE. See Fig. 8.16.

q3. The branch labeled INVERTED TRIANGLE leads to:
    q3(a) A node containing the decision value '?' (because there are no objects in P or in N whose shape is inverted triangle).

q3. The branch labeled TRIANGLE leads to:
    q3(b) A node containing the decision value '-' (because there is an object in N whose shape is triangle, but no such object in P).

q3. The branch labeled CIRCLE leads to:
    q3(c) A node containing the decision value '-'. The state of the decision tree and partition of U at this point is shown in Fig. 8.17.

q3. The branch labeled SQUARE leads to:
    q3(d) The root of a decision tree constructed for objects whose shape is square (because there are objects in both P and N whose shape is square). This decision tree is constructed for the revised sets

        P' = { object1a, object1b, object1c }
        N' = { object3a }

        as follows :

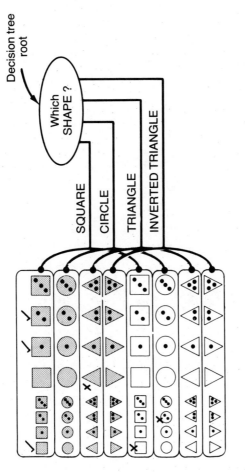

Fig. 8.16

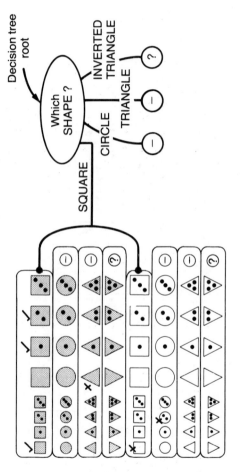

Fig. 8.17

q2. A category must be chosen to act as the test in the root of the decision tree under construction. Suppose that the category COLOR is chosen. This partitions the set of square objects into two subsets – gray square objects and white square objects. One branch leading from the root is created for each of the two values of color. The branches are labeled GRAY and WHITE.

q3. The branch labeled GRAY leads to:
    q3(b) A node containing the decision value '+' (because there is an object in P' whose color is gray, but no such object in N').

q3. The branch labeled WHITE leads to:
    q3(c) A node containing the decision value '−' (because there is an object in N' whose color is white, but no such object in P').

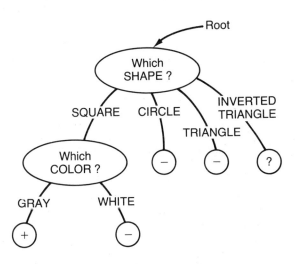

Fig. 8.18 Decision tree constructed by algorithm Q given the objects in Fig. 8.1 as positive examples and those in Fig. 8.3 as negative examples. This is the same decision tree as in Fig. 8.10.

Fig. 8.18 shows the final decision tree constructed by algorithm Q given the objects in Fig. 8.1 as positive examples and the objects in Fig. 8.3 as negative examples. This decision tree is the same as that in Fig. 8.10. When used in conjunction with algorithm DT it represents method 4 for classifying objects, as described above.

In algorithm Q, step q2 requires that a category be selected to act as the test in the node of the decision tree currently being constructed. One may ask, 'On what grounds is this selection made?' The answer is that category selection is not based on any single, universal criterion: different learning systems which use algorithm Q may employ different criteria in step q2. For instance, one system may choose whichever category minimizes the 'entropy' function* shown in Fig. 8.19. The decision trees produced using such a

---

if category takes on values $\{V_1, V_2, V_3, ...V_K\}$, its entropy is defined as:

$$\sum_{i=1}^{K} \left(-P_i \log_2 \left[\frac{P_i}{P_i + N_i} \right] - N_i \log_2 \left[\frac{N_i}{P_i + N_i} \right] \right)$$

Where P_i = the number of positive
examples,* x, for which CAT $(x) = V_i$

N_i = the number of negative
examples,* y, tor which CAT $(y) = V_i$

* In algorithm Q, P_i and N_i indicate the number of positive and negative examples *in the partition of U under consideration* for which CAT $(x) = V_i$

Fig. 8.19 The "Entropy" function is defined for a category

---

*   Taken from Quinlan (1979, 1982, 1983b).

criterion tend to be maximally compact. Notice that this
function depends on the distribution of category values
across the entire set of positive and negative examples.
Another system may have a fixed order of selection: for
instance, the category COLOR may be preferred over the
others because it is the easiest and most reliable property
of objects to measure under the conditions in which the
concept applying system will be operating. The decision tree
which is produced by algorithm Q on the example above when
COLOR is chosen first and SHAPE second is shown in Fig.
8.20. Note that this decision tree, when used in conjunction with algorithm DT, classifies white inverted triangles
as nonmembers whereas the decision tree in Fig. 8.18, when
used in conjunction with algorithm DT, offers no firm
classification (i.e. its classification is based on the
decision value '?') for white inverted triangles. Thus the
use of different criteria for selecting a category to use in
step q2 can result in a different method of classification.

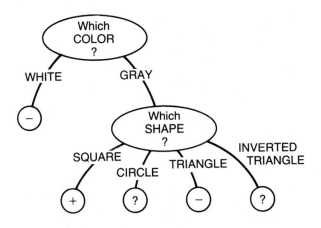

Fig. 8.20 An alternative decision tree

8.A.5

AN ALTERNATIVE REPRESENTATION OF METHODS OF CLASSIFICATION

We have just seen how an individual decision tree, when used
in conjunction with an interpretive algorithm such as DT,
represents a method for classifying an object as a member or
nonmember of a concept. In the following, the basis for
representation is not one decision tree but an ordered list
of decision trees. Such a list may be used in the classification of an object as follows: proceed one decision tree at
a time and classify the given object by interpreting according to Fig. 8.11 the first firm decision value ('+' or '-')
which is reached. Whenever a '?' is encountered, abandon
the current decision tree and classify the object on the
basis of the next decision tree in the list. If no decision
tree in the list delivers a firm decision value, classify
the object as 'unknown'.* This interpretation of an ordered
list of decision trees is employed by algorithm DTL.

8.A.5.1 Algorithm DTL

GIVEN:
      O - the object to be classified
      { T_1, T_2, ... ,T_K } - a list of decision trees
      K - the number of decision trees in this list

dtl1. Let I be an index into the list of decision trees,
      and T_I the decision tree currently under con-
      sideration. Initially, I=1.

dtl2. Begin with the root of decision tree T_I.

dtl3. Apply the test associated with the current node to O.
      Follow the branch which corresponds to the outcome of
      this test when applied to O.

dtl4. IF this branch leads to a leaf THEN classify O by
      interpreting the decision value at this leaf according
      to the table in Fig. 8.21. Finished.

dtl5. IF this branch leads to a non-leaf THEN repeat steps
      dtl3 through dtl5 for the node to which it leads.

---

* Michalski (1983 a,b) classifies all objects for which no
  firm decision value is reached as nonmembers.

Decision value	Interpretation
+	Classify the given object as a member
−	Classify the given object as a nonmember
?	If I<K, then set I to the value I+1, and classify the given object using steps DTL2 through DTL5.
	If I=K, then classify the given object as unknown

Fig. 8.21 The interpretation of decision values used by algorithm DTL

Algorithm DTL is a rather straightforward extension of algorithm DT to interpret a list of decision trees. This extension is achieved by interpreting the decision value '?' as 'classify the given object using the next decision tree in the list' in all the decision trees in the list except the last, where '?' is interpreted by DTL in the same way as it was by DT.[*] When there is only one decision tree in the given list of decision trees (i.e. when K=1) algorithm DTL is identical to algorithm DT. Since any single decision tree can be considered as a list containing one decision tree, algorithm DTL can be used whenever DT can be used: for instance as an interpreter of the output of algorithm Q.

---

[*] pp.183–84 in Quinlan (1979) does not overload the decision value '?' in this way, but instead introduces a fourth decision value which is always interpreted as 'classification must be done by some other means'. In his system, the 'other means' available was not another decision tree, as it is here, but rather an extremely time-consuming procedure for calculating the classification.

Given the list of decision trees in Fig. 8.22, algorithm DTL
would classify the object in Fig. 8.1(a) (named object1a) as
follows:

dt11. I = 1. T_1 is shown in Fig. 8.22.

dt12. Begin at the root of T_1.

dt13. Is SIZE(object1a)=large?
      Yes. Follow the branch labeled YES.

dt14. This branch does not lead to a leaf.

dt13. Is #SPOTS(object1a)=2?
      No. Follow the branch labeled NO.

dt14. This branch leads to a node containing the decision
      value '?'. The interpretation of this decision value
      is given in Fig. 8.21. The value of I (=1) is less
      than the value of K (=3), so set I to the value 2.

dt12. Begin at the root of T_2.

dt13. Is #SPOTS(object1a)=1?
      Yes. Follow the branch labeled YES.

dt14. This branch leads to a node containing the decision
      value '+'. The interpretation of this decision value
      is given in Fig. 8.21. Classify object1a as a member
      of the concept. Finished.

The classification method which is represented by the list
in Fig. 8.22 as interpreted by algorithm DTL is most clearly
understood when viewed as a partition of U into members,
nonmembers, and objects which are classified as unknown
(denoted in the figure as circled '+', '-', and '?', respectively). Figures 8.23 through 8.25 show the individual
decision trees of the list in Fig. 8.22 and the partitions
which correspond to each when interpreted by algorithm DT as
methods of classification. Notice that many elements of U
are classified in different ways by the different decision
trees, taken individually: for instance, a large white
object with two spots is classified as a member by T_1, as
unknown by T_2, and as a nonmember by T_3. Indeed the positive examples in Fig. 8.1(a) and 8.1(c) are classified as
nonmembers by T_3!

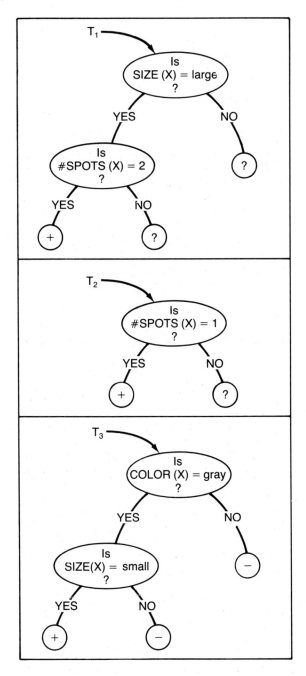

Fig. 8.22 A list of 3 decision trees

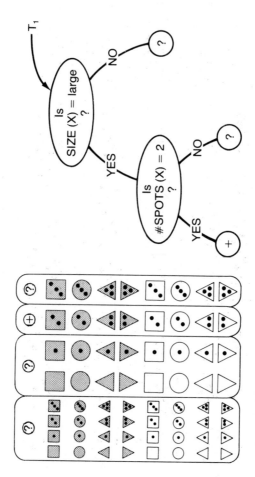

Fig. 8.23 Decision tree T_1 and its partition when interpreted by algorithm DT

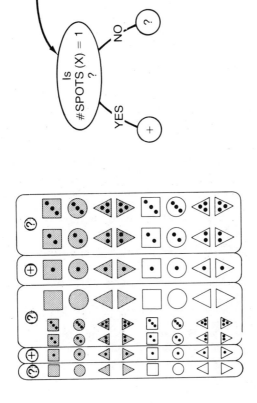

Fig. 8.24 Decision tree T_2 and its partition when interpreted by algorithm DT

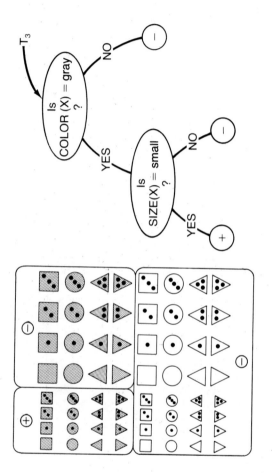

Fig. 8.25 Partition when interpreted by algorithm DT

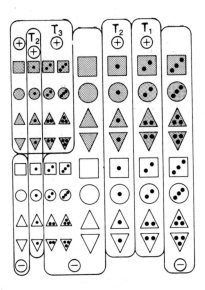

Fig. 8.26 The composite partition which corresponds to
$<T_1, T_2, T_3>$ as interpreted by DTL.
All $\ominus$ classifications are due to T_3. The source of the
$\oplus$ classification is indicated.

Algorithm DTL, or any other algorithm which interprets a collection of decision trees as a method of classification, provides a way of interpreting as a single classification, the several classifications which result when each decision tree in the collection is consulted separately.

In the case of algorithm DTL, the combining of classifications is based on the ordering of the decision trees: the classification of an object is the first firm classification which is encountered; if all of the decision trees individually classify an object as 'unknown' then its combined classification is 'unknown'. The ordered list of decision trees in Fig. 8.22, as interpreted by algorithm DTL, corresponds to the partition shown in Fig. 8.26. This composite partition is constructed from the individual partitions in Figs 8.23 through 8.25 as follows. All objects classified as members or nonmembers in the partition in Fig. 8.23 are classified similarly in the composite; this results in all large objects with two spots being classified as members. Then all objects which are not already classified in the composite and which are classified as members or nonmembers in the partition in Fig. 8.24 are classified similarly in the composite; this results in all objects with one spot being classified as members. Finally, all objects which are not already classified in the composite are classified in the same way as they are in the partition in Fig. 8.25.

8.A.5.2 Concept Learning Algorithm R*

Algorithm R is a concept learning algorithm which exploits the ability of algorithm DTL to interpret an ordered list of decision trees as a method for classifying an object as a member or nonmember of a concept. A concept is learned by constructing an ordered list of decision trees whose interpretation by algorithm DTL constitutes a satisfactory classification method for the concept. The relationship between R and DTL is shown in Fig. 8.27: it is the same as the relationship between Q and DT and representative of the general relationship which holds between a concept learning algorithm and a concept applying algorithm (see Fig. 8.39).

---

* in the spirit of the STAR methodology (pp. 113–117 in Michalski,1983a).

Fig. 8.27 The relationship between algorithm R and algorithm DTL

Algorithm R operates by choosing a positive example (object) and finding a subset of U which contains that object and no negative examples. If this subset does not contain all of the positive examples, then one of the positive examples which is not in the subset is chosen and the process repeated. Algorithm R terminates when a collection of subsets is found which jointly contain all of the positive examples and none of the negative examples. The subsets which algorithm R considers must be either subsets which correspond to category values or intersections of such subsets. Algorithm R is stated in the following in terms of the construction of an ordered list of decision trees: steps r3 through r5 construct the decision tree corresponding to a subset containing a positive example, D, and no negative examples, and steps r2 and r6 iterate this construction until every positive example is classified as '+' by at least one of the decision trees. The phrase 'object O is classified as '+' by decision tree T' is an abbreviation for 'object O is classified as a member by the method represented by decision tree T as interpreted by algorithm DT'.

Algorithm R

r1. Let I be an index for the ordered list of decision trees which will be constructed. T_I denotes the decision tree currently under construction. Initially, I=1. Let S be the ordered list of decision trees which constitutes the output of algorithm R. Initially, S is the empty list. Let POS be the set of positive examples which are not yet classified as '+' by any of the decision trees currently in S.

   Initially, POS = { all positive examples }.
   Finally, let NEG = { all negative examples }.

r2. Choose an object, D, from POS. Build a decision tree, T_I which classifies D (and perhaps other objects) as '+', but which classifies no negative example as '+', using steps r3 through r5. Two sets, P and N, will be maintained during the construction of this decision tree. P will contain all elements of POS which satisfy every test in the tree at the current stage of construction. Initially P=POS. N will contain all elements of NEG which satisfy every test in the tree at the current stage of construction. Initially, N=NEG. Ultimately (construction is complete when) N becomes empty. When construction of decision tree T_I is complete, advance to step r6.

r3. Choose a category, CAT. Let v be the value of CAT such that CAT(D)=v. The test in the current node is 'is CAT(X)=v?' (assuming that X stands for the object being classified). Create two branches leading from the current node, one labeled NO, the other labeled YES. The branches lead to nodes as specified in r4 and r5.

r4. The branch labeled NO leads to:

r4(a). A node containing the decision value '-' if there is no object, O, in P for which CAT(O) ≠ v.

r4(b). A node containing the decision value '?' if there is an object, O, in P for which CAT(O) ≠ v.

r5. The branch labeled YES leads to:

r5(a). A node containing the decision value '+' if there is no object, O, in N for which CAT(O)=v. Revise P to be
revised P = { all objects, O, in P for which
CAT(O)=v}

Construction of T_I is complete (advance to r6).

r5(b). The root of a decision tree which is constructed by applying r3 to the revised sets:

revised P = { all objects, O, in P for which
CAT(O)=v }
revised N = { all objects, O, in N for which
CAT(O)=v }

if there is at least one object, O, in N for which CAT(O)=v.

r6. Add T_I to the list S. Revise POS by removing from it all objects which are in P. If the revised POS is empty then finished. If the revised POS is not empty, then set I to the value I+1 and repeat steps r2 through r6.

The following demonstration of the operation of algorithm R assumes that the objects in Fig. 8.1 have been given as positive examples and that those in Fig. 8.3 have been given as negative examples. The object names used in demonstrating algorithm Q will be used here as well.

r1. I = 1. S = { }. POS = { object1a, object1b, object1c }.
                      NEG = { object3a, object3b, object3c }.

r2. Begin at the root of T_1. Suppose that D = object1c is
the chosen positive example.
        P = { object1a, object1b, object1c }
        N = { object3a, object3b, object3c }

r3. Suppose the category SIZE is chosen.
SIZE(object1c)=large. The root of T_1 contains the test
'is SIZE(X)=large?' Create a branch labeled NO and a
branch labeled YES leading from the root of T_1.

r4. The branch labeled NO leads to:
    r4(b). A node containing the decision value '?' (because
        SIZE(object1b)=small and SIZE(object3a)=small).

r5. The branch labeled YES leads to:
    r5(b). The root of a decision tree built by applying r3
        to the revised sets
        P' = { object1a, object1c }
        N' = { object3c }

        r3. Suppose the category #SPOTS is chosen.
        #SPOTS(object1c)=2. The current node con-
        tains the test 'is #SPOTS(X)=2?' Create a
        branch labeled NO and a branch labeled YES
        leading from this node.

        r4. The branch labeled NO leads to:
            r4(b). A node containing the decision value
            '?'.

        r5. The branch labeled YES leads to:
            r5(a). A node containing the decision value
            '+' (because the only object in N',
            object3c, does not have two spots). P'
            is revised to be P'' = { object1c }.

r6. T_1 is now complete (see Fig. 8.28) and it is added to
S, yielding S = { T_1 }. POS is revised by removing from
it the single object in P'', yielding
    POS' = { object1a, object1b } which is not empty.
Set I to the value 2.

r2. Begin at the root of T_2. Suppose that D = object1a is
the chosen positive example.
P = { object1a, object1b }
N = { object3a, object3b, object3c }

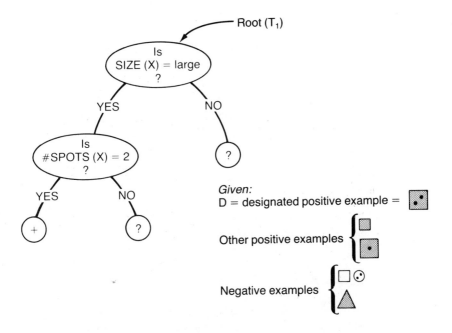

Fig. 8.28 The construction of T₁ by algorithm R

r3. Suppose the category #SPOTS is chosen.
#SPOTS(object1a)=1. The root of T$_2$ contains the test 'is
#SPOTS(X)=1?'. Create a branch labeled NO and a branch
labeled YES leading from the root of T$_2$.

r4. The branch labeled NO leads to:
    r4(b). A node containing the decision value '?' (because
           #SPOTS(object1b)=0 and #SPOTS(object3b)=2).

r5. The branch labeled YES leads to:
    r5(b). A node containing the decision value '+'. Revise
           P to be P' = { object1a }

r6. T$_2$ is now complete (see Fig. 8.29) and it is added
    to S, yielding S = { T$_1$, T$_2$ }. POS' is revised by remov-
    ing from it the single object in P', yielding
           POS'' = { object1b } which is not empty.
    Set I to the value 3.

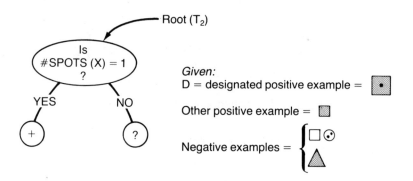

Fig. 8.29 The construction of T$_2$ by algorithm R

r2. Begin at the root of T₃. D = object1b is the only
remaining positive example.
P = { object1b }
N = { object3a, object3b, object3c }

r3. Suppose the category COLOR is chosen.
COLOR(object1b)=gray. The root of T₃ contains the test
'is COLOR(X)=gray?'. Create a branch labeled NO and a
branch labeled YES leading from the root of T₃.

r4. The branch labeled NO leads to:
r4(a). A node containing the decision value '-' (because
object1b is the only object in P, and
COLOR(object1b)=gray).

r5. The branch labeled YES leads to:
r5(b). The root of a decision tree built by applying r3
to the revised sets P' = { object1b }
N' = { object3c }

r3. Suppose the category SIZE is chosen.
SIZE(object1b)=small. The current node
contains the test 'is SIZE(X)=small?' Create
a branch labeled NO and a branch labeled YES
leading from this node.

r4. The branch labeled NO leads to:
r4(a). A node containing the decision value
'-'.

r5. The branch labeled YES leads to:
r5(a). A node containing the decision value
'+'. P' is revised to be
P'' = { object1b }.

r6. T₃ is now complete (see Fig. 8.30) and it is added
to S, yielding S = { T₁, T₂, T₃ }. POS' is revised by
removing from it the single object in P'', yielding POS'
= { } which is empty. Finished.

Thus, if the correct categories are chosen in step r3, the
ordered list of decision trees shown in Fig. 8.22 can be
constructed by algorithm R. The interpretation of this list
of decision trees by algorithm DTL has previously been
discussed.

As with the selection of a category in step q2 of algorithm
Q, there are many different criteria which can be used to
determine the selection of a category in step r3 of
algorithm R, and the different selections which result from
the use of different criteria can lead to vastly different
ordered lists of decision trees. For instance, if the
appropriate categories are selected in step r3, algorithm R
will produce the single decision tree shown in Fig. 8.31.
This decision tree, when used in conjunction with algorithm
DT or DTL, corresponds to method 3 above.

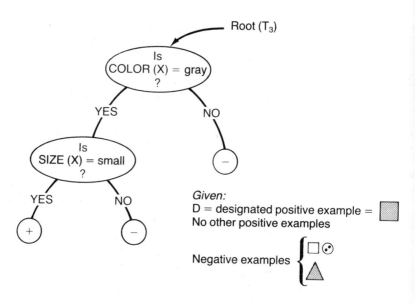

Fig. 8.30 The construction of T_3 by algorithm R

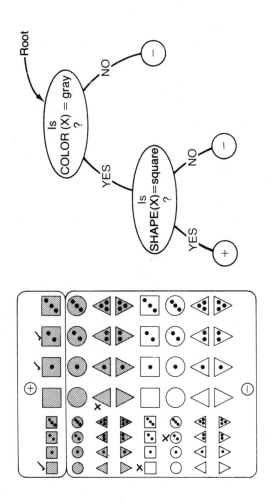

Fig. 8.31 A minimal decision tree for the given examples and the corresponding partition under interpretation by DTL.

One criterion which is very often employed in algorithm R
is to try to minimize the number of decision trees in the
final list. This criterion is difficult to satisfy perfectly, because one cannot always anticipate the precise
effect of choosing one or another category in step r3 on
the length of the final list of decision trees. Another
commonly employed criterion is to try to maximize the size
of subset containing each positive example. This criterion
plays a central role in the method of minimal modification
discussed in Section 8C. One should note that this criterion
is often in conflict with the criterion of minimizing the
number of decision trees in the final list: the subset
containing all three positive examples as determined by the
decision tree in Fig. 8.31 is considerably smaller than the
subsets (depicted in Figs 8.23 through 8.25) containing the
individual positive examples as determined by the decision
trees in Fig. 8.22.

8.A.6
AN ALTERNATIVE INTERPRETATION ALGORITHM FOR LISTS OF DECISION TREES

To emphasize that a method for classification is jointly
determined by the list of decision trees (in this particular
representation) and the algorithm for interpreting this
list, we shall consider briefly an alternative to algorithm
DTL which offers a distinct but equally legitimate interpretation of a list of decision trees as a method for
classifying an object as a member or nonmember of a concept.
This algorithm, called DTS, disregards the order of the
decision trees in the list. To classify a given object using
a list of decision trees, DTS first classifies the object
according to each decision tree in the list individually (in
this stage it is identical to algorithm DT), and then
combines these individual classifications to produce a final
classification.

8.A.6.1 Algorithm DTS

GIVEN:
        O - an object to be classified
        $\{ W_1, W_2, \ldots, W_K \}$ - a list of decision trees
        K - the length of this list

dts1. Classify O using each of the individual decision trees in the list in conjunction with algorithm DT. Let V_i be the classification of O resulting from the use of decision tree W_i by algorithm DT, for all values of i from 1 to K. Each V_i is either 'member', 'nonmember', or 'unknown'.

dts2. If at least one V_i='member' then classify O as a member of the concept.

dts3. If there is no V_i='member' and at least one V_i='nonmember' then classify O as a nonmember of the concept.

dts4. If every V_i='unknown' the classify O as unknown.

When there is only one decision tree in the list, DTS is identical to DT. When there is more than one decision tree in the list, DTS combines the classifications produced by considering the decision trees individually by giving the classification 'member' top priority: if the interpretation by DT of any decision tree in the list classifies the given object as a member of the concept, then DTS classifies the object as a member of the concept. The classification 'nonmember' is given second priority, and the classification 'unknown' is used only as a last resort.

To show that DTS and DTL do not always agree in their interpretation of a list of decision trees, consider the list {W1, W2} shown in Fig. 8.32. The partitions of U which correspond to these two decision trees individually are shown in Figs 8.33 and 8.34. There are two regions of conflict in these two partitions: small gray objects are classified as members by W1 and as nonmembers by W2, and large white square objects are classified as nonmembers by W1 and as members by W2. The composite partition which corresponds to the ordered list {W1, W2} as interpreted by DTL is shown in Fig. 8.35. The priority of the first decision tree over the second is evident here. Both areas of con-

flict are classified in this composite as they were in W1:
small gray objects as members, and large white square
objects as nonmembers. The composite partition which
corresponds to the list {W1, W2} as interpreted by DTS is
shown in Fig. 8.36. Here the priority of the classification
'member' over 'nonmember' is evident: objects in both areas
of conflict are classified as members in this composite.
Thus given the same list of decision trees, {W1,W2}, a large
white square would be classified as a member of the concept
under DTS's interpretation of the list, but as a nonmember
under DTL's interpretation. The method of classification of
an object as a member or nonmember of a concept is jointly
determined by the list of decision trees and by the
algorithm which interprets this list.

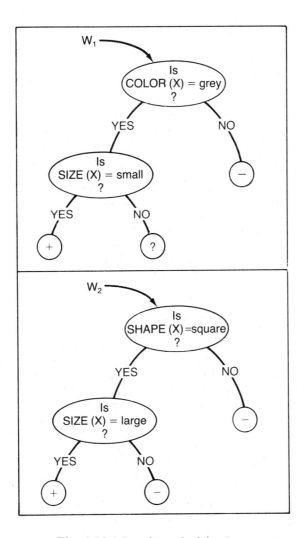

Fig. 8.32 A list of two decision trees

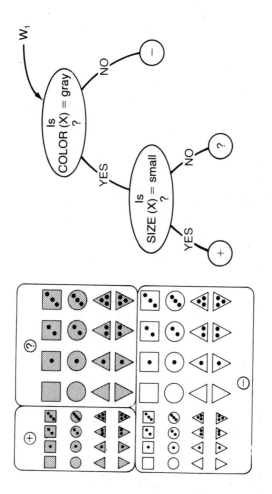

Fig. 8.33 The partition which corresponds to W_1 as interpreted by algorithm DT

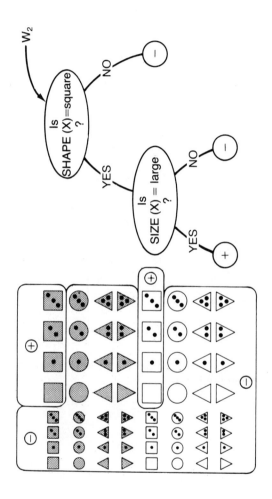

Fig. 8.34 The partition which corresponds to W_2 as interpreted by algorithm DT

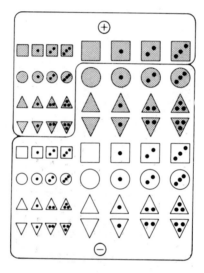

Fig. 8.35 The partition which corresponds to $\{W_1, W_2\}$ as interpreted by algorithm DTL.

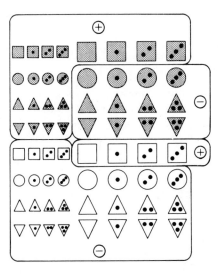

Fig. 8.36 The partition which corresponds to $\{W_1, W_2\}$ as interpreted by algorithm DTS.

8.B   Concept learning: central ideas and terminology

In the previous section a considerable number of terms and
ideas were introduced to describe the concept learning and
concept applying processes. In this section these terms and
ideas will be made more precise and more general. In
addition, several new terms and ideas which were implicit in
the previous section will be made explicit.

8.B.1 INTENSION, EXTENSION AND REPRESENTATION

The intension of a concept is a means of determining if a
given object instantiates that concept or not. A method for
classifying an arbitrary object as instantiating or not
instantiating a concept constitutes an intension of that
concept.

The extension of a concept is the set of all objects which
instantiate that concept. An object is a member of a concept
if it is in the extension of that concept. We shall use the
phrase 'concept C contains object O' to mean 'object O is a
member of concept C'. For the remainder of the chapter we
will assume that objects which are not members of a concept
are nonmembers, i.e. we will not consider learning systems
which produce classifications such as 'unknown'. Note that
the extension of a concept is not normally defined in terms
of its intension: objects may instantiate a concept independently of the existence of a method for classifying
them as members of that concept. Indeed, the concept learning task is precisely to construct a method for classifying
objects given a collection of objects whose classifications
are already known. If classification method M is the intension of concept C then the extension of C is the set which
contains all objects which would be classified by M as
members of C. In Section A the partition which corresponded
to a given method of classification indicated the extension
of the concept for which that method was the intension.

In Section 8.A.2, a distinction was made between objects and
entities. Entities are characterized by a small fixed
collection of properties of objects and instances of those

properties. An intension of an entity is a means of determining if a given object instantiates the given properties in the manner characteristic of that entity. An
intension of a particular instance of a property is a means
for determining if a given object instantiates that property
in that particular manner. Intensions of entities and
instances need not be trivial[*] but they will not be discussed in this chapter.

The extension of an entity is the set of all objects which
instantiate the given properties in the manner
characteristic of that entity. All of the objects in Fig.
8.6 are in the extension of 'large gray circular object with
two spots'. The extension of an entity is clearly relative
to a particular collection of properties and instances of
those properties. If it is true that whenever one object in
the extension of an entity is a member of a concept, every
object in the extension of the entity is a member of the
concept, then the collection of properties and instances of
those properties which is being used to characterize the
entities is said to be 'adequate'. The extension of a
particular instance of a property is the set of all objects
which instantiate that property in that particular way. The
distinction between objects and entities is not important
for the topics discussed in this chapter. Henceforth, we
will assume that the collection of properties and instances
of those properties is fixed and adequate, and we will use
the terms 'entity', 'object' and 'element of U' interchangeably to refer to entities.

For the purposes of manipulation and comparison within
concept learning and concept applying systems, the intensions of concepts and objects must be represented. A
number of representations for objects were described in
Section 8.A.3.[**] Intensions of concepts - i.e. methods of
classifying an object as a member or nonmember of a concept
- were represented with two components: a static or declarative component (e.g. a decision tree or ordered list of
decision trees) and an interpretive or procedural component
(e.g. algorithms DT, DTL, or DTS). The interpretive compon-

---

[*]   For example INTSUM (Lindsay et al.,1980; pp. 430-432 in
      Dietterich et al., 1982) is a complex program for
      calculating properties of chemical compounds.
[**] Fig. 8.9

ent of the representation of the intension of a concept shall be called the concept's 'membership determination process' or its 'procedural aspect'. The declarative component of the representation of the intension of a concept shall be called its 'declarative aspect' or simply 'the representation of the concept'.

That the declarative aspect of a concept should be called the representation of that concept strongly suggests that the procedural aspect of a concept plays only a trivial role in the representation of the intension of the concept. This, as we know from the difference in the concepts which result when algorithms DTS and DTL are used as membership determination processes, is clearly false in general. Ideally, we would prefer a term which acknowledged the important role which can be played by the membership determination process in the representation of concepts' intensions. Unfortunately, the use of 'the representation of the concept' to refer to the declarative aspect of the concept is virtually universal.

There are two reasons why this usage has not been found to be inadequate. First, in almost all extant learning systems the membership determination process is fixed. That is, in such learning systems, concepts are never learned or modified by constructing or altering the membership determination process: algorithms Q and R are representative of learning systems in this respect. In principle there is no obstacle to learning a concept by constructing or altering the membership determination process. In practice, this is extremely rare: the division of the representation of the intension of a concept into a declarative and a procedural component is always chosen so that all changes which might be necessary in the course of concept learning can be made on the declarative component.

Secondly, in most extant concept learning systems the membership determination process provides the natural interpretation of the declarative aspect of the concept. Thus the contribution of the membership determination process can be overlooked without penalty: for instance, algorithm DT merely echoes the intuitive interpretation of a decision tree as a method of classifying an object as a member or nonmember of a concept. These two features of most extant learning systems - that the procedural aspects of

the concepts they construct merely embody the natural
interpretation of the declarative aspects and are never
changed – encourage adopting the view that the declarative
aspect of a concept alone represents that concept. All
learning systems which are discussed in this chapter share
these two features, and we will adopt the common usage of
the phrase 'the representation of a concept'.

As in Section A, the properties of objects which are used
to characterize entities are represented as categories or
predicate families, and the instances of these properties
are represented as values of the appropriate category or
predicates within the appropriate predicate family. The
'extension' of a value refers, naturally, to the extension
of the property-instance which is represented by that value.
Similarly the 'extension' of the representation of an object
or the representation of a concept refers to the extension
of the object or concept represented.

8.B.2 REPRESENTATION LANGUAGES

The representation of a particular object or concept can be
viewed as a sentence (word, expression, string) in a formal
language. The symbols which stand for names of categories,
values, and names of objects are terminal symbols in this
formal language. So, too, are the connectives such as '&',
names for relational predicates such as '=', and miscellane-
ous 'punctuation' symbols such as '('. The formal language
in which objects are represented is called the object
representation language. Typical sentences in four distinct
object representation languages are shown in Fig. 8.9 and
discussed in the accompanying text. Note that in the vector
representation (Fig. 8.9(a)) each different assignment of
positions to categories constitutes a different object
representation language.

The categories which represent the properties with which
entities are characterized are called elementary categories.
It is common for a concept learning system to define
additional, 'derived' categories whose values correspond to
combinations of values of the elementary categories. For
instance, the category AREA and its values 'large',

'medium', and 'small' may be derived from the values of
categories SIZE and SHAPE as follows:

AREA(large)   corresponds to
                    SIZE(0,large) & SHAPE(0,circle)
                 OR SIZE(0,large) & SHAPE(0,square)

AREA(medium) corresponds to
                    SIZE(0,large) & SHAPE(0,triangle)
                 OR SIZE(0,large) & SHAPE(0,inverted triangle)
                 OR SIZE(0,small) & SHAPE(0,circle)
                 OR SIZE(0,small) & SHAPE(0,square)

AREA(small)   corresponds to
                    SIZE(0,small) & SHAPE(0,triangle)
                 OR SIZE(0,small) & SHAPE(0,inverted triangle)

Although they add nothing to the descriptive power of the
representation languages in which they occur, derived
categories can play an important role in concept learning.
They almost always add a 'bias' (see Section B.9) to the
representation language which has a significant effect
during concept learning. For instance, the derived category
AREA just defined could be used to smuggle disjunction of a
narrowly applicable kind into a representation language
which did not otherwise support disjunction. Alternatively,
in concept learning systems which, when all other criteria
are equally satisfied, prefer concepts whose representation
is short over those whose representation is long, a derived
category which shortens the representation of some concepts
but not all* effectively changes the preference ordering of
the concepts. Willshaw and Buneman (1972) used derived
categories to increase the compactness of the representation
of objects and concepts and the efficiency and simplicity
of the concept learning and concept applying processes.

The formal language in which (the declarative aspect of)
concepts are represented is called the concept representation language. Every concept learning system requires both
a concept representation language and an object
representation language. The two languages may be completely
different: there is clearly no relation between the decision

---

*   As defined above, AREA shortens the representation of all
     concepts equally.

tree representation used in Section A for concepts and the vector representation for objects.

8.B.2.1 The Single Representation Trick[*]

The extension of a concept is a subset of U. The extension of an object may be viewed as a subset of U which contains only one object. Thus a language for representing arbitrary subsets of U is sufficient to represent both concepts and objects. A concept learning system in which the object and concept representation languages are the same is said to employ the single representation trick. Use of a single representation language means that determining the membership of an object in a concept and determining if every member of one concept is a member of another are identical processes. It also means that an operation such as altering a concept so that it contains a particular positive example is identical with the operation of merging two concepts.[**]

8.B.3 VECTOR REPRESENTATION OF CONCEPTS

The vector representation of objects can easily be modified to serve as a representation language for concepts as well. Objects are represented in the usual way. The values which can occur in the representation of objects are called 'primary' values. To extend the representation to accommodate concepts (sets of objects), we introduce 'higher order' values each of which corresponds to a particular set of primary values. For instance, we can define the higher order value 'pointy' of the category SHAPE to correspond to the set of primary values {triangle, square, inverted triangle}. The extension of a higher order value is the union of the extensions of the primary values in the set of primary values to which it corresponds. Thus the extension of 'pointy' is the set of all objects which are triangular, square, or inverted triangular. Two standard higher order values of a category are 'anyvalue', which is the set of all primary values of the category, and 'novalue', which is the empty set.

---

[*] pp. 368-369 in Diettrich et al. (1982).
[**] This will be demonstrated in Section F.

The relations among the primary and higher order values of each category form a partial ordering, as shown in Fig. 8.37. This ordering is called the value containment ordering, and is defined as

value v CONTAINS value w   if and only if the extension
                       of w is a subset of the extension of v.

This ordering should not be confused with any magnitude orderings which might exist on the primary values. Consider the numerical values which can be taken by the #SPOTS category. Although 2 is (numerically) greater than 1, 2 does not CONTAIN 1 because the extension of the value 2 of the category #SPOTS does not contain the extension of the value 1 of the category #SPOTS. Had the category not been 'exactly S spots' but 'greater than S spots' (where S is the value of the category), then 1 would have CONTAINed 2, since the set of objects with 2 or more spots is a subset of the set of objects with 1 or more spots.

The membership determination process which is natural to use given the value containment ordering is called 'perfect matching': an object, O, is a member of a concept, C, if for every category F, F(C) CONTAINS F(O). A concept learning system in which concepts are represented by a vector of (possibly higher order) category values interpreted by the perfect match membership determination process is described under Focusing in Section E. An alternative membership determination process which is based on the value containment ordering is[*]

        let N be the total number of categories.
        let G be the number of categories for which
                F(C) CONTAINS F(O).
        Classify O as a member of C if and only if N-G < 2.

---

[*] This is just one of many possible definitions of 'imperfect match'. The significance of this kind of membership determination process is that it offers an escape to the objection that the 'concept of concept' which is employed in concept learning systems as studied in artificial intelligence is impoverished.   Johnson (1983,1981), among others, argues for a very different concept of concept.

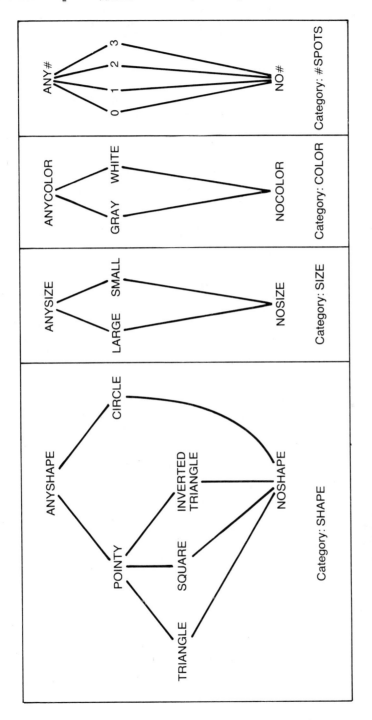

Fig. 8.37 Value Containment Partial Orderings for each of the categories. If value V_1 CONTAINS value V_2, then V_1 is above or coincides with V_2 in the diagram, and can be reached from V_2 by ascending zero or more arcs.

8.B.4 REPRESENTING CONCEPTS IN DISJUNCTIVE NORMAL FORM (DNF)

The predicate, relational and functional representations for objects can also be extended to represent concepts. First, higher order category values can be introduced in these representations in exactly the same way as they were introduced in the vector representation. For instance, the concept represented by the vector

$$< \text{pointy, anysize, gray, any\#spots} >$$

could be represented with the predicates

POINTY(C) & ANYSIZE(C) & GRAY(C) & ANY#SPOTS(C).

Because ANYSHAPE(C), ANYSIZE(C), ANYCOLOR(C), and ANY#SPOTS(C) are true for every object, they are usually omitted leaving, in this example,

POINTY(C) & GRAY(C).

Concepts such as this in which the only logical connective is AND (designated '&') are called conjunctive concepts.

A second way to extend the predicate, relational and functional representations so that they may represent concepts is to permit the use of the logical connective OR. Concepts whose representation contains an OR are called disjunctive concepts. In Disjunctive Normal Form (DNF) a concept is represented as the disjunction of conjunctive concepts. Of the following expressions

    (1) GRAY(C) & SQUARE(C)
    (2) GRAY(C) OR SQUARE(C)
    (3) (GRAY(C) & SQUARE(C)) OR SMALL(C)
    (4) GRAY(C) & SQUARE(C) OR SMALL(C)
    (5) GRAY(C) & (SQUARE(C) OR SMALL(C))

only (5) is not in DNF. Alternative bracketings of sub-expressions in (4) could yield either (3) or (5): since only one of these, (3), is in DNF, we interpret (4) as a conven-ient abbreviation for (3). Each conjunctive concept in a DNF expression is called a disjunct. The extension of a concept represented in DNF is the union of the extensions of the disjuncts in its representation. An alternative way of writing

    SHAPE(C)=SQUARE   OR   SHAPE(C)=TRIANGLE

is   SHAPE(C)=(SQUARE OR TRIANGLE).

The latter form is called internal disjunction:[*] it can only
be used with predicates in the same predicate family (i.e.
values associated with the same category). In a given
representation language there may be several distinct ways
of representing the same concept. For instance,

    SHAPE(C)=POINTY

    SHAPE(C)=SQUARE OR SHAPE(C)=TRIANGLE
                OR SHAPE(C)=INVERTED TRIANGLE

    SHAPE(C)=(SQUARE OR TRIANGLE OR INVERTED TRIANGLE)

    SHAPE(C)=(TRIANGLE OR INVERTED TRIANGLE OR SQUARE)

are all different representations of the same concept. Such
representations are said to be equivalent.

8.B.5 THE CONCEPT LEARNING TASK

The primary task, as originally described in Section A, is
that of classifying any given object as either instantiating
a concept or not. The basis for making such a classification
is a set of objects whose classification is known. An object
whose classification is known is called an example. Each
example is labeled as either a positive example, if it
instantiates the concept, or as a negative example, if it
does not. This primary task may be viewed as a kind of
inference in which the set of examples and the object to be
classified provide the premises and in which the ultimate
conclusion is a membership classification, i.e. a decision
to classify the given object as a member of the concept or
as a nonmember. This view is depicted in Fig. 8.38.

---

[*]   Michalski (1983a,b) gives a full rigorous account of
      internal disjunction and several other innovations in
      concept representation.

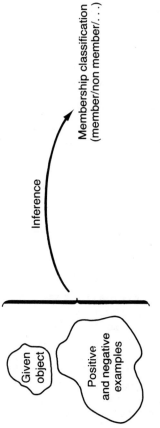

Fig. 8.38 The primary task: inferring a membership classification for a given object on the basis of a set of examples

The primary task may be divided into two subtasks: concept learning and concept application. Concept learning is viewed as an inference in which the set of examples provides the premises and in which the 'conclusion' is the declarative aspect of a concept. The algorithm which carries out this inference is called the concept learning algorithm. Concept application is also viewed as an inference: the premises here are provided by the declarative aspect which has been constructed by the concept learning algorithm, and the conclusion is a membership classification. The algorithm which carries out this inference is the membership determination process. This two stage view of the primary task is depicted in Fig. 8.39. Figures 8.14 and 8.27 should be seen as instances of the relationship between concept learning and concept application depicted in Fig. 8.39.

In principle there is no need to divide the primary task into these two stages: one could base each membership classification directly on the set of examples without reference to an intermediate structure such as the declarative aspect of a concept. In practice, however, this division is extremely useful. First, it is almost always the case that the set of examples changes extremely infrequently compared to the number of times a membership classification is requested. The overall cost (e.g. time) of inferring membership classifications for every object for which a classification is requested can be enormously reduced[*] by dividing the inferences involved in such classification into those which can be done once and hold for all objects, and those which must be repeated for each object because they depend on details particular to the object. The division of the original task into the subtasks of concept learning and concept application corresponds to such a division of the inferences: concept learning is based only on the set of examples, and need only be done when this set changes; concept application does not repeat all that has occurred during concept learning but uses the declarative aspect of the concept as a summary of the inferences which took place during concept learning. A second advantage of dividing the original task in this way is that the declarative aspects which are produced by the concept learning system can themselves be viewed as objects which can be compared, merged, inspected, and so on, by machines or by humans for many diverse purposes.

---

[*]   e.g. the ACORNS of Hayes-Roth and McDermott (1977).

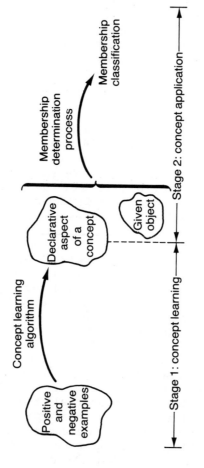

Fig. 8.39 Concept learning and concept application: 2 stages in the primary task

A third advantage of viewing concept learning and concept application as two stages of a single process, rather than two separate processes, is the emphasis which this view places on the relationship which exists between concept learning and concept application. For instance, it acknowledges the important role which is played by the membership determination process in the representation of an intension of a concept. It also suggests that the division of labor between the two stages is arbitrary to some extent. For instance, one could have as a declarative aspect a literal record of the the positive and negative examples and have all of the inference involved in the primary task done by the membership determination process. This is a rather extreme and unusual division of labor, but in a less extreme (but no less unusual) form, this describes the relation between concept learning systems which use the Example Set Method (Section 8.C.6) and the systems which interpret their output. It should be noted that according to the view depicted in Fig. 8.39, concept learning does not involve modifying the membership determination process. As mentioned previously[*] there is no reason in principle why this should be so, but in virtually every extant learning system learning is achieved by modifying or reconstructing the declarative aspect of the concept and leaving the procedural aspect unchanged. Throughout this chapter we shall equate 'learning a concept' with 'constructing a sentence in the concept representation language which, together with the (fixed) membership determination process, represents an intension of that concept'.

8.B.6 CRITERIA WHICH A CONCEPT SHOULD MEET

Implicit in the statement of the concept learning task is the understanding that the concept which is learned from a set of examples is not completely unrelated to those examples. That is, one insists that learning a concept is not merely a matter of, say, picking a concept at random, but rather a matter of finding or constructing a concept which is related to the examples in some particular predefined way. In other words, there are criteria which a concept which is learned must meet: the relation which must hold

---

[*]   Section 8.B.1.

between a concept and the set of examples on which it is based is one source of such criteria. There are other sources of such criteria as well. For instance, it may be a requirement that various costs associated with the process of concept learning or concept application be balanced in a particular way. Such a requirement inevitably restricts or prejudices the kind of concepts which are learned, and thus, at least indirectly, constitutes a criterion, or a set of criteria, which must be met by any concept which is learned. Or it may be that objects and concepts are being interpreted as phenomena in some particular domain, and that under that interpretation certain concepts are extremely unlikely or perhaps meaningless. One may use these domain-specific properties of concepts to restrict the kinds of concepts which are learned (e.g. one may insist that only concepts which have a meaningful interpretation be learned).

Some criteria are inviolable requirements which any concept which is learned must satisfy. These shall be called, simply, requirements. Other criteria are not inviolable but should be satisfied to as great a degree as possible. These shall be called preference criteria. A typical preference criteria is: 'the declarative aspect of every concept which is learned should have as few disjuncts as possible'.[*] Preference criteria can usually not be perfectly satisfied: either for practical reasons (e.g. the resources such as time or memory required to perfectly satisfy the criteria are unavailable) or because of conflicts with other preference criteria or requirements. Despite the fact that preference criteria are not strictly required, most concept learning systems invest a considerable percentage of their effort in trying to find a concept which best satisfies the preference criteria. This investment is justified because the preference criteria are usually related to a cost of some kind (memory, time, likelihood of a serious error, etc.) which is minimized by the best concept. Concepts which meet the requirements and satisfy the preference criteria to as great an extent as possible are called 'acceptable'.

Examples of some of the more common and important criteria are discussed in the following.

---

[*] 'As few as possible' is often written as 'minimum'. This substitution is unproblematic for requirements, but misleading for preference criteria.

8.B.6.1 Domain Specific Criteria

Objects and concepts are usually interpreted as phenomena in some particular domain. Known regularities or restrictions which are specific to this domain (henceforth these will collectively be called domain structure) can be used in a number of ways by a concept learning system: for instance, to justify particular inferences.

Domain structure can also provide constraints or criteria which concepts must satisfy. A common constraint on the extension of a concept stipulates a relationship between the membership of one (set of) object(s) and another. Suppose, for instance, that objects are interpreted as numbers, and domain structure is such that all meaningful concepts - that is, sets of numbers - in this domain are closed under the operation of addition. Then if the number 2 is included in the extension of a concept, domain structure requires that 2+2, 2+2+2, and so on, be in the extension of that concept. Conversely if 4 were excluded from the extension of a concept, domain structure would require that 2 (and 1) also be excluded from the extension of that concept.

A second kind of constraint which domain structure provides is more directly applicable to the representation of a concept. There are frequently interdependencies between two (or more) properties which constrain the way in which a single object can instantiate these properties. Such constraints translate into constraints on the combinations of category values which can occur in the representation of an object or concept. In categories whose values are numerical one often finds that the values of one category must vary continuously or monotonically with the values of another because of structure (such as physical or chemical laws) in the domain. For instance, the values of two categories may be constrained to vary in such a way that their product is equal to the value of a third category.

8.B.6.2
Domain Independent Criteria Related to the Extensions of Learned Concepts

A concept is said to be complete with respect to a set of examples if it contains all of the positive examples in that set. A concept is said to be consistent with respect to a set of examples if it contains none of the negative examples in that set. A set of examples is said to be consistent if there exists a consistent concept which meets the domain specific requirements. One normally requires that all concepts which are learned be both consistent and complete with respect to the entire set of examples. 'Complete' will be used as an abbreviation for 'complete with respect to the entire set of examples'. 'Consistent' will be used as an abbreviation for 'consistent with respect to the entire set of examples'.

There is often a penalty associated with the misclassification of each object. Since a concept (implicitly) constitutes a classification of every object, one can associate with each concept an overall penalty calculated from the penalties associated with individual objects under the assumption that, for instance, the concept misclassifies every object which is not an example. On this basis one can define the criterion that the concept which is learned should have an associated overall penalty which is as small as possible. A commonly occurring example of this kind of criterion is described in the following paragraph.

An 'error of omission' occurs when a member is misclassified as a nonmember. An 'error of commission' occurs when a nonmember is misclassified as a member. The penalty associated with the two types of error is usually different. Often the penalty associated with one kind of error is uniformly smaller than the penalty associated with the other kind of error. If errors of omission are uniformly less heavily penalized than errors of commission then the concept which is learned should contain as few objects as possible. If errors of commission are uniformly less heavily penalized than errors of omission then the concept which is learned should contain as many objects as possible.

Another kind of criteria relates the concept currently being learned to a collection of other concepts. One may require, for instance, that the concept currently being learned contain no objects which are contained in any of the given concepts.

8.B.6.3 Domain Independent Criteria Related to Concept Representation

A concept is representable in a given concept representation language if there is a sentence in that language which, together with the given membership determination process, represents an intension for that concept. Of the 256 possible concepts involving the eight objects shown in Fig. 8.40 only 22 are representable in the concept representation language shown in Fig. 8.41.[*] Clearly a concept which cannot be represented in a concept learning system cannot be learned by it.

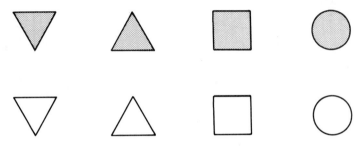

Fig. 8.40 A universe of eight objects

It is not necessarily true, however, that every concept which is representable in a concept learning system can be learned by that learning system. A concept may be representable in a concept learning system and satisfy all of the criteria which are demanded of concepts and yet still not be able to be learned by the system because the nature of the concept learning algorithm is such that no set of examples results in that concept being inferred by the concept learning system. Such a concept is said to be 'unreachable'. It is occasionally desirable that a concept be unreachable. For instance, it is an advantage if concepts which are representable but not acceptable are unreachable, or at least unreachable given consistent meaningful examples.[**]

---

[*] There are 4x8 distinct vectors, but every vector containing either 'noshape' or 'nocolor' represents the concept whose extension is empty. There are 3x7 vectors which represent distinct concepts whose extensions are not empty.

[**] p. 140 in Mitchell (1978) describes such conditions.

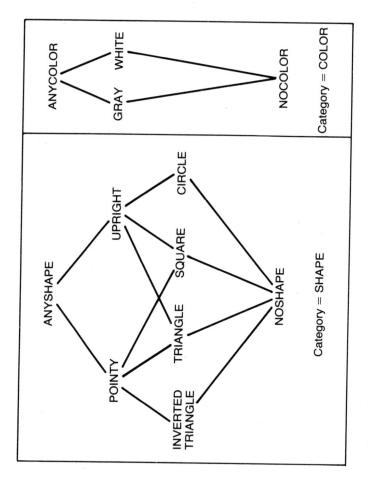

Fig. 8.41 A concept representation language for concepts based on the universe in Fig. 8.40. Disjunctive normal form will be used with the categories and values shown

Since there may be many distinct ways of representing a concept in a given concept representation language, we can also define the notion of a particular representation of a concept being unreachable: if no sequence of examples exists which results in a particular representation being inferred, then that representation is unreachable. It is often desirable that some representations of a concept be unreachable: for instance, amongst a set of equivalent representations it is an advantage if only the most 'preferred' representation is reachable. The undesirable aspect of unreachability is that an 'ideal' concept may be representable but fail to be inferred because an 'inferior' but acceptable concept is inferred instead.[*]

Criteria defined on various aspects of the sentences in the concept representation language may be employed to distinguish between equivalent sentences which are equally reachable. Particular categories, for instance, may be preferred over others. Factors which might determine such a preference ordering may be related to the 'cost' of obtaining a value for the category, or the effectiveness of the category in distinguishing concept members from nonmembers, or an a priori domain or problem specific category preference. Another such measure which is rapidly growing in importance is the comprehensibility of the sentence to a human.[**]

One criterion which is peculiar to Disjunctive Normal Form (DNF) is based on the number of disjuncts in the DNF expression which represents a concept. For instance, it is common to prefer concepts whose representation requires as few disjuncts as possible. Occasionally criteria involve aspects of both the extension and the representation of the concept: one such criterion prefers concepts in which the size of the intersection of the extensions of the disjuncts is as small as possible.

---

[*]   p. 361, Hayes-Roth and McDermott (1977);
      p. 415, Dietterich et al. (1982).
[**] Michie (1983); also pp. 122, 130-131 Michalski (1983b).

8.B.7 CONCEPT SPACE

Henceforth it will be assumed that the set of representable
concepts and the set of concepts meeting the domain-specific
(and other) requirements are the same. The specific topics
which will be investigated are methods which a concept
learning system may employ to (try to) ensure that the
concepts which it learns are complete and consistent, and
some issues surrounding reachability. For these purposes it
is useful to introduce the notion of concept space.

Generally, the preferences and requirements which define the
acceptability of a concept induce a partial ordering on the
set of representable concepts, as follows:

> For any two concepts, A and B, define
> A .<. B   if and only if   the acceptability of A is
>   guaranteed by the acceptability of B.

Concept space is the set of representable concepts under
this partial ordering. The ordering is sometimes called the
structure of concept space.

The orderings induced by the criteria of completeness and
consistency are duals of one another and both correspond
to extension containment. The completeness of A is
guaranteed by the completeness of B if and only if the
extension of B is a subset of the extension of A. On the
other hand, the consistency of A is guaranteed by the
consistency of B if and only if the extension of A is a
subset of the extension of B. We shall call this ordering
the 'extension containment ordering'. It is an example of a
'general to specific' ordering:

> A is more specific than B   if and only if   the extension of
>   (written A |< B)   A is a subset of the extension of B

This ordering will play a central role in the discussions of
concept learning in the subsequent sections. 'Concept A
contains concept B' shall be an abbreviation for 'the
extension of concept B is a subset of the extension of
concept A'. Two kinds of concepts which are of particular

importance are maximally specific and maximally general concepts, defined as follows.

A maximally specific concept (MSC) is any acceptable, complete concept which contains as few elements as possible. Thus an MSC contains only the positive examples and objects deemed necessary by domain-specific (and other) requirements given the examples.

A maximally general concept (MGC) is any acceptable, consistent concept which contains as many elements as possible. Thus an MGC contains all elements of U except the negative examples and those objects which domain-specific and other requirements prohibit given the examples.

When all subsets of U are acceptable, MSC and MGC will both be unique: MSC will contain all and only the positive examples, and MGC will be contain all objects except the negative examples. MSC or MGC may be unique when not all subsets of U are acceptable,[*] but in general neither will be unique. In Fig. 8.42, MGC is unique and MSC is not when only conjunctive concepts are acceptable. When disjunctive concepts are acceptable, MSC is unique and MGC, which is different from the conjunctive MGC, is unique up to the number of disjuncts in the representation. That is, there are equivalent representations of the unique MGC which contain between two and seven disjuncts.

Since each MGC is a maximal consistent concept according to the extension containment ordering, every consistent concept is contained in an MGC. Similarly every complete concept contains an MSC. A subspace of a partially ordered space which is linearly ordered and which has a maximum and a minimum element is called a 'chain'.[**] Every complete and consistent concept is an element of a chain in concept space in which the minimum element is a maximally specific concept and the maximum element is a maximally general concept (see Fig. 8.43).

---

[*] MGC is rarely unique. This asymmetry between MSC and MGC was pointed out in Bundy and Silver (1982).
[**] Standard mathematical usage does not require a chain to have a maximum or a minimum.

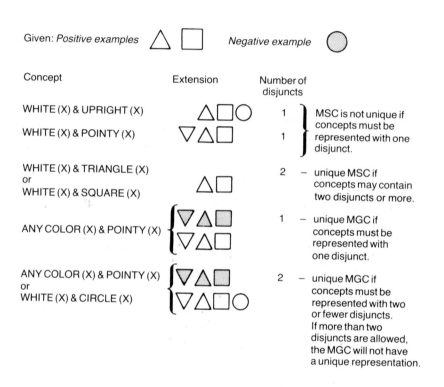

Given: *Positive examples* △ □   *Negative example* ◯

Concept	Extension	Number of disjuncts
WHITE (X) & UPRIGHT (X)	△□◯	1
WHITE (X) & POINTY (X)	▽△□	1

} MSC is not unique if concepts must be represented with one disjunct.

| WHITE (X) & TRIANGLE (X) or WHITE (X) & SQUARE (X) | △□ | 2 |

– unique MSC if concepts may contain two disjuncts or more.

| ANY COLOR (X) & POINTY (X) | ▽△■ ▽△□ | 1 |

– unique MGC if concepts must be represented with one disjunct.

| ANY COLOR (X) & POINTY (X) or WHITE (X) & CIRCLE (X) | ▽△■ ▽△□◯ | 2 |

– unique MGC if concepts must be represented with two or fewer disjuncts. If more than two disjuncts are allowed, the MGC will not have a unique representation.

Fig. 8.42 MSC and MGC

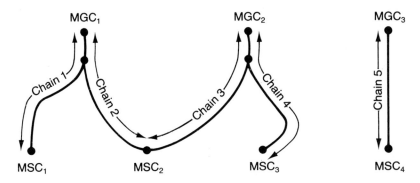

All consistent and complete concepts lie on a chain whose minimum is an MSC and whose maximum is an MGC.

Fig. 8.43 Typical chains of consistent and complete concepts.

8.B.7.1
Explicit Specification of a Structure for Concept Space

The recognition that preference criteria and requirements induce a partial ordering on the set of representable concepts has led some researchers to state the structure of concept space directly in terms of a partial ordering, bypassing an explicit statement of any criteria other than 'minimal according to the specified ordering'. These explicitly prescribed partial orderings are usually defined in terms of a concept's representation and not its extension. Consider the following:

Let A and B be concepts.
Let P, Q, R, and so on be categories.
Suppose that a_P and b_P are values of P such that $P(A,a_P)$
  and $P(B,b_P)$ are true.
Similarly let a_Q, b_Q, a_R, b_R be values of Q and R, and
  so on, such that

        A is represented as $P(A,a_P)$ & $Q(A,a_Q)$ & ... & $R(A,a_R)$
and   B is represented as $P(B,b_P)$ & $Q(B,b_Q)$ & ... & $R(B,b_R)$

Given this representation of concepts, the value containment ordering (of Section 8.B.3) can be used to define a 'general to specific' partial ordering on concepts as follows:

A is more specific than B   if and only if

$$b_P \text{ CONTAINS } a_P$$
$$\text{and } b_Q \text{ CONTAINS } a_Q$$
$$\text{and } \ldots$$
$$\text{and } b_R \text{ CONTAINS } a_R.$$

This ordering coincides with the extension containment ordering (which is induced by the criteria of completeness and consistency). Note, however, that this ordering is stated purely in terms of the representation of the concepts which are being compared, and not in terms of their extensions.   To emphasize this, recall that relational predicates involving the higher order values 'anyshape', 'anysize', etc.   need not be included in the representation of concepts (see Section 8.B.4). That is,

SHAPE(C,pointy) & SIZE(C,anysize) & COLOR(C,gray)
& #SPOTS(C,any#spots)

is equivalent to

SHAPE(C,pointy) & COLOR(C,gray).

This fact does not, of course, affect the definition of an ordering on concepts which is given in terms of concepts' extensions, such as the extension containment ordering. It does affect definitions of orderings which are stated in representational terms, as was the definition based on the value containment ordering just given. Since the representations of A and B may now be different lengths and contain different categories, the definition of this ordering in representational terms is considerably more involved:

If the number of categories in the representation of A is not the same as the number of categories in the representation of B, let us suppose that there are fewer categories in the representation of B than the representation of A.

If every category which occurs in the representation of B does not occur in the representation of A, then A and B are not comparable.

Otherwise, we have the following:

B is represented as $P(B,b_P)$ & ... & $Q(B,b_Q)$
and A is represented as $P(A,a_P)$ & ... & $Q(A,a_Q)$ & ...
& $R(A,a_R)$

(there need not be any predicates in the
representation of A beyond Q)

and we can define an ordering similar to that above:

A is more specific than B if and only if b_P CONTAINS a_P
and ...
and b_Q CONTAINS a_Q

(i.e. predicates in the representation of A beyond
Q are not considered when comparing A and B).

According to this ordering

SHAPE(A,triangle) & SIZE(A,small)
is more specific than SHAPE(B,pointy),
SIZE(A,small) is not comparable to SHAPE(B,pointy),
and SIZE(A,small) is not comparable to SIZE(B,large).

A convenient way to define a partial ordering on concept
space is to specify a set of operators on concept representations and define the ordering:

A is more specific than B if and only if
B can be derived from A using the given operators

By definition, the specified operators are used to derive
more 'general' concepts from more 'specific' ones. These
operators are thus called 'generalization operators'.[*] For
example, the concept comparison algorithm which has just
been described can be stated as[**]

A is more specific than B if and only if
B can be derived from A using the generalization
operators COM, DAC, and AVPO shown in Fig. 8.44

---

[*]   Michalski (1983a,b) discusses a number of generalization
operators.
[**] Similar to the ordering in Vere (1975,1977,1978).

Operator	transforms this conjunctive concept into	this conjunctive concept
COM (commute)	$P(A, a_P)\ \&\dots\ \&\ Q(A, a_Q)\ \&\ R(A, a_R)\ \&\dots\ \&\ S(A, a_S)$	$P(A, a_P)\ \&\dots\ \&\ R(A, a_R)\ \&\ Q(A, a_Q)\ \&\dots\ \&\ S(A, a_S)$
DAC (Drop a condition)	$P(A, a_P)\ \&\ Q(A, a_Q)\ \&\dots\ \&\ R(A, a_R)$	$Q(A, a_Q)\ \&\dots\ \&\ R(A, a_R)$
AVPO (Ascend the value containment partial ordering)	$P(A, a_P)\ \&\dots\ \&\ Q(A, a_Q)$	$P(A, a'_P)\ \&\dots\ \&\ Q(A, a_Q)$ where a'_P CONTAINS a_P

Fig. 8.44 Typical operators on the declarative aspect of a conjunctive concept

A typical derivation using these operators is shown in Fig. 8.45. The derivation shown establishes that the concept whose members are pointy objects is more 'general' than the concept whose members are small triangles.

GIVEN: SHAPE (A, TRIANGLE) & SIZE (A, SMALL)

APPLY CVPO: SHAPE (A, POINTY) & SIZE (A, SMALL)

APPLY COM: SIZE (A, SMALL) & SHAPE (A, POINTY)

APPLY DAC: SHAPE (A, POINTY)

Fig. 8.45 The derivation of the concept "SHAPE(A, POINTY)" from the concept "SHAPE(A, TRIANGLE) & SIZE(A, SMALL)" using the operators in Fig. 8.44

We have now seen four different definitions of the same partial ordering. The first definition was in terms of criteria on concepts' extensions. The fourth definition was in terms of seemingly arbitrary operators defined over a particular concept representation language. The properties of completeness and consistency, which originally motivated the definition of the partial ordering, can be related to the fourth definition of this partial ordering only with considerable effort. Despite the advantages inherent in using the partial orderings which are induced by the criteria which define the acceptability of a concept, most learning systems use orderings on concept space which are defined in terms of operators which are defined over the concept representation language. Such systems will be studied in detail in Sections C and F.

8.B.8
SIMULTANEOUS VERSUS SEQUENTIAL PRESENTATION OF EXAMPLES

Ideally, a concept learning system has the entire set of
examples available to it at the time when concept learning
occurs. When this condition, called the simultaneous presentation of examples, holds, the concept which is learned
can be guaranteed, in principle, to meet all requirements
and to satisfy all preference criteria to as great an extent
as possible. In particular, when examples are presented
simultaneously, the concept which is learned can be
guaranteed to be consistent and complete with respect to
all of the examples. Concept learning systems which operate
under the assumption that all examples will be presented
simultaneously are called 'nonincremental'. Algorithms Q and
R are nonincremental.

Nonincremental learning is not possible when either memory
limitations prohibit the storage of all of the examples or
the process of acquiring examples is interleaved with the
process of applying a concept which has been constructed on
the basis of the examples acquired to date. When examples
cannot be presented simultaneously, they are said to be
presented sequentially. We shall use the following
characterization of concept learning when examples are
presented sequentially.

Individual examples, or small sets of examples, are assumed
to be presented to the concept learning system from time
to time. Whenever additional examples are presented a new
concept or set of concepts, called the concept-to-date, is
calculated and output. The calculation of the concept-
to-date is based on a collection of concepts (e.g. recent
concepts-to-date) and previously seen examples, the total
number of which is limited by a fixed upper bound. The
phrase 'the set of examples' which has been used throughout
sections A and B is interpreted, when examples are presented
sequentially, as the set of all examples which have been
presented to date. Henceforth we shall refer to this set as
'all previously seen examples' or 'all examples seen to
date'. Learning systems which operate under these conditions
are called 'incremental'. Unless indicated otherwise, the
remainder of the chapter will be concerned with incremental
concept learning systems.

There are two important consequences of the conditions characterizing incremental learning. First, the entire set of examples seen to date will not in general be reconstructable from the collection of concepts and examples available at any given time to an incremental learning system. As a result, a major difficulty for incremental concept learning systems is to guarantee that every concept-to-date is acceptable with respect to ALL previously seen examples. This difficulty may be explained as follows. Every concept implicitly assigns a membership classification to every object. An object's classification is said to be 'required' if every concept which is acceptable with respect to any set of examples which contains all previously seen examples classifies the object in the same way. Otherwise the object's classification is said to be 'gratuitous'. When new examples are presented, a new concept will be constructed which may classify several objects differently from the previously constructed concept. Assuming that the previous concept was acceptable with respect to all previously seen examples, then if the new concept is to be similarly acceptable, every object whose classification by the new concept is different from its classification by the previous concept must have been gratuitously classified by the previous concept. For instance, if an object is classified as a member of the current concept because a requirement such as completeness demands such a classification, then that object must be a member of all subsequent concepts which are acceptable. Unfortunately, it is not generally possible to determine which objects have gratuitous classifications and which have required classifications. Thus an incremental learning system cannot guarantee that it will always construct a concept which is acceptable with respect to all previously seen examples.

Criteria which are based on the distribution of category values across all examples also become impossible to satisfy perfectly under the conditions characterizing incremental learning. The 'entropy' function (Fig. 8.19) which was used in algorithm Q was based on the number of occurrences among all positive and negative examples of every possible combination of category values. Such a comprehensive summary of all previously seen examples is generally not possible within the memory limitations imposed by the conditions of incremental learning. Incremental concept learning systems commonly keep a summary of the important aspects of the examples seen to date which will enable them to construct concepts which satisfy such demanding criteria in at least an approximate fashion:[*] for instance, a concept learning system might record the number of positive examples and the number of negative examples which have occurred for each category value.

The second major consequence of the conditions characterizing incremental learning is that the order of presentation of examples can be important: one must consider the example SEQUENCE, not just the example set. An incremental learning system which produces the same concept-to-date regardless of the order of presentation of the examples to date is said to be order-independent. Order independence is by no means certain - algorithm BDF in section C is not order independent.

In a sequence of examples one may consider the frequency with which a particular example recurs: the notion of recurring examples does not arise naturally in the non-incremental learning situation. Various assumptions are possible: for instance that examples do not recur, that they recur regularly, or that they recur with a particular, perhaps nonuniform, probability. The difficulties described above apply in their strongest form only when examples do not recur. For most purposes the recurrence of examples counteracts the memory limitations imposed in the incremental learning situation and allows incremental learning systems, if given enough time, to learn concepts of equal 'quality' to those learned by nonincremental concept learning systems. Several concept learning systems in the literature depend on examples recurring.[**]

---

[*]   e.g. the rule-strength parameters of Anderson et al. (1979) and Langley (1982,1983a,c), and the feature-confidence parameters of Lebowitz (1982,1983).

[**] e.g. Langley (1982,1983a,c); Wexler and Culicover (1980).

8.B.9
THE INACCESSIBILITY OF EXTENSIONS OF OBJECTS AND CONCEPTS

In this chapter it is assumed that concept learning systems are confined to inspecting and manipulating representations of objects and concepts and do not have direct access to the extensions of the objects and concepts. The impact of this restriction on concept learning systems is very large. One reason for its importance is that many of the operations and measures which play a natural role in concept learning are defined in terms of the extension of the objects and concepts: for instance, one may wish to measure the number of objects in the extension of a concept. Some such extensionally defined measures and operations have exact counterparts in some representation languages, but not in others. The representation language must be chosen so that extensionally defined measures and operations which are important to the success of the concept learning system can be accurately approximated as measures and operations on the representations of the objects and concepts.[*]

This restriction may have an even more direct influence on the nature of concepts which are learned by a concept learning system. The direct influence which a concept (or object) representation language has on the nature of concepts which are learned is called its 'bias'.[**] Bias is manifest in two ways. First, a particular concept (or object) may simply not be representable in the given language, or the categories and values which are provided in the language may be inadequate, that is, unable to distinguish two objects whose classification is required to be different, or unable to represent a concept which distinguishes between such objects. Secondly, the details of the representation of a concept may play a role in the fate of that concept during the concept learning process, so that some concepts will be more easily learned or more likely to be learned than others because of purely representational differences (e.g. a concept may be preferred over others because its representation is shorter than theirs).

---

[*] See p. 48 in Dietterich and Michalski (1983b).
[**] Mitchell (1980).

Investigating the effects of this restriction is an activity
which recurs throughout the entire chapter: in section C,
Lenat's Dictum and the motivation for the Method of Minimal
Modification are reflections on this restriction; in section
D, there is ongoing explicit concern for 'operational'
terms, and one area of particular concern is whether characteristics of the extension of a concept have 'operational'
counterparts - that is, whether thay can be accurately
calculated on the basis of characteristics of the representation of the concept; and in section E, the possibility that shortcomings in the representation language can be
automatically detected and corrected is briefly discussed.

This ends the introduction to the concept learning task. The
remainder of the chapter is a discussion of methods for
performing this task, i.e. concept learning methods. This
discussion will not focus on any particular system: descriptions of individual systems may be found elsewhere.[*]
Instead, three general approaches to concept learning -
CONCEPT MODIFICATION, HEURISTIC ENUMERATION, and CANDIDATE
ELIMINATION - will be discussed and algorithms typical of
each approach will be demonstrated.

The main point of difference between these approaches is the
way in which each characterizes the activity of concept
learning. For instance, from the point of view of Concept
Modification and Heuristic Enumeration, concept learning
involves the manipulation of individual concepts; from the
point of view of Candidate Elimination, concept learning
involves the manipulation of a vast partially ordered space
of concepts. Points of emphasis or explicit concern in one
approach may (apparently) be unattended in another. In the
learning systems which are typical of each approach, these
differences are significantly attenuated. The approach taken
in designing a learning system will leave its mark, but it
is always possible and often illuminating to view a system
from the perspective of the other approaches.

Each of the next three sections describes one of these
approaches. In Section F, several 'advanced' topics will be
considered from within the Concept Modification Approach.

---

[*]   cf. references in 'Overviews and Comparative Reviews' in
       Section G, especially Dietterich et al. (1982)

8.C   The concept modification approach

Within the Concept Modification Approach, a concept learning
system is characterized as having a (usually fairly small)
set of operators, called concept modification operators,
which are defined in terms of the concept representation
language: that is, they are relatively simple operations on
individual sentences in the concept representation language.
Some standard concept modification operators were shown in
Fig. 8.44. The concept-to-date is a set of concepts which
best fulfill the preference criteria and requirements.
Associated with the concept-to-date is a collection of previously seen examples; under the conditions of incremental
learning, the size of this collection may not exceed a fixed
bound. When an example is presented some of the concepts in
the concept-to-date may be deleted and some or all may be
modified, as necessary, through the application of the
concept modification operators. All concepts which come to
be members of the concept-to-date do so by being the result
of the application of concept modification operators to a
concept already in the concept-to-date. The decisions of
which operator to use, and where in the declarative aspect
of the concept to apply it, are important ones with lasting
consequences. Typically one compares the category values of
the example with each other and with those of the concepts
in the concept-to-date and its associated examples, and on
this basis chooses a category and concept modification
operator whose application to that category results (in the
ideal case) in a concept which meets all requirements and is
optimal according to the preference criteria.

A case worth noting is when there is only one operator/
category combination which will distinguish a concept in the
concept-to-date and the associated positive example(s) from
a given negative example. In this case the negative example
is called a 'near miss'.[*] Near misses are a highly desirable
kind of example: they leave no choice as to what action must
be taken, and therefore avoid all of the undesirable consequences associated with the strategies for coping with

---

[*]   The term 'near miss' originates with Winston (1970).
(Winston's work is described in Chapter 5.) Currently the
term is not used in a perfectly consistent way (e.g.
compare its use on p.52 and p.153 in Michalski, Carbonell
and Mitchell (1983)).

such choice. Unfortunately, examples are not always near
misses.[*] Three strategies for coping with the choice
afforded by 'far misses' will be discussed in the Method of
Minimal Modification.

An underlying premise of the Concept Modification Approach
is that simple changes in the representation of a concept
will generally produce desirable modifications of the
extension of the concept. Such a convenient relationship
between the extension and representation of a concept is far
from automatic. For instance, it is a somewhat unusual
property that small changes in the representation of an
integer always result in small changes in the value which
is represented: no radix number system has this property,
and neither does any representation language which has a
single syntactic symbol which stands for negation. While
this premise may be difficult to achieve, concept modification cannot succeed unless it holds. This may be restated as
Lenat's Dictum:[**]

> For concept modification to succeed,
> form must mirror content.

In Lenat's Dictum 'form' refers to the representation of the
entire intension of a concept, not just the concept's
declarative aspect, and 'content' refers to the concept's
extension. 'Mirror' means that the operations which are
performed on the declarative aspect of a concept closely
correspond to desirable operations on the extension of the
concept. In the discussion of 'bias' earlier, it was
asserted that 'content' was only accessible through 'form',

---

[*] When features are not independent it may be impossible
   for certain near misses to occur (Kibler, 1983, Bundy,
   1982).
[**] The appellation 'Lenat's Dictum' is mine. Lenat has
   actually been stressing this point for several years, but
   Lenat and Brown (1983) is the best, if not the first,
   explicit discussion of this issue. The reader is urged to
   read this paper. The fact that Lenat raises and discusses
   the issue in the context of concept discovery, which is
   quite different from concept learning, does not detract
   from the saliency of the Dictum for concept learning
   systems.

i.e. that only the representations of objects and concepts were accessible to a concept learning system, and that the choice of representation languages did indeed influence the concepts which a concept learner would produce. Lenat's Dictum is a significant expansion of the notion of 'bias' in the context of concept modification, which emphasizes that the primary consideration in choosing a manner of representing intensions of concepts is the degree to which desirable operations on a concept's extension can be achieved through operations on its declarative aspect.

Indeed, there are four separate decisions which the designer of a learning system must make within the Concept Modification Approach which together determine the degree to which concept modification operators will produce desirable effects on the extension of a concept. First, one must choose how the intension of a concept shall be divided into declarative and procedural components. The importance of this choice is that only the declarative component is accessible by the learning system. Second, one must choose a particular concept representation language. In addition to its bias, this language will determine the kind of concept modification operators which are possible. Third, one must choose which concept modification operators, of the many which are possible, will actually be used by the concept learning system. Finally, one may choose to impose restrictions on the conditions under which each chosen concept modification operator will be applied.

8.C.1 'PURE' versus HYBRID CONCEPT MODIFICATION SYSTEMS

'Generalization' refers to any operation which increases the size of the extension of a concept.[*] When an error of omission occurs the concept involved must be generalized to include the misclassified object. The opposite of generalization is discrimination: when an error of commission occurs the concept involved must be discriminated (or specialized) to exclude the misclassified object.

---

[*] Michalski (1983a,b) uses 'generalization' in a broader sense.

In a pure discrimination system, only operators which specialize the concept are used (discrimination operators). The concept-to-date initially contains those concepts whose extensions are as large as possible (e.g. the Universe). Negative examples which result in errors of commission initiate and guide the discrimination process. Positive examples are crucial to the efficiency of a pure discrimination system. Only categories in which a given negative example differs from the positive examples associated with the concept-to-date need be considered in the discrimination process. Retaining even a single positive example for this purpose drastically improves the efficiency of the learning process.

The roles of positive and negative examples just described for pure discrimination systems are reversed in pure generalization systems. Some systems[*] have worked under conditions in which only positive examples are available.[**]

A hybrid system is one which incorporates both generalization and discrimination operators. Within the Concept Modification Approach, there are many more pure systems than hybrid systems.[***]

Algorithms Q and R were nonincremental Concept Modification algorithms. In this section and in Section F, we will look at three methods for incremental learning within the Concept Modification Approach. The boundaries between these methods are not sharp, as we shall see, and these methods do not cover the entire spectrum of methods within the Concept Modification Approach.

---

[*]   Hayes-Roth and McDermott (1978,1977), Plotkin (1970), Vere (1978,1977,1975).

[**] Angluin (1980) gives a theoretical discussion of learning from positive examples only. Berwick (1983) discusses its psychological relevance.

[***] Anderson et al. (1979), Anderson (1981) and Shapiro (1981) are hybrids.

8.C.2 THE METHOD OF MINIMAL MODIFICATION

The Method of Minimal Modification requires that the modifications which are made in revising a concept which has misclassified an example be minimal according to a given measure of concept difference. Different measures, of course, will produce different concepts through the method of minimal modification. 'Minimal' modification, as measured by the extension containment partial ordering, is described in the following section. In subsequent sections representation-based measures of minimal modification will be investigated. Most systems designed from within the Concept Modification Approach use the Method of Minimal Modification in conjunction with an representation-based measure of the size of a modification.

8.C.3 'MINIMAL' AS MEASURED BY EXTENSION CONTAINMENT

The maximally specific and maximally general concepts (MSC and MGC, respectively) which are consistent and complete with respect to a given set of examples have been introduced in Section 8.B.7. Maximal and minimal are defined in terms of the size of the extension of these concepts. Concept learning systems whose concept-to-date is always the set containing all and only the current maximally specific concepts are called MSC-proposers. Similarly, concept learning systems whose concept-to-date is always the set containing all and only the current maximally general concepts are called MGC-proposers. The following discussion is about the properties of MSC-proposers only; similar properties hold for MGC-proposers.

Every concept which is complete with respect to a set of examples will contain one or more MSC. Also, a concept which is complete with respect to a set of examples is complete with respect to any subset of that set of examples. Together these imply that an MSC-proposer employs the Method of Minimal Modification in the sense that each MSC with respect to examples $\{ e_1, e_2,...,e_{n+1} \}$ will be minimally larger than some MSC with respect to $\{ e_1,e_2,...,e_n \}$. Consequently at least one member of every concept-to-date constructed by MSC-proposer will be consistent with all future examples.

One of the major difficulties which arises in incremental
learning is distinguishing those objects whose membership
classification is required, from those objects whose membership classification is gratuitous. It is necessary for a
learning system to distinguish these two kinds of objects so
that it can ensure that changes in the membership
classification which result from future examples affect only
gratuitously classified objects. MSC-proposer overcomes
this difficulty by having no gratuitously classified objects
in any of the concepts in its concept-to-date. That is, if
an object which is classified as a member of an MSC is later
required to be classified as a nonmember, its classification
is not changed, except in the sense that this entire MSC is
deleted from the concept-to-date.

8.C.4
'MINIMAL' AS MEASURED BY NUMBER OF CONCEPT MODIFICATION OPERATORS APPLIED

There are at least two circumstances in which it is not
practical to use MSC-proposer as a concept learning system.
First, the calculation of the set of MSCs often involves
repeated use of the membership determination process. When
this process is expensive, any system which requires its
frequent use will be impractical. Secondly, although MSC-
proposer was suggested as a solution to one of the
difficulties inherent in incremental learning, it is not
clear that the set of MSCs can be always be calculated
within the restrictions of incremental learning.

The Method of Minimal Modification is thus motivated by some
attractive properties of MSC-proposer, but implemented with
measures of minimal which support rapid concept modification
calculated on the basis of information which is certain to
be available under the conditions characterizing incremental
learning. The most common such measure of minimal is 'fewest
number of applications of concept modification operators'.
In order for a concept learning system using the method of
minimal modification with this measure of minimal to in-
herit, at least approximately, the attractive properties of

MSC-proposer it should be a pure generalization system;[*]
that is, all of its concept modification operators should
always have the effect of increasing the size of the extension of the concept.

Assuming that all of the MSCs are representable the only
differences between MSC-proposer and its counterpart which
uses a representation-based measure of 'minimal' will be
differences in the reachability of the MSCs. A concept, C,
may fail to be reachable in two ways: either no sequence of
concept modification operators can produce C from the
initial concept-to-date, or the application of concept
modification operators is regulated by conditions which
collectively prevent any of the C-producing sequences from
occurring.

8.C.5 THREE STRATEGIES[**]

Regardless of the choice of measure, there is often not a
unique minimal modification which can be made to a concept
to accomodate an example which it misclassifies. Concept
learning systems may handle this nonuniqueness with any of
three strategies, demonstrated in the following.

8.C.5.1 Strategy 1: Full Breadth

In this strategy every acceptable concept which is a minimal
modification of a concept in the current concept-to-date
is included in the subsequent concept-to-date. Any concept
in the concept-to-date which is replaced in this way or
otherwise proves unacceptable is eliminated from the subsequent concept-to-date. In a pure discrimination full
breadth system the concept-to-date will contain the best

---

[*] A pure discrimination system if modeled on MGC-proposer.
[**] These correspond closely to strategies in heuristic
     search. This is no accident: learning may be viewed as
     a search of concept space (e.g. Simon and Lea, 1974,
     Mitchell, 1982b,1979).   This view is often very useful,
     but it will not be exploited in the current chapter.

possible approximations to MGC under the given reachability restrictions. That is, it will contain the concepts whose extensions are maximal subsets of the MGCs. The degree of discrepancy between the extensions of the concepts in the concept-to-date and the MGCs may change after each example which results in a modification to the concept-to-date. All of the concepts in the concept-to-date will always be consistent but under incremental learning conditions some may be incomplete. This is demonstrated in the second example below.

There may be several equally attractive minimal modifications for each concept in the current concept-to-date: in the full breadth strategy all are included in the subsequent concept-to-date. Excessive memory consumption is thus a major drawback of the full breadth strategy. When two distinct members of the concept-to-date are equivalent one might be tempted to eliminate one of them. While this would have no effect on MGC-proposer, in systems in which the particular details of the representation of a concept play an essential role in that concept's fate during concept learning, such an action could result in concepts which were otherwise reachable becoming unreachable.

Full Breadth Pure Discrimination: algorithm FBD

Given:

   p - most recent positive example
   e - current example
   CTD - the concept-to-date
   F - set of categories
   CTD' - initially empty
   $x >= y$ - x CONTAINS y
   $x > y$ - x CONTAINS y, and is not equal to y
   $x >< y$ - x and y are not comparable under the CONTAINS ordering

fbd1. If e is a positive example, then include in CTD' all concepts in CTD except those which classify e as a nonmember. Replace CTD by CTD'. Replace p by e. Finished.

fbd2. If e is a negative example, then for each concept C_j in CTD perform fbd3 through fbd5. Replace CTD by CTD'. Finished.

fbd3. If e is a nonmember of C_j then include C_j in CTD'.

fbd4. If e is a member of C_j then : this means that for every category f, in F, that $f(C_j) >= f(e)$. Let L be the set of categories for which $f(p) >< f(e)$. For each category k in L perform fbd5.

fbd5. Find all maximally general values v_i such that

$$k(C_j) > v_i >= k(p) \text{ AND } v_i \text{ does not CONTAIN } k(e)$$

For each such v_i include in CTD' a concept D_i which is identical to C_j except that $k(D_i) = v_i$.

The following shows algorithm FBD operating on a sequence of examples. Examples are drawn from the Universe in Fig. 8.7. Vector representation will be used for objects and concepts: the values and value containment ordering are those shown in Fig. 8.38.

Initial concept C_0: ⟨anyshape, anysize, anycolor, any#⟩
Initial CTD: { C_0 }

Positive example p1: ⟨square, large, gray, 0⟩
    fbd1. CTD unchanged. Most recent positive example, p, is set to p1

Negative example n1: ⟨square, large, white, 0⟩
    fbd4. L = { COLOR }   (n1 is a near miss on p1)
    fbd5. COLOR: v_1 = gray
                C_1 = ⟨anyshape, anysize, gray, any#⟩

new CTD: { C_1 }

Negative example n2: ⟨triangle, small, gray, 3⟩
    fbd4. L = { SHAPE, SIZE, #SPOTS }

    fbd5. SHAPE: v_1 = square
                C_2 = ⟨square,   anysize, gray, any#⟩
        SIZE: v_1 = large
                C_3 = ⟨anyshape,   large, gray, any#⟩
      #SPOTS: v_1 = 0
                C_4 = ⟨anyshape, anysize, gray,   0 ⟩

new CTD: { C_2, C_3, C_4 }

Positive example p2: ⟨square, small, gray, 1⟩
    fbd1. Only C_2 classifies p2 as positive. p set to p2.

new CTD: { C_2 }

To demonstrate that this algorithm is not order independent, consider its behavior when the same examples are presented in the order p2, n1, p1, n2:

C_0 = ⟨anyshape, anysize, anycolor, any#⟩
CTD = { C_0 }

after examples p2 and n1:
    C_1 = ⟨anyshape, small,   anycolor, any#⟩
    C_2 = ⟨anyshape, anysize, gray,   any#⟩
    C_3 = ⟨anyshape, anysize, anycolor,   1 ⟩

CTD = { C_1, C_2, C_3 }

after example p1:

CTD = { C_2 }

after example n2:
    C_4 = ⟨square,   anysize, gray, any#⟩
    C_5 = ⟨anyshape, large,   gray, any#⟩
    C_6 = ⟨anyshape, anysize, gray,   0 ⟩

CTD = { C_4, C_5, C_6) }.

C_5 and C_6 do not appear in the concept-to-date at this stage in the previous sequence. It should be noted that these two concepts are actually incomplete: positive example p2 is not included in them! Were p2 to recur at this point in the example sequence they would be eliminated leaving only C_4.

8.C.5.2 Strategy 2: Bounded Breadth

This is a variation on the full breadth strategy in which the number of concepts in the concept-to-date, called its breadth, must not exceed a fixed bound. If the number of candidates for inclusion in the concept-to-date exceeds this bound, some must be pruned away using domain-specific knowledge or heuristic criteria. A danger associated with bounding the breadth is that one may inadvertently render all acceptable concepts unreachable. For instance, in the last step of the last example, if concept C_4 had been pruned away several concepts would have become unreachable, including C_4 itself (i.e. it is not reachable from C_5 or C_6). Despite this risk, the bounded breadth strategy is very often used because it offers a promising compromise between the potentially unmanageable memory demands of the full breadth strategy and the loss of information and the associated problems suffered by the backtracking strategy.

8.C.5.3 Strategy 3: Backtracking

In the backtracking strategy the concept-to-date always contains exactly one concept: thus one usually speaks of the concept-to-date as if it were a concept. A combination of concept-to-date and example for which there is more than one equally acceptable minimal modification is called a choice point. At such a point the backtracking strategy chooses one of the possibilities to serve as the concept-to-date, records the nature of the choice point and the unexplored alternatives, and proceeds as if the chosen concept had been unique. Should this choice ultimately lead to an unacceptable concept, one backtracks to a choice point and chooses one of the unexplored alternative concepts to serve as the concept-to-date.

Backtracking Pure Discrimination: Algorithm BD[*]

Given:
        S   - a set of choice points represented as individual
               concepts, initially empty
        p   - most recent positive example
        e   - current example
        CTD - the single concept which is the concept-to-date
        F   - set of categories
        R   - a set of concepts, initially empty
        x $\geq$ y - x CONTAINS y
        x $>$ y - x CONTAINS y and is not equal to y
        x $><$ y - x and y are not comparable under the CONTAINS
                                                          ordering

---

[*] Similar in spirit to SAGE (Langley, 1983a,c, 1982).

bd1. If e is classified correctly by CTD then: if e is a positive example replace p by e. Finished.

bd2. If an error of omission occurs then: replace CTD with a concept drawn from S. Replace p by e. Finished.

bd3. If an error of commission occurs then: initialize R to be empty. Perform bd4. Add all concepts in R to S and replace CTD with a concept drawn from this revised S. Finished.

bd4. Every category f, in F, is such that $f(CTD) >= f(e)$. Let L be the set of categories for which $f(p) >< f(e)$. For each category k in L perform bd5.

bd5. Find all maximally general values v_i such that

$$k(CTD) > v_i >= k(p) \text{ AND } v_i \text{ does not CONTAIN } k(e)$$

For each such v_i include in CTD' a concept D_i identical to CTD except that $k(D_i) = v_i$.

This algorithm will be demonstrated using slightly different examples from those used to demonstrate FBD.

positive example p2 : ⟨square, small, gray, 1⟩

```
CTD =   ⟨anyshape, anysize, anycolor, any#⟩
S   = { }
```

negative example n1 : ⟨square, large, white, 0⟩

```
CTD =   ⟨anyshape, small,    anycolor, any#⟩
S   = { ⟨anyshape, anysize, gray,     any#⟩
        ⟨anyshape, anysize, anycolor, 1  ⟩ }
```

positive example p1 : ⟨square, large, gray, 0⟩
An error of omission occurs, since CTD does not contain p1. One of the two concepts in S must be chosen. The chosen concept will be tested for completeness with respect to p1, but the concepts remaining in S will not be examined. If the selection procedure chooses, for instance, the first concept in S, it is tested and found to contain p1. No further testing is done, however, and the incompleteness of the other concept in S remains unnoticed.

```
CTD =   ⟨anyshape, anysize, gray,      any#⟩
S   = { ⟨anyshape, anysize, anycolor,  1 ⟩ }
```

negative example n3 : ⟨triangle, small, gray, 1⟩

An error of commission occurs, meaning that CTD must be specialized. The set R will contain concepts which are specializations of CTD on one of the categories for which p (p1, at this point) and n3 have values which are not comparable according to the CONTAINS ordering, namely SHAPE, SIZE and #SPOTS. In this example there is exactly one concept for each of those categories: R, then, contains three concepts. These are added to S and one of the (four) concepts in S is chosen to serve as CTD. Suppose the selection criteria were such that the one concept carried forward from the previous step is chosen, yielding

```
CTD =   ⟨anyshape, anysize, anycolor, 1 ⟩
S   = { ⟨anyshape,    large, gray,     any#⟩
        ⟨anyshape, anysize, gray,      0 ⟩
        ⟨square,   anysize, gray,      any#⟩ }
```

The new CTD can be checked for consistency against n3, the current example, and for completeness against the most recent positive example, p (p1, at this point). However, the incompleteness of this concept with respect to p2 cannot be detected by the BD algorithm. It should also be noted that although all of the variations created in steps bd4/bd5 are minimal modifications of the current CTD, the replacement for CTD is not necessarily chosen from among them - it is chosen from among them and all the others which were previously in S - and may not be a minimal modification of CTD.

A backtracking algorithm such as BD does not overcome the major drawback of the full breadth strategy: excessive memory consumption. In general, the list S which is used to record the backtracking options will be comparable in size to the set of concepts which constitutes CTD in the full breadth algorithm FBD.[*] BD should be viewed as an alternative to FBD as a means of dealing with the non-uniqueness of an acceptable minimal modification of the current concept-

---

[*] However, under specific conditions one may be very much smaller than the other.

to-date. Backtracking algorithms which do not represent the
set of choice points as an explicit list of alternative
concepts-to-date or which prune the list when it grows too
large may be memory efficient.

Backtracking is literally taking a step backwards in 'time'
(as measured by example presentation). In the process of
backtracking to a particular choice point, all examples
which have occurred between the first time a choice point is
recorded (in BD this is the time when the corresponding
concepts were placed in S) and the present are ignored,
except for the current example and the most recent positive
example. The concept-to-date which is chosen by backtracking
may be both incomplete and inconsistent with respect to all
previously seen examples.*   This effect can be minimized by
taking as small a backward step as possible by backtracking
to the most recent choice point. There are two reasons why
this backtracking strategy is not ideal. First, the most
recent choice point corresponds to the most specific concepts (in a pure discrimination system; the most general
concepts in a pure generalization system) which means that
one will almost certainly fail to achieve the objective of
having the concept-to-date as the maximally general concept.
Secondly, should all of the concepts which correspond to
the most recent choice point prove unacceptable, an even
larger step backwards in time will be required. Langley**
combats this dilemma by keeping a crude estimate of the
acceptability of the unchosen alternatives with respect to
the examples which have been presented subsequent to their
being considered but not chosen. When examples regularly
recur, the negative effects of stepping backwards in time
are largely neutralized. An alternative, effective means
of neutralizing these effects is to record a number of the
most 'informative' examples. The possibility of abandoning
the Method of Minimal Modification in favor of only recording informative examples is examined in the following.

---

*   The collection of choice points may be regarded as a kind
    of agenda of concepts to be considered. The effective
    maintenance and use of such an agenda has been studied in
    other contexts, e.g. Hayes-Roth and Lesser (1977),
    Lenat (1976).
** Langley (1983a,c,1982).

8.C.6 THE EXAMPLE SET METHOD

The conditions characterizing incremental learning stipulate that a concept learning system must determine the concept-to-date on the basis of previously seen examples and concepts whose combined memory requirements are below a given, fixed limit. The Method of Minimal Modification based its calculations on the most recent concept-to-date and one or two recent examples, the examples being used to determine which modifications should be made to the concept-to-date.

Concept learning systems using the Example Set Method determine the concept-to-date solely on the basis of a subset of previously seen examples, called the window. The concept learning process is a process of modifying the contents of the window. However, the output of a learning system employing the Example Set Method is not the window itself, but a 'rule' which is derived from the window. It is the rule and not the window which is interpreted during concept application as a method for classifying objects. The calculation of the rule from the window is straightforward, and will be described below. A typical example set algorithm is ES, as follows:

Algorithm ES[*]

Given:
>   WINDOW — as described above
>   RULE   — as described above
>   e   — the current example

es1. If, when interpreted, RULE correctly classifies e then no changes are required.

es2. If, when interpreted, RULE incorrectly classifies e then: include e in WINDOW; remove from WINDOW the minimum number of examples necessary to keep within memory limitations; derive a new RULE for this updated WINDOW. Finished.

---

[*] In the spirit of ID3 (Quinlan, 1979,1982,1983b).

The examples which are removed from the window are chosen
with the objective of maintaining the acceptability of the
resulting concept. For instance, if completeness or consistency is a requirement, one may try to choose examples
whose removal results in a minimal change in the extension
of the concept-to-date. Ideally, one will be able to remove
examples which are redundant with the other examples in the
window.

The derivation of the rule from the window is a matter of
extending the classifications of the examples in the window
to apply to any object. One method of doing this is to apply
a nonincremental concept learning technique to the examples
in the window and to use the resulting concept as the rule.
For instance, one could represent a rule as a decision tree
and use algorithm Q to construct a rule on the basis of the
examples in the window. We have seen that algorithm Q, when
it uses a category selection criterion like the entropy
function in Fig. 8.19 which is based on the distribution
of category values across all negative and positive examples, can produce considerably different decision trees
given similar examples: thus a small change in the window
can result in a significant modification of the rule.

The limit chosen for the size of the window will clearly
have a major influence on the reachability of rules. An
alternative to a fixed, a priori limit is to allow the
window size to increase indefinitely, but to control strictly the rate of increase. In either case, the usefulness of
this method depends on the ability to characterize a concept
with a relatively small set of positive and negative examples. Perhaps surprisingly, the method has proved
successful in all the cases in which it has been applied.

One of the intriguing aspects of the example set method is
that it is not perfectly clear whether it is the window or
the rule which constitutes the concept-to-date. Ross
Quinlan, the founder of the method, considers the rule
(represented as a decision tree) to be the declarative
aspect of the concept-to-date, and algorithm DT to be the
membership determination process. The window is regarded
merely as an intermediate structure which is used in the
calculation of the declarative aspect of the concept-
to-date. Supporting this view is the use of concept learn-

ing techniques to construct the rule from the window, and the direct involvement of the rule in the process of concept application.

An alternative view is that the example set method is really the Method of Minimal Modification where the window is the declarative aspect of the concept-to-date and the procedure which is used for constructing the rule from the window is part of the procedural aspect of the concept-to-date. That is, the membership determination process consists of two stages: the first stage is the process which derives the rule from the window, and the second stage is the algorithm which interprets the rule as a method of classification. The rule is regarded as a means of representing the concept which is efficient and convenient for the purposes of membership classification. This view is suggested by the facts that all modifications are made to the window and only indirectly to the rule, and furthermore that representation-related criteria are typically defined in terms of the representation of the window (e.g. its size) and not in terms of the representation of the rule.

The strategies discussed in the Method of Minimal Modification for coping with the nonuniqueness of the 'best' minimal modification are equally applicable to this method for coping with the nonuniqueness of the 'best' possible window modifications. For instance, a full breadth version of the example set method would maintain a set of windows, where each window in the set was equally compact and, to the extent that the extension of each could be determined, equally complete and consistent, and so on.

8.D   The heuristic enumeration approach

In the Heuristic Enumeration Approach concept space is
viewed as being linearly ordered. The concept-to-date is
always a single concept, initially the first concept in
concept space. The process of concept learning is this:
whenever a new example is presented, re-evaluate the acceptability of the concept-to-date; if it proves unacceptable, replace it by a concept 'later' in concept space
('later', as measured by the linear ordering); repeat this
process for the newly selected concept-to-date. In the
simplest enumeration algorithm, each concept is always
replaced by its immediate successor in the ordering. More
sophisticated versions may leap ahead (never back) in the
ordering, the distance leaped being determined by, for
instance, the nature of the unacceptability of the concept-
to-date.

The relation between successive concepts-to-date is viewed
very differently in the Enumeration and Concept Modification
Approaches. Enumeration is a matter of concept replacement,
not concept modification. The details of the unacceptable
concept-to-date are attended only insofar as they inform
the enumerator as to how far it may safely* leap ahead in
the ordering. In enumeration the declarative aspect of the
replacement concept bears no necessary relation to that of
the replaced concept. The role of the examples is also
quite differently construed in the two approaches: in the
Enumerative Approach the examples are used to select the
concept, whereas in the Concept Modification Approach the
examples are used to refine the concept.

The ordering chosen for enumeration is, of course, crucial,
in the very same ways that the concept modification
operators chosen play a crucial role in determining the
reachability of concepts, and the overall efficiency and
success in the Concept Modification Approach. The
reachability of a particular concept, for instance, can be
guaranteed by placing that concept earlier in the ordering
than any other concept which is consistent and complete with
respect to the same examples (one must also ensure that this

---

* 'safe' meaning that all of the concepts leaped over are
   unacceptable.

concept will not be inadvertently leaped over). Thus it is
extremely common to view the ordering as a preference
ordering with the most preferred concept earliest in the
ordering. Moreover, one may try to arrange that similar
concepts lie close together in the ordering so that one
large leap can bypass all of these concepts if any one
should prove unacceptable. Likewise, if one proves almost
acceptable, its neighbors will be good candidates. The
measure of similarity used must ensure the likely
(un)acceptability of 'similar' concepts.

In the context of incremental learning a difficult problem
for enumerative methods is that of ensuring consistency and
completeness. One approach to coping with this difficulty is
to use an enumerative approximation to MSC- or MGC-proposer:
i.e. to use an ordering of concept space which is based on
the extension containment ordering. A second approach is
to assume that examples recur often enough to ensure that a
complete and consistent concept will eventually be selected.

The Enumerative Approach differs significantly from the
Concept Modification Approach in that it demands an explicit
characterization of concept space and an explicit statement
of the relative order in which each concept should be
considered. As a consequence, the Enumerative Approach
demands a means of generating successive concepts-to-date
which is not based solely on the current concept-to-date and
examples. This often manifests itself as a visible difference between systems which are developed from the two
different approaches: whereas a system generated from the
Concept Modification Approach has concept modification
operators, a system developed from the Heuristic Enumeration
Approach has a concept-enumerator. The concept-enumerator is
the heart of any system developed in the Enumerative
Approach, and its character and construction are the subject
of the following section.

8.D.1 CONCEPT ENUMERATION

There are three qualities which any concept-enumerator must

possess. First, it must be exhaustive:* it must enumerate
all of concept space. Second, it must enumerate the concepts
in the specified order. Third, it should be as efficient as
possible. Efficiency is a less important consideration than
exhaustiveness and order-correctness, but is a major obstacle for the Enumerative Approach nonetheless. The
priorities of the Enumerative Approach dictate a method for
designing an enumerative learning system - make it right
(exhaustive and order-correct), then make it efficient. This
design method will be demonstrated in the example which
follows: first we will specify an algorithm for enumerating
all context-free grammars (the flexibility of this algorithm
with respect to the order of enumeration should be evident),
and then consider how it could be made more efficient.

8.D.1.1 Example - Enumerating Context-free Grammars

Context-free grammars, though adequate, are not a
particularly common mode of concept representation. The
correspondence between grammar-oriented terms and the
concept-learning terms introduced in Section B is:

Concept learning term	Grammar equivalent
object	sentence (string, expression)
concept	language (set of sentences)
declarative aspect	grammar

A membership determination process for a grammar is a method
for determining if a given sentence is in the language
generated by the grammar.

The Universe of Fig. 8.7 is represented by the grammar in
Fig. 8.46. The object in Fig. 8.1(a) would be represented by
the sentence

      ⟨square,large,gray,1⟩

---

*   'Complete' is often used to describe enumerators which
enumerate every member of a given set. This use should
not, of course, be confused with the completeness of a
concept with respect to a set of examples.

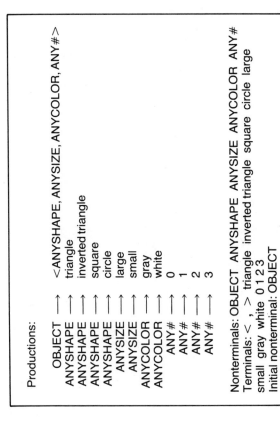

Productions:

OBJECT → <ANYSHAPE, ANYSIZE, ANYCOLOR, ANY#>
ANYSHAPE → triangle
ANYSHAPE → inverted triangle
ANYSHAPE → square
ANYSHAPE → circle
ANYSIZE → large
ANYSIZE → small
ANYCOLOR → gray
ANYCOLOR → white
ANY# → 0
ANY# → 1
ANY# → 2
ANY# → 3

Nonterminals: OBJECT ANYSHAPE ANYSIZE ANYCOLOR ANY#
Terminals: < , > triangle inverted triangle square circle large
small gray white 0 1 2 3
Initial nonterminal: OBJECT

Fig. 8.46 A grammar representing the universe in Fig. 8.7

A concept would be represented as a grammar which generated a language which was a subset of the language generated by the grammar in Fig. 8.46. A grammar representing the concept whose members are gray squares is shown in Fig. 8.47. If this representation is adopted, then enumerating concepts is identical with enumerating context-free grammars.

Grammars are ordinarily characterized as a 4-tuple
⟨ N, T, P, X ⟩ where

N is the set of nonterminals
T is the set of terminals
P is the set of production rules
X is the initial nonterminal

Productions:

GRAYSQUARE ⟶   <square, ANYSIZE, gray, ANY#>
ANYSIZE ⟶ large
ANYSIZE ⟶ small
ANY# ⟶ 0
ANY# ⟶ 1
ANY# ⟶ 2
ANY# ⟶ 3

Nonterminals: GRAYSQUARE ANYSIZE ANY#
Terminals: < , > large small 0 1 2 3
Initial nonterminal: GRAYSQUARE

Fig. 8.47 A grammar representing the concept "gray squares"

Thus in order to enumerate all possible grammars, one need only enumerate all possible combinations of values of these four parameters. The algorithm below demonstrates one method for doing this.[*] The notions of complexity-class, structure-class, and RHS-set, used in this enumeration algorithm are defined as follows:

COMPLEXITY-CLASS: Define the 'complexity' of a grammar, G, to be the triple
$$\langle n, p, m \rangle \quad \text{where}$$

n. is the number of non-terminals appearing in productions in G
p is the number of productions in G
m is the length of longest right-hand side of any production in G

The set of grammars which are characterized by a particular combination of values of n, p and m is called a 'complexity class'. There is exactly one (possibly empty) complexity class for each combination of values, and each grammar belongs to exactly one complexity class. The grammar in Fig. 8.47 is in the complexity class $\langle 3,7,9 \rangle$.

STRUCTURE-CLASS: For each combination of values of n and p define a 'structure vector' to be a vector of length n, $\langle s_1, s_2, \ldots, s_n \rangle$, such that each s_i is a non-negative integer and the sum of all of the s_i is equal to p. There are n nonterminals which we suppose are linearly ordered, named $N_1, N_2, \ldots, N_n$. We interpret s_i as indicating the number of productions which have N_i as their left-hand side. There will generally be several distinct structure vectors for given values of n and p. A 'structure class' is the set of grammars characterized by a particular structure vector. Each grammar is in exactly one structure class. The grammar in Fig. 8.47 is in structure class $\langle 1,2,4 \rangle$.

---

[*] This example is taken fairly directly from Wharton (1977). Many subclasses of context-free grammars can be enumerated with essentially the same algorithm by imposing extra constraints at various points in the procedure.

RHS-set: We assume that the set of possible terminal symbols
is fixed for all of the grammars to be enumerated (not all
grammars need use all of the terminal symbols). For each
combination of values of n and m, define the RHS-set to be
the set of all possible right-hand sides of productions. At
most this will be the set of all possible strings of
terminals and nonterminals whose length is m or smaller.
However, additional constraints usually arise from the
definition of a legal right-hand side,[*] and these constraints should be incorporated in the definition of RHS-
set so that it is kept as small as possible. A linear
ordering is imposed on the contents of RHS-set. Often this
ordering reflects the ordering of the nonterminals and an
implicit ordering of the terminals, and ranks shorter right
hand sides earlier than longer right-hand sides. There is a
unique RHS-set for each complexity class.

In addition to the orderings which have been imposed on the
terminals, the nonterminals, and the right-hand sides of
productions, we also impose a linear ordering on the complexity classes and on the structure classes within each
complexity class. These latter orderings are used as
follows: all of the grammars in one structure class are
enumerated (in an order determined by the orderings on the
terminals, nonterminals, and right-hand sides of productions) before any of the grammars in the 'next' structure
class, and all of the structure classes in one complexity
class are enumerated before any of the structure classes
in the 'next' complexity class. Thus, the overall ordering
on grammars is the product of the interaction of these five
separate linear orderings.[**] This method of enumerating
context-free grammars is used in the following algorithm:

---

[*]   For example, Greibach Normal Form insists that the
      leftmost character in every right-hand side be a
      terminal, and that all other characters (if there are
      any) be nonterminals.
[**] Although a large number of grammar-orderings are ac-
      commodated by this scheme, there are grammar-orderings
      which it cannot produce. The important property of this
      scheme is the clear separation of the steps, and not the
      particular complexity or structure definitions which are
      used. Adaptations of the scheme to accommodate other
      orderings should preserve its stepwise nature.

8.D.1.2 Algorithm GB

gb1. Perform gb2, beginning with the first complexity class.

gb2. Perform gb3 and gb4 for the current complexity class, $\langle n,p,m \rangle$. Then generate the next complexity class and repeat gb2 for it.

gb3. Determine the RHS-set for the current complexity class.

gb4. Perform gb5, beginning with the first structure class in the current complexity class.

gb5. Enumerate all grammars in the current structure class whose right-hand sides are drawn from the current RHS-set. Then generate the next structure class in the current complexity class and repeat gb5 for it.

Generating the complexity classes and structure classes in order, and generating the RHS-sets, are relatively straight-forward matters. The grammars in a given structure class, $\langle s_1, s_2, \ldots s_n \rangle$, whose right-hand sides are all drawn from a given RHS-set, $\langle n,m \rangle$, can be enumerated by enumerating all possible sequences of length 'p' consisting of elements drawn from RHS-set with replacement. Interpret the first s_1 elements in each such sequence as the right-hand sides of productions whose left-hand side is the first nonterminal, N_1; interpret the next s_2 elements as the right-hand sides of productions whose left-hand side is N_2; and so on. One method of performing this enumeration is the so-called 'counting' algorithm, as follows:

8.D.1.3 Algorithm C (the 'Counting' Algorithm)

c1. Let R = cardinality of RHS-set. Number the elements of RHS-set from 0 to R-1 according to the linear ordering imposed on RHS-set.

c2. Let the productions in the grammars of the given structure class be numbered (from 1 to p) in such a way that

<u>productions</u>

1	to	s_1	have	N_1	as their left-hand side
s_1+1	to	s_1+s_2	have	N_2	as their left-hand side

$$\cdot \qquad \cdot \qquad \cdot \qquad \cdot$$
$$\cdot \qquad \cdot \qquad \cdot \qquad \cdot$$
$$\cdot \qquad \cdot \qquad \cdot \qquad \cdot$$

$p-s_n+1$	to	p	have	N_n	as their left-hand side

c3. Count from 0 to $(p^R)-1$, representing each number as a p-digit numeral in base R (include leading zeroes). Each number may be interpreted as a grammar in the given structure class by interpreting the ith digit in each such number as an index into RHS-set specifying the right-hand side of the ith production in this grammar (the left-hand sides of all productions in all grammars in a particular structure class are the same, and are specified by step c2).

To demonstrate algorithm C, consider the following example:

Suppose   m = 2   (let N_1 be 'S' and N_2 be 'T'),
            p = 3,
            n = 2,
    that there are two terminals, 'a' and 'b',
    that right-hand sides of productions must begin
        with a terminal,
and that RHS-set = { a, b, aa, ab, aS, aT, ba, bb, bS, bT }

Step c1. The cardinality of RHS-set, R, is 10.   Assume that the order shown reflects the numbering assigned to RHS-set so that, for instance, RHS(4) is 'aS' (recall that the numbering begins at 0, not 1).

Step c2. The possible structure classes within the complexity class ⟨ 2,3,2 ⟩ are

    S1 = ⟨0,3⟩ S2 = ⟨1,2⟩ S3 = ⟨2,1⟩ and S4 = ⟨3,0⟩,

which correspond to the ordered sets of left-hand sides of productions:

S1	S2	S3	S4
(1) T -->	(1) S -->	(1) S -->	(1) S -->
(2) T -->	(2) T -->	(2) S -->	(2) S -->
(3) T -->	(3) T -->	(3) T -->	(3) S -->

that is, in structure class S2, for instance, the first production has 'S' as its left-hand side and the second and third productions have 'T' as their left-hand side.

Step c3. Suppose that the objective is to enumerate all grammars in structure class S2 whose productions' right-hand sides are drawn from RHS-set. This is done simply by counting (in this example) from 000 to 999 (base 10). Each number in that range corresponds to a grammar, for instance

number : 000   001   089   098   587

corresponds to grammar (in structure class S2)

```
S --> a    S --> a    S --> a    S --> a    S --> aT
T --> a    T --> a    T --> bS   T --> bT   T --> bS
T --> a    T --> b    T --> bT   T --> bS   T --> bb
```

The grammar enumerator just described is exhaustive but extremely inefficient in the sense that it enumerates a large number of grammars (concepts) which could not possibly be acceptable.* Concepts which cannot possibly be acceptable will be called 'extraneous'. A concept may be extraneous for a number of different reasons. The declarative aspect of the concept may be ill-formed or undesirable (e.g. it may contain too many disjuncts). Or, the extension of the concept may fail to meet all of the requirements; for instance, it may be inconsistent or incomplete with respect to the previously seen examples. Or, a concept may be extraneous because it has been previously enumerated and found unacceptable. Enumeration can be speeded up in two ways: (1) by adding to the enumerator knowledge characterizing additional kinds of extraneous concepts and (2) by modifying the enumerator to exploit more fully the knowledge which it has of extraneous concepts. Before looking at techniques of adding and exploiting knowledge of extraneous concepts, we shall look at how such knowledge may be represented in the enumerator.

---

* This enumerator is extremely efficient in terms of the amount of computation time and space needed to enumerate successive grammars.

8.D.2
REPRESENTING KNOWLEDGE CHARACTERIZING EXTRANEOUS CONCEPTS

The knowledge characterizing extraneous concepts manifests itself in the behavior of the enumerator as a failure to enumerate whole classes of concepts (namely those classes characterized as extraneous). This knowledge may be represented internally in the enumerator in either an implicit or explicit form. In the former case the enumerator is called a 'smart' enumerator, in the latter case it is called a 'generate and test' enumerator.

In either case the knowledge must be 'operationalized'* — that is, translated into terms and actions which are operational. An operational term is one that is computable on the basis of information available at the time and point in the process of enumeration at which the knowledge is to be applied. The conditions with which we have characterized concept learning, and incremental learning, restrict the kinds of terms which are operational. We have stipulated, for instance, that a learning system has access only to the representations of objects and concepts. To characterize a class of concepts in operational terms, then, is to characterize a class of sentences in the concept representation language. Or consider the predicate 'complete and consistent with respect to all previously seen examples'. This is operational when, for instance, all of the previously seen examples are explicitly recorded. Indeed the major difficulty of incremental learning is precisely that this term is not operational under the conditions with which we have characterized incremental learning.

An operational action is a computation defined over operational terms which can be taken at the moment when the knowledge proposing this action is applied. The action 'enumerate the best possible concept complete and consistent with respect to all previously seen examples', for a given operational definition of 'best possible' is not operational when it is impractical or impossible to be certain that a given concept is the 'best possible'. A typical operational

---

*   The term 'operationalization' is taken from Mostow (1981)
      where automatic operationalization is investigated.

action for a smart enumerator is altering the value of an
internal control variable, or altering a parameter to a
subsequent step in the enumeration process, or invoking a
particular enumeration subprocess.

8.D.3 SMART ENUMERATION

In a smart enumerator the knowledge characterizing extraneous concepts is implicitly represented: one arranges the
enumeration procedure to be such that the extraneous concepts simply never arise in the process of calculating
successive concepts in the enumeration sequence (that is,
they are effectively unrepresentable). For instance, the
following characterizations of extraneous grammars may be
represented implicitly.

Type-A grammar: contains nonterminals for which there are
                 no productions

Type-B grammar: is identical to an earlier grammar except
                 for the order of productions (e.g. grammar
                 098 is extraneous in this way, given grammar
                 089)

Type-C grammar: contains identical right-hand sides for the
                 same left-hand side (e.g. the last two
                 productions in grammar 000)

8.D.3.1
Implicitly Representing that Type-A Grammars are Extraneous

Type-A grammars are produced precisely when one of the s_i
entries in the structure vector has the value zero. One can
avoid enumerating all Type-A grammars by generating (in step
gb5) only those structure vectors which contain no zeroes.
This modification of the structure vector generator need
not require the introduction of explicit testing.

8.D.3.2
Implicitly Representing that Type-B and Type-C Grammars are Extraneous

One can avoid enumerating both of these types of grammars by requiring that the set of right-hand side indices associated with the same left-hand side nonterminal contain no duplicate indices (thus avoiding Type-C grammars) and also that each particular (unordered) set of distinct indices is enumerated exactly once (thus avoiding Type-B grammars but remaining exhaustive). For the example above (structure class $S2 = \langle 1,2 \rangle$) one sequence which meets both of these requirements is:

(0 01) (0 02) ... (0 09) (0 12) (0 13) ... (0 19) (0 23) ...
(0 89) (1 01) (1 02) ... (9 78) (9 79) (9 89)

There are a number of ways to generate (without explicit testing) sequences meeting these two requirements. That this sequence is in numerical order is a perhaps convenient but certainly not essential feature. Grammars 001 and 089 would be produced by this enumerator, but grammars 000 and 098 would not. Note that the enumeration of this structure class (which is exhaustive except for the extraneous grammars) produces approximately half the number of grammars that the original enumerator produced. In general the savings will be very much greater[*] than that: the speedup is greater than the product of the $\{s_i!\}$.

8.D.4 GENERATE AND TEST ENUMERATION

In this kind of enumerator, enumeration is viewed as a two step process consisting of a concept-generator (perhaps a 'smart' generator) and an internal tester, as depicted in Fig. 8.48. The tester consists of a bank of tests for extraneousness which are usually simple and fast. These tests are an explicit representation of the knowledge characterizing extraneous concepts: any concept which fails any of the tests is not enumerated.

---

[*] The magnitude of the speedup is due to the brutal inefficiency of the original enumeration algorithm.

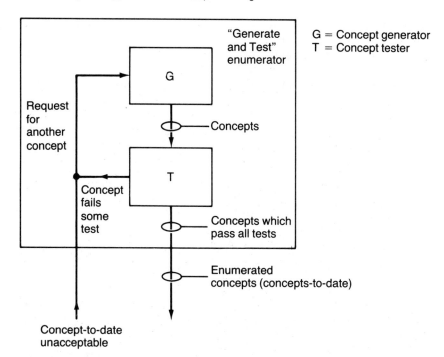

Fig. 8.48 The structure of a "Generate and Test" enumerator

The significance of enumerating a concept, as compared with merely generating it, is that each concept which is enumerated stands as the current concept-to-date until it proves unacceptable by failing to agree with the membership classification of an example. In situations where examples are expensive to gather or to record, it is desirable to enumerate as few concepts as possible. The 'test against the examples' may be regarded as the final, most expensive test: the tests in the tester act to screen out candidates which are clearly unacceptable.

For example, simple tests can be constructed which detect grammars which are characterized as follows:

(a) 'Disconnected' grammars - a disconnected grammar is one
    in which one or more nonterminals cannot be derived
    through a sequence of productions which begins with a
    production whose left-hand side is the initial non-
    terminal (grammar 089 would be disconnected if S were
    the initial nonterminal).

>   TEST: define the sets C_0 and D_0 to contain only the
>   initial nonterminal. Iterate the following until
> $C_{i+1} = C_i$:
>
> D_{i+1} = {all nonterminals which appear in the right-hand
>   side of a production whose left-hand side is a
>   nonterminal in D_i}
>
> $C_{i+1} = C_i$ UNION D_{i+1}
>
>   If there is any nonterminal which is not included in the
>   final C_i then the grammar is disconnected.

(b) Missing terminal symbol - if all terminal symbols which
    have appeared in positive examples are not present in
    the right-hand side of at least one production in a
    grammar, then the grammar is clearly unacceptable.

(c) Renaming-equivalent - if one grammar can be made iden-
    tical to another by simply renaming its nonterminals,
    the two grammars are said to be 'renaming-equivalent'.
    If two grammars are renaming-equivalent then the grammar
    which appears later in the enumeration sequence is
    extraneous.

>   TEST: initialize a set F of nonterminals to contain the
>   initial nonterminal. Nonterminals in F are said to
>   be 'fixed'; those not in F are said to be 'free'.
>   Two elements of RHS-set are said to be 'free-
>   renaming equivalent' if one can be made identical
>   with the other by a renaming of free nonterminals.
>   To test if a grammar, G, is renaming equivalent
>   with any grammar earlier in the enumeration
>   sequence, iterate the following over the right-
>   hand sides of all productions in G in order,
>   starting with the right-hand side of the first
>   production:

The current right-hand side is a member of RHS-set, and will therefore have an 'index', i, specified by the linear ordering imposed on RHS-set; that is, the current right-hand side will be the ith right-hand side in RHS-set for some value of i.

IF the current right-hand side is free-renaming equivalent with any right-hand side whose index in RHS-set is less than i,

THEN G is unacceptable (because a grammar re-naming-equivalent to G has already been enumerated),[*]

OTHERWISE add to set F all nonterminals which appear in the current right-hand side.

8.D.5 METHODS FOR EFFICIENT ENUMERATION

8.D.5.1 Method 1: Tight Specification of Concept Space

Perhaps the greatest danger in the Heuristic Enumeration Approach is the temptation to choose a concept space which is simple or rapid to enumerate, rather than one which properly fits the application. In a poorly chosen concept space, the acceptable concepts are hidden like so many needles in a haystack and the enumerator is likely to spend most of its time proposing 'straw concepts'. Heuristic Enumeration is not inherently slow, it is merely easy to misuse.

Given a characterization of the set of concepts to be enumerated and the required order of enumeration, one may have to invest a great deal of effort to find a suitable

---

[*] This is a consequence of the relationship between the order of grammar enumeration, the ordering on RHS-set, and the orderings of the terminals and nonterminals.

enumeration algorithm.[*] In the ideal enumeration sequence, of course, each concept in the given set occurs exactly once, in the position specified by the ordering, and no extraneous concepts occur. In practice, one must be ready to compromise on one or more of these points in the search for an efficient enumerator.

The possibility of 'tuning' an enumerator designed for one concept space for an application involving a characterizable (in operational terms) subspace has been investigated.[**] The user enters properties which concepts in the subspace of interest characteristically have (or do not have). A small degree of automatic operationalization takes place and the enumerator is subsequently configured to enumerate only concepts consistent with the user-specified properties.

8.D.5.2 Method 2: Hierarchical Enumerators

The structure of an hierarchical enumerator is shown in Fig. 8.49. The enumerator is a cascade of generators and testers. Each generator accepts from the tester(s) in the previous layer the specification of a class of concepts and it generates as its output a set of subclasses which are mutually exclusive and jointly cover the input class (or the cross product of the input classes if there are several). The final generator produces individual concepts as its output. A tester is associated with each generator which rejects outputs from its generator which are certain to be unacceptable.

There are two principal advantages in structuring the enumeration process in this way. First, this structure allows the two ways of representing knowledge (implicit and explicit) to both be used to full advantage: that is, one can choose to represent knowledge in whichever of the two ways is preferable. This hybrid architecture largely

---

[*]   Lindsay et al. (1980) provides an introduction to a nonredundant algorithm for enumerating cyclic molecular structures. The discovery of this algorithm constituted a major breakthrough in the Dendral project and enabled its scope to be vastly extended.

[**] CONGEN of the Dendral project. pp. 53-63 in Lindsay et al. (1980).

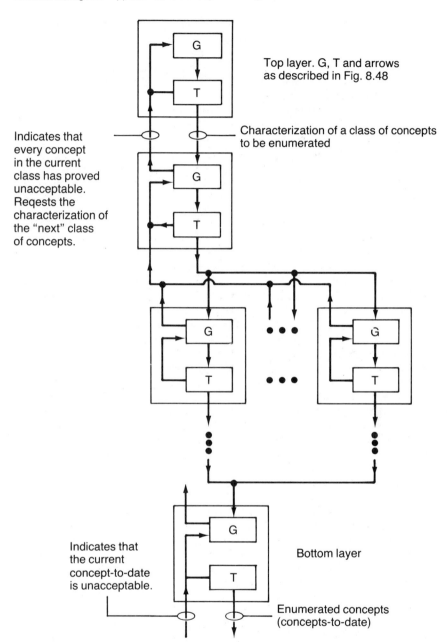

Top layer. G, T and arrows
as described in Fig. 8.48

Characterization of a class of concepts
to be enumerated

Indicates that
every concept
in the current
class has proved
unacceptable.
Reqests the
characterization of
the "next" class
of concepts.

Indicates that
the current
concept-to-date
is unacceptable.

Bottom layer

Enumerated concepts
(concepts-to-date)

Fig. 8.49 The structure of a hierarchical enumerator. The output of each
"layer" (except the bottom layer) is a characterization of the class of
concepts which is to be enumerated by the layers below. When this class has
been completely enumerated, the characterization of the "next" class of
concepts to be enumerated is generated.

captures the best of both representations. Second and more
importantly, in this architecture knowledge represented in
the form of explicit tests can be applied much earlier in
the enumeration process than in the pure generate and test
architecture. Except in the final layer, tests apply to
whole classes of concepts and not just to individual concepts: the higher up in the hierarchy the larger the class
of concepts which is being tested.

The grammar enumerator was structured in this way, although
few of the tests were left explicit. The cyclic structure
generator in CONGEN[*] achieves economical nonredundant
enumeration through extensive layering, with tests for
redundancy in every layer.

8.D.5.3 Method 3: Dynamic Enumeration

Currently, when a concept (class of concepts) is rejected by
a tester, the associated generator simply generates the next
concept (class of concepts) in sequence, and the tester is
applied to this new candidate. The enumeration process can
be made far more efficient if a characterization of the
aspects of previously tested (classes of) concepts which
caused them to be passed or rejected by the testers can be
made available to generators and testers throughout the
hierarchy. In extending the hierarchical architecture to
include feedback of this kind, the role of the testers can
be very differently construed. In the nonfeedback
architecture, the role of the tester was clearly to screen
out classes of concepts which were extraneous. In the new
architecture this role is secondary; the primary role of
the testers is to generate information characterizing
successful and extraneous classes of concepts which can be
fed back to higher layers in the hierarchy.

For example, the improved grammar enumerator described
earlier can itself be greatly improved[**] by utilizing

---

[*]   pp. 41-53 in Lindsay et al. (1980).
[**] These improvements are described and implemented in
      Wharton (1977). Empirical results (p.271) suggest that
      the speedup due to the adding of feedback was even
      greater than the speedup described earlier.

feedback in the form of a 'success point' or 'failure point' in a grammar with respect to a particular test. These points are defined in such a way that all grammars which are identical with a given grammar up to its success (failure) point for a particular test are certain to pass (fail) that test as well.

Success point information is redundant with the test with which it is associated in the sense that it merely indicates what the result of that test would be for those grammars to which the success point applies. The tester exploits this redundancy and uses the success point information as a computationally economical alternative to the test procedure itself. This is an example of a general technique[*] of speeding up the calculation of a function, say F(x), by keeping a table of pairs ⟨x,F(x)⟩ which have been previously calculated by a procedure for F(x), and replacing calculation by the procedure with a table lookup whenever possible. This technique is most effective when the table can be kept small and used frequently. In its application here, for speeding up the testing process, these qualities translate, roughly, into the quality that grammars which are identical up to a particular success point are clustered together in the generation sequence: this allows the table to be kept to a fixed length by eliminating success point information which has not been accessed by any of the more recently generated grammars. Failure point information can be used by the tester in a similar way.

Failure point information can be used by the generator to avoid generating grammars which are certain to fail because they are identical to a previously failed grammar up to its failure point. This is different than the use made of the failure point information by the tester: in this use the generator breaks its normal generation sequence and resumes generation some 'distance' ahead in the sequence. Grammars which have been leaped over in this way are never explicitly tested by either the tester or the generator. For example, the grammar

---

[*]   Called 'memo-izing' in Michie (1968) and Marsh (1969), and 'caching' in Lenat, Hayes-Roth and Klahr (1983).

```
P1:   X --> a
P2:   X --> XZ
P3:   Y --> b
P4:   Z --> XY
P5:   Z --> YZ
```

fails the renaming-equivalence test when production P2 is
considered.*   Any grammar which has these first two productions must also fail the test. Upon discovering the
failure point of this grammar, a dynamic generator would
generate as the next candidate a grammar whose second
production had a different right-hand side, bypassing a
large number of grammars which would have been generated had
the failure point information been ignored.**   In the
'counting' algorithm this would be achieved by immediately
'incrementing' a higher-order digit (in this example, the
second highest-order digit of five) and adjusting the lower
order digits accordingly, rather than simply 'incrementing'
the lowest order digit.

The degree to which failure point information can be exploited by the generator depends crucially on the relationship between the failure points and the internal structure
of the generation algorithm. Had the generation algorithm
modified the productions in forward, rather than reverse
order of production-number then the size of the leap would
have been very much smaller than in this example (and
correspondingly larger in the case where the failure point
was at production P4).

The extreme case of this is when the structure of the
generation algorithm is such that no leaping forward on the
basis of the failure point information is possible at all.

---

*   This test is given on in Section 8.D.4. We assume in this
     example that the right-hand side XY precedes XZ in the
     ordering imposed on RHS-set. The renaming equivalent
     grammar which is earlier in the enumeration sequence is
     identical to the one shown except that the roles of
     nonterminals 'Y' and 'Z' are reversed.
**   Assuming that grammars are generated by varying the
     right-hand sides of productions in the reverse order of
     the productions, as the generators which have been
     described here do.

An example of failure information which is inoperational with respect to the 'counting' grammar enumeration algorithm, is the information that a particular grammar has failed the 'missing terminal symbol' test:[*] there is simply no way (in this generation algorithm) to use that information to avoid generating subsequent grammars which suffer from the same deficiency. For the feedback from the tester to be maximally exploited it must be maximally operational as early in the enumeration process as possible. Thus the nature of feedback information acts as a constraint in the design of the structure of the enumerator and the concept representation language which it uses since these jointly determine which terms are operational and when in the enumeration process they become so.

So far the knowledge supplied by the examples has been represented as an explicit test and applied at the very end of the enumeration process. Efficiency can be gained by applying knowledge as early as possible (i.e. as soon as it is operational), and the knowledge supplied by examples is the same as knowledge from any other source in this regard. For instance, in the grammar enumerators which we have considered the knowledge that a particular terminal symbol must appear in the right-hand side of some production in every grammar is not acted upon until a grammar without this terminal is enumerated: yet this knowledge could have been acted upon as soon as the first example with that terminal was seen.

The examples will generally be represented in terms which are not operational at the points in the enumeration process where the knowledge they carry is to be applied. The (automatic) operationalization of the examples typically requires the use of domain-specific knowledge. In MetaDendral,[**] for instance, the program INTSUM uses a 'half-order' theory of mass spectrometry to associate the example data with particular combinations of values of the categories used to represent concepts in the concept enumerator, RULEGEN. When examples are to be applied at

---

[*] This test is described in Section 8.D.4.
[**] Lindsay et al. (1980).

several points in the enumeration process,[*] several different operationalizations of the examples may be necessary.

Operational knowledge derived from examples may be represented implicitly or explicitly in the enumerator.
MetaDendral represents the knowledge derived from positive
examples implicitly, as follows. The representation of concepts in MetaDendral is done in a manner akin to the vector
representation discussed in Section B. There a vector was a
fixed collection of categories, each of which could assume
one of a fixed number of values. In MetaDendral neither the
collection of categories which are used in representing a
concept nor the values which each category can assume is
fixed. MetaDendral, during concept learning, attempts to
minimize the number of categories which are used; the
collection of categories which it is using at any given
moment is called a 'schema'. The selection of values with
which to instantiate the current schema is based on the
values which have occurred in the positive examples seen to
date. That is, positive examples are operationalized into a
set of category-value combinations with which to instantiate
a schema: this is an implicit representation of the
knowledge 'any concept whose values (in the corresponding
categories) differ from these need not be considered'. In a
grammar enumerator, knowledge of the terminal symbols which
have occurred in positive examples may be operationalized
in this way. Knowledge from negative examples is usually
operationalized as explicit tests.

Learning systems which are described as fully exploiting
example derived knowledge in the 'language' of Heuristic
Enumeration can very often be equally well described in the
language of Concept Modification, especially when the
example derived knowledge is represented implicitly. The
converse is also true: an algorithm similar to algorithm
R, which is normally considered to be a concept modification
algorithm, has been described as a schema-instantiating
algorithm.[**]

---

[*]   For instance, when examples are interpreted by several
      'schema', as in SPARC (Dietterich and Michalski, 1983b).
[**] Dietterich and Michalski (1983b).

8.E   The candidate elimination approach

In the previous two approaches, the concept-to-date
contained only a small fraction of the total number of
acceptable concepts: the Full Breadth Pure Discrimination
(Generalization) Algorithm had the largest concept-to-date
of all, but its members were only those acceptable concepts
which were minimal modifications of concepts in the previous
concept-to-date. In the Candidate Elimination Approach every
acceptable concept is a member of the concept-to-date,
without exception. The set of all concepts which are
acceptable with respect to all examples seen to date is
called the 'version space' and each concept in it is called
a 'candidate'. The initial version space is the entire
space of concepts. When a new example is seen, the acceptability of all candidates is re-evaluated and any which
prove unacceptable are eliminated from the version space.

The policy of the Candidate Elimination Approach is thus not
to defer considering acceptable concepts, as did the
Backtracking and Full Breadth strategies, and not to prune
acceptable concepts prematurely on the basis of heuristic
measures for the sake of memory or time efficiency, as did
the Bounded Breadth Strategy, but to consider all acceptable
concepts at all times. Two consequences of this policy are:
first, a Candidate Elimination algorithm will perform
equally well in incremental and non-incremental learning
situations; and second, the final version space, which
ideally contains only one concept, is independent of the
order of presentation of examples.

The major difficulty facing the Candidate Elimination
Approach is the excessive consumption of time and memory:
there may be a vast number of candidates in a version space.
In order to be of practical use, a representation of the
version space must be found which has the following two
properties: it is always a manageable size yet can represent arbitrarily large version spaces; and it can be updated
quickly on every new example. For this purpose the Candidate Elimination Approach exploits a property of concept
space which neither of the earlier approaches explicitly

acknowledges: its structure.*

The extension containment partial ordering of concept space
is the basic constituent of the version space ordering on
top of which one may superimpose the preference orderings
and the orderings which draw on domain-specific structure.
This combined ordering shall be called the 'general-
to-specific' ordering. For the purposes of this chapter,
we shall use consistency and completeness as our criteria
for acceptability, and the extension containment ordering,
unaugmented, as the general-to-specific ordering. Recall
that in this ordering the most specific concept is the
'empty' concept - i.e. the concept whose extension is empty
Immediately above** this concept are those concepts which
contain precisely one element of U. The most general concept
is that concept whose extension is U itself.*** Recall too
that this ordering has the two properties: (1) if concept
C is inconsistent, then all concepts more general than C are
also inconsistent; and (2) if concept C is incomplete, then
all concepts more specific than C are also incomplete.

A consequence of these properties is that any version space
can be completely characterized by two sets called its
boundary sets: one which contains all of the maximally
general candidates, called G, and one which contains all of
the maximally specific candidates, called S. A concept is in
a version space characterized in this way if and only if it
is more specific than or equal to a concept in G and also
more general than or equal to a concept in S: the former
guarantees that the concept is consistent and the latter

---

*   One non-version space system which takes advantage of
       this structure is Holland (1975,1983), Holland and
       Reitman (1978).
**   'Above', 'more general' and 'less specific' will be used
       interchangeably, as will 'below', 'less general' and
       'more specific'. (Note that the relation between
       'above'/'below' and 'more/less general' is the opposite
       to that used by Mitchell 1977,1978.) These terms will
       be used without quotes throughout the remainder of this
       section and will always refer to the partial ordering
       for candidates in a version space as just described.
***   Assuming, of course, that these concepts are acceptable.

guarantees that it is complete.[*] In order to test the
acceptability of every candidate in the entire version space
one need only test the acceptability of the concepts in S
and G. All of the candidates which prove unacceptable when a
new example is presented can be eliminated from a version
space merely by modifying the individual concepts in S and G
which are unacceptable. This process is called 'updating
the version space'. The version space is updated for each
negative example, n, according to algorithm VSN:

Algorithm VSN

vsn1. Eliminate all concepts from S of which n is a member.

vsn2. For each s which remains in S after step vsn1, define
      g(s,n) to be the set of maximally general concepts
      above s which do not contain n, and which are more
      specific than some member of (unrevised) G. Update G
      to be the maximally general members in the union of
      all of the g(s,n).

The version space is updated for each positive example, p,
according to algorithm VSP:

Algorithm VSP

vsp1. Eliminate all concepts from G of which p is a non-
      member.

vsp2. For each s remaining in S after vsp1, define h(s,p) to
      be the set of maximally specific concepts above s
      which contain p and which are more specific than some
      concept in the revised version of G. Update S to be
      the maximally specific members in the union of all of
      the h(s,p).

One property of these algorithms is that eliminating a
concept from one boundary set in the first step will often
cause the elimination of a related concept from the other
boundary set. In VSN, any concept in G which is not more

---

[*]   Recall the properties of MSC and MGC (Section 8.B.7). S
      is the set of all MSCs and G is the set of all MGCs.

general than some concept remaining in S after step VSN1
cannot possibly occur in any of the g(s,n) in step VSN2 and
so will not appear in the updated G. In VSP, h(s,p) will
be empty for any s which is not more specific than some
concept in the revised version of G.

These algorithms update the version space by generalizing
(VSP; VSN discriminates) the individual concepts in S (G)
so that each includes (excludes) the given example. In
practice these algorithms are usually implemented using Full
Breadth Concept Modification techniques. This might lead
one to view Candidate Elimination as nothing more than
bidirectional Concept Modification in which the concept-
to-date is merely the set of concepts in S and G. This is
a misconstrual of the Candidate Elimination Approach. The
entire version space is the concept-to-date. The boundary
sets, S and G, are used to represent the current version
space in an economical fashion, but the concepts in them
have no special status as members of the concept-to-date.

8.E.1 EXAMPLE 1: THE FOCUSING ALGORITHM*

As an introductory example, let us consider a Candidate
Elimination Approach to learning concepts which are based on
the universe of Fig. 8.7. Objects and concepts will be
represented using value containment ordering diagrams, as
shown in Fig. 8.50, in which the values appropriate to that
object or concept are circled. For instance, Fig. 8.51
represents the concept whose members are pointy gray objects
with no spots. In the text, a vector representation will be
adopted. The concept in Fig. 8.51 is represented with the
vector

$$< \text{pointy, anysize, gray, 0} >.$$

The 'perfect match' membership determination process will be
used: object, O, is a member of concept, C, if for every
category, CAT (one of SHAPE, SIZE, COLOR, or #SPOTS)

$$\text{CAT(C) CONTAINS CAT(O)}.$$

---

* Bundy & Silver (1982).

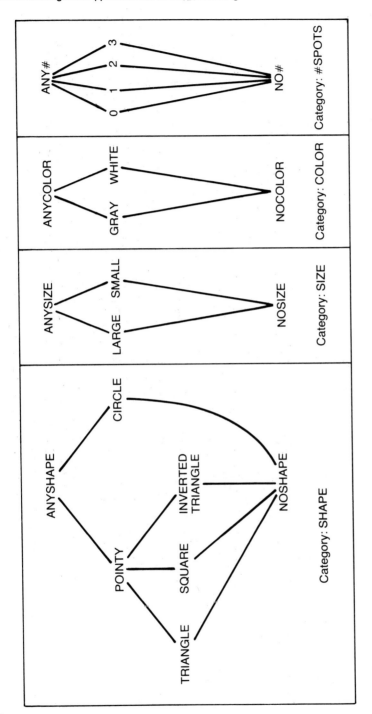

Fig. 8.50 Value containment partial orderings for each category

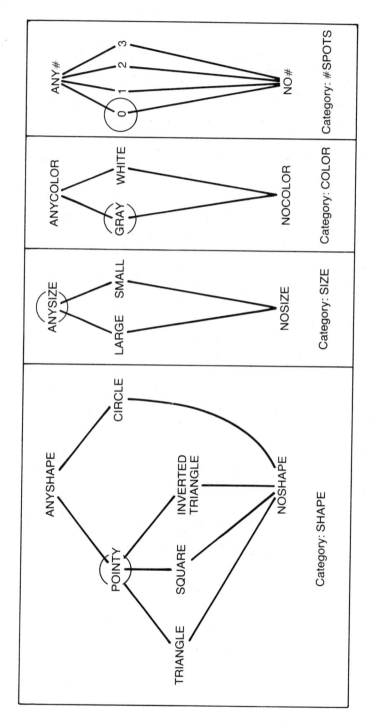

Fig. 8.51 Representation of the concept "pointy gray objects with no spots"

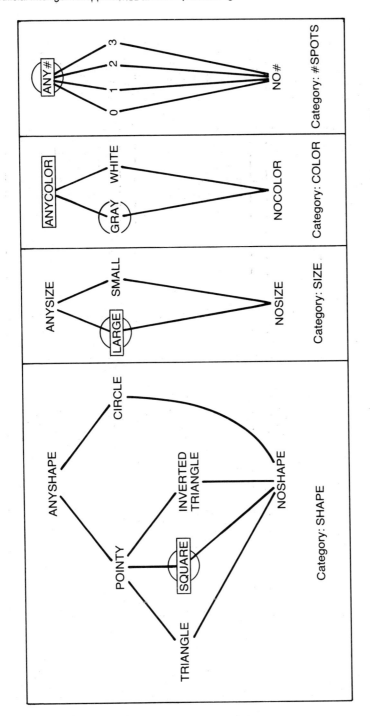

Fig. 8.52 Comparing the concepts "large squares" and "large gray squares"

□ – values of "large squares"
○ – values of "large gray squares"

In the diagrams this corresponds to every value associated
with 0 being below or coinciding with the value associated
with C. Similarly a concept, A, is more general than another
concept, B, if for every category, CAT (which, again, is one
of SHAPE, SIZE, COLOR, or #SPOTS)

       CAT(A) CONTAINS CAT(B).

In Fig. 8.52 the concept 'Large Square' is more general than
the concept 'Large Gray Square'.

This example will demonstrate a variation of the Candidate
Elimination Approach known as Focusing. In Focusing, each
boundary set always contains exactly one concept; the
concept in S is called the S-concept and that in G is called
the G-concept. Should the update algorithms find more than
one concept suitable for inclusion in a boundary set, one is
chosen to be put in the boundary set and the others are put
on the backtracking list associated with that boundary set.
Backtracking occurs when, in the course of applying the
update algorithms, one of the boundary sets becomes empty.*

In this example, a version space will be depicted by representing the S-concept and the G-concept in the same
picture. A concept is a candidate (i.e. is in the current
version space) if all of its category values fall between or
coincide with those of the current version space. The
initial version space, characterized by the most general
and most specific concepts (see Fig. 8.53), contains every
concept.

Version Space 0:
            G = {<anyshape, anysize, anycolor, any#>}
            S = {< noshape, nosize, nocolor, no#>}

---

*   The details of backtracking in Focusing have never been
     fully worked out. Bundy and Silver (1982) gives a
     backtracking algorithm which makes the simplifying
     assumption that all backtracking will involve the G-
     concept.

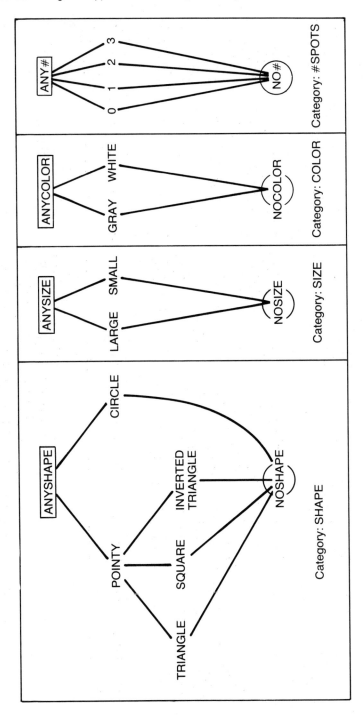

Fig. 8.53 Version space 0
☐ – values of G-concept
○ – values of S-concept

In this example the version space update algorithms, VSN and VSP, act as follows:

VSN1. If all of the category values of the S-concept are above or coincide with those of the negative example, n, backtrack.

VSN2. If the G-concept contains n, find a category for which the value of the G-concept may be moved towards that of the S-concept to a value above or coinciding with that of the S-concept which is not above the value of n in that category. If there are several such categories, choose one and put the others on the G-backtracking list. If no such category can be found, backtrack.

VSP1. If all of the values of the positive example, p, are not below or coinciding with those of the G-concept, backtrack.

VSP2. Move all of the category values of the S-concept towards those of the G-concept until they are above or coincide with those of p. If this is not possible, backtrack.

The following is a description of the Focusing Algorithm being applied to a sequence of examples. The initial version space is Version Space 0, above.

Positive Example: <Square, Large, Gray, 0>
(see Fig. 8.54)

    VSP1. G is satisfactory.
    VSP2. Move each S-value up to coincide with the example values.

Version Space 1:

                    G = {<anyshape, anysize, anycolor, any#>}
                    S = {<Square,   Large,   Gray,   0 >}

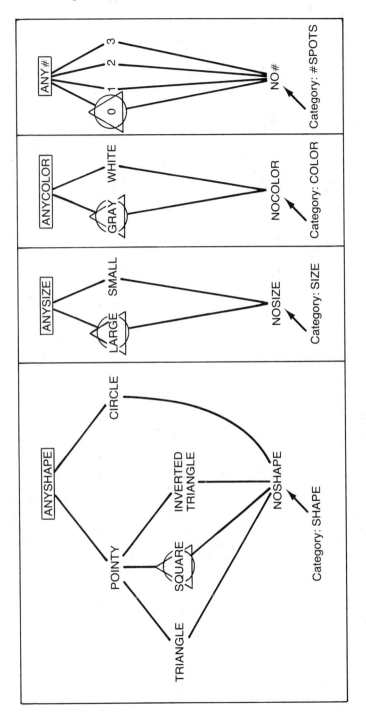

Fig. 8.54 Version Space 1

△ – values of the given positive example
☐☐ – values of the G-concept
◯◯ – values of the S-concept in Version Space 1
↗ – values of the S-concept in Version Space 0 which have changed

Positive Example: <Square, Small, Gray, 1>
(see Fig. 8.55)

VSP1. G is satisfactory.
VSP2. The lowest SIZE value which is above both 'Large'
and 'Small' is 'anysize'. Similarly for #SPOTS.

Version Space 2:

$$G = \{<anyshape, anysize, anycolor, any\#>\}$$
$$S = \{<Square,\quad anysize, Gray,\quad\quad any\#>\}$$

This version space contains all concepts which specify
any combination of values between those specified by S
and G, namely:

SHAPE : Square, Pointy, anyshape
SIZE   : anysize - i.e. no concept in this
         version space can place a restric-
         tion on the SIZE of its members
COLOR : Gray, anycolor
#SPOTS : any#

One concept which is not in this version space is 'Large
Square', since the value 'Large' is lower than the S-
value for the SIZE category ('anysize').

Negative Example: <Square, Large, White, 0>
(see Fig. 8.56)

VSN1. The value 'White' is not below the S-value ('Gray')
and therefore the concept in S does not contain
this example. S is satisfactory.

VSN2. The G-concept must be altered to exclude this
negative example but remain more general than S.
This negative example happens to be a near miss:
there is a unique category (COLOR) whose G-value
can be changed to meet these two requirements.

Version Space 3:

$$G = \{<anyshape, anysize, Gray, any\#>\}$$
$$S = \{< Square,\quad anysize, Gray, any\#>\}$$

This version space contains three concepts:
'Gray Object'   : <anyshape, anysize, Gray, any#>,
'Gray Pointy Object' : <Pointy,   anysize, Gray, any#>,
and 'Gray Square'   : <Square,   anysize, Gray, any#>

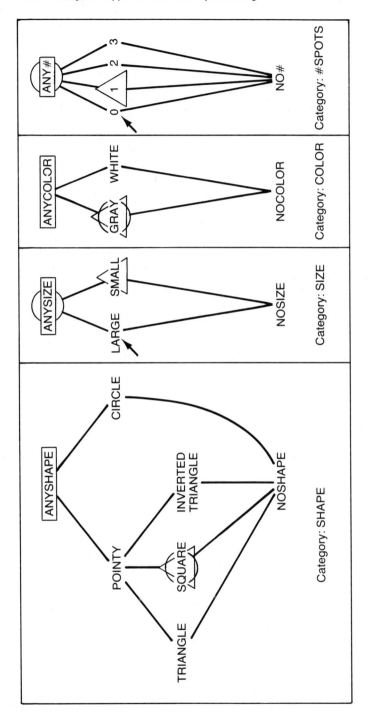

Fig. 8.55 Version Space 2

△ – values of the given positive example
☐○ – values of the G-concept
○ – values of the S-concept in Version Space 2
↗ – values of the S-concept in Version Space 1 which have changed

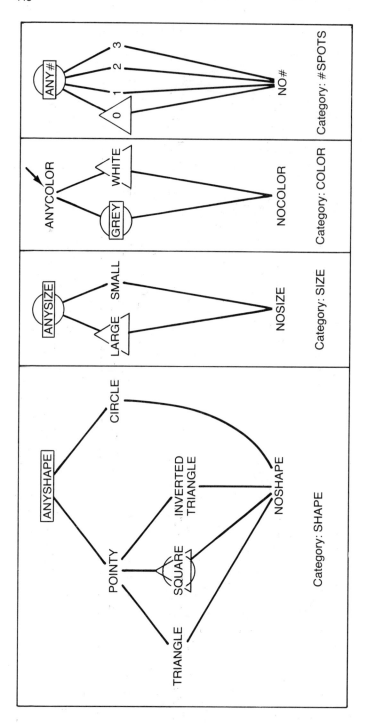

Fig. 8.56 Version Space 3

△ – values of the given negative example

☐ – values of the S-concept

◯ – values of the G-concept in Version Space 3

↗ – value of the G-concept in Version Space 2 which has changed

Category: SHAPE

Category: SIZE

Category: COLOR

Category: #SPOTS

Negative Example: <Triangle, Small, Gray, 2>
(see Fig. 8.57)

VSN1. Because 'Triangle' is not below 'Square', this
example is not a member of the S-concept. S is
satisfactory.

VSN2. The example is contained the G-concept, and so the
G-concept must be revised to exclude the example
yet remain more general than S. Since the concepts
in S and G agree in all categories except SHAPE, it
is the SHAPE value of the G-concept which must be
changed. It may be changed to either 'Pointy' or
'Square' : the higher of these values which is not
above 'Triangle' is 'Square'.

Version Space 4:

G = {<Square, anysize, Gray, any#>}
S = {<Square, anysize, Gray, any#>}

This version space contains exactly one concept,
'Gray Square'.

8.E.2 A MORE COMPLEX EXAMPLE

The following example demonstrates a Candidate Elimination
Approach to learning concepts whose extensions are 30-60-90
triangles in a bounded region in 2-space which have one
side, called the base, lying on the x-axis. Objects are
single points: positive examples are points inside or on the
perimeter of the extension of a concept, and negative
examples are points outside the extension of a concept.

The partial ordering will be based only on extension containment: concept C1 is more general than C2 if the
triangular region which is the extension of C2 is wholly
contained in the region which is the extension of C1. If
the extensions of two concepts only partially overlap then
neither concept is more general than the other.

In the figures which accompany this example, objects and
concepts will be depicted in the natural way. A version

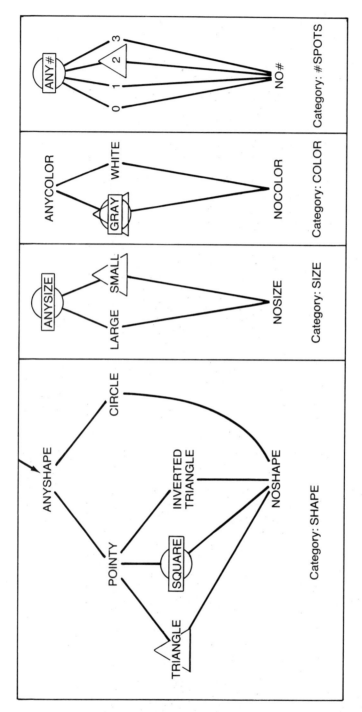

Fig. 8.57 Version Space 4

△ – values of the given negative example
☐ – values of the S-concept
◯ – values of the G-concept in Version Space 4
⟋ – value of the G-concept in Version Space 3 which has changed

space with exactly one concept in each boundary set will be
depicted by drawing on the same figure the two triangles
which are the extensions of the concepts in the boundary
sets, as in Fig. 8.58. The G-triangle will always contain
the S-triangle and the version space is all 30-60-90
triangles which contain the S-triangle and are contained by
the G-triangle: these lie in the shaded area in Fig. 8.58.

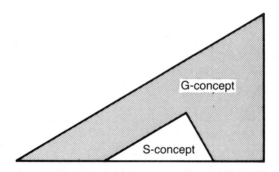

Fig. 8.58 Version space in which S and G each contain one concept. The
version space contains all concepts entirely in the shaded region

We define a 'primitive constituent' of a version space to be
a chain in concept space whose maximum element is a concept
in the G boundary set of the given version space and whose
minimum element is a concept in the S boundary set of the
given version space. Since every concept in a version space
lies on at least one such chain, we may view a version space
as the collection of all distinct primitive constituents
which are defined on its boundary sets. Primitive constituents, of course, are version spaces with exactly one
concept in each boundary set, and so can be depicted as described in the previous paragraph. A version space with more
than one concept in either of its boundary sets will be
depicted by individually depicting all of the primitive
constituents of that version space.

G is initialized to contain the largest possible 30-60-90 triangles wholly contained in the bounded region. The six triangles shown in Fig. 8.59 have maximal bases, but only two of these, G1 and G2, are maximal according to the general-to-specific (i.e. the extension containment) ordering. G is initialized to { G1,G2 }.

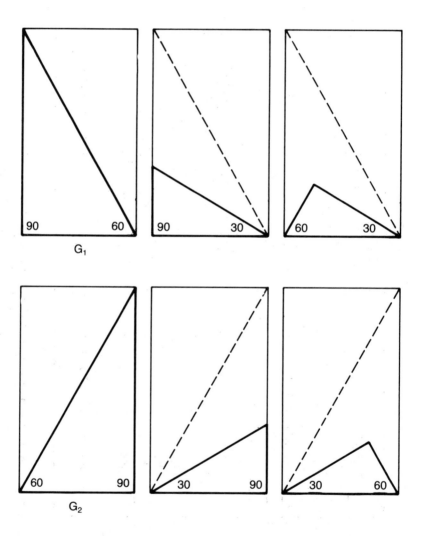

Fig. 8.59 Maximal baseline 30-60-90 triangles for the six possible orientations. Only G_1 and G_2 are maximally general concepts

S is initialized to {[empty]}. The [empty] region contains
no points and is indicated in Fig. 8.60 by the absence of a
lower boundary indicator.

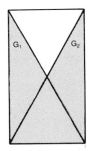

Fig. 8.60 Version Space 0

The initial version space is region shown in Fig. 8.60 with
the restriction* that all concepts must be wholly in either
G1 or G2.

Version Space 0: G = {G1,G2}   S = {[empty]}
                  is interpreted as all concepts contained
                  in either G1 or G2.

Positive example P.

   VSP1. P is contained by both G1 and G2, so G remains
         unchanged.
   VSP2. The minimal triangles containing P for each of the
         six possible orientations are shown in Fig. 8.61
         Since either s0 or s1 is contained in each of the
         others, h([empty],P) = {s0,s1}.

Version Space 1: G = {G1,G2}   S = {s0,s1}
                  both s0 and s1 are more specific than
                  both G1 and G2.

    is interpreted as all concepts containing either s0 or
    s1 and contained by either G1 or G2. See Fig. 8.62.

_____

*   Since there is no concept whose extension does not meet
     this 'restriction' it is more a reminder to the reader on
     the interpretation of the figures than a real re-
     striction.

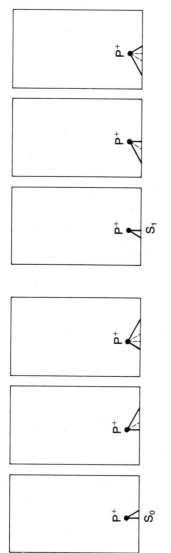

Fig. 8.61 Minimal triangles containing P for each possible orientation. Only S_0 and S_1 are maximally specific

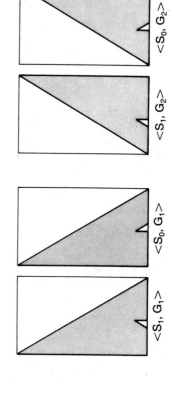

Fig. 8.62 Primitive constituents of Version Space 1

Positive example Q.

VSP1. G remains unchanged.
VSP2. The calculation h(s0,Q) = {s2,s3,s4,s5} is shown in
      Fig. 8.63. h(s1,Q) = {s3,s4,s5} is similar.

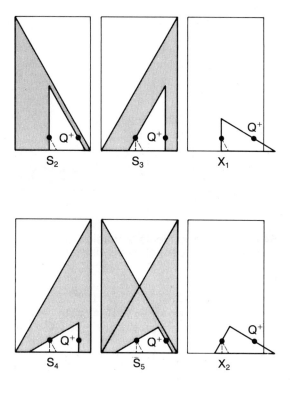

Fig. 8.63 h $(S_0, Q) = \{S_2, S_3, S_4, \bar{S}_5\}$. X_1 and X_2 are not contained in either G_1 or G_2. Shaded areas are the primitive constituents of Version Space 2

Version Space 2:   G = {G1,G2}   S = {s2,s3,s4,s5}
                   s2 is more specific than G1.
                   s3 and s4 are more specific than G2.
                   s5 is more specific than both G1 and G2.

Negative example M (see Fig. 8.64).

  VSN1. M is in s2, so s2 is eliminated from S.
  VSN2. g(s3,M) = {G3};   g(s4,M) = {G4};   g(s5,M) = {G4}

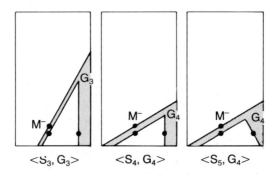

Fig. 8.64 Primitive constituents of Version Space 3. Adding negative example M directly above P eliminates S_2

Version Space 3:   G = {G3,G4}   S = {s3,s4,s5}
                   s3 is more specific than G3.
                   s4 and s5 are more specific than G4.

Negative example N (see Fig. 8.65).

  VSN1. S remains unchanged.
  VSN2. g(s3,N) = {G5};   g(s4,N) = {G6};   g(s5,N) = {G7}

        Up until now, s4 and s5 had a common upper boundary.
        N forces this upper boundary to be 'specialized' in
        different ways for s4 and s5. For s4 the 90 degree
        base angle is maintained and N is accommodated by
        shortening the length of the base, yielding G6. For
        s5, the base angle must be reduced from 90 to 60
        degrees, yielding G7.

Version Space 4: G = {G5,G6,G7}   S = {s3,s4,s5}
                     s3 is more specific than G5.
                     s4 is more specific than G6.
                     s5 is more specific than G7.

is interpreted as any concept which contains either s3, s4, or s5, and is contained in the corresponding member of G (see Fig. 8.66).

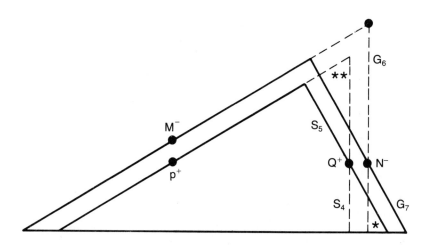

Fig. 8.65 Negative example N. Enlarged view showing that G_6 is more general than S_4 but not S_5 (region *) and G_7 is more general than S_5 but not S_4 (region **)

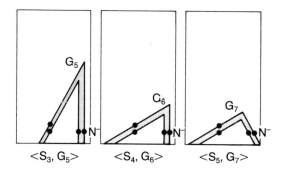

Fig. 8.66 Primitive constituents of Version Space 4

Positive example R (drawn from region * in Fig. 8.65).

> VSP1. R is not contained by either G5 or G6 and since these are maximally general they must simply be eliminated, along with any members of S which are not more specific than a member of G which does contain R. This leaves only G7 in G and s5 in S.

> VSP2. Since R is in s5, h(s5,R) = {s5}.

Version Space 5: G = {G7}   S = {s5}
                      s5 is more specific than G7.

this is version space <s5,G7> in Fig. 8.66.

After only five examples the space of possible concepts has been reduced to those in the narrow band lying between s5 and G7. The interaction of positive and negative examples was largely responsible for the rapid convergence of the algorithm. Note that at no point in this example were the boundary sets very large, although the version space contained an infinite number of candidates at every step. Unfortunately the boundary sets are not always so small and controlling their size is one of the main obstacles to be overcome in applying a Candidate Elimination algorithm to large scale problems.

In the Candidate Elimination Approach one has available at all times a characterization of all concepts which are acceptable with respect to all previously seen examples. There are a number of ways of exploiting this characterization to improve the efficiency and economy of the concept learning process. These are described briefly in the following paragraphs.

8.E.3 DETECTING EXCEPTIONAL CONDITIONS

Two exceptional conditions which can be detected in the Candidate Elimination Approach are (1) when a concept has been uniquely identified, and (2) when the examples are inconsistent in the sense that there is no concept which is acceptable with respect to all previously seen examples. The former condition holds whenever there is exactly one concept remaining in the version space - which is whenever S and G are identical. It can be used, for example, to suspend the example gathering process.

The condition that the examples are inconsistent is indicated when G (or S) has all of its members eliminated in one of the steps in algorithms VSP or VSN. For instance, if a negative example were introduced at the end of the above example which was contained in s5, then step VSP1 would eliminate s5 from S leaving S empty. This condition represents an incompatibility between the examples and the space of representable concepts. It is extremely useful to detect this condition although the action required when the condition arises is not perfectly clear. Most frequently the source of the incompatibility is taken to be that the example data has been contaminated with 'noise'. In this case the typical action is to attempt to identify and eliminate the noisy examples from the set of examples, for instance by using the largest consistent subset of the set of examples. An alternative interpretation of this condition is that it signals a 'Representation Crisis' - that the examples are correctly labeled and presented but that the current concept representation language is inadequate. In this case the corrective action must be aimed at adjusting the bias of the concept representation language.*

It is ironic that the one approach which allows the explicit detection of this incompatibility condition is considered a poor approach for coping with the condition when it arises. The major difficulty is that candidate elimination cannot be undone: the current contents of S and G do not indicate uniquely which examples have been seen and which have not; its order independence means that even the most recent examples cannot be restored knowing only S and G. Despite this, the Candidate Elimination Approach has been used successfully in situations where the data was inherently noisy.**

---

* The reader is referred to the entries listed under NOISE and ADJUSTING BIAS in Further Reading (Section G).
** Mitchell (1978).

8.E.4 THE VERSION SPACE AS A BASIS FOR ACTION

Despite the fact that many candidates still remain in
Version Space 5 .in the above example, a great deal can be
inferred about the 'final' concept by considering the nature
of all candidates which remain. For instance, the length of
its sides can be closely estimated. Also, the correct
membership classification of most objects (points) is known
with certainty, and the correctness of the membership
classification of the other objects can be estimated, for
instance, probabilistically.

All this is possible because the version space provides a
characterization of all concepts which are acceptable with
respect to all seen examples. Any characteristics shared by
all concepts in a version space are certain to be shared
also by the final concept. But this is only one way in which
the explicit characterization of all acceptable concepts
which is provided by the version space can be used. Perhaps
more importantly, differences which exist among the
candidates can be determined, as can the distribution of
these differences throughout the version space. Correlations
between the presence or absence of various characteristics
of the candidates can be tallied. All of this and more can
be computed at any time and used as the basis for membership
classification in lieu of the final (as yet unknown) concept. It is this ability to classify an object on the basis
of all concepts which are acceptable with respect to all
previously seen examples, more than any other, which is the
distinguishing mark of the Candidate Elimination Approach.

8.E.5 EXAMPLE SELECTION

The characterization provided by the version space can also
be used to determine which examples would be most informative. Various measures of 'informativeness' are
possible. One measure which could be used to accelerate the
convergence of the version space to a single candidate is
'number of candidates which would be eliminated by this
example'. An estimate of this measure could be based on the
distribution of differences amongst the candidates in the
version space. Selection of the example must take into

account both possible labelings of the example.

A method of controlling the size of the boundary sets is to
select examples which will reduce or at worst minimally
increase the size of the boundary sets. By this measure of
informativeness, point P in the above example was not
particularly informative since both G1 and G2 were consistent with it. Given Version Space 2, an extremely informative point would be one directly above Q, outside of G1 but
inside s3 (e.g. point I in Fig. 8.67). If this point turns
out to be a negative example, then s3 and s4 would be
eliminated from S. Also all concepts more specific than G2
which contain P and Q but not 'I' are more specific than G1,
and so would not be included in the revised version of G.
No changes would be needed for s2, s5 or G1, and no new
concepts would be added to either boundary set. If 'I' turns
out to be a positive example, then G1, and therefore s2,
would be eliminated. s5 would also be effectively eliminated
since the least general concept which contains s5 and 'I'
also contains s4 (note that h(s4,I)={s4}) and would
therefore not be included in the revised version of S. Both
the size of S and the size of G are reduced by half regardless of the labeling of example 'I'.

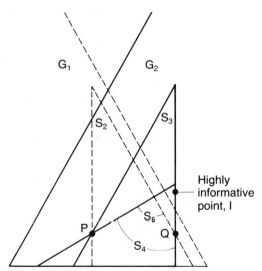

Boundary set concepts containing I (solid sides): G_2, S_3, S_4
Boundary set concepts not containing I (broken sides): G_1, S_2, S_5

Fig. 8.67 A highly informative point. Whether I is a positive or a negative
example, the size of both G and S will be reduced by half

8.F   Extending the notion of 'object'

The number of category values required to characterize a
particular object has so far been fixed. Every object was
characterized by a single value for each category. This
allowed us to represent objects with a fixed length vector
of category-values. In this section we will call such
objects 'primitive objects' and extend the notion of object
to include arbitrary collections of primitive objects. Such
a collection will be called a compound object. A number of
new issues arise when U is assumed to consist of compound
objects. For instance, relational predicates may be necessary to describe the relations (left-of, above, inside, same-
size, etc.) which may hold between the constituent objects
in a single compound object.

The single representation trick will be employed in this
section. Concepts and objects will be represented in either
the predicate or relational format. Only conjunctive
concepts will be considered. Sentences in the representation language will be called descriptions. Generally, the
primitive objects wil be characterized with only two
categories: SHAPE, with values CIRCLE and SQUARE, and COLOR,
with values GRAY and WHITE. Typical objects are E1, E2, E3,
E4 and E5, shown in Fig. 8.68. These objects and object
names will be used throughout most of the section.
Descriptions will also be given names, for purposes of
clarity and reference in the discussion. The same name will
be used for an object O and a description D only when D is a
description of O. Alternative descriptions of the same
object, say E1, will be distinguished by being subscripted
with a letter, as in $E1_a$, $E1_b$, and so on.

We shall adopt the Concept Modification Approach for describing concept learning in this section. The learning
method which will be developed is similar in some ways to a
Pure Generalization algorithm in the Method of Minimal
Modification, where minimal is measured by the number of
generalization operators applied. We assume that only
positive examples are available. The current method is
unlike the previously seen Concept Modification methods in

---

*   This section draws heavily on Kodratoff and Ganascia
     (1983) and Kodratoff (1982) which in turn draw on an
     unpublished manuscript Vere (1981).

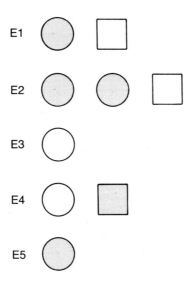

Fig. 8.68 Typical compound objects

that in this method the concept and the new example are treated in a perfectly symmetrical fashion: the method is best described as the Description Merging Method. Learning is achieved by 'merging' two descriptions; that is, by constructing a third description which is minimally more general than the given descriptions. Merging, then, is a way of generalizing.

8.F.1 OBJECT NAMES

To represent a collection of primitive objects, it is insufficient to merely conjoin the descriptions of the individual primitive objects. For instance

        E1 = SHAPE(circle) & COLOR(gray) & SHAPE(square)
                & COLOR(white)

    is not distinct from

        E4 = SHAPE(circle) & COLOR(white) & SHAPE(square)
                & COLOR(gray)

given that & is associative and commutative.

A mechanism is required to distinguish the categories and values pertaining to one primitive object from those which pertain to a different primitive object in the same compound object. There are many such mechanisms; the one which shall be adopted here is to give a distinct (otherwise arbitrary) name to each object in a given collection and to add an extra argument, for object names, to every predicate. Thus

        E1 = SHAPE(o1,circle) & COLOR(o1,gray)
                    & SHAPE(o2,square) & COLOR(o2,white)

        (where o1 and o2 are the arbitrarily assigned names of
                                            the two objects in E1)
        is entirely distinct from

        E4 = SHAPE(o1,circle) & COLOR(o1,white)
                    & SHAPE(o2,square) & COLOR(o2,gray)

in the sense that there is no uniform renaming of objects in description E4 which will result in a description identical to E1. Object names are local to a given description: the object names used in description E1 bear no relationship whatsoever to those used in E4. The object names used for the constituent objects in two descriptions of the same compound object are also entirely unrelated. For instance

        SHAPE(o2,circle) & COLOR(o2,gray) & SHAPE(o1,square)
                    & COLOR(o1,white)

is a perfectly satisfactory description for object E1, even though it is different from description E1 above. Neither the object names nor their indices (if they have any) imply or represent an order on the objects that they name. If the constituents of a compound object are ordered (or otherwise structured), this fact must be explicitly represented by a 'structural' predicate, that is a predicate which has more than one object name as an argument. For example,

        E1 =   SHAPE(o1,circle) & COLOR(o1,gray)
                    & SHAPE(o2,square) & COLOR(o2,white)
                                & LEFT-OF(o1,o2)

is one possible way of indicating that (in E1) the gray circle is to the left of the white square.

8.F.2 OBJECT MATCHING

The fact that object names are assigned arbitrarily creates a difficulty which did not occur in the simpler universes:[*] how can one determine if two descriptions are equivalent, i.e. represent the same concept?

The answer is straightforward although it may be computationally expensive:[**] given that the same predicates occur the same number of times in each description (call two such descriptions 'structurally identical'), look for a renaming of objects which renders the two descriptions identical. Renamings shall be indicated as follows

$$R = X/(o2\ o1)$$ which is read as 'rename both o2 in description 1 and o1 in description 2 as X'

For example, given

$$E1_a = SHAPE(o1,circle)\ \&\ SHAPE(o2,square)$$
$$\&\ COLOR(o1,gray)\ \&\ COLOR(o2,white)$$

$$E1_b = SHAPE(o2,circle)\ \&\ SHAPE(o1,square)$$
$$\&\ COLOR(o2,gray)\ \&\ COLOR(o1,white)$$

applying the renaming R, one gets

$$E1_a' = SHAPE(o1,circle)\ \&\ SHAPE(X,square)$$
$$\&\ COLOR(o1,gray)\ \&\ COLOR(X,white)$$

$$E1_b' = SHAPE(o2,circle)\ \&\ SHAPE(X,square)$$
$$\&\ COLOR(o2,gray)\ \&\ COLOR(X,white)$$

---

[*]   This general problem exists whenever there is redundancy in the description language. We shall limit our discussion to matters arising from the use of object names.

[**] p.464, Quinlan (1983b) remarks that the computational costs of concept learning increase linearly with the 'difficulty' of the concept to be learned when one is restricted to considering concepts which are characterizable as fixed-length vectors of category values, but increases exponentially with 'difficulty' when a richer representation language, such as we are now considering, is used.

to which one may apply the renaming Y/(o1 o2) to get

$$\text{E1}_a{}'' = \text{E1}_b{}'' = \text{SHAPE(Y,circle)} \ \& \ \text{SHAPE(X,square)}$$
$$\& \ \text{COLOR(Y,gray)} \ \& \ \text{COLOR(X,white)}$$

Finding a renaming which renders two descriptions identical, or showing that no such renaming exists, may be done by considering all possible renamings. For a pair of descriptions which each contain two object names there are only two possible renamings, namely

    R1 = X/(o1 v1) and Y/(o2 v2)
    R2 = X/(o1 v2) and Y/(o2 v1)

R1 is used for introducing a common set of object names (X and Y) into descriptions which may have object names drawn from different 'pools' (for example o's and v's). In the case where the two descriptions use the same object names R1 has no real effect - if the two descriptions were not identical prior to its being applied, then they will not be identical afterwards. R2 is the renaming just used (in two steps) to uncover the similarity of E1_a and E1_b. To establish that objects E1 and E4 are different, one need only determine if a description of E1 can be made identical to a description of E4 through either one of these two renamings. This, as we have seen above, is not possible, and therefore objects E1 and E4 are different.

Considering all possible renamings rapidly becomes impractical - the number of possible renamings grows as a factorial of the number of object names. The first way to speed the process of testing all renamings is to proceed in a stepwise fashion as was done in the $\text{E1}_a/\text{E1}_b$ example. In each step one considers just one object in the first description and one in the second description. These are renamed to be the same and the resulting descriptions (or rather the sub-descriptions which were affected by this renaming) are compared. If they are not identical, or cannot possibly be made identical by subsequent renaming, then no renaming which renames these two variables to be the same can possibly lead to the two descriptions being identical. Such a renaming is called 'unacceptable'.* A renaming which results in identical subdescriptions is called 'acceptable'. Assuming that there are no structural predicates the number of such steps required to test for description identity now grows in proportion to the square of the number of object names.

To demonstrate this stepwise process, consider the following two descriptions of E2

$$E2_a = \text{SHAPE(o1,circle)} \& \text{COLOR(o1,gray)}$$
$$\& \text{SHAPE(o2,circle)} \& \text{COLOR(o2,gray)}$$
$$\& \text{SHAPE(o3,square)} \& \text{COLOR(o3,white)}$$

$$E2_b = \text{SHAPE(o3,circle)} \& \text{COLOR(o3,gray)}$$
$$\& \text{SHAPE(o1,circle)} \& \text{COLOR(o1,gray)}$$
$$\& \text{SHAPE(o2,square)} \& \text{COLOR(o2,white)}$$

The renaming X/(o1 o1) results in identical subdescriptions in both $E2_a$ and $E2_b$ – SHAPE(X,circle) & COLOR(X,gray) – and therefore is acceptable. The next step tries the renaming Y/(o2 o2) which results in the subdescriptions

SHAPE(Y,circle) & COLOR(Y,gray)   in $E2_a$
SHAPE(Y,square) & COLOR(Y,white)   in $E2_b$

which are not identical and cannot be made so through subsequent renaming. This particular renaming is thus rejected leaving Y/(o2 o3) and Z/(o3 o2) as the only remaining possibility. This renaming renders the two descriptions identical.

The test 'and cannot be made so through subsequent renaming' becomes significant when the subdescription contains a structural predicate. When this happens, subsequent renamings may result in apparently identical relational predicates becoming distinct or vice versa. Since this cannot generally be anticipated, renamings involving a

---

* Kodratoff feels that 'unacceptable' is too forceful. When the objective is to merge two descriptions, and not to test them for equivalence, renamings which by this definition are 'unacceptable' can be very useful.

particular object name must be accepted 'tentatively' (i.e. with the possibility of being undone) until all the objects in all predicates involving that object name have been renamed. Consider the two descriptions of E2 which include the structural predicate LEFT-OF (where LEFT-OF(o1,o2) means that object o1 is to the left of object o2):

$$E2_c = \text{(same as } E2_a) \ \& \ \text{LEFT-OF(o1,o2)} \ \& \ \text{LEFT-OF(o2,o3)}$$
$$E2_d = \text{(same as } E2_b) \ \& \ \text{LEFT-OF(o3,o1)} \ \& \ \text{LEFT-OF(o1,o2)}$$

As above, one considers the renaming X/(o1 o1) which yields subdescriptions

SHAPE(X,circle) & COLOR(X,gray) & LEFT-OF(X,o2)   in $E2_c$
SHAPE(X,circle) & COLOR(X,gray) & LEFT-OF(X,o2)   in $E2_d$

This does not provide firm grounds for rejecting this renaming, but because the object names in the second argument of the LEFT-OF predicate have not yet been renamed (that they are both 'o2' is a mere coincidence), neither does this provide firm grounds for concluding that this renaming is acceptable. It can only be concluded to be acceptable if the renaming Y/(o2 o2) also proves to be acceptable. This renaming yields subdescriptions

SHAPE(Y,circle) & COLOR(Y,gray) & LEFT-OF(X,Y)   in $E2_c$
SHAPE(Y,square) & COLOR(Y,white) & LEFT-OF(X,Y)   in $E2_d$

which is unacceptable. Rejecting this renaming forces the rejection of the X/(o1 o1) renaming. The X/(o1 o2) renaming fails immediately (on the SHAPE and COLOR predicates), leaving X/(o1 o3) as the only possible renaming involving the 'o1' in $E2_c$. This yields subdescriptions

SHAPE(X,circle) & COLOR(X,gray) & LEFT-OF(X,o2)   in $E2_c$
SHAPE(X,circle) & COLOR(X,gray) & LEFT-OF(X,o1)   in $E2_d$

The difference in the object names in the second argument of the LEFT-OF predicate is not grounds for rejecting this renaming, since they may be renamed to be the same. Indeed only under that condition can this renaming be acceptable, and so the renaming Y/(o2 o1) is applied yielding subdescriptions

$$\text{SHAPE}(Y,circle) \& \text{COLOR}(Y,gray) \& \text{LEFT-OF}(X,Y)$$
$$\& \text{LEFT-OF}(Y,o3) \qquad \text{in } E2_c$$

$$\text{SHAPE}(Y,circle) \& \text{COLOR}(Y,gray) \& \text{LEFT-OF}(X,Y)$$
$$\& \text{LEFT-OF}(Y,o2) \qquad \text{in } E2_d$$

Again, this renaming (and thus also the ones which depend on it) is only acceptable if the renaming $Z/(o3 \ o2)$ is acceptable. This renaming yields subdescriptions

$$\text{SHAPE}(Z,square) \& \text{COLOR}(Z,white) \& \text{LEFT-OF}(Y,Z) \quad \text{in } E2_c$$

$$\text{SHAPE}(Z,square) \& \text{COLOR}(Z,white) \& \text{LEFT-OF}(Y,Z) \quad \text{in } E2_d$$

which is unconditionally acceptable. Thus the previous renamings are confirmed as acceptable, and the identity of the objects represented by $E2_c$ and $E2_d$ has been established.

The process of discovering an acceptable renaming (or discovering that no such renaming exists) can be accelerated by renaming first those objects which occur in infrequently occurring predicates, called rare predicates, or predicates which have a large number of object names as arguments, called populous predicates. The former strategy, called the rare predicate strategy, is effective because the number of possible renamings which will result in an acceptable renaming of objects which are arguments of a rare predicate is small. The latter strategy, called the populous predicate strategy, is effective because it will spawn renaming dependencies (as seen in the last example) which will reduce the number of renamings which need be considered.

To demonstrate the rare predicate strategy, observe that the predicate SHAPE(__,square) occurs only once in each of $E2_c$ and $E2_d$:

$$E2_c : \text{SHAPE}(o3,square) \quad \text{and} \quad E2_d : \text{SHAPE}(o2,square)$$

The only possible renaming which will make these two subdescriptions identical is $X/(o3 \ o2)$. If this renaming fails, then no other renaming need be considered. In this particular example all renamings subsequent to this one are forced by renaming dependencies which arise through structural predicates, in the same way that the renamings were forced in the above example once the renaming $X/(o1 \ o3)$

had been asserted. In the above example, however, two
unsuccessful renamings (X/(o1 o1) and X/(o1 o2)) had to be
considered before an acceptable one was found. The rare
predicate strategy introduces renaming constraints from the
very start.

Objects involved in rare predicates need not also be involved in populous predicates. Populous predicates are
extremely effective at accelerating the search for an
acceptable renaming because once one object in a particular
populous predicate is renamed the number and details of all
potentially acceptable renamings of all of the other objects
in that predicate are determined (there is one such renaming
for each occurrence of that predicate-name in the description). In other words, renaming dependencies are
exposed as rapidly as possible by renaming objects in
populous predicates.

8.F.3 MERGING TWO STRUCTURALLY IDENTICAL DESCRIPTIONS

As indicated in the introduction to this section, concept
learning is viewed as the merging of two concept (or object)
descriptions. For the moment we will assume that the two
descriptions which are to be merged are structurally
identical. Once the alternative ways of merging two such
descriptions have been discussed, this assumption will be
relaxed.

The object matching and renaming process just described will
play an important part in the merging process. A part of
each description will be made identical through renaming and
the remaining (non-identical) part will be dealt with
according to one or another of the merging processes which
will be described below. In general no uniform renaming can
make the entirety of the descriptions identical. Different
parts may be made identical through different renamings.
The decision of which renaming to choose is based on the
biases, requirements, preference criteria, and heuristic
measures typically found in any concept learning system.
Note that the rare predicate strategy and the populous
predicate strategy, which were strategies for improving the
efficiency of testing the equivalence of two descriptions,

become biases in a description merging process.* That is, if these strategies are used during description merging, one is implicitly expressing a preference for merging objects or values which occur in predicates which are neither rare nor populous, since the later a predicate is considered in the merging process, the more likely the need to merge the objects or values which occur in it.

Let us consider how E1 and E4 might be merged.

        E1 =   SHAPE(o1,circle) & SHAPE(o2,square)
                 & COLOR(o1,gray) & COLOR(o2,white)

        E4 =   SHAPE(o3,circle) & SHAPE(o4,square)
                 & COLOR(o3,white) & COLOR(o4,gray)

No uniform renaming can get both the SHAPE predicates and the COLOR predicates in the two descriptions to agree. Since our purpose is to merge these two descriptions and not to test their equivalence, we do not stop at this point, but choose one of the ('unacceptable') renamings and proceed as follows. Suppose that the renaming X/(o1 o3) and Y/(o2 o4) was chosen. Then one has the identical subdescription ID and the non-identical subdescriptions NID1 (in E1) and NID4 (in E4) as follows

        ID = SHAPE(X,circle) & SHAPE(Y,square)

        NID1 = COLOR(X,white) & COLOR(Y,gray)   (in E1)
        NID4 = COLOR(X,gray) & COLOR(Y,white)   (in E4)

Let M be the name of the description which will be the ultimate the product of merging E1 and E4. Then

        M = ID & XXX

where XXX is calculated on the basis of NID1 and NID4 using one of the following three methods.

---

* I thank Yves Kodratoff for this observation.

8.F.3.1 Method 1: Condition Dropping

This method of merging asserts that only subdescriptions of
the two descriptions to be merged which are identical under
the chosen renaming are included in M. That is, the non-
identical subdescriptions, NID1 and NID4, and the information which they carry, are simply ignored. In the current
example, merging by condition dropping yields:

   M = ID = SHAPE(X,circle) & SHAPE(Y,square)

which represents the concept whose members are compound
objects in which 'there are two distinct objects, one of
which is a circle and one of which is a square'. All COLOR
information from the examples (E1 and E4) has been lost.

8.F.3.2 Method 2: Value Merging

Most of the generalization operators which were described in
previous sections merge category values, and differ only in
the assumptions they make about the structure of the domain
from which the values were drawn.* Let us name the value
merging operator VM. Then two of the possible ways of
merging values are

   VM(triangle,square) = pointy
            (VM = ascend the value containment ordering)

   VM(triangle,square) = [triangle or square]
                     (VM = internal disjunction)

To apply the value merging method to two structurally
identical descriptions, A and B, we must decide which of the
values in A will be merged with each of the values in B.
That is, we must establish a 1-1 correspondence between the
values in A and the values in B. We do this by establishing
a 1-1 correspondence between the instances of the predicates
in A and in B. For each distinct occurrence of the predicate P(a,b,c,...) in A we choose a distinct occurrence of
the same predicate P(j,k,l,..) in B. This choice determines
a 1-1 correspondence between the instances of values and
object names in A and B as follows:

---

*   pp. 126-127 in Michalski (1983b) discuss   this in some
    detail.

```
argument a   corresponds to   argument j
argument b   corresponds to   argument k
argument c   corresponds to   argument l
```

and so on, where each of these arguments is either a value or an object name.* Generally there will be several such 1-1 correspondences, and we may choose to use any one of them. In the current example, there are two:

```
value in NID1      corresponds to     value in NID4

white  in COLOR(X,white)  ...   gray   in COLOR(X,gray)
gray   in COLOR(Y,gray)   ...   white  in COLOR(Y,white)
```

and,

(*)

```
white  in COLOR(X,white)  ...   white  in COLOR(Y,white)
gray   in COLOR(Y,gray)   ...   gray   in COLOR(X,gray)
```

Of these two possible 1-1 correspondences, suppose we choose the one in which the object names are in agreement, i.e. the first correspondence. Then, if internal disjunction were used as the value merging operator, the final outcome of merging E1 and E4 would be

```
M  =  SHAPE(X,circle) & SHAPE(Y,square)
      & COLOR(X,[gray or white])
      & COLOR(Y,[white or gray])
```

Unlike the condition dropping method, the value merging method retains some of the COLOR information. M represents the concept whose members are compound objects consisting of 'two distinct objects, one of which is a circle and is either gray or white, the other of which is a square which is either white or gray'.

---

* One usually prefers correspondences in which the object names which correspond can be acceptably renamed to be the same.

8.F.3.3 Method 3: Object Merging

The 1-1 correspondence marked (*) implicitly requires that object X be identified with object Y. This amounts to a relaxation of the requirement that a renaming must be 'acceptable' when applied uniformly across entire descriptions. Relaxing this requirement tends to erode the distinctness of the constituent objects in the compound objects that these descriptions represent. For instance, one of the consequences of relaxing this requirement is that it becomes possible to merge descriptions of compound objects which have different numbers of constituent objects. This amounts to neglecting, to some extent, the number of distinct objects in these compound objects. In order to relax the requirement that a renaming must be 'acceptable' when applied across entire descriptions with as little erosion of the distinctness of constituent objects as possible, a mechanism must be introduced to indicate whether the objects referred to by two different object names in a given description are definitely different, definitely the same, or possibly the same and possibly different (analogous to having values for the category COLOUR which mean definitely white, definitely gray, or either gray or white). This may be done by introducing two new predicates:*

SAME(o1,o2) means that objects o1 and o2 must be the same

MBS(o1,o2) means that objects o1 and o2 may be the same or they may be different

In a given description, if o1 and o2 do not occur in either a SAME() or an MBS(), then they must be different objects (as has been assumed up to this point). SAME(o1,o2) need never appear in an example, since the example could be rewritten with only one of the two object names. It provides a useful mechanism for keeping track of the object name relations during the course of description merging. The final step of this merging process is to replace all of the SAMEs with the appropriate MBSs, as illustrated in the following.

$$NID1 = COLOR(X,gray) \& COLOR(Y,white)$$
$$NID4 = COLOR(Y,gray) \& COLOR(X,white)$$

---

* Hayes-Roth and McDermott (1978) chooses to introduce the predicates SAME(o1,o2) and DIFFERENT(o1,o2).

may be rewritten as

$$NID1' = COLOR(Q1,gray) \ \& \ COLOR(Q2,white)$$
$$\& \ SAME(X,Q1) \qquad \& \ SAME(Y,Q2)$$

$$NID4' = COLOR(Q3,gray) \ \& \ COLOR(Q4,white)$$
$$\& \ SAME(X,Q4) \qquad \& \ SAME(Y,Q3)$$

The object matching and renaming process may now be applied to these two descriptions to find the renaming $U/(Q1 \ Q3)$ and $V/(Q2 \ Q4)$ which yields

$$NID1'' = COLOR(U,gray) \ \& \ COLOR(V,white)$$
$$\& \ SAME(X,U) \qquad \& \ SAME(Y,V)$$

$$NID4'' = COLOR(U,gray) \ \& \ COLOR(V,white)$$
$$\& \ SAME(X,V) \qquad \& \ SAME(Y,U)$$

These are identical except for the SAME() predicates which are merged according to the rule: every SAME(K,L) which does not occur in all of the descriptions which are being merged is replaced by MBS(K,L).

The resulting description is

$$NID1''' = NID4''' = \quad COLOR(U,gray) \ \& \ COLOR(V,white)$$
$$\& \ MBS(X,U) \ \& \ MBS(X,V)$$
$$\& \ MBS(Y,U) \ \& \ MBS(Y,V)$$

This result is conjoined with ID to produce the final version of M:

$$M = \quad SHAPE(X,circle) \ \& \quad SHAPE(Y,square)$$
$$\& \ COLOR(U,gray) \ \& \quad COLOR(V,white)$$
$$\& \ MBS(X,U) \ \& \ MBS(X,V) \ \& \ MBS(Y,U) \ \& \ MBS(Y,V)$$

M represents the concept whose members are compound objects in which 'there are two distinct constituent objects, of which one is a square and the other is a circle. These two objects are distinctly colored: one being gray and the other white'. This maintains a great deal of the information available from the examples. In contrast to the value merging method, object merging (in this example) retains the fact that the circle and square may not be the same color.

The information that there are exactly two distinct objects
is lost by object merging only if it is possible for some
objects to have shape but no color and for other objects to
have color but no shape (for the predicates SHAPE and COLOR
and objects in the macroscopic world this may seem un-
important, but for other predicates or in other domains,
this is an important consideration in choosing whether to
use value merging or object merging).

In the example just considered, there was a choice between
using value merging and using object merging. This choice
will be made on the basis of domain and other requirements,
and preference and other heuristic measures (such as an
estimate of which loses the least amount or least important
'information'). In the following example object merging is
the only applicable merging process. The compound objects
to be merged are shown in Fig. 8.69 (descriptions contain
LEFT-OF information only).

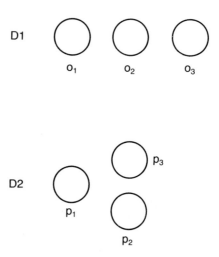

Fig. 8.69 Object merging is necessary

$$D1 = \text{LEFT-OF}(o1,o2) \ \& \ \text{LEFT-OF}(o2,o3)$$
$$D2 = \text{LEFT-OF}(p1,p2) \ \& \ \text{LEFT-OF}(p1,p3)$$

There is no uniform renaming which renders these identical. Suppose the renaming $X/(o1 \ p1)$ is chosen yielding the subdescriptions involving X

$$\text{LEFT-OF}(X,o2) \qquad\qquad\qquad (\text{from } D1)$$
$$\text{LEFT-OF}(X,p2) \ \& \ \text{LEFT-OF}(X,p3) \qquad (\text{from } D2)$$

In all previous examples, the subdescriptions have been structurally identical: here they are not. The solution suggested by the object merging process is to rewrite all predicates which appear in one subdescription but not the other in terms of a novel object name and assert that the two object names are the same.

$$D1' = \text{LEFT-OF}(X,o2) \ \& \ \text{LEFT-OF}(o2,o3)$$
$$D2' = \text{LEFT-OF}(X,p2) \ \& \ \text{LEFT-OF}(Y,p3) \ \& \ \text{SAME}(X,Y)$$

This maneuver introduces its own discrepancies which can be dealt with in a similar fashion. Renaming $Z/(o2,p2)$ yields subdescriptions

$$\text{LEFT-OF}(X,Z) \ \& \ \text{LEFT-OF}(Z,o3) \qquad (\text{from } D1')$$
$$\text{LEFT-OF}(X,Z) \qquad\qquad\qquad (\text{from } D2')$$

A similar rewriting is done for Z in D1' yielding

$$D1'' = \text{LEFT-OF}(X,Z) \ \& \ \text{LEFT-OF}(U,o3) \ \& \ \text{SAME}(Z,U)$$
$$D2'' = \text{LEFT-OF}(X,Z) \ \& \ \text{LEFT-OF}(Y,p3) \ \& \ \text{SAME}(X,Y)$$

As in the object merging process described above, object names introduced during object merging must themselves be renamed. Thus the final renaming is $V/(U \ Y)$ and $W/(o3 \ p3)$ which yields

$$D1''' = \text{LEFT-OF}(X,Z) \ \& \ \text{LEFT-OF}(V,W) \ \& \ \text{SAME}(Z,V)$$
$$D2''' = \text{LEFT-OF}(X,Z) \ \& \ \text{LEFT-OF}(V,W) \ \& \ \text{SAME}(X,V)$$

These two descriptions can finally be merged to get

$$M = \text{LEFT-OF}(X,Z) \ \& \ \text{LEFT-OF}(V,W) \ \& \ \text{MBS}(Z,V) \ \& \ \text{MBS}(X,V)$$

which represents the concept whose members are compound objects in which 'there are at least three distinct constituent objects (X,Z and W) and there is a unique leftmost object (X)'. As in the above example, the number of objects in the examples (three) has been compromised somewhat: if not for the semantics of LEFT-OF (in Euclidean two-space) it might be possible for a fourth distinct object (V) to be 'LEFT-OF' the object W, but for no 'LEFT-OF' relation to hold between the pairs of objects (X,Z) and (V,W). For example if the predicate 'CONTAINS' is substituted for LEFT-OF then the object merging remains the same (being purely syntactic) yielding

$$M = \text{CONTAINS}(X,Z) \ \& \ \text{CONTAINS}(V,W) \ \& \ \text{MBS}(Z,V) \ \& \ \text{MBS}(X,V)$$

in which it is plausible for V to be a fourth distinct object. This concept has as members compound objects in which (roughly) 'there are three, possibly four, distinct constituent objects (X, Z and W are definitely distinct), two of which (W,Z) are contained by some other constituent object(s)'. All of the members of this concept (the two examples and one other) are shown in Fig. 8.70.

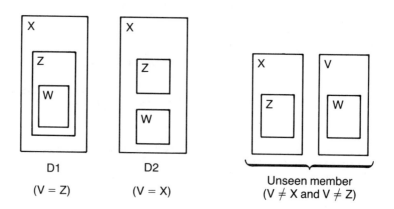

D1   D2   Unseen member
(V = Z)   (V = X)   (V ≠ X and V ≠ Z)

Fig. 8.70 All members of the concept "CONTAINS (X, Z) & CONTAINS (V, W) & MBS (Z, V) & MBS (X, V)"

This example suggests that the object merging process:

$$SAME(X,Y) \ \& \ SAME(X,Z) \ ---> MBS(X,Y) \ \& \ MBS(X,Z)$$

is not always appropriate. In the same way that there are many different value merging operators, so there are many possible object merging operators. An alternative object merging operator which preserves information about the number of constituent objects in the above example is analogous to internal disjunction:

$$SAME(X,Z) \ \& \ SAME(X,Y) \ ---> SAME(X, \ Z \ or \ Y)$$

where this latter predicate is interpreted as 'X must be the same as either Z or Y but not both'.

8.F.4 ACHIEVING STRUCTURAL IDENTITY

At this point, a method for merging two structurally identical descriptions has been outlined. Our attention now turns to the problem of transforming two non-identical descriptions into structurally identical forms (in order that the above method may be applied). This problem will not be addressed in its most general form. Instead, two methods will be described which are widely applicable (in the sense of being largely domain independent) but which by no means provide a full solution to the problem of achieving structural identity.[*] When two descriptions cannot be made structurally identical, there seems to be no alternative to simply dropping the non-identical subdescriptions.

---

[*] In particular, the general use of domain knowledge to replace a predicate with a semantically equivalent predicate will not be described (predicate families reflect one use of domain knowledge). Kodratoff and Ganascia (1983), page 86, demonstrates a more general use of domain knowledge for rendering two descriptions structurally identical.

8.F.4.1 Predicate Families

In most representations[*] predicate names are distinguished from object names and category values. This preempts the possibility of directly using value or object merging methods to cope with descriptions which are not structurally identical. The method of 'predicate families'[**] attempts to rewrite non-identical predicate names as different values in an identical (higher order) predicate. Once this is done, the usual value merging operators can be used to merge the two predicate names (since these are now simply values). An example will make this idea clear.

$$E5 = CIRCLE(o1) \ \& \ GRAY(o1)$$
$$E3 = CIRCLE(o1) \ \& \ WHITE(o1)$$

These two descriptions are not structurally identical, but they are equivalent to

$$E5' = CIRCLE(o1) \ \& \ COLOR(o1,gray)$$
$$E3' = CIRCLE(o1) \ \& \ COLOR(o1,white)$$

which are structurally identical. Merging $E5'$ and $E3'$ yields

$$M = CIRCLE(X) \ \& \ COLOR(X,gray \ or \ white)$$

using internal disjunction as the value merging operator. The transformation which produced $E5'$ and $E3'$ from the original descriptions makes use of the knowledge that both 'Gray' and 'White' are colors - i.e. that these predicates belong to the same predicate family. Similarly the predicate family 'SHAPE' has been used throughout this section so that objects with different shapes could be represented with structurally identical descriptions.

8.F.4.2 The Method of &-Idempotence

'&-idempotence' refers to the fact that conjoining a sub-description to a description which already contains a copy of that subdescription does not affect the meaning of the

---

[*]   Vere (1975,1977,1978) is an exception. He treats predicate names, object names, and values perfectly uniformly.
[**] The name and idea originate in Kodratoff and Ganascia (1983).

description. Thus the two descriptions below are equivalent (both represent E3):

$$W HITE(o1) \& CIRCLE(o1)$$
$$W HITE(o1) \& WHITE(o1) \& CIRCLE(o1)$$

The use of &-idempotence is similar to that of predicate families in that both change the structure of a description without altering its meaning. &-idempotence can be used to introduce one or more additional instances of a predicate name. An example of the use of &-idempotence is given in the merging of E1 and E2 (colors are disregarded in this example, but would be treated precisely the same as shapes):

$$E1 = \qquad\qquad CIRCLE(o1) \& SQUARE(o2)$$
$$E2 = CIRCLE(o1) \& CIRCLE(o2) \& SQUARE(o3)$$

E1 is apparently deficient in an instance of the CIRCLE predicate. Using &-idempotence it can be transformed:

$$E1' = CIRCLE(o1) \& CIRCLE(o1) \& SQUARE(o2)$$
$$E2 \ = CIRCLE(o1) \& CIRCLE(o2) \& SQUARE(o3)$$

Apply the renaming X/(o1 o1) and Y/(o2 o3) to get

$$E1'' = CIRCLE(X) \& CIRCLE(X) \ \& SQUARE(Y)$$
$$E2' \ = CIRCLE(X) \& CIRCLE(o2) \& SQUARE(Y)$$

Object merging is required in order to resolve the incompatibility between the CIRCLE(X) predicate in E1'' and the CIRCLE(o2) predicate in E2'. The usual rewriting yields:

$$E1''' = CIRCLE(X) \& CIRCLE(A) \ \& SQUARE(Y) \& SAME(X,A)$$
$$E2' \ = \quad CIRCLE(X) \& CIRCLE(o2) \& SQUARE(Y)$$

and the renaming Z/(A o2) results in two descriptions which can be merged to yield the final description

$$CIRCLE(X) \& CIRCLE(Z) \& SQUARE(Y) \& MBS(X,Z)$$

which represents the concept whose members are compound objects in which 'there are two or three distinct constituent objects, exactly one of which is a square, the other(s) being a circle'.

8.F.5 EXAMPLE

The following example* is intended to demonstrate all of the
methods described above working together to merge the three
examples shown in Fig. 8.71.

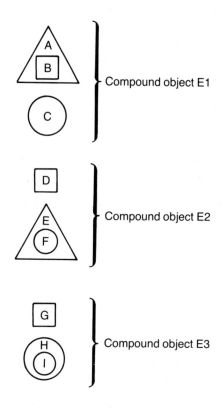

Fig. 8.71 Three compound objects to be merged

The original descriptions of these examples are:

```
E1 = TRIANGLE(A) & SQUARE(B) & CIRCLE(C)
     & INSIDE(B,A) & ABOVE(A,C) & ABOVE(B,C)

E2 = TRIANGLE(E) & SQUARE(D) & CIRCLE(F)
     & INSIDE(F,E) & ABOVE(D,F) & ABOVE(D,E)

E3 = SQUARE(G)   & CIRCLE(H) & CIRCLE(I)
     & INSIDE(I,H) & ABOVE(G,H) & ABOVE(G,I)
```

These descriptions are structurally identical except for the SHAPE predicates which can be replaced using the predicate family SHAPE. Rather than bias the possible object and value mergings at this premature stage by selecting only one of the SHAPE predicates from each description to be modified, modify all of the occurrences of SHAPE predicates in all descriptions.

```
E1 = SHAPE(triangle,A) & SHAPE(square,B)
     & SHAPE(circle,C) & INSIDE(B,A) & ABOVE(A,C)
                       & ABOVE(B,C)

E2 = SHAPE(triangle,E) & SHAPE(square,D)
     & SHAPE(circle,F) & INSIDE(F,E) & ABOVE(D,F)
                       & ABOVE(D,E)

E3 = SHAPE(square,G)   & SHAPE(circle,H)
     & SHAPE(circle,I) & INSIDE(I,H) & ABOVE(G,H)
                       & ABOVE(G,I)
```

The notation for descriptions will be abbreviated in the following account of the merging process. Predicate arguments will be written in columns with the predicate name at the head of the column. The values of the SHAPE category will be abbreviated 't' for 'triangle', 'c' for 'circle' and 's' for 'square'. The comma separating arguments will be omitted (all value and object names are single letters).

```
Predicate: SHAPE        INSIDE      ABOVE              SAME

   E1 = (tA)(sB)(cC)    (BA)        (AC)(BC)
   E2 = (tE)(sD)(cF)    (FE)        (DF)(DE)
   E3 = (sG)(cH)(cI)    (IH)        (GH)(GI)

Rename: Z/(A E H)

   E1 = (tZ)(sB)(cC)    (BZ)        (ZC)(BC)
   E2 = (tZ)(sD)(cF)    (FZ)            (DF)(DZ)
   E3 = (cZ)(sG)(cI)    (IZ)            (GI)(GZ)
```

There are three troublespots here:
  1. The SHAPE of Z is not the same in all three de-
     scriptions. In this example use value merging and
     replace each SHAPE value with the value 'anyshape',
     which will be abbreviated '*'.
  2. In E1 there is an ABOVE(Z,C) but there is no ABOVE(Z,_)
     in either E2 or E3. Rewrite this occurrence of Z using
     the new object name J.
  3. Similarly, the ABOVE(_,Z) predicates in E2 and E3 have
     no counterpart in E1. These occurrences of Z are
     rewritten using new object names K and L in E2 and E3.

```
Predicate: SHAPE        INSIDE      ABOVE              SAME

   E1 = (*Z)(sB)(cC)    (BZ)        (JC)(BC)           (ZJ)
   E2 = (*Z)(sD)(cF)    (FZ)            (DF)(DK)       (ZK)
   E3 = (*Z)(sG)(cI)    (IZ)            (GI)(GL)       (ZL)

Rename: Y/(C F I)

   E1 = (*Z)(sB)(cY)    (BZ)        (JY)(BY)           (ZJ)
   E2 = (*Z)(sD)(cY)        (YZ)    (DY)(DK)           (ZK)
   E3 = (*Z)(sG)(cY)        (YZ)    (GY)(GL)           (ZL)
```

There are two troublespots here:
  1. There are two different ABOVE(_,Y) in E1 but only one
     ABOVE(_,Y) in each of E2 and E3. Using &-idempotence,
     make a duplicate of these predicates in E2 and E3 which
     use object names M and N instead of D and G.
  2. In order to be able to match INSIDE(B,Z) in E1 with
     INSIDE(_,Z) in E2 and E3 rewrite these occurrences Y in
     E2 and E3 using the new object names O and P.

Predicate: SHAPE	INSIDE	ABOVE	SAME
E1 = (*Z)(sB)(cY)	(BZ)	(JY)(BY)	(ZJ)
E2 = (*Z)(sD)(cY)	(OZ)	(MY)(DY)(DK)	(ZK)(YO)(DM)
E3 = (*Z)(sG)(cY)	(PZ)	(NY)(GY)(GL)	(ZL)(YP)(GN)

Rename: X/(B D G)

E1 = (*Z)(sX)(cY)	(XZ)	(JY)(XY)	(ZJ)
E2 = (*Z)(sX)(cY)	(OZ)	(MY)(XY)(XK)	(ZK)(YO)(XM)
E3 = (*Z)(sX)(cY)	(PZ)	(NY)(XY)(XL)	(ZL)(YP)(XN)

Two troublespots:
1. INSIDE(X,Z) in E1 has no counterpart in E2 and E3.
   Rewrite this occurrence of X in E1 using the new object
   name Q.
2. ABOVE(X,_) in E2 and E3 have no counterpart in E1.
   Using &-idempotence, duplicate the ABOVE(X,Y) in E1
   using the new object name R instead of Y.

Predicate: SHAPE	INSIDE	ABOVE	SAME
E1 = (*Z)(sX)(cY)	(QZ)	(JY)(XY)(XR)	(ZJ)(YR)(XQ)
E2 = (*Z)(sX)(cY)	(OZ)	(MY)(XY)(XK)	(ZK)(YO)(XM)
E3 = (*Z)(sX)(cY)	(PZ)	(NY)(XY)(XL)	(ZL)(YP)(XN)

The final renaming U/(Q O P) and V/(J M N) and W/(R K L)
yields the common description

E = (*Z)(sX)(cY)	(UZ)	(VY)(XY)(XW)

and the following SAMEs to be merged

(in E1) :	SAME(Z,V) & SAME(Y,W) & SAME(X,U)
(in E2) :	SAME(Z,W) & SAME(Y,U) & SAME(X,V)
(in E3) :	SAME(Z,W) & SAME(Y,U) & SAME(X,V)

The final concept is

SHAPE(anyshape,Z) & SHAPE(square,X) & SHAPE(circle,Y)
   & INSIDE(U,Z)
(A)   & ABOVE(V,Y) & ABOVE(X,Y) & ABOVE(X,W)
   & MBS(Z,V) & MBS(Z,W) & MBS(Y,W) & MBS(Y,U)
   & MBS(X,V) & MBS(X,U)

It is not particularly easy to give an interpretation of
this concept. In each of its members there are at least
three distinct constituent objects (X,Y,Z), and at most six
(when U, V, and W are all distinct from X, Y and Z). There
are only two distinct members of this concept which contain
exactly three constituent objects: SAME(X,U) & SAME(Y,W) &
SAME(Z,V), which corresponds to example E1, and SAME(X,V) &
SAME(Y,U) & SAME(Z,W), which corresponds to both example E2
and example E3, since the shape of Z is unspecified in this
concept. Of the remaining sixteen possible members of this
concept, very few meet the semantic demands of the ordinary
meanings of the predicates ABOVE and INSIDE. For instance,
SAME(X,U) & SAME(Z,W) & DIFFERENT(Y,V) creates the situation
ABOVE(X,Z) & INSIDE(X,Z). As with a previous example, there
may be predicates for which this combination is perfectly
valid (e.g. if ABOVE referred to the center of an object,
and not the object in its entirety).

It should also be emphasized that the sequence of renamings
which occurred in this example was not the only possible
one. Indeed there are a great many possible orders of
renaming and choices of which objects to merge. In general
each different sequence of renamings will produce a different final concept. All of these final concepts will be
equally general in the sense that all will be more general
than all of the given examples, and none of the final
concepts will be more general than any of the other final
concepts. For instance, another final concept which can be
produced by merging these examples using a different sequence of renamings is:[*]


```
      SHAPE(anyshape,X) & SHAPE(anyshape,Y) & SHAPE(anyshape,Z)
         & INSIDE(Y,X)
(B)      & ABOVE(W ,T) & ABOVE(U,V)
         & MBS(Z,W ) & MBS(Z,V) & MBS(Z,U) & MBS(Z,T)
         & MBS(Y,W ) & MBS(Y,V)                  & MBS(X,T)
         & MBS(V,T) & MBS(U,W).
```


The renamings which were used to generate (B) were determined by the relational predicates INSIDE and ABOVE. In
comparing this with (A) one should observe that the shapes

---

[*]   From Kodratoff and Ganascia (1983).

which were preserved in (A) are lost in (B), but that the number of objects which are ABOVE is more closely preserved in (B) than in (A). This reflects the priorities which were used to determine which renamings to apply. It is also interesting that the number of MBSs is considerably greater in (B). Both (A) and (B) admit the possibility of only one object being ABOVE only one other object, with the third object off to the side – a possibility which was not represented in any of the examples.

One way to test if a given object is a member of a concept is to merge the description of the object with that of the concept. If the resulting description is a description of the concept, then the object is a member of that concept. Otherwise, it is not. The merging process thus serves as both concept learning algorithm and membership determination process. Although this is the natural interpretation of concept membership, given the rich representation language which is being used, the merging process is anything but trivial. The complexity of the membership determination process has increased dramatically under the extension of the notion of 'object' to include compound objects.

The single representation trick has been fully exploited by the concept learning method described in this section. First, it enabled a process such as description merging to be used as a learning algorithm. Secondly, the description merging process can merge the descriptions of two concepts as easily as it can merge an object description with a concept description. That is, an entire concept can be treated as a single positive example. Merging two concept descriptions corresponds to finding that concept which is minimally more general than both of the given concepts.*

---

* Mitchell (1983,1982a), Utgoff and Mitchell (1982) have made use of concept merging. Michalski's AQ11, as described on pp. 423-426 in Dietterich et al. (1982), is a discrimination algorithm which is able to treat a concept as if it was a single negative example. This enables him to ensure that the concept which is learned has no members in common with a particular other concept.

8.G Further reading

This section is meant to provide pointers into the literature for topics of interest to the student of concept
learning systems which have not been covered in this
chapter. The list of pointers for each topic by no means
provides a comprehensive or even fully representative
bibliography for that topic, but rather guides the reader
to a few of the more accessible papers which are typical of
recent work. I have drawn heavily on the valuable papers
listed under 'Overviews and Comparative Reviews' in preparing this chapter and I recommend them as useful, perhaps
even necessary, supplements to the material and outlook
provided in this chapter.

Bibliography - the reader will find a complete bibliography
    on Machine Learning in Nudel and Utgoff (1980).

Overviews and Comparative Reviews -
    Angluin and Smith (1982), Buchanan et al. (1977),
    Bundy and Silver (1982), Carbonell et al. (1983),
    Dietterich et al. (1982),
    Dietterich and Michalski (1983a,b,1981,1979),
    Langley (1980), Michalski (1983a,b).

Noise - Quinlan (1983a), Mitchell (1978), Rendell (1983).

Applications -
    Buchanan and Mitchell (1978), Lindsay et al. (1980),
    Langley (1983b), Lenat, Sutherland and Gibbons (1982),
    Lenat (1983b), Michalski and Chilausky (1980),
    Michalski and Baskin (1983), Michalski et al. (1982),
    Michie (1983), Mitchell (1977,1978), Sleeman (1983).

Psychological Models -
    Anderson (1981), Anderson et al. (1979),
    Selfridge (1983), Klahr, Langley and Neches (1984).

Formal Learning Theory -
    Angluin and Smith (1982), Wexler and Culicover (1980),
    Angluin (1980), Osherson et al. (1983,1982).

Learning by Analogy -
    Several papers in IMLW , e.g. Carbonell (1983a) and
    Winston (1983). Carbonell (1983b), Carbonell (1982),
    Winston (1980).

Strategy Learning –
  Carbonell (1983a), Langley (1983a,c,1982),
  Mitchell (1983), Mitchell et al. (1983),
  Silver (1983a,b), Sleeman et al. (1982),

Automatic Bias Revision –
  Lenat (1983a,b), Utgoff and Mitchell (1982),
  Utgoff (1983).

Operationalization –
  Mostow (1983a,b,1981), Mostow and Hayes-Roth (1979),
  pp. 350-359 in Dietterich et al. (1982).
(data sensitive:) Mitchell (1982,1983),
                  Utgoff and Mitchell (1982).

ACKNOWLEDGEMENTS

I am indebted to David Kirsh and Alan MacDonald for the many
hours they spent carefully reviewing drafts of this chapter.
Many improvements in both presentation and technical content
resulted from their advice. Yves Kodratoff was very helpful
during the preparation of Section F. I thank Bruce Buchanan
and Larry Rendell for their encouraging comments on an early
draft. I gratefully acknowledge the financial support which
made this work possible: a War Memorial Scholarship from
the Imperial Order of the Daughters of the Empire (Canada);
a Postgraduate Scholarship from the Natural Sciences and
Engineering Research Council (Canada); and an Overseas
Research Student Scholarship from the Committee of Vice-
Chancellors and Principals (UK). Finally, many thanks to
Lee Flanagan and Y. H. Ng for their generous assistance in
preparing the text of this chapter.

REFERENCES

The following abbreviations have been used:

ECAI-82 Proceedings of the European Conference on Artificial
    Intelligence, Orsay, France, 1982.

IJCAI-n   Proceedings of the 'n-th' International Joint
    Conference on Artificial Intelligence. Available from
    William Kaufmann Inc., Los Altos, California.

IMLW Proceedings of the 1983 International Machine Learning
    Workshop, Department of Computer Science, University of
    Illinois, Urbana.

Machine Learning refers to Michalski, Carbonell, and
    Mitchell (1983).

NCAI-n   Proceedings of the 'n-th' National Conference on
    Artificial Intelligence. Available from William
    Kaufmann Inc., Los Altos, California.

PDIS refers to Waterman and Hayes-Roth (1978)

Anderson, J.R. (1981), 'A Theory of Language Acquisition
    Based on General Learning Principles',pp. 97-103 in
    IJCAI-7.

Anderson, J.R., Kline, P.J., and Beasley, C.M. Jr.   (1979),
    'A General Learning Theory and its Application to
    Schema Abstraction', pp. 277-318 in G.H. Bower (ed.),
    The Psychology of Learning and Motivation, vol. 13,
    Academic Press.

Angluin, D. (1980), 'Inductive Inference of Formal Languages
    From Positive Data', Information and Control 45, pp.
    117-135.

Angluin, D., and Smith, C.H.   (1982), 'A Survey of Inductive
    Inference: Theory and Methods', technical report 250,
    Computer Science Department, Yale University.

Berwick, R.C. (1983), 'Domain-Specific Learning and the
    Subset Principle', pp. 228-233 in IMLW.

Buchanan, B.G., and Mitchell, T.M. (1978), 'Model-Directed
    Learning of Production Rules', pp. 297-312, in PDIS.

Buchanan, B.G., Mitchell, T.M., Smith, R.G., and Johnson,
    C.R. Jr. (1977), 'Models of Learning Systems', in J.
    Belzer, A.G. Holzmán, and A. Kent (eds), 'Encycloped-
    ia of Computer Science and Technology', Volume 11, pp.
    24-51, Marcel Dekker Inc., New York.

Bundy, A. (1982), 'The Indispensability of Inference in Focussing', Note 122, Department of Artificial Intelligence, University of Edinburgh.

Bundy, A., and Silver, B. (1982), 'A Critical Survey of Rule Learning Programs', pp. 151-157, in ECAI-82. (To appear in Artificial Intelligence.)

Carbonell, J.G. (1983a), 'Derivational Analogy in Problem-Solving and Knowledge Acquisition', pp. 12-18 in IMLW.

Carbonell, J.G. (1983b), 'Learning by Analogy: Formulating and Generalizing Plans From Past Experience', pp. 137-162 in Machine Learning.

Carbonell, J.G. (1982), 'Experiential Learning in Analogical Problem Solving', pp. 168-171 in NCAI-2.

Carbonell, J.G., Michalski, R.S., and Mitchell, T.M. (1983), 'Machine Learning: A Historical and Methodological Analysis', in The AI Magazine, 4(3), 69-79.

Cohen, P.R., and Feigenbaum, E.A. (1982), 'The Handbook of Artificial Intelligence', volume 3, William Kaufmann Inc., Los Altos, California.

Dietterich, T.G., London, B., Clarkson, K., and Dromey, G. (1982), 'Learning and Inductive Inference', Chapter 14 in Cohen and Feigenbaum,(1982). Also Dept of Computer Science report STAN-CS-82-913, Stanford University.

Dietterich, T.G., and Michalski, R. (1983a), 'A Comparative Review of Selected Methods for Learning from Examples', pp. 41-82, in Machine Learning.

Dietterich, T.G., and Michalski, R.S. (1983b), 'Discovering Patterns in Sequences of Objects', pp. 41-57 in IMLW.

Dietterich, T.G., and Michalski, R.S. (1981), 'Inductive Learning of Structural Descriptions: Evaluation Criteria and Comparative Review of Selected Methods', Artificial Intelligence, 16, 257-294.

Dietterich, T.G., and Michalski, R.S. (1979), 'Learning and Generalization of Characteristic Descriptions: Evaluation Criteria and Comparative Review of Selected Methods', pp. 223-231 in IJCAI-6.

Hayes-Roth, F., and Lesser, V. (1977), 'Focus of Attention
    in the HEARSAY-II Speech Understanding System', pp. 27–
    35 in IJCAI-5.

Hayes-Roth, F., and McDermott, J. (1978), 'An Interference
    Matching Technique for Inducing Abstractions',
    Communications of the ACM 26, pp. 401–410.

Hayes-Roth, F., and McDermott, J. (1977), 'Knowledge Acqui-
    sition From Structural Descriptions', pp. 356–362, in
    IJCAI-5.

Holland, J.H. (1983), 'Escaping Brittleness', pp. 92–95 in
    IMLW .

Holland, J.H. (1975), 'Adaptation in Natural and Artificial
    Systems', University of Michigan Press, Ann Arbor.

Holland, J.H., and Reitman, J.S. (1978), 'Cognitive Systems
    Based on Adaptive Algorithms', pp. 313–329 in PDIS.

Johnson, L. (1983), 'Epistemics and the Frame Conception of
    Knowledge', Kybernetes 12, 177–181.

Johnson, L. (1981), 'Medical Concepts', Man-Computer Studies
    Group technical report TR-15, Brunel University,
    England. Forthcoming in 'Clinical and Behavioural
    Science', L. Kohout and W. Bandler (eds), Abacus Press.

Kibler, D. (1983), personal communication.

Klahr, D., Langley, P., and Neches, R. (1984), 'Production
    System Models of Learning and Development', MIT Press.

Kodratoff, Y. (1982), 'Generalizing and Particularizing as
    the Techniques of Learning', Proc. International
    Conference on Artificial Intelligence and Information –
    Control of Robotics, Bratislava, pp. 131–134 (1982).
    Also forthcoming in Computers and Artificial
    Intelligence.

Kodratoff, Y., and Ganascia, J.-G. (1983), 'Learning as a
    Non-Deterministic But Exact Logical Process', pp. 81–91
    in IMLW .

Langley, P. (1983a), 'Learning Search Strategies Through Discrimination', International Journal of Man-Machine Studies 18, 513-541.

Langley, P. (1983b), 'Student Modelling as Strategy Learning', Proceedings of the 5th Conference of the Cognitive Science Society, University of Rochester.

Langley, P. (1983c), 'Learning Effective Search Heuristics', pp. 419-421 in IJCAI-8.

Langley, P. (1982), 'Strategy Acquisition Governed by Experimentation', pp. 171-176 in ECAI-82.

Langley, P. (1980), 'A Review of Research on Learning and Discovery', CIP Working Paper No. 415, Dept of Psychology, Carnegie-Mellon University.

Lebowitz, M. (1983), 'Concept Learning in a Rich Input Domain', pp. 177-182 in IMLW.

Lebowitz, M. (1982), 'Correcting Erroneous Generalizations', Cognition and Brain Theory 4, 367-381.

Lenat, D.B. (1983a), 'The Role of Heuristics in Learning by Discovery', pp. 243-306 in Machine Learning.

Lenat, D.B. (1983b), 'EURISKO: A Program That Learns New Heuristics and Domain Concepts. The Nature of Heuristics III: Program Design and Results', Artificial Intelligence 21, 61-98.

Lenat, D.B. (1976), 'AM: An Artificial Intelligence Approach to Discovery in Mathematics as Heuristic Search'. Dept of Computer Science STAN-CS-76-570, Stanford University. Also in R. Davis and D.B. Lenat, 'Knowledge-Based Systems in Artificial Intelligence', McGraw-Hill, 1980.

Lenat, D.B., and Brown, J.S. (1983), 'Why AM and Eurisko Appear to Work', pp. 236-240 in NCAI-3.

Lenat, D.B., Hayes-Roth, F., and Klahr, P. (1983), 'Cognitive Economy in a Fluid Task Environment', pp. 133-146 in IMLW.

Lenat, D.B., Sutherland, W.R., and Gibbons, J. (1982), 'Heuristic Search for New Microcircuit Structures: An Application of Artificial Intelligence', AI Magazine 3(3), 17-33.

Lindsay, R.K., Buchanan, B.G., Feigenbaum, E.A., and Lederberg, J. (1980), 'Applications of Artificial Intelligence for Organic Chemistry: The Dendral Project', McGraw-Hill.

Marsh, D. (1969), 'Memo Functions, the Graph Traverser, and a Simple Control Problem', pp. 281-300 in Machine Intelligence 5, B. Meltzer and D. Michie (eds), Edinburgh University Press.

Michalski, R.S. (1983a), 'A Theory and Methodology of Inductive Learning', pp. 83-134 in Machine Learning.

Michalski, R.S. (1983b), 'A Theory and Methodology of Inductive Learning', Artificial Intelligence 20, 111-161.

Michalski, R.S. (1980), 'Pattern Recognition as Rule-Guided Inductive Inference', IEEE Transactions on Pattern Analysis and Machine Intelligence, PAMI-2, 349-361.

Michalski, R.S., and Baskin, A.B. (1983), 'Integrating Multiple Knowledge Representations and Learning Capabilities in an Expert System: the ADVISE system', pp. 256-258 in IJCAI-8.

Michalski, R.S., Carbonell, J.G., and Mitchell, T.M. (1983), 'Machine Learning - An Artificial Intelligence Approach', Tioga Publishing Company.

Michalski, R.S., and Chilausky, R.L. (1980), 'Knowledge Acquisition by Encoding Expert Rules versus Computer Induction From Examples: A Case Study Involving Soybean Pathology', International Journal of Man-Machine Studies 12, 63-87.

Michalski, R.S., Davis, J.H., Bisht, V.S., and Sinclair, J.B. (1982), 'PLANT/ds: An Expert System for the Diagnosis of Soybean Diseases', pp. 133-138 in ECAI-82.

Michie, D. (1983), 'Inductive Rule Generation in the Context of the Fifth Generation', pp. 65-70 in IMLW.

Michie, D. (1968), '"Memo Functions" and Machine Learning', Nature 218, 19-22.

Mitchell, T.M. (1983), 'Learning and Problem-Solving', pp. 1139-1151 in IJCAI-8 (Computers and Thought lecture).

Mitchell, T.M. (1982a), 'Toward Combining Empirical and Analytical Methods for Inferring Heuristics', report LCSR-TR-27, Laboratory for Computer Science Research, Rutgers University.

Mitchell, T.M. (1982b), 'Generalization as Search', Artificial Intelligence, 18(2), 203-226.

Mitchell, T.M. (1980), 'The Need for Biases in Learning Generalizations', report CBM-TR-117, Computer Science Department, Rutgers University.

Mitchell, T.M. (1979), 'An Analysis of Generalization as a Search Problem', pp. 577-582 in IJCAI-6.

Mitchell, T.M. (1978), 'Version Spaces: An Approach To Concept Learning', technical report CS-78-711, Dept of Computer Science, Stanford University.

Mitchell, T.M. (1977), 'Version Spaces: A Candidate Elimination Approach to Rule Learning', pp.305-310 in IJCAI-5.

Mitchell, T.M., Utgoff, P., and Banerji, R. (1983), 'Learning by Experimentation: Acquiring and Refining Problem-Solving Heuristics', pp. 163-190 in Machine Learning.

Mostow, D.J. (1983a), 'Operationalizing Advice: A Problem-Solving Model', pp. 110-116 in IJCAI-8.

Mostow, D.J. (1983b), 'Machine Transformations of Advice into a Heuristic Search Procedure', pp. 367-404 in Machine Learning.

Mostow, D.J. (1981), 'Mechanical Transformations of Task Heuristics into Operational Procedures', report CMU-CS-81-113, Department of Computer Science, Carnegie-Mellon University, Pittsburgh.

Mostow, D.J., and Hayes-Roth, F. (1979), 'Operationalizing Heuristics: Some AI Methods for Assisting AI Programming', pp. 601-609 in IJCAI-6.

Nudel, B., and Utgoff, P.E. (1980), 'A Bibliography on Machine Learning', report CBM-TR-120, Laboratory for Computer Science Research, Rutgers University. Also pp. 54-64 in ACM SIGART Newsletter, No. 76, April 1981. Also pp. 511-549 in Machine Learning.

Osherson, D.N., Stob, M., and Weinstein, S. (1983), 'Formal Theories of Language Acquisition: Practical and Theoretical Perspectives', pp. 566-572 in IJCAI-8.

Osherson, D.N., Stob, M., and Weinstein, S. (1982), 'Ideal Learning Machines', Cognitive Science 6, 277-290.

Plotkin, G.D. (1970), 'A Note on Inductive Generalization', pp. 153-163 in Machine Intelligence 5, B. Meltzer and D. Michie (eds), Edinburgh University Press.

Quinlan, J.R. (1983a), 'Learning From Noisy Data', pp. 58-65 in IMLW.

Quinlan, J.R. (1983b), 'Learning Efficient Classification Procedures and their Application to Chess End Games', pp. 463-482 in Machine Learning.

Quinlan, J.R. (1982), 'Semi-autonomous Acquisition of Pattern-Based Knowledge', pp. 159-172 in Machine Intelligence 10, J.E. Hayes, D. Michie and Y-H Pao (eds), Ellis Horwood Ltd.

Quinlan, J.R. (1979), 'Discovering Rules From Large Collections of Examples: A Case Study', in 'Expert Systems in the Microelectronic Age', D. Michie (ed.), Edinburgh University Press.

Rendell, L.A. (1983), 'A Learning System Which Accommodates Feature Interaction', pp. 469-472 in IJCAI-8.

Selfridge, M. (1983), 'How Can CHILD learn about Agreement? Explorations of CHILD's Syntactic Inadequacies', pp. 218-220 in IMLW.

Shapiro, E.Y. (1981), 'An Algorithm That Infers Theories from Facts', pp. 446-451 in IJCAI-7.

Silver, B. (1983a), 'Learning Equation Solving Methods from Examples', pp. 429-431 in IJCAI-8.

Silver, B. (1983b), 'Learning Equation Solving Methods from Worked Examples', pp. 99-104 in IMLW.

Simon, H. and Lea, G. (1974), 'Problem-Solving and Rule Induction: A Unified View', pp. 105-127 in L. Gregg (ed.), 'Knowledge and Cognition', Lawrence Erlbaum Associates.

Sleeman, D.H. (1983), 'Inferring Student Models for Intelligent Computer Aided Instruction', pp. 483-510 in Machine Learning.

Sleeman, D.H., Langley, P., and Mitchell, T.M. (1982), 'Learning From Solution Paths: An Approach to the Credit Assignment Problem', The AI Magazine, 3(2), 48-52.

Utgoff, P.E. (1983), 'Adjusting Bias in Concept Learning', pp. 105-109 in IMLW.

Utgoff, P.E., and Mitchell, T.M. (1982), 'Acquisition of Appropriate Bias for Inductive Concept Learning', pp. 414-417 in NCAI-2.

Vere, S.A. (1981), 'Constrained N-to-1 Generalizations', unpublished.

Vere, S.A. (1980), 'Multilevel Counterfactuals for Generalizations of Relational Concepts and Productions', Artificial Intelligence 14, 139-164.

Vere, S.A. (1978), 'Inductive Learning of Relational Productions', pp. 281-296 in PDIS.

Vere, S.A. (1977), 'Relational Production Systems', Artificial Intelligence 8, 47-68.

Vere, S.A. (1975), 'Induction of Concepts in the Predicate Calculus', pp. 281-286 in IJCAI-4.

Waterman, D.A., and Hayes-Roth, F. (1978), (eds), 'Pattern-Directed Interence Systems', Academic Press.

Wexler, K., and Culicover, P.W. (1980), 'Formal Principles of Language Acquisition', MIT Press.

Wharton, R.M. (1977), 'Grammar Enumeration and Inference', Information and Control, 33, 253–272.

Willshaw D.J. and Buneman, O.P. (1972), 'Parallel and Serial Methods of Pattern Matching', pp. 357–367 in Machine Intelligence 7, B. Meltzer and D. Michie (eds), Edinburgh University Press.

Winston, P.H. (1983), 'Learning by Augmenting Rules and Accumulating Censors', pp. 2–11 in IMLW.

Winston, P.H. (1980), 'Learning and Reasoning by Analogy', Communications of the ACM, 23(12), 689–703.

Winston, P.H. (1970), 'Learning Structural Descriptions From Examples', report TR-231, AI Laboratory, MIT, Cambridge, Massachusetts. Also pp. 157–209 in P.H. Winston (ed.), 'The Psychology of Computer Vision', McGraw-Hill, 1975.

Chapter 9

Introduction to CAD

Vivienne Begg

9.1 WHY DO WE NEED CAD?

Computer aided design (CAD) for electronics is what an aqualung is for a diver. It allows him to go, without unnecessary stress, where previous to its invention only unusually gifted people had gone. The levels of **complexity** seen in ICs produced today (1983, with a minimum feature size of 1 micron) are equivalent to the complexity of a city street map covering 700 square miles, with all its road, river and rail routes detailed. That's about three and a half times the size of the London 'A to Z'.

The effort of producing a design with the complexity equivalent to just one London street map represents perhaps the limit of processing power for unaided humans. Ten years ago (when minimum feature sizes were about 5 times larger) many designers of MSI circuits were laying out chips by hand using vast sheets of Mylar, a lot of sticky tape and Stanley knives. Checking this sort of wall-sized design ('eye-balling' as it is still known in the States) is a prodigious task, with success hardly guaranteed. The logic design of such chips was a feat which forced people to lock themselves in quiet back rooms for months. The designer of the Motorola M6800, having produced one of the most complex chips ever designed in the unstructured style, was reputed to have vowed when it was finished that 'that's the last of the big mothers.' That anecdote is told by Carver Mead, whose techniques of structured design have done so much to make learning to design VLSI systems easier (Mead and Conway, 1980). But CAD started out as something very much less sophisticated than a methodology.

9.2 WHAT IS CAD?

CAD comes as a system. In order to use even one **design tool** (see Section 9.5 below for a description of some design tools) one has to put the design into the computer in such a way that it can act as input data to a program or programs. At present, this means that the design has to be expressed in a **design language**, which will be a variant of some programming language. The simplest design tools take a description of the connectivity of a layout and check for simple faults like open circuits, missed connections and also for violations of design rules. The most complicated design tools attempt the simulation of complete circuits. So a typical CAD system comprises:

A design database (libraries of components, etc.)

A set of design tools (software packages)

A set of interface programs (editors, interpreters, pre- and post-processors, etc.)

The interface programs are there to form a **man-computer interface**. This, as you will find out, can be more or less helpful, or ´user-friendly´.

The first CAD systems to be developed were large ´turnkey´ systems (Fig. 9.1), so called because they were delivered as a single package. The package included a large mainframe computer, mass storage, between 20 and 50 terminals and output peripherals of various kinds, and several suites of software. In theory, the user only had to ´turn the key´ to start it up, and the whole system went into action. This seldom happened in practice.

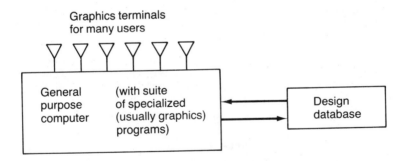

Fig. 9.1 A 'turnkey' CAD system

At present, there is a move towards single-user ´dedicated´ systems (see Fig. 9.2). These consist of a fairly conventional microcomputer, plus graphics terminal and printer/plotter. Since most CAD applications require large amounts of storage capacity for large databases and equally large amounts of processor power, this sort of system is often linked into a local area network (LAN), sharing the facilities of a large host computer. However, the single-user system provides a level of security and flexibility to the user which is often appreciated by designers. Their job is such that they cannot always predict exactly when they want to 'book in' to a multi-user system.

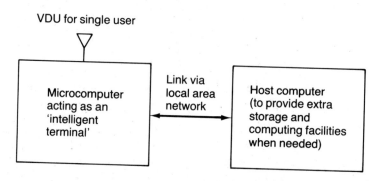

VDU for single user

Microcomputer acting as an 'intelligent terminal'

Link via local area network

Host computer (to provide extra storage and computing facilities when needed)

Fig. 9.2 The single-user CAD 'workstation'

9.3 THE DESIGN PROCESS

In most situations where CAD is in use in Britain today, the design process in electronic engineering is carried out by groups of people working in teams. This is because CAD is only used when there is a large throughput of big, high complexity designs to be produced, since the equipment on which a CAD system runs is at present very expensive (perhaps 250,000 pounds for a large turnkey system or 10,000 pounds upwards for a dedicated single-user system). Only large firms have been able to afford such capital intensive operations. Hence the CAD system is used by a design team rather than a single designer. Team work requires co-ordination and top-down design. One of the strategies for controlling complexity is the maxim 'divide and conquer'. In order to partition a complex design it is necessary to have an over-view of the system to be designed. The design team structure reflects the stages of partitioning or **functional decomposition** which occur in the design process.

Level of abstraction	Output	Produced by
System	System specification	System designer
Module	Module specification	Project manager(s)
Logic	Logic diagram	Electronic engineers
Circuit/device	Layout	Draughtsmen/designers

Fig. 9.3 **The design process for large digital applications**

These stages of digital design are illustrated in Fig. 9.3: other fields of electronics follow a similar pattern of decomposition. At each level the design is split into smaller and smaller **modules.**

Each of these levels of decomposition is represented in a different way. Logical and electrical design principles are largely the same in each case, but designers tailor the representation of the circuit to exploit properties unique to that level of design. Hence a systems designer will use the very abstract flow diagram to represent his view of the system, while the board or chip designer produces a very detailed (refined) map of the components of a particular sub-module. The I/O characteristics of the modules must be carefully mapped in order to ensure a correct result when the design is recomposed.

9.4 WHO USES CAD?

The introduction of computer aids into industry has proceeded in a uniform direction: backwards from concerns with production and distribution of the end product to the design process. As payroll programs begat accounting programs which begat stock control programs, eventually it became obvious that calculation and archiving were not the only functions a computer could perform. Combined with some techniques from robotics, manufacture and testing could be computer-assisted. In the case of design, the particular advantages of computer aids are that they are tireless and that they make no copying

errors. These characteristics are most important in the last
stages of electronic design, layout and layout verification.

True CAD tools in electronics were first developed for the
draughtsman. The difficulties of laying out large designs
became obvious very quickly: they could be drawn, but they
couldn't be verified. The computer can hold a library of
shapes for use in design and accurately check the
connectivity of a large circuit. It can also perform the
boring job of design rule checking. **Design rules** are
necessary to ensure that the design can be executed in the
available technology. They are a list of things you can't do
if you want your design to work. Just as the use of computers
in industry was increased with the development of robotics,
CAD tools have become more popular as the graphics interfaces
of systems have improved. Output from the first interactive
layout programs was displayed on very inadequate CRTs and
response times were very slow. Facilities for computer
assisted draughting have become very much more satisfactory
over the last 5 years, though there are still problems (see
Section 9.5, below).

CAD for layout is only one side of the story. There are many
CAD programs which perform analysis and simulation of
circuits. These are used by electronic engineers in circuit
design and testing. Working our way back up the design
process, it is salutary to notice that the different kinds of
programs used at different stages (e.g. design, test and
layout) were not made compatible in the beginning. You could
not take the output of one program and plug it into the input
of the next in line to form an integrated system.

If we extrapolate from the current direction of development
in CAD, we come to functional **specification**, an area in which
very little as yet has been accomplished. Systems designers
very seldom use CAD tools, and specification methods are
generally lacking in the rigor which would be necessary
before a specification could be used by a computer program.
Just as the topology of a circuit has to be translated into a
design language before it can be used in a CAD system, so has
the logic diagram and the specification. It would be
convenient if these design languages were translatable, one
into the other. This is very often not the case in real life.
If you cast your mind back to Fig. 9.3 you will realize what
all those pre- and post-processors are for.

9.5 WHAT CAD TOOLS ARE AVAILABLE?

The kind of CAD tool that is used by a designer varies between analog and digital applications and between PCB and chip technologies because these applications and technologies have very different requirements of the designer's knowledge and skill. (See Fig. 9.4 for summary of application areas in which CAD is used.)

Digital Design		Analog
Printed circuit boards	Integrated circuits	Design
Logic simulation		Circuit Analysis
Layout and layout verification		
Design rule checking		
Artwork	Mask-making	Artwork

Fig. 9.4 **Areas of design where CAD tools are used**

9.5.1 Circuit Analysis

Analog applications are declining, but are not disappearing entirely. **Circuit analysis** makes use of mathematical models to check the function of a circuit. They are circuit simulators into which a wide range of ideal component models can be plugged. The SPICE program is perhaps the most commonly used at present, and was designed for analysis of integrated circuits. However, the mathematical models on which these programs are based are only approximate. Generally speaking they do not give the designer the accuracy that is required, especially when dealing with a complex design with many variables, but they are used to provide a starting point for further (human) analysis. For low power digital requirements, circuit analysis is not necessary and hardly used.

9.5.2 Logic Simulation

The logic simulator is a complex suite of software which models behavior of a circuit in terms of logic in the time domain. It is a level of abstraction above circuit simulation (which is sometimes called 'device level simulation'). Logic simulation programs represent the circuit with signal states and logic gate operations rather than the electrical parameters of components. The output of a gate-level logic simulator is usually a time table of state transitions as a response to input waveforms.

The four flip-flop circuit in Fig. 9.5 is described in the HILO design language statements below:

```
CCT REG4 (Q[1:4],NQ[1:4],IP[1:4],P)
CCNAND
FF[1:4](IP[1:4],P,Q[1:4],NQ[1:4]),
UNID Q[1:4] NQ[1:4];
INPUT P IP[1:4].
```

The command: DISPLAYCHANGE (TIME,,S,,R,,,Q,,NQ).

will result in output from the specified monitor points at specified time intervals being displayed, as below:

```
                       N
            S  R  Q  Q     <-- monitor points

---TIME---
        0   1  1  X  X     <-- The X indicates an unknown
      120   1  0  X  X         initial state
      125   1  0  X  1
      130   1  0  0  1
      190   1  1  0  1
      220   0  1  1  1
      225   0  1  1  0
      225   0  1  1  1
      230   0  1  1  0
      290   1  1  1  0
```

Hilo input and output (from 'HILO User Manual' Sec. 4)

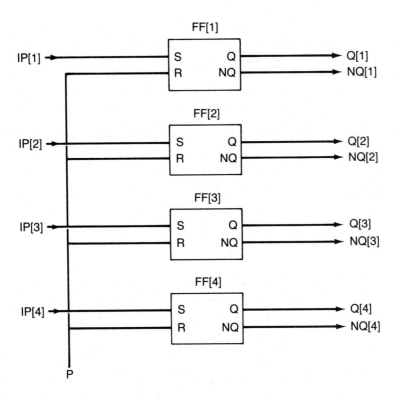

Fig. 9.5 An example circuit

There is a level of simulation above device-level and gate-level known as register-transfer level (RTL), in which a high level design language (usually based on Pascal or Algol) is used to specify the behavior of a machine and then compiled, not into machine code, but into sets of logical expressions which define synchronous finite state machines. Such a simulation is concerned only with function and hardly at all with structure, since its smallest primitives are registers. The invention of this kind of **specification language** has been important in the development of silicon compilers (see below).

9.5.3 Automatic Layout Routines

Computer aids for layout help in the task of transforming the circuit or logic diagram into a map of the positions of actual components and wires. Although all layout programs perform the same sort of functions (e.g. placement, routing, compaction), applications for printed circuit boards (PCBs) and integrated circuits (ICs) are slightly different and will be treated separately.

9.5.4 PCB Layout Routines

Input to a layout routine is a description of the components and the connectivity of a circuit (sometimes called a **netlist**). This description is sometimes generated automatically, using a **circuit extractor**, but may be put into the computer by hand using a **digitizer**. Connectivity will be the same at the logic and the device levels, but components will differ: individual logic-level gates have to be **packaged** into standard components which perform the same function. Once gates have been packaged, the resulting components can be **placed**. Automatic placement programs divide a board area into a matrix of ´slots´ into which only one component can fit. Then the most connected components are selected first for placement, starting roughly in the middle of the board.

Automatic packaging programs do exist, but results are not satisfying to many designers. A draughtsman can see and appreciate the contents of the whole board: the program only has the netlist description, which is at a level of representation too low to incorporate much information about function. The experienced draughtsman/designer has a store of knowledge about packaging and placement (which components will be sensitive, where screening is required, when to place components near edge connectors) which have not as yet be incorporated into the programs.

9.5.5 Automatic Routing

Once components have been placed, automatic routing programs can be used to connect components together in the specified way. This sounds like a simple process, but there is one more set of constraints to be taken into consideration: the design rules. There could be 15 to 150 design rules laid down for a particular project, those for routing covering width of tracks, clearances, acceptable angles of turn, etc. Even without incorporating such constraints (and others, like making the most economical use of metal) the routing algorithms used are complex in themselves. Commonly used algorithms, like the Manhattan or Lee algorithms, are constantly being enhanced, but their performance suffers from underlying formal problems.

The algorithms treat the circuit as a tree. They are designed to make branching decisions as routes round the circuit are completed. Early decisions are crucially important, since a badly placed wire can obstruct later progress. The form in which the problem is represented is liable to generate a multiplicity of alternative routes which results in a combinatorial explosion of branching decisions. Like the 'travelling salesman' problem, the routing problem in this form is mathematically intractable. New forms of algorithm are being invented (river-routing, wave propagation models, (DA Conf. 1982 and 1983) which overcome some of these problems.

CAD operators find that automatic routers can be used in some areas of a board and not in others. The performance of a program in specific conditions depends on the algorithm used. Routers tend to be interactive to a large degree, allowing the user to set up the board in such a way as to present an easier problem, and to finish the routing when no more tracks can be completed by the program. Most autorouters will complete up to 75-90% of a board. Given that the program is unlikely to produce a 100% complete routing in a reasonable time (under a couple of hours), the draughtsman is happy to finish off manually. However, the solution provided by the computer may seem very odd to the draughtsman, perhaps using

far too many via holes, or not leaving any room for the last
tracks to be routed through.

9.5.6 Design Rule Checkers

Design rule checkers (DRCs) are universally considered to be
the most boring kind of CAD tool. They are basically a
codification in the form of a set of rules of the limitations
of the implementation technology. A design rule set is
prefaced with a set of definitions, and comprises a list of
rules of the following form:

```
      RULE MAX LENGTH                    [rule name
           FAIL '' IF LENGTH(WIRE) < 8   [fail condition
      END
```

This is a very simple rule with only one condition. An error
message (textual or in the form of a graphical pointer) is
returned if the length of any wire in the circuit is over 8
units long. Some rules may have four or five conditions
linked in a Boolean expression.

Since most DRCs use the technique of exhaustive search to
detect such violations, they are painfully slow: so slow that
one often does not know whether or not the system has hung
up! If more than a few errors are discovered in a design, the
resulting superimposed graphical pointers can be very
difficult to read. Moreover, DRCs have a reputation for
producing spurious errors (errors are signalled where they do
not exist). There are many sources of spurious errors: where
design data is digitized, for instance, spurious errors can
be avoided if digitizing is done in a particular order. Many
of the faults of existing DRCs could be eliminated by
redesign of bad software, but not all.

9.5.7 Automatic Layout for ICs

Moving from CAD tools for PCB layout to those for chip design
is a major step. The materials and manufacturing methods for
ICs are so different from those of boards that design styles
are bound to differ, and the newness of IC technology has
lead to developments of design methodology which have been
affected by the necessity for using CAD tools.

The output of the design process for ICs is not a single
diagram, but a set of masks in metal on glass, for etching,
vapor deposition or ion implantation on the silicon wafer.
Drawing the artwork for those masks by hand would be
completely out of the question. The data to produce mask sets
must be generated from CAD output. Computer aids for design
and manufacture have been heavily relied on in the semiconductor industry for years, and their use is taken for
granted to a greater extent than in other areas of electronic
design.

A selection of tools for IC design

Level of abstraction	Representation used	Product
Register transfer level	High level programming language	Specification
Logic level	Logic description	Logic simulation
Circuit level	Loose layout plan	Sticks diagram
Geometry level	Standard code (e.g. CIF)	Mask generation data

Fig. 9.6 **The design process for integrated circuits**

If you are using a silicon compiler (see below) then the
first step in design (and maybe your last) will be the
specification of the behavior of the system to be designed in
a high level specificaton language. Otherwise, the first step
in IC design is **floor-planning.** This is equivalent to the
functional decomposition of a system design. The chip area is
partitioned into **functional blocks** (e.g. control section,
ALU, memory, etc.) which are then refined further. Blocks may
be decomposed into sub-modules before logic diagrams are
completed for each section (e.g. the INMOS CAD system).

Logic diagrams can be used to generate layout, but designers
often choose to work interactively with a **sticks diagram**
editor, which provides an intermediate format which indicates
relative placement and interconnection of layout symbols.
This loose symbolic layout plan is then expanded into the
real geometry using the design rules, thus removing the need
for design rule checking. The results can be used directly
for simulation and layout verification (e.g. GAELIC).

Few designs are completely original. Some elements of IC
designs can be used over and over again: these are called
standard cells. CAD systems have large **cell libraries** which
can be used both by designers and by programs which generate
particular parts of a design, like data paths (e.g. Shrobe,
1982). The use of automatic generation techniques not only
reduces the chance of human errors being introduced, but cuts
down the (high) cost of design rule checking.

9.5.8 Silicon Compilers

´A silicon compiler translates a behavioural
description of a function into a set of geometric
images which can be used to fabricate an
integrated circuit that performs that function. A
sophisticated silicon compiler has the potential
of allowing the design of very large circuits
based on the same methodology that allows modern
software compilers to generate very large complex
programs.´   (Rupp, 1981)

Silicon compilers bring together all the functions performed
by the tools mentioned above and provide an integrated system
which produces mask generation data from a formal
specification. The function of the IC designer who uses this
kind of design tool has changed considerably from the that of
the board designer, who used to produce circuit diagrams ´on
the back of an envelope´. The designer who uses a silicon
compiler has to have the skills of a programmer: instead of
drawing diagrams, he has to be able to write specifications
in a high level programming language.

The big difference between using a conventional CAD system
and a silicon compiler is that with a silicon compiler one
cannot access the intermediate stages of the design. The

process is executed as if by a ´black box´, with no
opportunities to modify what the program produces. The
silicon compilation process has advantages in that it is very
quick, compared with other CAD techniques, and almost
completely error free (barring errors in the specification).

There are disadvantages, too. Most silicon compilers are
limited in scope, because they are fixed programs working
with a limited range of standard cells from a library. They
tend to be designed to produce ICs for a particular range of
applications (e.g. FIRST (Bergmann, 1983), the Edinburgh
University silicon compiler for VLSI digital signal
processing systems). General purpose silicon compilers are
under development, (e.g. Rupp, 1981 , Siskind et al. 1982,
Anceau, 1983) but will be some time before they are widely
used in industry. One reason for this is the inefficiency of
designs produced in this way. They tend, because they are
generated from standard cells and optimized automatically, to
be somewhat wasteful of silicon and this leads to poor
performance compared with that of a design optimized by a
human designer.

9.5.9 Summary of Effect of IC Technology on Design Methods

The impact of computers on this area of industry has
proceeded from the lower levels of the design process towards
the upper levels of specification in the same backwards
fashion as everywhere else. First the ´easy´ jobs (working
through checklists, archiving) are automated, then the more
demanding tasks (big calculations, simulation of complex
processes). Yet it is only when the demands of technology,
driven by the demands of the market, force engineers into
using CAD tools in their everyday work that a change in
design methodology is brought about. Historically, design
methods have changed over periods of centuries, not decades.
Yet developments in semiconductor technology have made
designers look at electronic design in completely different
ways.

One example is that of the development of parallel
architectures. The technology has provided the opportunity to
put a whole computer on a chip. In order to increase
processor speeds, some designers have abandoned the
conventional Von Neuman serial architecture and schemes for
parallel processing have had to be invented. Invention has

flourished in many areas: at the formal level (e.g. Milner's
calculus of communicating systems, Milner, 1980); in
programming languages (e.g. occam, Taylor and Wilson, 1982)
the language INMOS developed for implementing concurrent
systems; in the field of system architectures (e.g. systolic
array processing, Kung, in Mead and Conway, 1979).

9.6 HOW COULD WE GO ABOUT DESIGNING A BETTER SYSTEM?

In the opening paragraphs, you may have noticed that whenever
early CAD systems were referred to, a criticism was made of
their man-computer interface. They lacked adequate display
facilities, methods of representation of design data were
inappropriate and different parts of the CAD system were not
linked together, thus creating opportunities for errors to be
introduced into the system. Just as computer systems were
introduced into industry by the back door, and were first
used in the electronics field at the bottom level of the
design process, the man-computer interface (being at the top
level of the system) is usually the last thing to be
considered in a system design. It is at this point that some
of the knottiest problems in software and hardware
engineering come to the surface.

9.6.1 A Better Man-Computer Interface

In hardware terms, peripherals have to be provided that are
physically suitable media for human 'data input': the science
of ergonomics determines what can be termed suitable for us,
which provides some long-standing headaches for peripherals
manufacturers. (e.g. in providing large, flat, flicker-free,
touch-sensitive display screens.) In software terms, programs
have to be produced which communicate to the user what the
system is doing, and which allow the user to control system
output. It is assumed by most researchers in the field of
man-computer interaction that successful modeling of the
user's task will improve the degree of communication and
control that a person has with a computer (Gaines and Facey,
1975).

If we take this argument to its logical conclusion, the first
step in designing a CAD system will be to construct a model

of the design task and from that build the system's man-
computer interface <u>first</u>, and then think about I/O
characteristics for the kind of machine we could build behind
it. After all, this is only an application of the top-down
design method! We know, from asking engineers who work with
CAD, that:

* User interaction is desirable at all levels of the
  system in order to provide a true general purpose
  system. Otherwise a silicon compiler will fit the bill.

* The output of one design tool should be compatible with
  the input of the next in line, to reduce human
  transcription errors.

* There should be a range of appropriate representations
  of the design available at each level of abstraction
  (system, RTL, logic (gate), circuit, geometry and
  perhaps others?).

* All aspects of the man-machine interface should be
  supportive (i.e. crash-proof, with on-line documentation
  available, etc.)

                                              (from Begg, 1983)

This provides a start point for a better system. If we
collect together all the design tools at our disposal, how
can we best link them together? Are they sufficient to
perform the whole task we have in mind?

9.6.2 What Goes Behind the Interface?

Remembering the discussion on automatic layout, particularly
the effects of technological developments on IC design,
reminds us that a true design aid will not be only a symbolic
representation of the objects which a designer manipulates to
produce a design, but also of the methods that he uses to do
this manipulation. The biggest problem facing CAD system
designers is how to build systems flexible enough to allow
the representation of different design methodologies. A
frequently cited criterion for a successful CAD system is
that it should embody an abstract design methodology which is
technology independent. If this is achieved, designs can be
implemented in whatever technology becomes available. The
technique of structured (top-down) design, borrowed from
software engineering, represents an element of such a

methodology,   the evolution of formal specification languages
is   another.   Structured   design gives   a   framework,   formal
specification   gives a language for description,   but what is
required   to make a really flexible system is a set of   plans
of action which represent different design methodologies,   or
design styles.

Most   silicon   compilers   do not provide an   answer   to   this
question,   because   they   implement   only   a   part   of   one
particular   design   methodology   for   a   small   range   of
applications. To do more than this, one has to start applying
different   programming   techniques   which   will   supplement
conventional procedures.   In short,   it is necessary to go to
the   field of artificial intelligence (AI) to get some   ideas
on how to represent new design alternatives.

9.7 TECHNIQUES FROM ARTIFICIAL INTELLIGENCE FOR CAD

CAD   presents   a number of problems to the   systems   designers
which are canonical problems in AI: particularly in knowledge
representation   and   acquisition,   language   translation   and
search   through   large   and   complex   spaces.   Some   basic
characteristics of the problems that design poses are thought
to   be inherently intractable to automation.   Which are they,
and   which parts of the design process are easy to   put   into
the   form of a program?   Which of the armory of   programming
techniques   from AI should we use and where   in   the   system
should they be used? If we can answer some of these questions
it   will   take   us   a little closer to a   more   flexible   and
effective CAD system.

9.7.1 Design as an Ill-structured Problem

Herbert   Simon is one of the founding fathers of AI.   He   was
the   co-author of GPS (General Problem Solver),   one   of   the
first   attempts at an ´intelligent´ program,   a program   that
didn´t have to be told how to perform a procedure,   but found
out   for   itself how to do it.   It was the foundation of   the
´problem-solving´ paradigm.   GPS was not a success,   in   one
sense, for it failed to solve anything but a limited range of
types of problem.   But its results lead to an appreciation of
the   importance of the way that a problem was **represented** in

the computer, and the way that the relative tractability of problems was related to this representation. Simon has looked at the problems of automating design (Simon, 1973), and his conclusions are relevant to our field.

Design is considered to be an 'ill-structured problem', i.e. one which is difficult to formalize and thus difficult to solve, especially for man-made problem solvers. The design can be seen as a solution proposed to the problem: 'Find a machine whose performance matches this specification.' A well-structured problem has a well-defined **initial state**, a **goal state** and intermediate states which can be brought about by the application of **plans.**

In the first place, for electronic design, the goal state is not well-defined. There is no fixed criterion by which one can judge a design to be a good solution to the problem posed by the specification. In effect, the final criterion for a successful electronic design is that the customer judges the performance of a prototype, or breadboard, version of the design. Since the initial specification was almost certainly not a formal, rigorous or complete statement of expected behavior (a sort of functional equation), then a mechanizable test for a 'correct solution' is not possible.

Moreover, it is difficult to say exactly what the initial state is, in our design problem. In a sense it is 'the state of the art': a description of all the machines it is possible to make in the available technology. This is difficult to describe, since the technology in question is at present undergoing rapid development. This means that it is not only not well understood, but very volatile. Obviously, if we cannot completely describe the initial state or the goal state, transitions between the two are not going to be easy to represent.

Besides all this, Simon points out that in a problem area like design, one has to plan actions on the world outside the computer: if this is so, then one's representations must take into account the laws of nature, so that the designs that are created are physically possible. This sounds very obvious, but is in fact an area of disagreement within the field of engineering. In describing the kinds of representations of the design used at different stages, the term 'levels of abstraction´ was used. At high levels of abstraction, the representation is not concerned with the physical details of the implementation (e.g. a logic diagram does not map onto any particular layout of a board or chip). It is not necessary to take the laws of nature into account at that level. However, at lower levels, as we have pointed out in the case of the design rules, it is necessary to incorporate information about the implementation technology into the design. The degree to which a design is efficient and effective will depend to a large extent on how well these low level constraints are incorporated into the design process.

Most people will have come across at least two types of engineer. There are those who consider that electronic design can be done with only the most gross considerations of the materials in which the design is to be carried out. There are others who swear by their ´feel´ for the materials, and neglect the use of high level design aids. Part of the reason for this difference in cognitive style is in an engineer´s education and training, part in his working environment. Those who advocate the use of silicon compilers and technology independent design methods are in the former camp, but the opinions of the practical engineer deserve a hearing, too. Some parts of the design process have been automated, but other aspects resist formalization. These less formal aspects constitute the real ´expertise´ of the engineer, and it is those aspects which it is hoped that AI techniques will capture.

9.7.2 Design as Problem Solving

Although the prognosis for a successful ´problem-solving´ approach to electronic design looks gloomy, it is possible to attack from this angle. Gerald Sussman, in the SLICES program (Sussman, 1978) took as an initial state, the specification of a circuit, then decomposed it into ever smaller sub-units, until a unit matched an item in a database of partial designs. The decomposition was guided by several types of constraint embodying different kinds of knowledge, including one technique which Sussman termed ´knowing the form of the answer´. To develop this technique, Sussman used observations of expert circuit designers who ´use terminal equivalence and power arguments to reduce the apparent synergy of the circuit so that their computational power can be focused.´ Sussman knew perfectly well that the problems posed by circuit analysis were algebraically intractable, and so he used expert heuristics to guide the decomposition of the circuit into units which were simple enough to describe, analyze and match with known circuit elements.

Once the circuit was represented in terms of known partial designs, a new problem arose. How were the partial designs to be recomposed? The level of decomposition of the designs was so low that many of the composition rules invented for the purpose were similar to each other. A method of inventing more general composition rules was needed. The form of the representation (a rule-based language) was very far from known methods and techniques in engineering, so one could not go to human experts to look for such general rules. Also, the final design had to be debugged: the procedure of ´problem solving by debugging almost-right plans´ works well when the plans are on a small scale, but it threatens to break down when applied to very complex designs. Sussman´s early work demonstrates that a simple approach to decomposition and to problem representation will not be enough to master the complexity of large designs. We need a more sophisticated decomposition method which will break up the design in a more intelligent fashion, and a form of representation which tells us much more about specific sets of attributes of a system that we are interested in at different stages of the design.

9.7.3 Design as Expertise

The KBVLSI project at Xerox PARC and Stanford, led by Mark Stefik, took a different approach (Stefik et al., 1982b). They used the paradigm of **expert systems** to tackle the design problem: an expert system is basically a collection of facts and **inference rules** about an expert **domain**, called a **knowledge base**, plus an **inference engine** which checks the validity of sets of statements about the domain by a simple pattern matching search process.

PALLADIO, the KBVLSI expert system, is based on a series of representations which are designed to capture specific aspects of knowledge about design, termed ´description levels´.

Description level	Concerns	Terms	Composition rules	Bugs avoided
Linked module abstraction LMA	Event sequencing	Modules Forks Joins Buffers	Token conservation Fork/join rules	Deadlock Data not ready
Clocked registers and logic CRL	Clocking 2 phase	Stages Register transfer Transfer functions	Connection of stages	Mixed clk bugs Unclocked feedback
Clocked primitive switches CPS	Digital behavior	Pull-ups Pull-downs Pass Transistors	Connection of switch networks Ratio rules	Charge sharing Switching levels
Layout	Physical dimensions	Colored rectangles	Lambda rules	Spacing errors

Fig. 9.7 **Levels of description for VLSI**
(from Stefik et al., 1982b)

'Each description level has a set of terms that are
composed to form systems and a set of composition
rules that define legal combinations of the terms.
The concerns of each level are characterised by
specific classes of bugs that can be avoided when
the composition rules are followed.'
(p.45 Stefik et al., 1982b)

Design is seen as a search through a space of possible
designs which can be generated dynamically according to known
specification constraints. These designs are defined in ever
increasing detail at successive levels of abstraction. Stefik
and his colleagues discriminated between the notion of
abstraction   and   that   of   functional   decomposition.
Decomposition splits up designs into a 'component hierarchy',
of function/ structure correspondences, while abstraction
serves a different purpose. Abstraction is a way of stating
design problems so that specific issues can be faced at the
appropriate stage of a design, and across the breadth of the

design. Pre-emptive design decisions can be made early on, to
prevent faulty designs being generated.

This radically different way of looking at electronic design
offered the opportunity of capturing some types of knowledge
about design decision-making which was previously un-
formalizable. However, this form of representation still
poses the problem of translation between levels: how are we
to be sure that the scheme proposed in the abstract will be
implemented accurately? We can be sure that certain classes
of bugs are eliminated, but we cannot vouch for others.

The work of Stefik and his colleagues shows how far we can
get in substituting a new kind of representation for
electronic designs, relevant to design constraints which are
of increased importance in VLSI technology. It also shows how
the models we have of decomposition and abstraction levels
are crucially important in the timing of design decisions,
and how necessary it is to have some degree of formal
correspondence between design descriptions so that designs
can be verified.

9.7.4 The Nature of Expertise

It should now be clear that CAD system design is a problem
area which exercises all the skills of the conventional
programmer and the ´knowledge engineer´. In order to make the
design of large complex electronic systems tractable, some
parts of the design process have to be automated. This
involves capturing knowledge about electronic engineering in
at least three ways: as various **forms of representation**
which give us easy access to specific aspects of a problem in
design, as **algorithms** which embody well-known procedures, and
as **heuristics**, the rules of thumb which allow us to overcome
the drawbacks of a developing and poorly understood
technology.

How do all these different ways of capturing knowledge fit
together? The structure of a CAD system that uses all three
methods will have to be different from that of currently used
CAD systems, which have too little structure, being no more
than loose collections of tools, and from silicon compilers
and the like, which have a very firm structure which does not
allow for human intervention. We assume human intervention to

be necessary and to a certain degree desirable, because the designs created by CAD have to show a responsiveness to change (in technological possibilities and in the demands of the market) which is at present not part of the behavioural repetoire of computer programs. Some forms of expertise can be more or less fossilized: in the domain of medicine, there are just so many symptoms detectable in a patient, even though the range of diseases may increase every day; but design remains for the time being an ´ill-structured´ and partially intractable problem for the computer scientist.

Given that we want to use all the available means to use knowledge about electronic design, and that users are a crucial part of the system, we should investigate the possibility of improving human-computer communication, and propose a flexible and comprehensible structure for CAD.

9.7.5 New Ways to Communicate with Programs

Part of the spin-off from large AI projects has been a range of tools for effective communication between people and programs which can be loosely grouped under the heading **knowledge acquisition systems** (KAS). These systems consist of a set of programs to do with making communication easier, and a more complex set to do with storing, organizing and retrieving information from a knowledge base.

Examples of facts about the domain of electronic engineering could be definitions of primitive components or units of decomposition (like the block called ´control section´ on a chip). In the case of CAD, some of the rules would be composition rules, others would perhaps be concerned with interpretation of simulation data, or with choice of style of design with respect to the technology being used. The contents of the knowledge base are usually arranged in a semantic network so that related concepts can be readily identified.

A KAS is founded on a natural-language-like **command language.** This enables users to talk to the computer in a subset of English including all of the expert jargon necessary to concisely express key concepts in the domain. New concepts can be added to the computers lexicon by the user. In this excerpt from a session with PROSPECTOR (Duda and Hart,

(1980), a consultant for mineral exploration, the computer is asking the questions and the geologist is giving estimates of probability and issuing commands to the system. (User's input underlined.)

```
1 -- To what degree do you believe that the prospect is in a
       volcanic province ? 5
P(H|E) = .02

2 -- To  what degree do you believe that there are dikes  in
       the area ? 5
P(H|E) = .02

3 -- What is the pyrite concentration (in %) ? ??
```

Legal answers are:

1 ... The lower and upper bounds of an interval, or a single number.
2 ... A taxonomy name for an interval.
3 ... A PROSPECTOR-command.

Type '??n' for more information about option n.

```
3 -- What is the pyrite concentration (in %) ? 4.6 5.8
       What is your confidence in this estimate? 4
P(H|E) = .0265661

4 -- To what degree do you believe that there is biotite? -2
P(H|E) = .0645086

5 -- To  what degree so you believe that hornblende has been
       altered to biotite ? SUMMARIZE
```

    My certainty in

1. XYZ-type deposit is now 1.21547

Do you wish to see additional information? YES

I suspect that
1 - (*XYZ-type deposit) (1.21547)

There is one favourable factor:
1: 1. favourable intrusives in target area 4.99999

There is one positive factor with neutral effect that, if
negative, could have been significant:

1: 2. You were sure that the prospect is in a volcanic
      province   5.0
                      ** would have hurt if negative **

There is one uncertain factor whose score may be subject to
                                                     change:

1: 3. favourable zones .227085

For which of the above do you wish to see additional
information? (etc.)

                                            (from Reboh, 1981)

This particular excerpt demonstrates the way in which the new
information being gathered by the system can be summarized
for the user so that missing data can be added and also how
explanations are given for inferences which the system has
made.

The man-computer relationship can be strained by the fact
that computers usually do not accept bad spelling or typing
errors, whereas people invariably make mistakes. This can be
eased by a concept from natural language understanding
programs usually called DWIM (´do what I mean (not what I
say)´) which allows the computer to guess at what was meant
when commands are garbled. Commands are only carried out
after the computer´s interpretation is confirmed with the
user.

Another useful tool for communication is the **browser**, which
allows the user to locate and read files and databases in the
system. Its structure is rather like that of a thesaurus: one
can choose classes and subclasses of information to look at.
For example, if the user wants to learn something specific
about the system, the class ´teaching programs´ can be
chosen, and within it the subclass containing the relevant
documentation, rather than having to start at the beginning
of a more elementary teaching session.

The inside of a KAS consists of programs which check the
validity of new facts and rules before storing them away in
appropriate places. When the user presents the KAS with a new
piece of information, the system checks to see whether it has
that information already in an identical or similar form, or
whether it actually contradicts anything in the knowledge
base. If the information is anomalous in some way, the new
statement (fact or rule) is presented to the user alongside
the similar or contradictory old statement, and the user can
make the necessary adjustments. If the statements are
similar, they might be grouped together under the same
heading. If they are contradictory, rephrasing of either
statement or perhaps restructuring of the knowledge base may
be necessary.

One of the most useful aspects of the expert systems paradigm
is the **explanation** facilities provided by knowledge based
programs. The system can give an account of its reasons for
recommending a particular action, or for performing a
procedure. This sort of facility would be very useful in CAD
systems for debugging designs. Communication on this level
with programs gives us a much better chance to recognize and
capture high level heuristics for design which are used every
day by designers, but remain implicit, unstated and
unformalized.

9.8 WHAT WILL CAD SYSTEMS OF THE FUTURE LOOK LIKE?

There are several sorts of constraint on the future
development of CAD of electronics. Firstly, developments in
hardware equipment for CAD are producing smaller, cheaper,
yet more complex systems, which are able to be customized to
a particular user's requirements, and which can be connected
to existing computer networks. Peripherals are becoming more
and more sophisticated, with some functions being put into
hardware which used to be implemented in large software
suites, e.g. graphics programs. We can look forward to many
different modalities of man-computer interaction, too, like
voice input and output, and touch-sensitive screens. Other
basic requirements, like parsers for languages and inference
engines for expert systems are likely to be put onto
comparatively cheap chips.

For some applications, computers will not continue to 'aid' design, but will take it over completely, and with automatic manufacturing plant and test equipment, eliminate the human element in the design and manufacture of some types of electronic goods. The concept of a 'silicon foundry', a commercial service which takes specifications and turns them very quickly, with the help of silicon compilers, into chips, is part of this direction for CAD. Constraints that affect this kind of development are a) the volatility of the market (how important is it to reduce design times?), b) the tractability of the technology (how far can the technology be stretched to fit a rigidly structured design methodology?), c) volume of production (how much of the product do we need to sell before we make a profit?) and d) the familiarity of the application (is the design already well known, or do we have to start from scratch?).

For well-known, high volume products in a stable market, an automatic design and manufacturing system is ideal. If the market is volatile and volume low, then a silicon foundry delivers the goods. There are still a good number of applications for which the capital expenditure on a completely automatic system is too high and the output of a silicon foundry unsuitable. Human designers, working with intelligent CAD tools, have a considerable part to play in the development of electronic technology.

One of the changes which increasing computer automation brings about is an increased interest in the nature of the high levels of systems. When the low levels are well understood enough to be left to machines, the higher, abstract levels of design are thrown into relief. Research in CAD will be directed toward acquiring knowledge about abstract representations of designs and their relationship to each other, and especially about the nature of specification. As well as providing the 'technology independence' which is sought after by some researchers, this sort of interest borders on the realms of applied mathematics and is as yet far removed from the gritty pragmatics of electronic system manufacturing.

Intelligent CAD tools will act as store-houses for our developing knowledge, to which we can add and from which we can learn. There is no doubt that interaction with CAD systems will change the face of electronic engineering. Many of the skills thought indispensable for an engineer will be lost and other skills, so far neglected, will have to be acquired. Some distinctions between engineering disciplines must be ignored before progress can be made. Hardware and software engineering, for instance, which are becoming indistinguishable from each other in practice, are disciplines in which interchange of ideas can be very fruitful. There must be radical changes in engineering education now, so that people can keep up with the pace of change in the future.

QUESTIONS

Think back to the last circuit you designed ´by hand´:

Did you do preliminary drawings?
How did you represent the design?
Did you use more than one form of representation (e.g. block
diagram, logic diagram, Petri net, state transition table)?

If you have used CAD tools, compare your procedure when
designing manually with the one you used with the CAD system.

What are the differences between designing hardware and
designing software?

If you can cook, write down the design rules for making meat
pies:

What aspects of culinary technology are crucial for
successful pie-making in general?
Can you conceive of some levels of abstraction for cookery?
(Look at the structure of a cookery book.)
Design a CAD tool for pie-makers that pie-makers can
understand.

If you can´t cook, write a specification for a bedroom:

How much of the specification is a description of
environmental parameters and how much a description of the
required ´behavioral characteristics´ of a ´machine for
living in´? (Le Corbusier)

How far can you go in ´abstracting´ a description of a
bedroom? What new ideas does your most abstract description
give you about the design of rooms in general?

Would implementation of your bedroom specification require
lots of custom design, or could it be put together from
ready-made components? (Are you excessively tall? Have you
got a bad back, like me? What sort of things do you do in
bed?)

When you are furnishing your room at home, what sort of
compromises are you forced to make because you can´t design
your own furniture? Could you live in a ´standard cell´?

REFERENCES

Anceau, F. (1983) ˊCAPRI: a Design Methodology and a Silicon Compiler for VLSI Circuits Specified by Algorithms ́, in Bryant (ed.) (1983).

Begg, V. (1983) ˊMaking CAD Tools for Electronic Design more Usable ́, Technical Report, M.C.S.G., Department of Computer Science, Brunel University.

Bergmann, N. (1983) ˊA Case Study of the F.I.R.S.T. Silicon Compiler ́ in Bryant (ed) (1983).

Bobrow, D.G., and Goldstein, I.P. (1980) ˊRepresenting Design Alternatives ́, Proc. AISB-80.

Bryant, R. (ed) (1983) Proc. 3rd Caltech Conf. on VLSI, Computer Science Press.

DA Conf. (1982) and (1983) Proceedings 19th and 20th EE Design Automation conferences, IEEE.

Duda, R.O. (1980) ˊThe Prospector System For Mineral Exploration ́, Final report, SRI project 8172, AI Center, SRI International, 333 Ravenswood Road, Menlo Park, Cal. (April 1980).

Frank, E.H., and Sproull, R.F. (1981) ˊTesting and Debugging Custom ICs ́, ACM Computing Surveys 13 (4), 425-451.

Gaines, B.R., and Facey, P.V. (1975) ˊSome Experience in Interactive System Development and Application ́, Proceedings of the Inst. of Electrical and Electronic Engineers 63, 894 - 911.

Maguire, M. (1982) ˊAn Evaluation of Published Recommendations on the Design of Man-computer Dialogues ́ Int. J. Man-Machine Studies 16, 237-261.

Mead, C., and Conway, L. (1979) ˊAn Introduction to VLSI Systems ́, Addison Wesley.

Michie, D. (ed.) (1979) ˊExpert Systems in the Micro-electronic Age ́, Edinburgh University Press.

Milner, R. (1980) ˊA Calculus of Communicating Systems ́, Lecture Notes in Computer Science no. 92, Springer Verlag.

Reboh, R. (1981) ´Knowledge Engineering Techniques and Tools in the Prospector Environment´, Technical Note 243, SRI International.

Rupp, C.R. (1981) ´Components of a Silicon Compiler System´ in Proceedings VLSI 81, (Edinburgh), J.P. Gray (ed.), Academic Press.

Shrobe, H.E. (1982) ´The Data Path Generator´ in Penfield, P. (ed.), Proceedings, Conference on Advanced Research in VLSI., MIT.

Simon, H.A. (1973) ´The Structure of Ill-structured Problems´, Artificial Intelligence 4, 145.

Siskind, J.M., et al. (1982) ´Generating Custom High Performance VLSI Designs from Succinct Algorithmic Descriptions.´ in Penfield (ed) (1982), Proc. Conf. on Advanced Research in VLSI, MIT Press, 1982.

Stefik, M., et al. (1982a) ´The Organisation of Expert Systems: a Tutorial´, Artificial Intelligence 18, 135-173.

Stefik, M., et al. (1982) ´The Partitioning of Concerns in Digital System Design´, Proc. MIT Conference on Advanced Research in VLSI 1982, p.43.

Sussman, G.J. (1977) ´Electrical Design: a Problem for AI´, MIT AI Memo No.425.

Sussman, G.J. (1978) ´SLICES: At the Boundary Between Analysis and Synthesis´, in Latombe, J.C.(ed.) ´Artificial Intelligence and Pattern Recognition in Computer Aided Design,´ North Holland.

Sussman, G.J., et al. (1979) ´Computer Aided Evolutionary Design for Digital Integrated Systems´, MIT AI Memo No.526.

Taylor, R., and Wilson, P. (1982) ´Process Oriented Language Meets Demands of Distributed Processing´, Electronics, 30 Nov. 1982.

Weiss, S., et al. (1981) ´Building Expert Systems for Controlling Complex Programs´, Proc. IJCAI 81, p.322.

Chapter 10

Associative processing

R. M. Lea

10.1 INTRODUCTION

An increasing proportion of the work-load of modern computer systems involves the representation and manipulation of mainly non-numerical data structures. For example, editing, compiling, file-processing, table sorting and searching all involve extensive processing of symbolic data which have no numerical meaning. Moreover, the ´information explosion´, seen in recent years in all fields of human endeavor, has already stimulated the development of computer-based ´information systems´ to assist the creation, modification, classification, storage, retrieval and dissemination of mainly ´textual´ data. Furthermore, the current interest in ´database management systems´, ´expert systems´ and ´intelligent knowledge-based systems´ will inevitably increase the demand for non-numerical information processing. Nevertheless, minicomputer and microcomputer hardware is almost invariably designed for mainly numerical computation. Clearly, design optimization for fast high-precision arithmetic provides little benefit for non-numerical information processing. Indeed, the lack of flexible data structuring facilities is a major impediment to cost-effective information system design.

The lack of suitable hardware for structured data processing has forced system analysts and programmers to develop software techniques for non-numerical information processing. For example, non-numerical programming languages such as LISP, SNOBOL, SETL and PROLOG have become well established and text string processing extensions to less specialized languages such as BASIC and PASCAL are widespread. However, the implementation of such software techniques on numerically-oriented computers can lead to complex, expensive, inefficient and possibly unreliable information processing systems. Indeed, the ´software mountains´ required for flexible ´database management systems´ and ´intelligent knowledge-based systems´ are daunting prospects.

Fortunately, there are signs that the future for non-numerical information processing systems is rather more encouraging. The increasing cost of software development is already seriously limiting its cost-effectiveness over an increasingly wide range of computer applications. Moreover, at the same time, the rapidly growing interest in ´information technology´ and the prospect of VLSI (Very Large

Scale Integration) are stimulating proposals for radically
new microcomputer chip architectures. In particular, VLSI
offers the potential of low-cost building-blocks for the
flexible support and manipulation of non-numerical data
structures.

This chapter reviews the fundamental features of non-
numerical information processing and considers the design
requirements for a new computer architecture to be dedicated
to relational data processing. In particular, the suitability
of the associative parallel processor is discussed and
progress towards its integration on a VLSI chip is reported.
The application of this associative processing component in
a ´back-end relational data processing architecture´ is also
discussed.

10.2 NON-NUMERICAL INFORMATION PROCESSING

The fundamental features of an information processing machine
are manifest in the need to

(1) represent information by means of, possibly
    complex, data structures (viz. an ensemble of related
    data elements)

    e.g. consider a ´family tree´: a common data structure
         in which the data elements are named persons
         related by birth or marriage

(2) reference data elements via relevant relationships
    within the data structure

    e.g. ´grandfather of´
         ´sister of wife of brother of´
         etc.

(3) execute simple logical and relational (as opposed to
    arithmetic) operations on referenced data elements

    e.g. name the father-in-law of person X
         list the first-born of the male descendants of
         person Y, etc.

(4)   interact meaningfully with the user

      e.g. in terms of recognizable names and relationships
      in a cost-effective manner.

10.2.1 Data Modelling

There   are three fundamental models of structured data [1],
these being the

(1) hierarchic model: a   'tree'   of   data   elements,
                        supporting 'one-way navigation' from
                        the 'root-node' to a 'referenced
                        leaf-node', as indicated in Fig.
                        10.1,

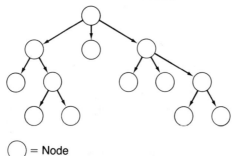

○ = Node

Fig. 10.1 Hierarchic data model

(2) network model: a 'directed graph' of data elements,
                        supporting   'one-way   navigation'
                        from any 'node' to any 'node' as
                        indicated in Fig. 10.2;

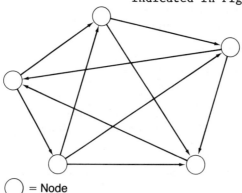

○ = Node

Fig. 10.2 Network data model

(3) relational model: a 'table' comprising a 'set' of
                        'tuples' of 'attributes' of data
                        elements, supporting all 'entities'
                        and all 'associations' between them
                        in a single and uniform manner, as
                        indicated in Fig. 10.3.

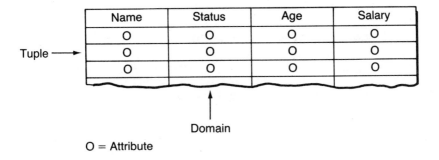

Fig. 10.3 Relational data model

The hierarchic and network data models enable a 'single data
element' to be referenced, via 'navigational links', by
virtue of its 'unique location' within the data structure. In
contrast, the relational data model enables a 'set' of data
elements, 'associated' with a common attribute, to be
referenced by virtue of the 'value' of that attribute and
independently of its location within the data structure.   For
example, 'an item' of information within a textbook can be
accessed, either by reference to its position in the
hierarchy of numbered chapters, sections and sub-sections, or
'all occurrences' of the item <u>and</u> 'all associated items' of
information can be accessed by reference to the index at the
back of the book.

Whereas the hierarchic and network data models are clearly
based on linked-list structures (comprising a block of
storage for each node, which contains data and the addresses
(viz. pointers) of immediately linked nodes) for 'navigation'
by 'expert' system programmers, the relational model is not
concerned with access strategy. Instead, the relational model
offers a very high-level (viz. set-oriented) language for
'non-expert' system users. In fact, the relational data model
is supported by a 'relational algebra' which comprises a
well-defined collection of set operations, as defined in the
following sub-section.

Hence, the hierarchic/network and the relational data models need not be in competition. Indeed they could complement each other within a single information processing system. A hierarchic data structure classifies data elements into more easily manageable categories, whereas a relational data structure provides flexible access to groups of related data elements.

10.2.2 Relational Data Processing

The fundamental operations of a ´relational algebra´ create a new relation from either one or two existing relations, as illustrated in the following examples.

P	Q	R
p	q	r
s	p	t
r	q	s

Relation [X]

S	T	U
q	u	p
s	p	t

Relation [Y]

(1) Intersection of [X] and [Y]

s	p	t

(2) Union of [X] and [Y]

(i.e. [X] + [Y])

p	q	r
s	p	t
r	q	s
q	u	p

(3) Difference of [X] and [Y]
(i.e. [X] − [Y])

p	q	r
r	q	s

(4) Projection of [X] to P and R

(i.e. [X] } P,R)

p	r
s	t
r	s

(5) Selection of [X] for P > Q
(i.e. [X] : P > Q)

s	p	t
r	q	s

(6) Mapping of [X] into P and R for
Q = q
(i.e. [X] : Q = q } P,R)

p	r
r	s

(7) Cartesian product of [X] and [Y]

(i.e. [X] * [Y])

p	q	r	q	u	p
p	q	r	s	p	t
s	p	t	q	u	p
s	p	t	s	p	t
r	q	s	q	u	p
r	q	s	s	p	t

(8) Join of [X] and [Y] for Q <> T

(i.e. [X] * [Y] : Q <> T)

p	q	r	q	u	p
p	q	r	s	p	t
s	p	t	q	u	p
r	q	s	q	u	p
r	q	s	s	p	t

Information processing with the relational model involves the execution of a sequence of algebraic expressions, constructed from such relational operations. The following simple examples concern ´retrieval´ and ´update´ processes with the relation [TD], supporting a ´telephone directory´ for which the relevant segment is shown in Table 10.1.

Name	Style	Dept	Room	Num
Scholes	Mr	AC	127	137
Scorer	Dr	RE	64	109
Scott	Mrs	SA	201	193
Scowen	Miss	AC	127	137
Scrips	Mr	SA	202	194
Scriven	Dr	RE	65	110
Scroggs	Mrs	AC	127	137
Scroll	Dr	RE	64	109
Scrow	Mr	AC	128	135

Table 10.1. Segment of an internal telephone directory

Example 1: Finding the telephone numbers of all personnel named Scott in the SAles department involves the listing of a new relation [NR] created by a ´selection´ followed by a ´projection´ operation, as follows

$$[NR] := [[TD]:(Name = Scott) \text{ and } (Dept = SA)]\} Num$$

Example 2: Changing the telephone numbers of all ACcounts personnel, in room 127, to 134 involves the creation of working relation [WR1] with a ´selection´ operation, working relation [WR2] with

a 'projection' followed by a 'cartesian product'
and completion with a 'difference' and 'union'
operations to create the updated relation [UTD],
as follows

[WR1] := [TD] : (Dept = AC) and (Room = 127);
[WR2] := [[WR1] } Name,Style,Dept,Room]*[Num=134];
[UTD] := [TD] - [WR1] + [WR2]

10.2.3 Commercial Data Processing Systems

The hierarchic and network data models have been extensively
implemented in commercial data processing systems. For
example, IBM's IMS [2], SDC's TDMS [3], Informatics' Mark IV
[4] and MRI's System 2000 [5] are all based on hierarchic
data modeling. In addition, systems conforming to the
recommendations of the DBTG (Data Base Task Group of the
CODASYL (Conference On DAta management SYstem Languages)
programming language committee) [6] are based on network data
modelling, examples include DEC's DBMS [7], Univac's EDMS
[8], Cullinane's IDMS [9], Cincom's TOTAL [10], IBM's DBOMP
[11] and Honeywell's IDS [12].

A major problem confronting the implementation of information
systems based on the relational data model, is the lack of
suitable hardware facilities to support its computational
needs. Consequently, despite many academic projects (e.g.
MacAIMS (MIT) [13], ZETA (University of Toronto) [14] and
INGRES (University of California at Berkeley) [15]), there
are remarkably few commercial implementations of relational
data base management systems. Nevertheless, commercial
interest is evident in the development of Tymshare's MAGNUM
[16], IBM's System R [17], Relational Software Incorporated's
ORACLE and Logica's RAPPORT.

10.3 IMPLEMENTATION OF RELATIONAL DATA PROCESSING

Typical commercial data processing systems comprise a large
file-store and a powerful computer for query, record and
display processing. In the case of relational data processing
systems, these units can be considered as a 'relation-store'
and a 'relation-processor'.

Since current relational databases require storage for increasingly larger sets of relations, a cost-effective direct-access mass-storage device is an essential component for the implementation of relation-stores. In fact, moving-head magnetic disk stores are likely to remain unchallenged in this application for at least the current decade.

Equally important is the choice of the relation-processor. Since unknown numbers of tuples may be retrieved or updated in a single information processing transaction, quite high speed data processing is required to maintain acceptable transaction rates.

The conventional Von Neumann SISD (Single Instruction and Single Data streams) computer architecture is well suited to the sequential store-addressing required by the ´dynamic pointer structures´ underlying the hierarchic and network data models. Indeed, traversing ´navigational links´, in search of a single data element, is a sequential process. In contrast, the relational model requires a different style of information processing, namely ´associative set processing´. However, the SISD architecture does not support ´value referencing´, ´association linking´ and ´parallel processing´ as primitive operations. Hence, these operations must be ´simulated´ in software or ´emulated´ in firmware (with the ´dynamic pointer structures´ of the hierarchic and network models and consequent loss of simplicity and computational efficiency) or, indeed, be supported by special-purpose hardware (with consequent consequent questions of cost-effectiveness). In fact, two main approaches to the architecture of relation-processors are evident, these being the

(1) centralized uni-processor architecture

> In this case, the relation-processor is implemented ´indirectly´ in the software or firmware of a powerful general-purpose maxi or minicomputer, as discussed in the next section.

(2) distributed multiprocessor architecture

> In this case, the relation-processor incorporates a special-purpose SIMD (Single Instruction but Multiple Data streams) processor which is dedicated to associative relation processing. Operating under the

control of a small SISD processor, which implements a
hierarchic (network) data model for query and display
processing, this Associative Parallel Processor
implements the relational model 'directly'. Such
distributed multiprocessor computer architectures can
be further classified, according to size and location
of the Associative Parallel Processor, as follows

    (a) large main-frame Associative Parallel Processor
    (b) small back-end Associative Parallel Processor

These form the subject of subsequent sections.

10.3.1 Conventional Relation-processors

As an illustration of the inadequacy of the SISD computer
architecture for relational data processing, consider its
representation of the 'selection' operation (defined in
Section 10.2.2). Assuming that 'tuples' are to be selected
according to the values of some logical combination of 'key'
attributes, Fig. 10.4 clearly shows that the execution time
would be critically dependent on the ordering of the tuples
within the relation.

In the simplest ordering, a particular key-domain is
specified and the tuples are sequenced in order of its
attribute values. For example, the 'name' domain in
Table 10.1 has been sorted to ease tuple selection. Hence, if
all 'search keys' are also 'sort keys', the 'sequential-scan'
(assuming that the 'search keys' are also sorted) and the
'binary-chop' searching techniques would be very much more
efficient than the 'random-ordering' of tuples. More complex
ordering, involving 'key-transformation' (e.g. 'hash-coding')
would enable a 'computed-search' to achieve still higher
searching efficiency. In short, faster tuple selection can be
bought at the further expense of relation ordering.

Selection based on non-key domains involves the searching of
effectively non-sorted tuples. Consequently, in such cases,
selection efficiency falls to that of 'random ordering'. Of
course, the provision of auxiliary indices (viz. a sorted
index for each search-domain) can help to ease this problem.
In fact, an 'inverted list' (viz. each attribute is assigned
a list of the tuples in which it occurs) can greatly improve

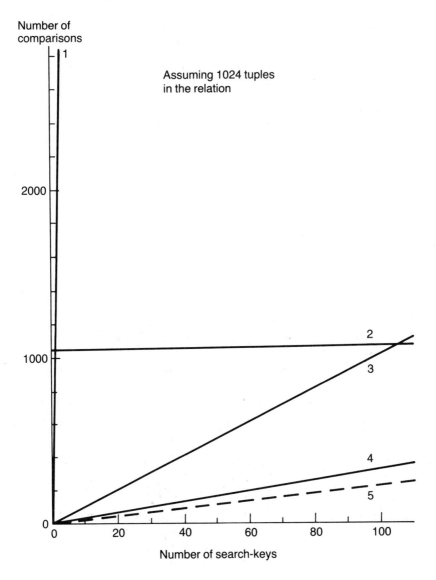

Number of
comparisons

1

Assuming 1024 tuples
in the relation

2000

1000

2

3

4

5

0

0   20   40   60   80   100

Number of search-keys

1. Random order – sequential scan
2. Sequential order – sequential scan
3. Sequential order – binary chop
4. Transformed order – computer search
5. Random order – associative search

Fig. 10.4 Comparison of tuple selection techniques

searching efficiency. However, all such searching techniques incur considerable expense in terms of index creation and maintenance and, indeed, in terms of extra storage (auxiliary indices may be larger than the original relation).

In summary, the searching inefficiency of the SISD computer hardware can be improved with additional software or firmware complexity, which can lead to unpredictable, expensive, inflexible and possibly unreliable information processing systems.

10.4 MAIN-FRAME ASSOCIATIVE PARALLEL PROCESSORS

Since the conventional SISD computer architecture is not well suited to relational data processing, it follows that the specification and design of a main-frame 'associative parallel processing' architecture could be considered for this application. Such a machine could provide the consistantly high computational efficiency indicated in Fig. 10.4. Indeed, much academic research has been directed towards this objective. A common feature of this work is the suggestion of an SIMD (Single Instruction but Multiple Data streams) computer architecture incorporating an Associative Memory (viz. Content Addressable Memory), as shown in idealized form in Fig. 10.5.

10.4.1 An Ideal Associative Parallel Processor

The ideal main-frame Associative Parallel Processor would comprise a large Content Addressable Memory (CAM) and flexible means of access to its word-rows and data-columns[18]. As indicated in Fig. 10.5, a word-row would be allocated to each tuple and the CAM would be large enough to accommodate an entire relation. The Field Masking Logic would allocate data-columns of the CAM to the attribute-fields of the stored tuples.

In operation, the data contents of the non-masked attribute-fields of all tuples in the CAM would be compared simultaneously with the corresponding attribute-values held in the Tuple Input Register. The subset of matching tuples

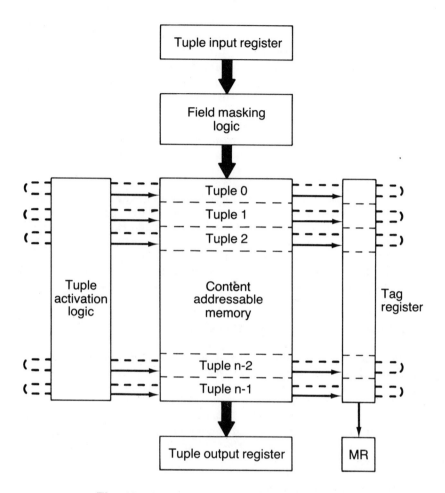

Fig. 10.5 Ideal associative relation processor

would be marked by ´tags´ in the Tag Register. Particular tuples could then be activated for ´retrieval´ or ´update´ by the Tuple Activation Logic, which implements a selected mapping on the state of the Tag Register. ´Retrieval´ involves the transfer of an activated tuple to the Tuple Output Register, whereas ´update´ involves the transfer of the un-masked attribute-values of the Tuple Input Register to the corresponding attribute-fields of all activated tuples.

Ideally, the word-size and column-length of the CAM would be sufficiently long to accommodate many different relations. However, the very wide diversity of information processing requirements ensures that, to achieve this objective, the CAM would have to be very large indeed. Moreover, the diversity of relation size is such that, except for special-purpose applications, most of the CAM would be redundant for most of the time. Consequently, practical proposals for main-frame Associative Parallel Processors usually support multi-word CAM allocation for tuples and some form of virtual CAM management for ´the ´overlaying´ of relation segments.

10.4.2 Associative Relation Processing

The ideal main-frame Associative Parallel Processor, shown in Fig. 10.5, would implement a form of ´associative set processing´, on all tuples in the stored relation, in which

(1) a subset of tuples would be referenced by the value(s) of one or more common attributes (viz. by ´content address´ rather than by their locations in addressable storage);

(2) ´association links´ between the attributes of the referenced tuples would be traversed simply in any direction;

(3) all associated attributes, in all referenced tuples, would be processed in parallel.

Applying the ideal main-frame Associative Parallel Processor to examples 1 and 2 in Section 10.2.2 and using the construct

forall i : <conditional values of attributes of tuple[i]> do
    <assignment statement(s) concerning attributes of tuple[i]>

to imply the parallel processing of all tuple[i]s satisfying
the selection condition, the examples could be coded as
follows:

Example 1: forall i : (Name[i] = Scott) and (Dept[i] = SA) do
            TOR.Num := Num[i]

            i.e. the tuple(s) containing both the attributes
                 Mrs Scott and SA would be tagged and its
                 (their) data content transferred to the Tuple
                 Output Register

Example 2: forall i : (Dept[i] = AC) and (Room[i] = 127) do
            Num[i] := 134

            i.e. all tuples containing both the attributes AC
                 and 127 would be tagged and then the number
                 attributes of tagged tuples would be updated
                 to 134

Clearly, a main-frame Associative Parallel Processor is
ideally suited to relational data processing [18].
Nevertheless, the CAM must be sufficiently large to support
an entire relation and the data processing requirement
sufficiently extensive, such that the benefit of associative
relation processing is not undermined by the overheads of
loading the data. Since both relations and processing
requirements vary considerably in size and extent, a cost-
effective implementation of the ideal main-frame Associative
Parallel Processor is very difficult to achieve and would,
probably, need to be ‛tailor-made‛ for each application.

10.4.3 Practical Main-frame Associative Parallel Processors

The implementation of main-frame Associative Parallel
Processors has been of interest for over twenty years. Many
designs, for structures similar to that shown in Fig. 10.5
have been proposed and several associative parallel
processing machines have been built, for mainly military
applications [19 - 24]. Prominent among these are the
Goodyear STARAN [25] and ASPRO [26], Bell Laboratories PEPE
[27] and Honeywell ECAM [28]. The feasibility of applying
such machines to relational database management has been
investigated by many researchers. Prominent among these

studies have been the work of Savitt, Love and Troop [29]
with ASP, of DeFiore, Stillman and Berra [30 - 32] and
Moulder [33] with STARAN, of Linde, Gates and Peng [34] with
APCS and of Anderson and Kain [28] with ECAM. The design of
microelectronic Associative Parallel Processors for
information processing has also been of interest to the
author [35 - 38].

Emerging from this wave of endeavor is the growing
realization that the ideal main-frame Associative Parallel
Processing structure shown in Fig. 10.5 does not provide a
cost-effective means of implementing relational data
processing systems. Despite considerable effort to develop
cheap building-blocks for associative hardware, it is
increasingly evident that such large Associative Parallel
Processors can very rarely justify their implementation cost.
More importantly, it is becoming clear that such use of a
large Associative Parallel Processor is a naive approach to
relational data processing. Indeed, the very extensive search
for a suitable fabrication technology for the manufacture of
low-cost associative hardware has masked the inherent fallacy
in this approach.

10.5 BACK-END ASSOCIATIVE PARALLEL PROCESSORS

In general, compared with the size of relations, relatively
few tuples are retrieved or updated in a single information
processing transaction. Thus, the 'filtering' of relevant
tuples requires the redundant processing of irrelevant
tuples. Indeed, since such 'filtering' must also be performed
on large relations, quite high speed tuple selection is
required to maintain acceptable transaction rates. Clearly,
the application of a powerful main-frame processor to this
rather mundane task, not only detracts from its main purpose,
but is also cost-ineffective.

A more efficient alternative is to delegate the 'filtering'
operation to a small Associative Parallel Processor
incorporated in-line with the disk controller, as indicated
in Fig. 10.6. A very simple auxiliary processor of this kind
would free the main-frame processor from tuple selection,
avoid data transmission delays and the protocol processing

normally associated with data-block transfers. Indeed, the delegation of more complex associative relation processing to a more sophisticated auxiliary processor could gain further advantages. The reduced load on the main-frame processor would allow more time for query and display processing and general system management or even allow the use of a cheaper machine. Such dedicated Associative Relation Processors are now known as 'Back-End Processors' [39 - 54].

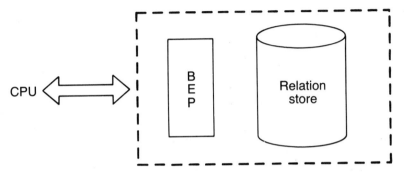

Fig. 10.6 Back-end processor

Two styles of 'Back-End Processor' (BEP) are in evidence, these being the

(1) 'load-and-process' BEP

A tuple-block is loaded into the CAM of the BEP, formatted as shown in Fig. 10.5, for subsequent associative relation processing. For those applications requiring access to consecutive tuple-blocks, the blocks are loaded alternately into the twin CAMs of a doubly-buffered BEP, one block being processed while the other is being loaded. A further store supports the associative relation processing algorithm.

(2) 'on-the-fly' BEP

Each tuple-block is 'scanned' (i.e. read but not stored) character-by-character and relevant tuples are selected 'on-the-fly' for subsequent, possibly 'in flight', processing; thereby avoiding the unnecessary storage of irrelevant tuples. The tuple selection terms are stored in the BEP, thereby minimizing the storage requirements of the associative relation processing algorithm.

It should be noticed that the underlying data representations of the two BEP styles are different. The 'load-and-process' BEP supports 'associative table processing', whereas the 'on-the-fly' BEP supports 'associative string processing'. For both BEP styles, maximum effiency is achieved when each tuple block is processed, any results passed to the main-frame processor and, if appropriate, (modified) tuples written to a new relation within one block read-time.

10.5.1 Back-end Processor Architecture

Back-end processor architecture is now a well established field of research and commercial products for the maxicomputer [42,43] and minicomputer [44,45] environments are already evident. Clearly, 'load-and-process' BEPs are potentially more expensive than 'on-the-fly' BEPs and, therefore, they apply only to those to database computers for which the required tuple processing is too complex to be performed at the relation-store data-rate. For this reason, most research has been directed towards the specification and design of high-speed comparison logic to be incorporated in-line with the read-heads of relation-store disk-drives for 'on-the-fly' relation processing. Logic-per-track fixed-head disk-drives provide very fast scans of entire disks, whereas the lower-cost moving-head devices tend to share a single block of comparison logic situated further down the disk data channel.

'On-the-fly' back-end Associative Parallel Processors can be distinguished by the relative extent of the 'scanning' and 'indexing' facilities which they incorporate. Designs range from a straight scan of a large block of randomly ordered tuples to the full indexing of tuples ordered according to a set of 'search keys'.

Scanning has the merits of efficient use of storage media and flexible (e.g. 'free text') access with simple software, but transaction times depend on block-length and for long blocks this delay can be unacceptable.

Indexing avoids long search delays by structuring relations for direct-access and creating an auxiliary index of pre-selected 'search keys', at the expense of extra storage and software complexity.

Thus research is directed towards cost-effective compromises involving 'indexed scan-blocks' [46]. Analysis of disk accesses reveals that, due to 'head-move' and 'latency' delays, the average time to access one disk-sector is roughly equivalent to the time to 'scan' two or three disk-tracks. Hence, 'scan-block' sizes tend to be multiples of disk-tracks up to a disk-cylinder. Consequently, the advantage of indexing 'scan-blocks' rather than disk-sectors approaches two orders-of-magnitude, in terms of scanned data [46].

An attractive option, which can considerably enhance the cost-effectiveness of 'on-the-fly Back-End Processors', is that of data compression [45 - 47]. Typical relations contain considerable redundancy. For example, attribute values may be chosen for readability rather than for coding efficiency, such that some relations may be up to an order-of-magnitude larger than necessary. Thus by encoding relations more efficiently, larger tuple volumes can be compressed into the scan-blocks, with consequent savings in storage space and access time. Moreover, research has shown that dedicated hardware providing in-line data encoding and decoding can easily support 50% compression of natural text at typical disk speeds [47] . Higher degrees of data compression can be supported [45], but with increasing difficulty and further research is required to establish levels of cost-effectiveness.

10.5.2 Practical Back-end Associative Parallel Processors

Despite many academic proposals for back-end Associative Parallel Processors, very few commercial products have been announced. Of these, ICL's CAFS [42] and the Britton-Lee's IDM [44] are the best known. Nevertheless, it is clear that several back-end machines are in development and their availability as commercial products will soon be announced [45]. Prominent among the more practical proposals, stimulating such development, are RAPID [50], CASSM [52], RAP [53], MEMEX [45] and the machines being developed at the Universities of Illinois [54], Ohio [39] and Braunschweig (Germany) [43].

10.6 ASSOCIATIVE PARALLEL PROCESSING AT BRUNEL UNIVERSITY

For over a decade the Computer Architecture group at Brunel
University has been investigating the problems of building
associative processing modules, programming them and applying
them cost-effectively to relational data processing tasks. In
particular, research has been directed towards the provision
of hardware modules for the 'load-and-process' and 'on-the-
fly' BEPs (back-end processor) described in Section 10.5. A
major result of this research has been the specification of
the design philosophy, structural organization and
operational principles of the Associative Parallel Processor.

The Associative Parallel Processor (APP) executes three
primitive operations (viz. 'search', 'read' and 'write')
under the control of an external 'microprogram sequencer'. In
fact, the APP comprises seven functional blocks, as shown in
Fig. 10.7, namely the

DIR: Data Input Register storing an n-bit word for
       'search' and 'write' operations.

BCL: Bit Control Logic selecting 0 or more of the n AMA
       bit-columns in support of a bit-parallel 'search' or
       'write' operations on selected (viz. un-masked) AMA
       fields.

AMA: Associative Memory Array, a Content Addressable
       Memory (CAM) comprising m n-bit word-rows. During a
       'search' operation, each AMA bit-cell compares its
       content with the corresponding bit in the Data Input
       Register and generates the appropriate match or
       mismatch signal, the bit-cells in each masked bit-
       column generate match signals. If no bit-cell in
       particular word-row generates a mismatch signal, then
       that word-row is deemed to have matched the 'search'
       word. A 'read' operation transfers the contents of an
       activated word-row to the Data Output Register,
       whereas a 'write' operation updates selected fields
       of activated word-rows with the un-masked contents of
       the Data Input Register.

DOR: Data Output Register storing the output resulting
       from a 'read' operation.

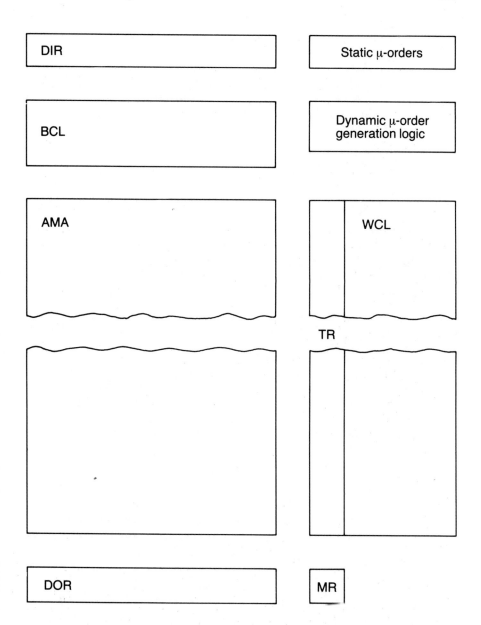

Fig. 10.7 APP schematic organisation

WCL: Word Control Logic activating 0 or more of the m AMA
       word-rows,   for   'read'   and   'write'   operations,
       according to a defined mapping on the response to a
       'search'   operation,   which   is   stored   in   a   Tag
       Register. Activation mappings include the resolution
       of the first (last) matching word-row, neighbor and
       group activation and linking between remote matching
       AMA word-rows.

MR: Match   Reply,   a   1-bit   flag   which   indicates   the
       presence of 1 or more tags in the Tag Register.

MOGL: Micro-Order Generation Logic issuing 'dynamic micro-
       orders to the BCL and WCL, derived from the 'static
       micro-order'   of the current   'micro-instruction'   of
       the controlling microprogram.

10.6.1 APP Structures

Much of the investigation of APP structures has been
stimulated by application studies, which have included many
aspects of information retrieval, database management and
general text string processing. In many cases, these studies
were   commissioned   and   sponsored   by   industrial   and
institutional interests in the progress of the APP project.
One   of   the   results   of   this   research   has   been   the
identification of three structural variants of the APP [18],
which   are   described   below   in   terms   of   relational   data
processing.

(1) Fixed Record-Length APP (FRL-APP)

       A   practical   implementation   of   the   ideal   main-frame
       associative relation processor,   shown in Fig. 10.5, in
       which the smallest feasible number of long-length CAM
       word-rows   are   allocated to each   'tuple',   to allow
       parallel association between 'attributes'. Thus, the
       CAM width is fixed by the longest 'tuple' and the
       storage of shorter 'tuples' entails CAM redundancy.

(2) Field-Organized Variable Record-Length APP (FO-VRL-APP)

       One   shorter-length   CAM word-row is allocated to   each
       'attribute',   to   support   different   length   'tuples'
       (comprising fixed-length 'attributes') with   sequential
       association   between   'attributes'   and   less   CAM
       redundancy.

(3) Byte-Organized Variable Record-Length APP   (BO-VRL-APP)

   One short-length CAM word-row is allocated to each
   character, to support different length 'attributes' in
   different length 'tuples' with sequential association
   between both characters and 'attributes' and minimum
   CAM redundancy.

The structures of the FRL-APP and BO-VRL-APP have been
extensively modeled with both software simulations   and
hardware emulations. This work has confirmed that the FRL-APP
structure is very well suited to high-speed support of
specific relational data processing applications,   which
require extensive processing of relations with similar tuple
lengths. In such cases, an FRL-APP module would provide ideal
support for the implementation of the 'load-and-process' BEP
(back-end processor, discussed in Section 10.5. However, in
general, when tuple lengths vary considerably, the BO-VRL-APP
structure provides a lower-speed, but more cost-effective,
support of relational data processing. Indeed, the BO-VRL-APP
is ideally suited to the implementation of the 'on-the-fly'
BEP (discussed in last section) since the data stream of the
disk-store is in character string form.

10.6.2 APP Software

A major result of the APP research project was   the
development of an APP assembly language.

As with all parallel processing computer architectures, the
specification of the primitive APP instruction set is of
crucial importance to the eventual cost-effectiveness of the
machine. If the instruction level is placed too low, then
very few programmers can achieve a high overall processing
performance. In fact, extensive research has shown that even
'expert' programmers can allow computational efficiency
(viz. ratio of useful parallel processing operations to the
total number of operations) of the parallel processor to fall
below 5% in this case. In fact, it is very difficult to avoid
'sapping the power' of the parallel   processor with
essentially sequential algorithms. If the instruction level
is placed too high, then the programmability of the machine
falls to the level where only a few specific applications of
the parallel processor are likely to be cost-effective. Thus,
the instruction level for the APP was the subject   of

extensive experimental research, which resulted in the APP software structure described below.

APP application programs are written entirely in Pascal (or a similar block-structured high-level language). Such programs include calls to ´external´ pre-compiled procedures which support associative processing in the APP. These ´associative procedures´ (also known as ´APP macros´) are written with the ´APP assembly language´. Hence, the application programmer selects suitable APP macros from the ´APP macro library´ and only if it is necessary does he resort to APP macro creation. In operation, selected APP macros are stored as microprograms for APP control. Thus, APP macros are called by the application program, which is suspended during macro execution.

APP macros are written in terms of ´Associative Processing Instructions´ (APIs), which are notional constructs comprising the ´APP micro-instructions´ MIDA and MIDMFN, as defined in simplified form below

```
<API>  ::= <MIDA> {<MIDMFN>}

<MIDA> ::= <domain address> <conditional branch>

<domain address>      ::= S(<input specification>)
<conditional branch>  ::= <empty> | BMR <conditional address>
<conditional address> ::= <address_if_mismatch>, |
                          <address_if_mismatch>,
                          <address_if_match>

<MIDMFN>::=<domain modification><function execution><branch>

<domain modification> ::= <clear option> <activation>
<clear option>        ::= <empty> | M(<clear mnemonic>)
<activation option>   ::= <empty if true tags> |
                          M(<activation mnemonic>)
<function execution>  ::= R(<output destination>) |
                          W(<input specification>)
<branch>              ::= <empty> | BRN <address>
```

For example, expressing examples 1 and 2 (see Sections 10.2.2 and 10.4.2) in the APP assembly language would yield the following code

Example 1:   S(Name=Scott,Dept=SA) BMR addN,addM
             R(TOR.Num) BRN addN

Example 2:   S(Dept=AC,Room=127) BMR addN,addM
             W(Num=134) BRN addN
             where ´addM´ refers to the MIDMFN given and
             ´addN´ refers to the next API.

A third example of an APP assembly language coding will be found later under the description of the SCRIPT chip.

10.6.3 The Micro-APP Project

Much of the research has been directed towards the specification, design, fabrication and evaluation of microelectronic building-blocks for cost-effective APP implementation. In fact, this work has led to the definition of the ´Micro-APP module´, a single printed-circuit-board supporting a ´chain´ of VLSI Micro-APP chip blocks operating under microprogram control, as indicated in Fig. 10.8.

The Micro-APP ´chain controller´ comprises the standard bit-slice microprocessor components of typical high-speed microprogram controllers. ´APP macros´, stored as microprograms, can be called from a program running in the host machine. The controller also buffers data transmitted between the Micro-APP ´chain´ and the host.

The Micro-APP ´chain´ comprises a linear array of singly-linked Micro-APP blocks, each connected to the common ´Micro-APP chip bus´ which supports input-output data, commands derived from the current APP micro-instruction and a status feedback signal.

10.6.4 Micro-APP Chips

There is a choice of VLSI chip architectures for the construction of Micro-APP chip blocks, which are described below with reference to Fig. 10.7.

3-chip block: chip M an m-word by n-bit AMA
              chip B an n-bit section of the BCL, DIR and DOR
              chip W an m-word section of the WCL

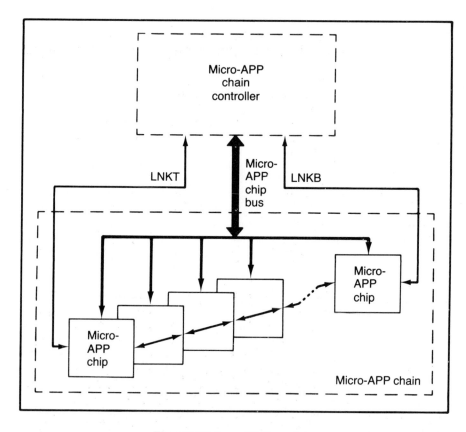

Fig. 10.8 Micro-APP module

Although many bipolar and MOS examples of chip M have been reported [35,36], few achieve the speed requirement for APPs. However, it is clear that both technologies can meet this target. Most of the chips were developed for specific military applications [18,36], but sample quantities of a bipolar chip M have been released by Ferranti and MOS chips M by Texas Instruments, GEC-Marconi and Solid-State Scientific Incorporated for general application [36]. No examples of chips B and W have yet been reported.

2-chip block: chip MB a combination of chips M and B on a single VLSI chip, as shown in Fig.10.9.
chip MW a combination of chips M and W on a single VLSI chip, as shown in Fig.10.9.

Small bipolar versions of chip MB have been marketed by Intel, Fairchild, Signetics and Motorola, but these are much too expensive for the construction of cost-effective Micro-APP modules. An MOS version of chip MB has been reported by Philips [55] and an MOS version of chip MW has been proposed [37]. Simulation studies for the latter indicate cost-effective performance for a limited range of associative processing tasks.

1-chip block: chip MBW a combination of chips M, B and W on a single VLSI chip, as shown in Fig. 10.10

Apart from the Micro-APP project, no other chip MBW has yet been reported.

The 3-chip block offers the most versatile approach to the construction of Micro-APP modules and, therefore it best suited to the implementation of the ideal main-frame APP described in Section 10.4.1. However, it is the most expensive to develop and its cost-per-function is very dependent on packaging costs due to the unavoidably high pin-counts. Indeed, the development of 3 different VLSI chips, for such a radically new application area, remains a daunting prospect for even the most speculative chip manufacturer.

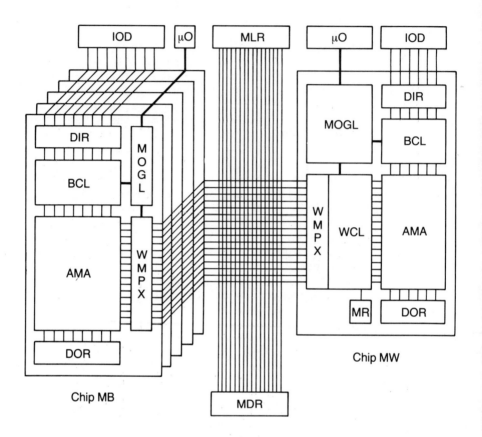

Fig. 10.9 2-chip micro-APP block

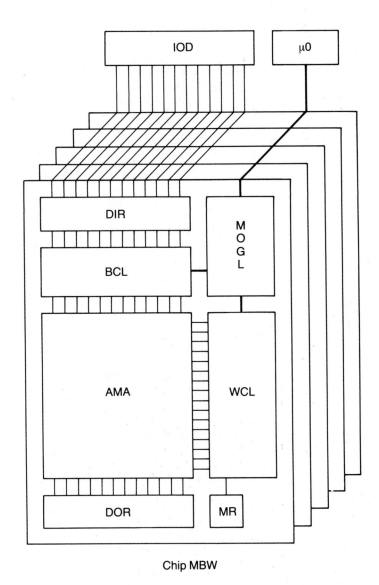

Chip MBW

Fig. 10.10 1-chip micro-APP block

The 2-chip block offers savings in chip development and
production costs at the expense of function packing-density
or speed, depending on the choice of fabrication technology.
Hence, it is more suitable for the implementation of the
'load-and-process' BEP (Back-End Processor, described
earlier). Although more attractive than the 3-chip block, the
cost-per-function of the 2-chip block is still markedly
dependent on pin-count. Clearly, the chip MBW offers the
lowest cost compromise and, hence, it provides the most
suitable means of implementation for the 'on-the-fly' BEP
(described in Section 10.5).

10.6.5 The Brunel Micro-APP Composite Test Chip

In 1977 the UK Department of Industry funded a program of
work to investigate the feasibility of the Micro-APP chip
proposals.

Design requirements were derived from a survey of previous
and existing application studies and comprehensive
rationalizations of the BCL and WCL specifications were
undertaken, such that the particular requirements of a
specific Micro-APP variant would be a subset of the general
specification. Thus, the requirements of the different Micro-
APP variants (for FRL-APP, FO-VRL-APP and BO-VRL-APP
implementation) were embodied in a common specification.

The choice of chip fabrication technology presented some
problems; since Micro-APP chips share memory and logic in
roughly equal proportions, whereas the technologies available
in 1977 were optimized for one or the other but not both. ECL
offered ample speed and line-driving power for the BCL and
WCL, but its power dissipation and cell packing-density would
severely restrict its suitability for the AMA. Available nMOS
processes, although suitable for the AMA, would severely
restrict the performance of the BCL and WCL. Hence, the
compromise of I^2L was considered. Indeed at that time the
future of I^2L seemed very promising. Eventually, SFL
(Substrate Fed Logic, an optimized version of I^2L) was chosen
for chip fabrication at Plessey Research Ltd. (Caswell).

In view of the high cost of mask and chip fabrication, it was
considered that the development of the three different Micro-
APP chip architectures (viz. chips MB, MW and MBW) would be

too expensive for the purposes of the feasibility study. Hence, a ´composite test chip´, as shown in Fig. 10.11, which could be packaged to emulate each chip architecture was attempted. In addition, the ´drop-in´ sites on each SFL wafer, which normally accommodate process test devices, were used to provide independent access to ´dismembered´ layout blocks. Thus, the two chip types provided adequate opportunity for future evaluation of the Micro-APP chip variants [38].

Design and layout work was completed (by Brunel staff) during the Spring of 1979, the final ´composite test chip´ comprising 1760 gates on a total chip area of 20.8 mm^2. A minor layout error was found on testing the first wafers (fabricated by Plessey staff). Having corrected the error, subsequent wafers were produced at intervals throughout the following year. All probe-testing and packaged-chip testing was completed (by Brunel staff) with equipment specially designed for these tasks. By the Autumn of 1980, a sufficient number of fully-working chips had been assembled for evaluation of the three fundamental Micro-APP variants.

Analysis of the ´composite test chip´ proved the feasibility of the Micro-APP concept and enabled the following Micro-APP chip predictions [38,56].

2-chip block: chip MB

AMA size	16 words x 8 bits
No. of gates	1579
chip area	19.3 mm^2
package	40-pin

chip MW

AMA size	16 words x 4 bits
No. of gates	921
chip area	11.8 mm^2
package	40-pin

The range of API execution times, covering all activations, was estimated to be 351 ns - 593 ns

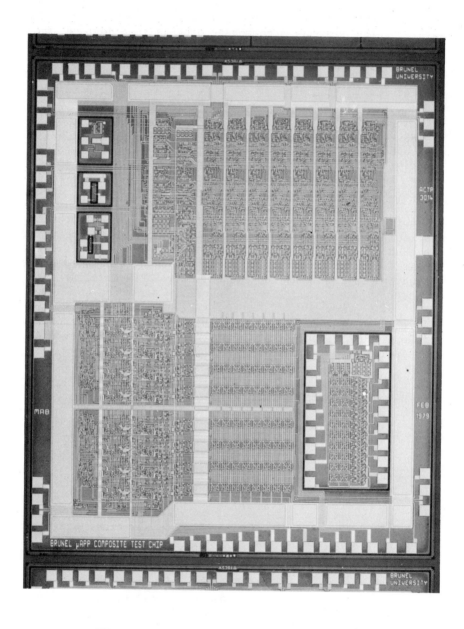

Fig. 10.11 Brunel micro-APP composite test chip

1-chip block: chip MBW

AMA size   16 words x 12 bits
No. of gates   2166
chip area   26.4 mm^2
package   40-pin

The range of API execution times, covering
all activations, was estimated to be 335 ns -
770 ns.

It should be noted that the above API timing forecasts assume
'worst-case' design with the SFL technology of 1979. Indeed,
fabrication with an I^{2}L technology of 1983 would provide at
least a 3-fold increase in API execution rate.

10.6.6 Micro-APP Evaluation

Various associative relation processing application studies
have proceeded in parallel with Micro-APP chip development.
Indeed, in many cases, the existence of the Micro-APP project
stimulated the initial interest in such studies. In most
studies, a Micro-APP module has been specified as an
alternative to a traditional microprocessor-based module
applied to operate autonomously, under microprogram control,
as a peripheral to a conventional host machine; its purpose
being to increase the performance or cost-effectiveness of
the overall system. Hence, it has been expedient to compare
the cost and performance of the alternative modules. Studies
have included particular aspects of information retrieval,
relational database management, word processing and general
symbolic string processing.

The comparative advantages of Micro-APP modules over
traditional microprocessor-based modules, applied to the same
dedicated relational data processing tasks, are summarized in
Fig. 10.12.

10.6.7 The SCRIPT Chip Project

As discussed earlier, the 'load-and-process' and 'on-the-fly'
BEPs (Back-End Processor) offer the potential of cost-
effective relational data processing. Indeed, the Micro-APP
project has demonstrated that, for specific applications

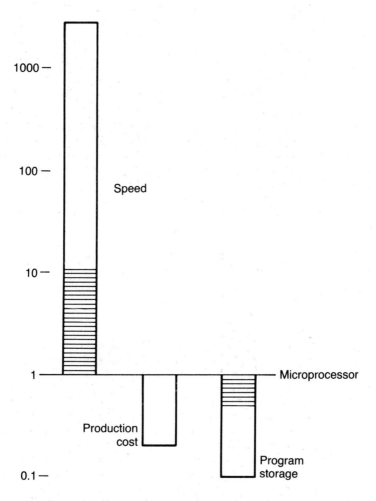

Fig. 10.12 Comparative benefits of micro-APP modules

requiring extensive processing of relations with similar
tuple lengths, an FRL-APP module comprising chips MB and MW
would provide a cost-effective implementation of a 'load-and-
process' BEP. Similarly, a BO-VRL-APP built with chip MBW
would provide a cost-effective implementation of an 'on-the-
fly' BEP.

The major architectural challenge of relational data
processing is that, in general, tuples and attributes vary in
length between relations, which in turn vary considerably in
size. Thus, except for certain specific applications, a
'load-and-process' BEP incorporating an FRL-APP module, for
'associative table processing', is unlikely to be cost-
effective for general relational data processing. However,
this presents no problem for the 'on-the-fly' BEP, since its
BO-VRL-APP module supports 'associative string processing'.
Indeed, the relations would be stored as a 'string', with
special characters to delimit contiguous attributes and
tuples. Hence, the BO-VRL-APP is well-suited to the
fundamental constraints of relation storage. It follows,
therefore, that 'load-and-process' BEPs for general
relational data processing are better implemented with a BO-
VRL-APP, supporting 'associative string processing'.

Of the three Micro-APP chip architectures, the chip MBW is
clearly the most attractive Micro-APP chip variant for
further development. Moreover, the regular memory-oriented
structure of chip MBW is very well-suited to VLSI fabrication
techniques, whereas the high pin-counts of chips MB and MW
severely limit their further development.

Thus, for the reasons outlined above, the Micro-APP project
has stimulated further research, leading towards the
specification of a VLSI chip MBW for the cost-effective
implementation of 'load-and-process' and 'on-the-fly' BEPs
supporting 'associative string processing'. This VLSI chip
has become known as the SCRIPT (Single-Chip Relational
Information Processing elemenT) chip.

The SCRIPT chip is targeted to integrate 512 AMA word-rows,
each comprising an 8-bit character field and 4 control-bits,
on a 2 um CMOS chip. SCRIPT chips would be linked to form a
'SCRIPT chain' and the 'SCRIPT chain controller' would
support a set of 'SCRIPT macros'. Thus a single printed-

circuit-board could accommodate a ´SCRIPT module´ supporting a BO-VRL-APP with a sufficiently large associative memory to store a ´scan-block´ comprising one track of most Winchester disks. Feasibility studies indicate that such a SCRIPT module could support at least 5 APIs (Associative Processing Instructions, as described earlier) per character at typical Winchester disk data rates.

To illustrate the application of a ´SCRIPT module´ to general text string processing, the following Pascal procedure finds and marks all occurrences of the sub-string ´PROCESS´ in the ´SCRIPT chain´.

```
procedure FIND_SUB_STRING (ss:string);
var i : 1..n,  {assuming sub-string length of n}

begin {FIND_SUB_STRING}
   MARKALL_B1;
   i := 1,
   MARK_HEADS (ss[i]);
   repeat
     i := i + 1;
     FOLLOW_TAILS (ss[i])
   until (i=n) or (MR=mismatch), {MR=Match Reply (see Fig. 7)}
   if MR = mismatch
     then writeln (´Sub-string ´,ss,´ not found´)
     else ISOLATE_SUB_STRINGS
end {FIND_SUB_STRING}
```

The SCRIPT Macros MARKALL_B1, MARK_HEADS, FOLLOW_TAILS and ISOLATE_SUB_STRINGS are defined below (in the APP assembly language and their effects are illustrated in Tables 10.2, 10.3, 10.4, 10.5 and 10.6 respectively.

```
SCRIPTMACRO MARKALL_B1
   001 S(* XXXX)   {Set all tags in Tag Register 1}
   002 W(* 1000)
ENDMACRO
```

Search data	Write data	Content of the Associative Memory Array
X	0	B4
X	0	B3
X	0	B2
X	1	B1 1 1 1 1 1 1 1 1 1 1 1 1 1 1 1 1 1 1 1 1 1 1 1 1 1 1 1
*	*	Ch S T R I N G P R O C E S S I N G P R O G R A M

Table 10.2 State of the ´SCRIPT chain´ after MARKALL_B1

```
SCRIPTMACRO MARK_HEADS (Ch:char)
   001 S(Ch 1XXX) BMR 2,3
   002 M(CMT) W(* 0000) BRN END   {CMT complements Tag Register 1}
   003 M(CLBM) M(PRR) W(* X2XX)   {CLBM clears unwanted B1s}
ENDMACRO                         {PRR propagates right}
```

Search data	Write data	Content of the Associative Memory Array		
X	X	B4		
X	X	B3		
X	2	B2	2	2
1	X	B1	1	1
P	*	Ch S T R I N G P R O C E S S I N G P R O G R A M		

Table 10.3 State of the ´SCRIPT chain´ after MARK_HEADS (P[1])

```
SCRIPTMACRO FOLLOW_TAILS (Ch:char)
   001 S(Ch X2XX) BMR 2,3
   002 M(CMT) W(* 00XX) BRN END   {CMT complements Tag Register 1}
   003 M(CLAB) M(PRR) W(* X2XX)   {CLAB clears all B2s}
ENDMACRO                         {PRR propagates right}
```

Search data	Write data	Content of the Associative Memory Array
X	X	B4
X	X	B3
X	X	B2
R,2	2	B2 2 2
0,2	2	B2 2 2
C,2	2	B2 2
E,2	2	B2 2
S,2	2	B2 2
2	2	B2 2
X	X	B1 1 1
S	*	Ch S T R I N G P R O C E S S I N G P R O G R A M

Table 10.4 State of the 'SCRIPT chain' during FOLLOW_TAILS (P[i])

```
SCRIPTMACRO ISOLATE SUB_STRINGS
   001 S(* 1XXX).TRI2 BMR 6,2        {Set ´stops´  in Tag Register 2}
   002 S(* X2XX) BMR 6,3            {Set ´starts´ in Tag Register 1}
   003 M(GRUNL) W(* XX3X)           {GRUNL = Group Run Left}
   004 S(* 1X3X) BMR 6,5
   005 M(CLAB) W(* 1XXX) BRN END    {CLAB clears all B1s and B3s}
   006 M(CMT) W(* 0000)             {CMT complements Tag Register 1}
ENDMACRO
```

Search data	Write data	Content of the Associative Memory Array
X	X	B4
X	3	B3 3 3 3 3 3 3 3
2	X	B2 2
X	X	B1 1 1
*	*	Ch S T R I N G P R O C E S S I N G P R O G R A M

Table 10.5 State of the ´SCRIPT chain´ after micro-instruction 3 of ISOLATE_SUB_STRINGS

Search data	Write data	Content of the Associative Memory Array
X	X	B4
3	X	B3
X	X	B2 2
1	1	B1 1
*	*	Ch S T R I N G P R O C E S S I N G P R O G R A M

Table 10.6 State of the ´SCRIPT chain´ after ISOLATE_SUB_STRINGS

10.7 CONCLUSIONS

The increasing demand for non-numerical information processing, the inadequacy of the conventional Von Neumann computer for such tasks, the rapidly growing interest in 'information technology' and the prospect of VLSI have combined to stimulate interest in radically new computer architectures dedicated to relational data processing. Indeed, it has been argued that the Associative Parallel Processor (APP) is ideally suited to this task.

The encouraging results of the Micro-APP project confirm that Micro-APP chips offer major architectural advantages in the field of non-numerical information processing. Freed from the rigors of representing relational data structures with complex list processing techniques, the design of information processing systems is greatly simplified. Moreover, the conceptual simplicity of associative relation processing leads to significant savings in software development and storage, as indicated in Fig. 10.6.

The commercial availability of VLSI Micro-APP chips, such as the SCRIPT chip (described in Section 10.6.4), could lead to the development of information systems incorporating organizations of traditional microprocessors and Micro-APP chips, which could be simply tailored to exploit the natural parallelism of both the hierarchic (or network) and relational data structures of specific non-numerical information processing tasks. In particular, SCRIPT modules offer the potential of cost-effective 'back-end relational data processing architectures' (discussed in Section 10.5). Such flexible systems could have a major impact on the new growth areas of 'database management', 'expert systems' and 'intelligent knowledge-based systems' where the limitations of traditional microcomputer architectures are manifestly evident.

REFERENCES

[1] Date, C.J. ´An Introduction to Database Systems´, Addison-Wesley, 1977.

[2] IBM Corporation, ´Information Management System/Virtual Storage General Information Manual, IBM Form No. GH20-1260.

[3] Bleier, R.E. ´Treating Hierarchical Data Structures in the SDC Time-shared Data Management System (TDMS)´, Proc. ACM Nat. Mtg, 1967.

[4] Informatics Inc., ´Mark IV Reference Manual´, No. SP-681810-1.

[5] MRI Systems Corporation, ´System 2000 General Information Manual´, 1972.

[6] Olle, T.W. ´The CODASYL Approach to Data Base Mangement´, Wiley, New York, 1978.

[7] Wiederhold, G. ´Data Base Design´, McGraw Hill, New York, 1977.

[8] Cardenas, A.F. ´Data Base Management Systems´, Allyn and Bacon, Boston, 1979.

[9] Cullinane Corporation, ´Integrated Data Base Management Systems (IDMS) Brochure´, 1975.

[10] Gallaire, H., and Minker, J. ´Logic and Data Bases´, Plenum Press, New York, 1978.

[11] IBM Corporation, ´System 360 Data Base Organisation and Maintenance Processor Application Description Manual´, IBM Form No. GH20-0771.

[12] Bachman, C.W., and Williams, S.B. ´A General Purpose Programming System for Random Access Memories´, Proc. AFIPS (FJCC), 1964.

[13] Goldstein, R.C., and Strand, A.J. ´The MacAIMS Data Management System´, Proc. ACM SIGFIDET workshop on data description and access, 1970.

[14] Mylopoulos, J., et al. ´A Multi-level Relational System´, Proc. NCC, 44, 1975.

[15] Stonebraker, M., et al. ´The Design and Implementation of INGRES´, ACM Trans. on data base systems, pp. 189 - 222, 1976.

[16] Tymshare Inc. ´MAGNUM Reference Manual´, 1975.

[17] Astrahan, M.M., et al. ´System R: A Relational Approach to Data Management, ACM Trans. on data base systems, pp. 97 - 137, 1976.

[18] Lea, R.M. ´Associative Processing of Non-numerical Information´, in Boulaye, G.G., and Lewin, D.W. (eds), ´Computer Architecture´, D. Reidel, Dordrecht-Holland, 1977.

[19] Hanlon, A.E. ´Content Addressable and Associative Memory Systems - A Survey´, IEEE Trans. EC-15, 509 - 521, 1966.

[20] Minker, J. ´An Overview of Associative or Content Addressable Memory Systems and a KWIC Index to the Literature 1956 - 1970´, Computing Reviews 12, 453 - 504, 1971.

[21] Parhami, B. ´Associative Memories and Processors - an Overview and Selected Bibliography´, Proc. IEEE 61, 722 - 730, 1973.

[22] Thurber, K.J. ´Associative and Parallel Processors´, Computing Surveys 7, 215 - 255, 1975.

[23] Higbie, L.C. ´Associative Processors: a Panacea or a Specific?´, Computer Design, pp. 75 - 82, July 1976.

[24] Yau, S.S., and Fung, H.S. ´Associative Processor Architectures - A Survey´, Computing Surveys 9, 3 - 27, 1977.

[25] Rudolph, J.A. ´A Production Implementation of an Associative Array Processor - STARAN´, Proc. AFIPS (FJCC) 41, 229 - 241, 1972.

[26] DiGiacinto, T. ´Airborne Associative Processor (ASPRO)´, Proc. AIAA Comput. in Aerospace III Conf., pp. 202 - 205, October 1981.

[27] Crane, B.A., et al. ´PEPE Computer Architecture,´ IEEE Compcon., pp. 57-60, 1972.

[28] Anderson, G.A., and Kain, R.Y. ´A Content–addressed Memory Design for Data Base Applications´, Proc. IEEE Conf. on parallel processing, 191 – 195, 1976.

[29] Savitt, B.A., Love H.H., and Troop, R.E. ´ASP – A New Concept in Language and Machine Organisation´, Proc. AFIPS (SJCC) 30, 87 – 102, 1967.

[30] DeFiore, C.R., Stillman, N.J., and Berra, P.B. ´Associative Techniques in the Solution of Data Management Problems´, Proc. ACM Nat. Conf., pp. 28 – 36, 1971.

[31] DeFiore, C.R., and Berra, P.B., ´A Data Management System Utilising an Associative Memory´, Proc. AFIPS (NCC) 42, 181 – 185, 1973.

[32] DeFiore, C.R., and Berra, P.B. ´Quantitative Analysis of the Utilisation of Associative Memories in Data Management´, IEEE Trans. C-23, 121 – 133, 1974.

[33] Moulder, R. ´An Implementation of a Data Management System on an Associative Processor´, Proc. AFIPS (NCC) 42, 171 – 176, 1973.

[34] Linde, R.R., Gates, R., and Peng, T. ´Associative Processor Applications to Real–time Data Management´, Proc. AFIPS (NCC) 42, 187 – 195, 1973.

[35] Lea, R.M. ´Building–blocks for Low–cost High–speed Associative Memory´, Electronic Engineering 49, 77 – 80, 1977.

[36] Lea, R.M. ´The Comparative Cost of Associative Memory´, The Radio and Electronic Engineer 45, 487 – 496, 1976.

[37] Lea, R.M. ´Micro–APP: A Building–block for Low–cost High–speed Associative Parallel Processors´, The Radio and Electronic Engineer 47, 91 – 99, 1977.

[38] Lea, R.M. ´I^{2}L Micro–associative Processors´, ESSCIRC 79 Dig. of Tech. Papers, pp. 104 – 106, 1979.

[39] Hsiao, D.K. ´Data Base Computers´, Advances in Computers 19, 1 – 64, 1980.

[40] Bray, O., and Freeman, H. ´Data Base Computers´, Lexington Books, 1979.

[41] Rosenthal, R.S. 'The Data Management Machine, A Classification', Proc. ACM SIGIR-SIGARCH-SIGMOD third workshop on computer architecture for non-numeric processing, pp. 35 - 39, 1977.

[42] Maller, V.A.J. 'The Content Addressable File Store - CAFS', ICL Tech. J., pp. 265 - 279, 1978.

[43] Leleich, H.O., Stiege, G., and Zeidler, H. 'A Search Processor for Data Base Management Systems', Proc. IEEE fourth very large data base conf., pp. 280 - 287, 1978.

[44] Epstein, R., and Hawthorn, P. 'Design Decisions for the Intelligent Data Base Machine', Proc. AFIPS 49, 237 - 241, 1980.

[45] Smith, K. 'Disk Store Finds Text References from Simple Queries', Electronics, pp. 73 - 74, February 24, 1982.

[46] Lea, R.M., and Schuegraf, E.J. 'An Associative File Store using Fragments for Run-time Indexing and Compression', in Oddy, R.N., Robertson, S.E., van Rijsbergen, C.J., Williams, P.W., (eds.), 'Information Retrieval Research' Butterworths, London, pp. 280 - 295, 1981.

[47] Lea, R.M. 'Text Compression with an Associative Parallel Processor', The Computer 21, 45 - 56, 1978.

[48] Slotnick, D.L. 'Logic-per-track Devices', Advances in Computers 10, 291 - 296, 1970.

[49] Parker, I.L. 'A logic-per-track Retrieval System, Proc. IFIPS, pp. 146 - 150, 1971.

[50] Parhami, B. 'A Highly Parallel Computer System for Information Retrieval', Proc. AFIPS (FJCC) 41, 681-690, 1972.

[51] Lin, S.C., Smith, D.C.P., and Smith, J.M. 'The Design of a Rotating Associative Memory for Relational Data Base Application', ACM Trans. on data base systems, pp. 1 - 8, 1976.

[52] Heaty, L.D., Lipovski, G.J., and Doty, K.L. 'The Architecture of a Context Addressed Segment-sequential Memory', Proc. AFIPS (FJCC) 41, 691 - 701, 1972.

[53] Schuster, S.A., Nguyen, H.B., and Ozkarahan, E.A. 'RAP-2 An Associative Processor for Data Bases', IEEE Trans. on Computers C-28 (6), 446 - 458, 1979.

[54] Hollaar, L.A. 'Text Retrieval Computers', IEEE Computer, pp. 40 - 50, March 1979.

[55] Nederlof, L., Veendrick, H.J.M., and van Zanten, A.T. 'Content Addressable Memory with Parallel Write Facilities', ESSCIRC 78 Dig. of Tech. Papers, pp. 94 - 96, 1978

[56] Kheder, M.A.G.A. 'Three General-purpose Micro-associative Parallel Processor chips: A Feasibility Study', Brunel University MPhil thesis, 1983.

Index